DATE DUE

OC 17 05			

DEMCO 38-296

THE GUINNESS BOOK OF SPORTS RECORDS

Editor
Mark C. Young

Guinness Media, Inc.

THE GUINNESS BOOK OF SPORTS RECORDS
Copyright © 1997 by Guinness Publishing Ltd.

Guinness Media, Inc.
Six Landmark Square
Stamford, CT 06901-2704

This book is taken in part from The Guinness Book of World Records © 1997

ISBN 0-9652383-2-6 (hardcover)
ISBN 0-9652383-1-8 (paperback)
ISSN 1054-4178

"Guinness" is a registered trademark of Guinness PLC for Publications

Text design by Ron Monteleone
Jacket design by Sanford C. & Marilena Vaccaro/Smart Graphics
Composition by Ron Monteleone

Printed in the United States of America

RRD GUINNESS MEDIA 10 9 8 7 6 5 4 3 2 1

This book is printed on acid-free paper.

CONTENTS

ARCHERY

Origins

The date of the invention of the bow is unknown, but historians agree that it was at least 50,000 years ago. The origins of archery as a competitive sport are also unclear. It is believed that the ancient Olympic Games (776 B.C. to 393 A.D.) featured archery, using tethered doves as targets. The legends of Robin Hood and William Tell indicate that archery prowess was highly regarded in Europe by the 13th century.

Archery became an official event in the modern Olympics in 1900. In 1931, the *Federation Internationale de Tir à l'Arc* (FITA) was founded as the world governing body of the sport.

United States It is believed that Native American tribes in the eastern part of North America were familiar with the bow by the 11th century. The National Archery Association (NAA) was founded in 1879 in Crawfordsville, IN and is the oldest amateur sports organization in continuous existence in the United States. The NAA is currently located in Colorado Springs, CO.

Archer Justin Huish won two gold medals at the 1996 Olympics, making him the first American to achieve a Games double.
(Rick Stewart/Allsport)

TARGET ARCHERY

The most widely practiced discipline in archery is Olympic-style target archery (also known as FITA style). Olympic-style target archery competition is based on the FITA round system of scoring.

A FITA round consists of 36 arrows shot from four distances: 90, 70, 50 and 30 meters for men; 70, 60, 50 and 30 for women, for a total of 144 arrows. The maximum possible score for a FITA round is 1,440 points.

Olympic Games

Archery made its first appearance in the 1900 Games in Paris, France. It was also featured in 1904, 1908 and 1920, but then was omitted until 1972, when enough countries had adopted FITA standardized rules to allow for a meaningful international competition. In Olympic competition, archers are only allowed to use a recurve (Olympic) bow.

Most gold medals Hubert van Innis (Belgium) has won six gold medals (au cordon dore—33 meters, au chapelet—33 meters, 1900; moving bird target, 28 meters, 33 meters, moving bird target [team], 33 meters, 50 meters, 1920).

United States Two American archers have won two gold medals: Darrell Pace (individual titles, 1976 and 1984) and Justin Huish (individual and team titles, 1996).

Most medals Hubert van Innis has won nine medals in all: six gold (see above), and three silver (au cordon dore—50 meters, 1900; moving bird target, 50 meters, moving bird target [team] 28 meters, 1920).

United States Darrell Pace is the only American archer to win three Olympic medals, two gold (see above) and one silver (team, 1988).

World Championships

Target archery world championships were first held in 1931 in Lvov, Poland. The championships have been staged biennially since 1959. In 1995 the tournament was divided into two categories: Recurve (Olympic) Bow and Compound Bow. World indoor archery championships have been held biennially since 1991.

Most titles, outdoor (archer) The most titles won is seven, by Janina Spychajowa-Kurkowska (Poland) in 1931–34, 1936, 1939 and 1947. The most titles won by a man is four, by Hans Deutgen (Sweden) in 1947–50.

United States Rick McKinney is the only American archer to win three individual world titles: 1977, 1983 and 1985. The most successful woman archer is Jean Lee. She won two world titles in 1950 and 1952.

Most titles, outdoor (country) The United States has a record 13 men's (1959, 1961, 1963, 1965, 1967, 1969, 1971, 1973, 1975, 1977, 1979, 1981, 1983) and nine women's (1952, 1957, 1958, 1959, 1961, 1963, 1965, 1977, 1995 [Compound Bow]) team titles.

Most titles, indoor (archer) The most titles is two, by Natalia Valeeva (Moldova) in 1991 and 1993.

United States Two Americans have won individual world indoor titles: Joe Asay, Compound Bow, 1991; and Michael Hendrikse, Compound Bow, 1993.

Most titles, indoor (country) The United States has won two men's team titles, 1991 and 1993.

United States Championships

The U.S. national championships were first held in Chicago, IL, August 12–14, 1879, and are staged annually.

Most titles The most archery titles won is 17, by Lida Howell between 1883 and 1907. The most men's titles is nine (three individual, six pairs), by Rick McKinney, 1977, 1979-83, and 1985-87.

▐▶ Fantastic Feats

Greatest draw on a longbow Gary Sentman of Roseberg, OR drew a longbow weighing a record 176 pounds to the maximum draw on the arrow of 28¼ inches in Forksville, PA on September 20, 1975.

Highest score The highest recorded score over 24 hours by a pair of archers is 76,158, during 70 Portsmouth Rounds (60 arrows per round at 20 yards at 2-foot FITA targets) by Simon Tarplee and David Hathaway in Evesham, England on April 1, 1991. During this attempt Tarplee set an individual record of 38,500.

Flight Shooting World Records

The object in flight shooting is to fire the arrow the greatest distance possible. There are two flight shooting classifications: regular flight and broadhead flight.

REGULAR FLIGHT

Bow Type	Distance	Archer	Date
Men			
Crossbow	2,047 yds. 0 ft. 2 in.	Harry Drake	July 30, 1988
Unlimited Footbow	2,028 yds. 0 ft. 0 in.	Harry Drake	October 24, 1971
Conventional Footbow	1,542 yds. 2 ft. 10 in.	Harry Drake	October 6, 1979
Unlimited Recurve Bow	1,336 yds. 1 ft. 3 in.	Don Brown	August 2, 1987
Unlimited Compound Bow	1,320 yds. 1 ft. 3 in.	Kevin Strother	July 31, 1992
Unlimited Longbow	408 yds. 1 ft. 4 in.	Don Brown	October 7, 1995
Unlimited Recurve Field	611 yds. 2 ft. 5 in.	Don Brown	October 5, 1996
Women			
Unlimited Recurve Bow	1,039 yds. 1 ft. 1 in.	April Moon	September 13, 1981
Conventional Footbow	1,113 yds. 2 ft. 6 in.	Arlyne Rhode	September 10, 1978
Unlimited Compound Bow	807 yds. 1 ft. 3 in.	April Moon	August 1, 1987
Unlimited Longbow	271 yds. 2 ft. 4 in.	April Moon	October 6, 1995

BROADHEAD FLIGHT

Bow Type	Distance	Archer	Date
Men			
Unlimited Compound Bow	784 yds. 2 ft. 9 in.	Bert McCune Jr.	August 2, 1992
Unlimited Recurve Bow	526 yds. 0 ft. 5 in.	Don Brown	June 26, 1988
Unlimited Longbow	332 yds. 2 ft. 0 in.	Don Brown	August 2, 1992
Unlimited Primitive Bow	244 yds. 2 ft. 7 in.	Daniel Perry	June 24, 1990
Unlimited Simple Composite	240 yds. 0 ft. 2 in.	David Hayes	October 6, 1996
Women			
Unlimited Compound Bow	481 yds. 0 ft. 7 in.	April Moon	June 24, 1989
Unlimited Recurve Bow	364 yds. 0 ft. 4 in.	April Moon	June 28, 1987
Unlimited Longbow	237 yds. 2 ft. 3 in.	April Moon	August 2, 1992
Unlimited Primitive Bow	107 yds. 1 ft. 5 in.	Gwen Perry	June 24, 1990

Source: U.S. National Archery Association

World Records (Single FITA Rounds)

Event	Archer	Country	Points	Year
Men				
FITA	Kyo-Moon Oh	South Korea	1,368	1995
90 m	Vladimir Esheev	USSR	330	1990
70 m	Hiroshi Yamamoto	Japan	344	1990
50 m	Seung Hun Han	South Korea	348	1994
30 m	Seung Hun Han	South Korea	360	1994
Women				
FITA	Jung-Rye Kim	South Korea	1,377	1995
70 m	Altin Kaynak	Turkey	339	1996
60 m	He Ying	China	349	1995
50 m	Hyun-Ji	South Korea	342	1996
30 m	Joanne Edens	Great Britain	357	1990

Source: U.S. National Archery Association

AUSTRALIAN RULES FOOTBALL

Origins

A cross between soccer and rugby, Australian Rules Football was developed in the mid-19th century by Henry Harrison and Thomas Wills, who helped form the Melbourne Football Club in 1858. In 1877, the Victorian Football Association was founded. Eight clubs broke away to form the Victorian Football League. Four more teams had been admitted by 1925, and in 1987 teams from Queensland and Western Australia joined the league, which was renamed the Australian Football League. Another team, Adelaide, joined in 1991.

Highest score The highest recorded score in football is 634 points (100–34) by Campbell's Creek in a Maryborough Castlemaine District League match against Primrose (18) on June 23, 1990.

Most goals (career) 2,191 by Peter Hudson (Hawthorn), 1963–81.

Most games (career) 426 by Michael Tuck (Hawthorn), 1972–91.

GRAND FINAL

The sport's premier event is the Grand Final, played annually since 1897. Staged at the Melbourne Cricket Ground, it had a record attendance of 121,696 people in 1970.

Most wins The greatest number of League Premierships is 16, by Carlton: 1906–08, 1914–15, 1938, 1945, 1947, 1968, 1970, 1972, 1979, 1981–82, 1987 and 1995.

Dating back to the mid-19th century, Australian Rules Football is one of the world's oldest organized sports; it has a reputation for being one of the world's most rugged as well.
(Allsport)

AUTO RACING

The nationality of the competitors in this section is U.S. unless noted otherwise.

Origins

There is a claim that the first race was held in the United States in 1878, from Green Bay to Madison, WI, won by an Oshkosh steamer. However, France discounts this, claiming that *La Velocipede*, a 19.3-mile race in Paris on April 20, 1887, was the first race. The first organized race did take place in France: 732 miles from Paris to Bordeaux and back, on June 11–14, 1895. The first closed-circuit race was held over five laps of a one-mile dirt track at Narragansett Park, Cranston, RI on September 7, 1896. Grand Prix racing started in 1906, also in France. The Indianapolis 500 was first run on May 30, 1911 (see below).

INDIANAPOLIS 500

The first Indianapolis 500 was held on May 30, 1911 at the Indianapolis Motor Speedway, where the event is still run. The Speedway was opened on August 19, 1909. The race track is a 2¹/₂-mile-square oval that has two straightaways of 3,300 feet and two of 660 feet, all 50 feet wide. The turns are each 1,320 feet, 60 feet wide and banked 9 degrees, 12 minutes.

Victory Lane

Most wins Three drivers have won the race four times: A. J. Foyt Jr., in 1961, 1964, 1967 and 1977; Al Unser, in 1970–71, 1978 and 1987; and Rick Mears, in 1979, 1984, 1988 and 1991.

Fastest win The record time is 2 hours 41 minutes 18.404 seconds (185.981 mph) by Arie Luyendyk (Netherlands), in a 1990 Lola-Chevrolet on May 27, 1990.

Slowest win The slowest time is 6 hours 42 minutes 8 seconds (74.602 mph) by Ray Harroun in the inaugural race in 1911.

Consecutive wins Four drivers have won the race in consecutive years: Wilbur Shaw, 1939–40; Mauri Rose, 1947–48; Bill Vukovich, 1953–54; and Al Unser, 1970–71.

Oldest winner Al Unser became the oldest winner when he won the 1987 race at age 47 years 11 months.

Youngest winner Troy Ruttman became the youngest winner when he won the 1952 race at age 22 years 2 months.

Closest finish The closest margin of victory was 0.043 seconds in 1992 when Al Unser Jr. edged Scott Goodyear (Canada).

Lap leader Al Unser has led the race for a cumulative 644 laps during his 27 starts, 1965–93.

Highest earnings The record prize fund is $8,114,600 awarded in 1996. The individual prize record is $1,373,813, by Al Unser Jr. in 1994. Rick Mears leads the field in career earnings at $4,299,392 from 15 starts, 1978–92.

Qualifying

Most starts A. J. Foyt Jr. has started a record 35 races (1958–92).

Pole position Rick Mears has gained a record six poles, in 1979, 1982, 1986, 1988–89 and 1991.

Fastest qualifier The record average speed for four laps qualifying is 236.986 mph by Arie Luyendyk (Netherlands) in a Reynard-Ford-Cosworth on May 12, 1996. On the same day he set the one-lap record of 237.498 mph.

INDY CAR RACING

The first Indy Car Championship was held in 1909 under the sponsorship of the American Automobile Association (AAA). In 1956 the United States Automobile Club (USAC) took over the running of the Indy series. Championship Auto Racing Teams Inc. (CART) was founded on November 25, 1978 and is the governing body for the PPG Indy Car World Series. In 1996 the Indy Racing League (IRL) was formed, creating two Indy Car racing series. The Indianapolis 500 is the final event of the IRL series. *Indy Car records in this section reflect the combined records of the AAA, USAC and CART. IRL records are included in the Indianapolis 500 section.*

Victory Lane

Most championships A. J. Foyt Jr. has won seven Indy Car National Championships: 1960–61, 1963–64, 1967, 1975 and 1979.

As Fast As You Can Go

Officially, CART stands for Championship Auto Racing Teams, Inc., but racing fans recite the acronym as "Continuing Albuquerque Racing Tradition." The Unser family, New Mexico's auto racing dynasty, has dominated the Indy Car record book for two generations. Of the first generation, Al and Bobby Unser won seven Indy 500's between them. Al's son, Al Jr., has extended the family tradition, winning the Indy 500 twice and laying down his own indelible skid marks on the sport.

"Little Al," as he is fondly called, holds pole position in several CART record categories, including fastest driver and career earnings leader. "My father influenced me big time. I was very fortunate to be born where I was," says Unser. He attributes his success, however, to his team: "The team is critical. I'm nothing without the team behind me. The car owner, sponsor, and mechanics all work together with the driver to win the race. They are just as important as the driver."

That teamwork was critical in Unser's most famous victory, his 1992 Indy 500 win. In the closest finish in history, Unser edged out Scott Goodyear by 0.043 seconds. "My first reaction was, that's way too close. I could tell you that I was sitting down, but my gut wasn't in the seat. I knew I had won. I knew he didn't get past me when we hit the bricks. It was very exciting and exhilarating," recalls Unser. The driving ace has excelled at other oval tracks. His Michigan 500 victory in 1990 was the fastest 500-mile race in history. "We were lucky to win a heck of a race. Bobby Rahal, my teammate, and I passed each other five or six times in the last 10 laps," says

David Taylor/Allsport

Unser. "I didn't know it was a record until well after the race."

Speeds of 200 mph are commonplace for a CART driver, but Unser understands the risks involved. "Danger is part of the sport. I love the speed and I love the sport enough where fear doesn't come into play." Adds Unser, "Racing drivers are very calm, smart people. We are not daredevils." Driving at such phenomenal speeds is a physically demanding experience. Unser describes the sensation: "We pull about three and a half lateral gs. It goes straight to the thigh. You feel it in your chest and stomach." He cautions aspiring drivers: "It's hot as hell. You have to drink plenty of fluids to cope with that."

In 1996 Indy Car racing was marred by CART's boycott of the Indy 500. Unser joined the protest. "We miss the Indy 500 very much. My family has enjoyed racing in the Indianapolis 500 for many years. It [the current situation] is beyond our control," says Unser. His main concern is for the fans: "What made the Indianapolis 500 so great is what it meant to the fans. They are the ones who are losing out because the best drivers in the world are not competing in the Indy 500."

The Indy great is optimistic, though: "There's always hope and I'm sure it will be resolved. I honestly see myself racing in the Indy 500 again." Until then Unser will continue to extend the family tradition in the PPG-CART series, in the trademark Unser style: "wide open and going as fast as you can go."

Indianapolis 500

Year	Driver	Av. Speed (mph)
1911	Ray Harroun	74.602
1912	Joe Dawson	78.719
1913	Jules Goux	75.933
1914	Rene Thomas	82.474
1915	Ralph DePalma	89.840
1916	Dario Resta	84.001
1917	(not held)	
1918	(not held)	
1919	Howard Wilcox	88.050
1920	Gaston Chevrolet	88.618
1921	Tommy Milton	89.621
1922	Jimmy Murphy	94.484
1923	Tommy Milton	90.954
1924	L. L. Corum and Joe Boyer	98.234
1925	Peter DePaolo	101.127
1926	Frank Lockhart	95.904
1927	George Souders	97.545
1928	Louis Meyer	99.482
1929	Ray Keech	97.585
1930	Billy Arnold	100.448
1931	Louis Schneider	96.629
1932	Fred Frame	104.144
1933	Louis Meyer	104.162
1934	William Cummings	104.863
1935	Kelly Petillo	106.240
1936	Louis Meyer	109.069
1937	Wilbur Shaw	113.580
1938	Floyd Roberts	117.200
1939	Wilbur Shaw	115.035
1940	Wilbur Shaw	114.277
1941	Floyd Davis and Mauri Rose	115.117
1942	(not held)	
1943	(not held)	
1944	(not held)	
1945	(not held)	
1946	George Robson	114.820
1947	Mauri Rose	116.338
1948	Mauri Rose	119.814
1949	Bill Holland	121.327
1950	Johnnie Parsons	124.002
1951	Lee Wallard	126.244
1952	Troy Ruttman	128.922
1953	Bill Vukovich	128.740
1954	Bill Vukovich	130.840
1955	Bob Sweikert	128.209
1956	Pat Flaherty	128.490
1957	Sam Hanks	135.601
1958	Jim Bryan	133.791
1959	Rodger Ward	135.857
1960	Jim Rathmann	138.767
1961	A. J. Foyt Jr.	139.131
1962	Rodger Ward	140.293
1963	Parnelli Jones	143.137
1964	A. J. Foyt Jr.	147.350
1965	Jim Clark [1]	150.686
1966	Graham Hill [1]	144.317
1967	A. J. Foyt Jr.	151.207
1968	Bobby Unser	152.882
1969	Mario Andretti	156.867
1970	Al Unser	155.749
1971	Al Unser	157.735
1972	Mark Donohue	162.962
1973	Gordon Johncock	159.036
1974	Johnny Rutherford	158.589
1975	Bobby Unser	149.213
1976	Johnny Rutherford	148.725
1977	A. J. Foyt Jr.	161.331
1978	Al Unser	161.363
1979	Rick Mears	158.899
1980	Johnny Rutherford	142.862
1981	Bobby Unser	139.084
1982	Gordon Johncock	162.029
1983	Tom Sneva	162.117
1984	Rick Mears	163.612
1985	Danny Sullivan	152.982

1986	Bobby Rahal	170.722
1987	Al Unser	162.175
1988	Rick Mears	144.809
1989	Emerson Fittipaldi [2]	167.581
1990	Arie Luyendyk [3]	185.981
1991	Rick Mears	176.457
1992	Al Unser Jr.	134.477
1993	Emerson Fittipaldi [2]	157.207
1994	Al Unser Jr.	160.872
1995	Jacques Villeneuve [4]	153.616
1996	Buddy Lazier	147.956

(1)=Great Britain; (2)=Brazil; (3)=Netherlands; (4)=Canada

Source: Indianapolis Motor Speedway

Most consecutive championships Ted Horn won three consecutive national titles, 1946–48.

Most wins (career) A. J. Foyt Jr. has won a career record 67 Indy Car races, 1957–92. Foyt's first victory came at the DuQuoin 100 in 1960 and his last at the Pocono 500 in 1981.

Most wins (season) The record for most victories in a season is 10, shared by two drivers: A.J. Foyt Jr. in 1964 and Al Unser in 1970.

Consecutive winning seasons Bobby Unser won at least one race per season for 11 seasons from 1966–76.

Most wins (road course) Mario Andretti won a record 21 road course races, 1964–94.

Most wins (500-mile races) A. J. Foyt Jr. has won nine 500-mile races: Indianapolis 500 in 1961, 1964, 1967 and 1977; Pocono 500 in 1973, 1975, 1979 and 1981; California 500 in 1975.

Closest races The closest margin of victory in an Indy Car race was 0.02 seconds on April 10, 1921 when Ralph DePalma edged Roscoe Sarles to win the Beverly Hills 25.

The closest finish in a 500-mile event was Al Unser Jr.'s 0.043-second victory in the 1992 Indianapolis 500.

Mario Andretti pulled off the closest finish in an Indy road race, when he won the Portland 200 by 0.07 seconds on June 15, 1986. The loser in this memorable showdown was Andretti's son, Michael.

Youngest winner Al Unser Jr.'s victory in the 1984 Portland 200 at age 22 years 1 month 29 days is the youngest age any driver has won an Indy Car race.

Buddy Lazier celebrates his 1996 Indy 500 victory.
(Andy Lyons/Allsport)

Oldest winner   On April 4, 1993 Mario Andretti won the Valvoline 200 at the Phoenix International Raceway. At 53 years 52 days Andretti became the oldest driver to win an Indy Car race.

Highest earnings (season)   The single-season earnings record is $3,535,813, set in 1994 by Al Unser Jr.

Highest earnings (career)   Through the 1996 season, Al Unser Jr. has the highest career earnings for Indy drivers with $17,735,906.

Qualifying

Most starts   Mario Andretti made a record 407 starts in Indy Car racing, 1964–94.

Most poles and laps led (career)   Mario Andretti earned a record 66 pole positions, 1964–94. He also holds the record for laps led (7,587).

Most poles (season)   A. J. Foyt Jr. earned 10 poles in 1965.

Most poles (road courses)   Mario Andretti has earned 26 poles on road courses, 1964–94.

Most poles (500-mile races)   Rick Mears has earned a record 16 poles in 500-mile races.

Fastest qualifiers   The fastest qualifying lap ever for a PPG Indy Car race was 234.275 mph by Mario Andretti on August 1, 1993 in qualifying for the Marlboro 500.

NASCAR (National Association for Stock Car Auto Racing)

The National Association for Stock Car Auto Racing, Inc., was founded by Bill France Sr. in 1947. The first NASCAR-sanctioned race was held on February 15, 1948 on Daytona's beach course.

The first NASCAR championship, the Grand National series, was held in 1949. Since 1970, the championship series has been called the Winston Cup Championship. The Winston Cup is won by the driver who accumulates the most points during the season series.

Victory Lane

Most championships   Two drivers have won a record seven NASCAR titles: Richard Petty, 1964, 1967, 1971–72, 1974–75 and 1979; and Dale Earnhardt, 1980, 1986–87, 1990–91, and 1993–94.

Most consecutive titles   Cale Yarborough is the only driver to "threepeat" as NASCAR champion, winning in 1976–78.

Most wins (career)   Richard Petty has won 200 NASCAR Winston Cup races out of 1,185 in which he competed, 1958–92.

Most wins (season)   Richard Petty won a record 27 races in 1967.

Fastest average speed   The fastest average speed in a Winston Cup race is 186.288 mph, set by Bill Elliott at Talladega Superspeedway, AL on May 5, 1985.

Highest earnings (season)   Jeff Gordon earned a record $4,347,343 in 1995.

Highest earnings (career)   Dale Earnhardt holds the career earnings mark at $28,234,471, 1975–96.

DAYTONA 500

The Daytona 500 has been held at the 2 1/2 mile oval Daytona International Speedway in Daytona Beach, FL since 1959. The Daytona 500 is the most prestigious event on the NASCAR calendar.

Victory Lane

Most wins   Richard Petty has won a record seven times: 1964, 1966, 1971, 1973–74, 1979 and 1981.

Consecutive wins   Richard Petty and Cale Yarborough are the only drivers to have repeated as Daytona 500 winners in consecutive years. Petty's double was in 1973–74 and Yarborough's in 1983–84.

Oldest winner   Bobby Allison became the oldest winner in 1988 at age 50 years 2 months 11 days.

Youngest winner   Jeff Gordon won in 1997 at age 25 years 6 months.

NASCAR Winston Cup Champions

Terry Labonte won the 1996 Winston Cup title, edging '95 champ Jeff Gordon.
(David Taylor/Allsport)

1949	Red Byron	1974	Richard Petty
1950	Bill Rexford	1975	Richard Petty
1951	Herb Thomas	1976	Cale Yarborough
1952	Tim Flock	1977	Cale Yarborough
1953	Herb Thomas	1978	Cale Yarborough
1954	Lee Petty	1979	Richard Petty
1955	Tim Flock	1980	Dale Earnhardt
1956	Buck Baker	1981	Darrell Waltrip
1957	Buck Baker	1982	Darrell Waltrip
1958	Lee Petty	1983	Bobby Allison
1959	Lee Petty	1984	Terry Labonte
1960	Rex White	1985	Darrell Waltrip
1961	Ned Jarrett	1986	Dale Earnhardt
1962	Joe Weatherly	1987	Dale Earnhardt
1963	Joe Weatherly	1988	Bill Elliott
1964	Richard Petty	1989	Rusty Wallace
1965	Ned Jarrett	1990	Dale Earnhardt
1966	David Pearson	1991	Dale Earnhardt
1967	Richard Petty	1992	Alan Kulwicki
1968	David Pearson	1993	Dale Earnhardt
1969	David Pearson	1994	Dale Earnhardt
1970	Bobby Isaac	1995	Jeff Gordon
1971	Richard Petty	1996	Terry Labonte
1972	Richard Petty		
1973	Benny Parsons		Source: NASCAR

Dale Earnhardt has won seven Winston Cup titles, a record he shares with Richard Petty.
(David Taylor/Allsport)

Daytona 500

Year	Driver	Av. Speed (mph)
1959	Lee Petty	135.521
1960	Junior Johnson	124.740
1961	Marvin Panch	149.601
1962	Fireball Roberts	152.529
1963	Tiny Lund	151.566
1964	Richard Petty	154.334
1965	Fred Lorenzen	141.539
1966	Richard Petty	160.627
1967	Mario Andretti	149.926
1968	Cale Yarborough	143.251
1969	LeeRoy Yarborough	157.950
1970	Pete Hamilton	149.601
1971	Richard Petty	144.462
1972	A. J. Foyt Jr.	161.550
1973	Richard Petty	157.205
1974	Richard Petty	140.894
1975	Benny Parsons	153.649
1976	David Pearson	152.181
1977	Cale Yarborough	153.218
1978	Bobby Allison	159.730
1979	Richard Petty	143.977
1980	Buddy Baker	177.602
1981	Richard Petty	169.651
1982	Bobby Allison	153.991
1983	Cale Yarborough	155.979
1984	Cale Yarborough	150.994
1985	Bill Elliott	172.265
1986	Geoff Bodine	148.124
1987	Bill Elliott	176.263
1988	Bobby Allison	137.531
1989	Darrell Waltrip	148.466
1990	Derrike Cope	165.761
1991	Ernie Irvan	148.148
1992	Davey Allison	160.256
1993	Dale Jarrett	154.972
1994	Sterling Marlin	156.931
1995	Sterling Marlin	141.710
1996	Dale Jarrett	154.308
1997	Jeff Gordon	148.295

Source: NASCAR

Jeff Gordon's victory in the 1997 Daytona 500 made him the youngest driver to win NASCAR's premier event.
(David Taylor/Allsport)

Fastest win The record average speed is 177.602 mph, by Buddy Baker in 1980.

Slowest win The slowest average speed is 124.740 mph, by Junior Johnson in 1960.

Highest earnings The individual race earnings record is $377,410, by Jeff Gordon in 1997. The career earnings record is $1,724,256, by Dale Earnhardt in 19 races, 1979–97.

Qualifying

Most starts Richard Petty competed in 32 Daytona 500 races, 1959–92.

Fastest qualifying time The record average speed for qualifying for the race is 210.364 mph, set by Bill Elliott in 1987.

Most poles Cale Yarborough has earned a record four poles at the Daytona 500, in 1968, 1970, 1978 and 1984.

FORMULA ONE (Grand Prix)

The World Drivers' Championship was inaugurated in 1950. Currently the championship is contested over 16 races in 14 different countries worldwide. Points are awarded to the first six finishers in each race; the driver with the most points at the end of the season is the champion.

Victory Lane

Most championships Juan-Manuel Fangio (Argentina) has won the drivers' championship five times, 1951 and 1954–57. He also holds the record for consecutive titles with four straight, 1954–57.

Oldest champion
Juan-Manuel Fangio is the oldest world champion, winning the 1957 title at age 46 years 41 days.

Youngest champion
Emerson Fittipaldi (Brazil) became the youngest champion in 1972, at age 25 years 273 days.

Most wins (career)
Alain Prost (France) has won 51 Formula One races (from 200), between 1980 and 1993.

Most wins (season) The most victories in a season is nine, by two drivers: Nigel Mansell (Great Britain) in 1992, and Michael Schumacher (Germany) in 1995.

Oldest winner The oldest driver to win an official race was Luigi Fagioli (Italy), who was 53 years 22 days old when he won the 1951 French Grand Prix.

Youngest winner The youngest driver to win an official race was Troy Ruttman, who was 22 years 80 days old when he won the 1952 Indianapolis 500, which counted in the World Drivers' Championship that year.

Damon Hill's 1996 Formula One World Drivers' Championship made him the first second-generation F1 world driving champion. His father, Graham Hill, won the F1 title in 1962 and 1968.
(Alain Patrice/Vandystadt/Allsport)

Closest finish The narrowest margin of victory in a Formula One race was when Ayrton Senna (Brazil) held off Nigel Mansell by 0.014 seconds to win the Spanish Grand Prix on April 13, 1986.

United States Two Americans have won the Formula One title—Phil Hill in 1961 and Mario Andretti in 1978.

Qualifying

Most starts Riccardo Patrese (Italy) has raced in a record 256 Grand Prix races from 1977–93.

Most poles Ayrton Senna earned a record 65 poles in 161 races, 1985–94.

Fastest qualifying time Keke Rosberg (Finland) set the fastest qualifying lap in Formula One history, when he qualified for the British Grand Prix at Silverstone with an average speed of 160.817 mph on July 20, 1985.

DRAG RACING

Drag racing is an acceleration contest between two cars racing from a standing start over a precisely measured, straight-line, quarter-mile course. Competition is based on two-car elimination heats culminating in a final round. The fastest elapsed time wins the race. Elapsed time is measured over the distance of the course; the top speed is a measurement of the last 66 feet of the track, where a special speed trap electronically computes the speed of the dragster. There are several classifications in drag racing, based on the engine size, type of fuel and vehicle weight limitations of the car.

The most prominent drag racing organization is the National Hot Rod Association (NHRA), which was founded in 1951. The NHRA recognizes 12 categories of racers, with the three main categories being Top Fuel, Funny Car and Pro Stock.

TOP FUEL

Top Fuel dragsters are 4,000-horsepower machines that are powered by nitromethane. The engines are mounted behind the driver, and parachutes are the primary braking system.

Speed Records

Quickest elapsed time in an NHRA event
The quickest elapsed time recorded by a Top Fuel dragster from a standing start for 440 yards is 4.592 seconds by Blaine Johnson at the Western Auto Nationals, Topeka, KS on July 7, 1996.

Fastest top speed in an NHRA event The fastest speed recorded in a Top Fuel race is 316.23 mph by Shelly Anderson on October 12, 1996 at the Chief Auto Parts Nationals in Ennis, TX.

Victories

Most wins (career) Joe Amato has won a record 36 Top Fuel races (1982–96).

Most wins (season) Six drivers have won six Top Fuel races in a season: Don Garlits, 1985; Darrell Gwynn, 1988; Gary Ormsby, 1989; Joe Amato, 1990; Kenny Bernstein, 1991; and Eddie Hill, 1993.

FUNNY CAR

A Funny Car is a short-wheelbase version of the Top Fuel dragster. Funny Cars mount a fiberglass replica of a production car with the engine located in front of the driver.

Speed Records

Quickest elapsed time in an NHRA event
The quickest elapsed time recorded in the Funny Car class is 4.889 seconds, by John Force on July 7, 1996 in Topeka, KS.

Fastest top speed in an NHRA event John Force was timed at 311.20 mph in Topeka, KS, on July 7, 1996.

Victories

Most wins (career) John Force has won a record 61 Funny Car races (1975–96).

Most wins (season) John Force won a record 13 races in 1996.

PRO STOCK

Pro Stock dragsters look like their oval-racing counterparts, but feature extensive engine modifications. A maximum 500-cubic-inch displacement and a minimum vehicle weight of 2,350 pounds are allowed under NHRA rules.

Quickest elapsed time in an NHRA event
The quickest elapsed time in the Pro Stock class is 6.947 seconds, by Jim Yates on September 16, 1996 at the Keystone Nationals in Mohnton, PA.

Fastest top speed in an NHRA event
The fastest speed ever achieved in a Pro Stock race is 199.15 mph by Warren Johnson on March 10, 1995 at the Slick 50 Nationals, Baytown, TX.

Most wins (career)
Bob Glidden has won a record 85 races (1972–96), the most victories of any driver in NHRA events.

Most wins (season)
Darrell Alderman won a record 11 races in 1991.

NHRA Winston Drag Racing Series
The NHRA World Championship Series was inaugurated in 1951. Since 1975 the series has been known as the NHRA Winston Drag Racing Series.

Most Titles

Top Fuel
Joe Amato has won a record five national titles: 1984, 1988 and 1990–92.

Funny Car
John Force has won a record six national titles, in 1990–91 and 1993–96.

Pro Stock
Bob Glidden has won a record 10 national titles, in 1974–75, 1978–80 and 1985–89.

➡ Fantastic Feats

Longest skid marks
The skid marks made by the jet-powered *Spirit of America*, driven by Craig Breedlove, after the car went out of control at Bonneville Salt Flats, UT on October 15, 1964, were nearly six miles long.

Two-side-wheel driving
On May 24, 1989 Bengt Norberg of Åppelbo, Sweden drove a Mitsubishi Colt GTi-16V on two side wheels nonstop for a distance of 192.873 miles in a time of 7 hours 15 minutes 50 seconds.

Sven-Erik Söderman (Sweden) achieved a speed of 102.14 mph over a 100-meter (328.1-foot) flying start on two wheels of an Opel Kadett at Mora Siljan Airport, Mora, Sweden, August 2, 1990.

Bobby Ore (Great Britain) drove a double-decker bus 810 feet on two wheels at North Weald Airfield in England on May 21, 1988.

The fastest sport on wheels, NHRA races regularly top 300 mph.
(Jamie Squire/Allsport)

AVIATION SPORTS

AEROBATICS

Origins

The first aerobatic "maneuver" is generally considered to be the sustained inverted flight in a Blériot flown by Célestin-Adolphe Pégoud (France), in Buc, France on September 21, 1913. Stunt flying became popular in the United States during the 1920s and 1930s. In the late 1950s aerobatic contests regained popularity at air shows. In 1970 the International Aerobatic Club formed standardized rules for the sport, establishing four categories of competition: unlimited, advanced, intermediate and sportsman.

World Championships

First held in 1960, the world championships are a biennial event. The competition consists of three flight programs: known and unknown compulsories and a free program. The judges award scores based on a system devised by Col. José Aresti (Spain).

Most titles (team) The USSR won the men's title six times, 1964, 1966, 1976, 1982, 1986, and 1990.

Most titles (individual) Petr Jimus (Czechoslovakia) has won two men's world titles: 1984 and 1986. Betty Stewart (U.S.) has won two women's world titles, 1980 and 1982.

AIR RACING

Air racing, or airplane racing, consists of piloted aircraft racing a specific number of laps over a closed circuit marked by pylons. The first plane to cross the finish line is the winner. Air races are divided into several categories, depending on the type of plane and engine. The top level of the sport is the unlimited class.

Origins

The first international airplane racing competition, the Bennett Trophy, was held in Rheims, France, August 22–28, 1909.

United States The first international air race staged in the United States was the second Bennett Trophy competition at Belmont Park, NY in 1910. Air racing became very popular in the 1920s. Competitions, such as the National Air Races (inaugurated in 1924) and the Thompson Trophy (inaugurated in 1930), drew enormous crowds—500,000 people attended the 1929 National Air Races in Cleveland, OH. Following World War II the popularity of the sport declined. During the mid-1950s, enthusiasts revived the sport, racing smaller World War II military planes. In 1964 Bill Stead staged the first National Championship Air Races (NCAR) in Reno, NV; this is now the premier air racing event in the United States.

National Championship Air Races (NCAR)

Staged annually in Reno, NV since 1964, the NCAR has been held at its present site, the Reno/Stead Airport, since 1986. Races are staged in four categories: Unlimited class, AT-6 class, Formula One class and Biplane class.

Unlimited Class

In this class the aircraft must use piston engines, be propeller-driven and be capable of pulling six *g*s. The planes race over a pylon-marked 9.128 mile course.

Most titles Darryl Greenmyer has won seven unlimited NCAR titles: 1965–69, 1971 and 1977.

Fastest average speed (race) Lyle Shelton won the 1991 NCAR title recording the fastest average speed at 481.618 mph in his *Rare Bear*.

Fastest qualifying speed The one-lap NCAR qualifying record is 482.892 mph, by Lyle Shelton in 1992.

AT-6 CLASS

Only World War II Advanced Trainers (AT), complying with the original stock configuration, are allowed to compete. Seats can be removed and the engines stripped and reassembled, but the cubic inch displacement of the 650-horsepower 1340-R Pratt & Whitney engine cannot exceed the original level.

Most titles Eddie Van Fossen has won seven AT-6 NCAR titles: 1986–88, 1991–94.

Fastest average speed (race)   Eddie Van Fossen won the 1992 NCAR title recording the fastest average speed at 234.788 mph in *Miss TNT*.

Fastest qualifying speed   The one-lap NCAR qualifying record is 235.223 mph, by Eddie Van Fossen in 1992.

⇒ Fantastic Feats

Inverted flight   The duration record is 4 hours 38 minutes 10 seconds by Joann Osterud (U.S.) from Vancouver to Vanderjoof, Canada on July 24, 1991.

BALLOONING

The earliest recorded ascent of a hot-air balloon in public occurred on June 5, 1783. The unmanned balloon, made of linen and paper, was designed and built by Joseph and Etienne Montgolfier. It lifted off from Annonay, France, and flew one mile, attaining an altitude of 5,906 feet. The modern-day sport of ballooning developed in the United States in the early 1960s. Official World Championships were first staged in Albuquerque, NM in 1973.

Distance

Longest balloon flight   The record distance traveled by a balloon is 9,672 miles, by Steve Fossett in a helium balloon, *Solo Spirit*. Fossett left St. Louis, MO on January 13, 1997 and landed near Sultanpur, India on January 20, 1997.

Longest hot-air balloon flight   Richard Branson and Per Lindstrand (both Great Britain), crossed the Pacific Ocean in the *Virgin Otsuka Pacific Flyer* from the southern tip of Japan to Lac la Matre, Yukon, Canada, January 15–17, 1991. The 2.6 million-cubic-foot capacity hot-air balloon flew 4,768 miles.

Altitude

Highest balloon altitude   The official record for altitude gained in a helium balloon is 113,740 feet. Piloted by Cdr. Malcolm D. Ross (U.S.N.R.) and Lt. Cdr. Victor A. Prother (U.S.N.), the 12-million-cubic-foot closed-gondola balloon rose from the deck of the U.S.S. *Antietam* in the Gulf of Mexico on May 4, 1961.

Highest balloon altitude (unpressurized) Scientists Harold Froelich and Keith Lang of Minneapolis, MN made an "unplanned" ascent in an open gondola, without pressure suits or goggles, to an altitude of 42,126 feet on September 26, 1956.

Highest hot-air balloon altitude   Per Lindstrand reached 64,997 feet in a Colt 600 hot-air balloon over Laredo, TX on June 6, 1988.

Duration

Longest flight   Steve Fossett's record-setting 9,672 mile journey from St. Louis, MO to Sultanapur, India, January 13–20, 1997 lasted 146 hours 54 minutes, the longest ever.

American balloonist Steve Fossett failed in his circumnavigation bid in January 1997, but he set marks for distance and duration.
(AP Photo/Bill Stover, HO; AP Photo/John Moore)

PARACHUTING

Origins

The sport of parachuting traces its origins to the early 20th century, when daredevils performed parachute stunts at fairs and carnivals across the United States. Target jumping contests were first organized in the 1930s. In 1952 the sport was organized internationally by the *Fédération Aeronautique Internationale*. The sport is now contested in two main formats: target jumping and display formation.

World Championships

Most wins (team)
The USSR won seven men's world titles, 1954, 1958, 1960, 1966, 1972, 1976 and 1980; and six women's world titles, 1956, 1958, 1966, 1968, 1972, 1976.

Most wins (individual) Nikolay Ushamyev (USSR) is the only jumper to have won two world titles, 1974 and 1980.

▥➡ Fantastic Feats

Total descents (men) Don Kellner (U.S.) parachuted 22,500 times in various locations through March 17, 1997.

Total descents (women) Cheryl Stearns (U.S.) made 10,100 jumps in various locations through August 2, 1995.

Total descents—24 hours (men) Jay Stokes (U.S.) jumped 331 times on May 30–31, 1995.

Total descents—24 hours (women) Cheryl Stearns (U.S.) parachuted 352 times on November 8–9, 1995.

Oldest (men) Edwin Townsend (U.S.), 89 years of age, jumped on February 5, 1986.

Oldest (women) Mrs. Sylvia Brett (Great Britain), 80 years, 166 days, completed her jump on August 23, 1986.

To celebrate her 99th birthday, Hildegarde Ferrera set the world record as the oldest tandem parachute jumper.
(Courtesy of Lavonne West)

The modern sport of soaring developed in the mid-1930s, allowing French pilots training for the World Championships the added perk of wonderful vistas of the French Riviera.
(Bernard Desestres/Vandystadt)

Oldest tandem parachutist Hildegarde Ferrera (U.S.) made a tandem parachute jump in Mokuleia, HI on February 17, 1996, her 99th birthday.

Oldest tandem parachutist (men) Edward Royds-Jones, 95 years, 170 days, made a tandem parachute jump in Dunkeswell, Great Britain on July 2, 1994.

SOARING

Origins

Research by Isadore William Deiches has shown evidence of the use of gliders in ancient Egypt c. 2500–1500 B.C. Emanuel Swedenborg of Sweden made sketches of gliders c. 1714. The earliest human-carrying glider was designed by Sir George Cayley and carried his coachman (possibly John Appleby) about 500 yards across a valley in Brompton Dale, North Yorkshire, England in the summer of 1853.

World Championships

World championships were instituted in 1937.

Most individual titles The most individual titles won is four, by Ingo Renner (Australia) in 1976 (Standard class), 1983, 1985 and 1987 (Open).

United States The most titles won by an American pilot is two, by George Moffat, in the Open category, 1970 and 1974.

WORLD RECORDS (SINGLE-SEATERS)

Distance and Height

Straight distance 907.7 miles, Hans-Werner Grosse (Germany), Lubeck, Germany to Biarritz, France, April 25, 1972.

Declared goal distance 779.4 miles, by three pilots: Bruce Drake, David Speight and Dick Georgeson (all New Zealand), who each flew from Te Anau to Te Araroa, New Zealand, January 14, 1978.

Goal and return 1,023.2 miles, Tom Knauff (U.S.), Williamsport, PA to Knoxville, TN, April 25, 1983.

Absolute altitude 49,009 feet, Robert R. Harris (U.S.), over California, February 17, 1986. The women's record is 41,449 feet, by Sabrina Jackintell (U.S.) on February 14, 1979.

Height gain 42,303 feet, Paul Bikle (U.S.), Mojave, CA, February 25, 1961. The women's record is 33,506 feet, by Yvonne Loader (New Zealand) in Omarama, New Zealand on January 12, 1988.

Speed Over Triangular Course

100 km 121.35 mph, Ingo Renner (Australia), December 14, 1982.

300 km 105.32 mph, Jean-Paul Castel (France), November 15, 1986.

500 km 105.67 mph, Beat Bunzli (Switzerland), January 9, 1988.

750 km 98.43 mph, Hans-Werner Grosse (Germany), January 8, 1985.

1,000 km 105.4 mph, Helmut H. Fischer (Germany), January 5, 1995.

1,250 km 82.79 mph, Hans-Werner Grosse (Germany), January 9, 1980.

ULTRALIGHTING

The National Aeronautic Association (NAA) rules define ultralights as fixed wing craft with an empty weight of no more than 254 pounds, maximum airspeed of 55 knots, and a fuel capacity of no more than 5 gallons. For record attempts, ultralights fit into the microlight class. FAI regulations allow for a single place landplane with a maximum gross weight of 661 pounds, and a two place landplane with a maximum weight of 992 pounds. The stall speed at maximum gross weight must be less than 35 knots.

WORLD RECORDS

The following are a selection of world records officially recognized by the FAI in the Class R Microlights division.

Landplanes, Solo

Distance in a straight line without landing 850.68 miles, Bernard d'Otreppe (Belgium), Frejus la Palud, France to Teesside, England, September 6, 1988.

Distance in a closed circuit without landing 665.58 miles, Michel Serane (France), in Besancon-Thise, France, August 5, 1991.

Altitude 31,889 feet, Serge Zin (France), in Saint Auban, France, September 18, 1994.

Speed over a 50 km closed circuit 97.82 mph, Serge Ferrari (France), in Belleville sur Saone, France, June 30, 1995.

Landplanes, Multiplace

Distance in a closed circuit without landing 312.79 miles, Robert Mair and Dietmar Spekking (Germany), in Griesau, Germany, September 29, 1996.

Altitude 23,434 feet, Walter Mauri and Heike Goettlicher (Italy), in Udine, Italy, April 16, 1993.

Speed over a 500 km closed circuit 51.00 mph, Robert Mair and Dietmar Spekking (Germany), in Griesau, Germany, September 29, 1996.

BADMINTON

Origins

Badminton is a descendant of the children's game of battledore and shuttlecock. It is believed that a similar game was played in China more than 2,000 years ago. Badminton takes its name from Badminton House in England, where the Duke of Beaufort's family and guests popularized the game in the 19th century. British army officers took the game to India in the 1870s, where the first modern rules were codified in 1876. The world governing body is the International Badminton Federation, formed in 1934.

United States The earliest known reference to badminton in the United States is a description of battledore and shuttlecock in the 1864 *American Boy's Book of Sports and Games*. The first badminton club formed in the United States was the Badminton Club of New York, founded in 1878. The game was not organized at the national level until 1935, when the American Badminton Association (ABA) was founded in Boston, MA. In 1978 the ABA was renamed the United States Badminton Association.

Olympic Games

Badminton was included in the Olympic Games as an official sport for the first time at the Barcelona Games in 1992. The game was included as a demonstration sport at the Munich Games in 1972.

Most medals Gil Young-ah (South Korea) has won three medals: one bronze, women's doubles, 1992; one gold, mixed doubles, 1996; and one silver, women's doubles, 1996.

World Championships

The first championships were staged in Malmo, Sweden in 1977. Since 1983 the event has been held biennially.

Most titles (overall) Park Joo-bong (South Korea) has won a record five world titles: men's doubles in 1985 and 1991; mixed doubles in 1985, 1989 and 1991. Three women have won three titles: Lin Ying (China), doubles in 1983, 1987 and 1989; Li Lingwei (China), singles in 1983 and 1989, doubles in 1985;

Guan Weizhan (China), doubles in 1987, 1989 and 1991.

Most titles (singles) Yang Yang (China) is the only man to have won two world singles titles, in 1987 and 1989. Two women have won two singles titles: Li Lingwei (China), 1983 and 1989; Han Aiping (China), 1985 and 1987.

United States National Championships

The first competition was held in 1937.

Most titles Judy Hashman (née Devlin) has won 31 titles, including a record 12 singles titles: 12 women's singles, 1954, 1956–63 and 1965–67; 12 women's doubles, 1953–55, 1957–63 and 1966–67 (10 with her sister Susan); and seven mixed doubles, 1956–59, 1961–62 and 1967. Wynn Rogers won a record 18 men's titles: 10 men's doubles, 1948–53, 1955, 1961–62 and 1964; eight mixed doubles, 1949–52, 1955 and 1961–62. David G. Freeman has won a record seven men's singles titles: 1939–42, 1947–48 and 1953.

Bang Soo-hyun (South Korea) won the 1996 women's Olympic gold medal.
(Gary Prior/Allsport)

BASEBALL

Origins

In 1907, baseball's national commission appointed a committee to research the history of the game. The report, filed in 1908, concluded that Abner Doubleday had invented the game in 1839 in Cooperstown, NY. At the time, the report was viewed with some skepticism because of the friendship between Doubleday and the committee chairman, A. G. Mills; however, in 1939, major league baseball celebrated its centennial and cemented the legend of Doubleday's efforts in American folklore. Sports historians today discount the Doubleday theory, claiming that baseball in North America evolved from such English games as cricket, paddleball and rounders.

Uncontested is that Alexander Cartwright Jr. formulated the rules of the modern game in 1845, and that the first match under these rules was played on June 19, 1846, when the New York Nine defeated the New York Knickerbockers, 23–1, in four innings. The first professional league in the United States, the National Association of Professional Base Ball Players, was formed on March 17, 1871. Today there are two main professional baseball associations, the National League (organized in 1876) and the American League (organized in 1901, recognized in 1903), which together form the major leagues, along with approximately 20 associations that make up the minor leagues. The champions of the two leagues first played a World Series in 1903 and have played one continuously since 1905. (For further details on World Series history, see page 40.)

THE MAJOR LEAGUES

Records listed in this section are for the all-time major league record. Where an all-time record is dated prior to 1900, the modern record (1900–present) is also listed.

GAMES PLAYED

Career 3,562, by Pete Rose, Cincinnati Reds (NL), 1963–78, 1984–86; Philadelphia Phillies (NL), 1979–83; Montreal Expos (NL), 1984.

Consecutive 2,315, by Cal Ripken Jr., Baltimore Orioles (AL), May 30, 1982 through September 29, 1996.

BATTING RECORDS

Batting Average

Career .367, by Ty Cobb, Detroit Tigers (AL), 1905–26; Philadelphia Athletics (AL), 1927–28. Cobb compiled his record from 4,191 hits in 11,429 at-bats.

Season .438, by Hugh Duffy, Boston Beaneaters (NL) in 1894. Duffy compiled 236 hits in 539 at-bats. The modern record is .424, by Rogers Hornsby, St. Louis Cardinals (NL), in 1924. Hornsby compiled 227 hits in 536 at-bats.

Hits

Career 4,256, by Pete Rose, Cincinnati Reds (NL), 1963–78, 1984–86; Philadelphia Phillies (NL), 1979–83; Montreal Expos (NL), 1984. Rose compiled his record hits total in 14,053 at-bats.

Season 257, by George Sisler, St. Louis Browns (AL), in 1920, in 631 at-bats.

Game Nine, by John Burnett, Cleveland Indians (AL), during an 18-inning game on July 10, 1932. The record for a nine-inning game is seven hits, by two players: Wilbert Robinson, Baltimore Orioles (NL), on June 10, 1892; Rennie Stennett, Pittsburgh Pirates (NL), on September 16, 1975.

Singles

Career 3,215, by Pete Rose, Cincinnati Reds (NL), 1963–78, 1984–86; Philadelphia Phillies, 1979–83, Montreal Expos, 1984.

Season 206, by Wee Willie Keeler, Baltimore Orioles (NL) in 1898. The modern-day record is 198, by Lloyd Waner, Pittsburgh Pirates, in 1927.

Game Seven, by John Burnett, Cleveland Indians (AL), in an 18-inning game on July 10, 1932. In regulation play the record for both the National and American leagues is six hits by several players.

Doubles

Career 793, by Tris Speaker, Boston Red Sox (AL), 1907–1915; Cleveland Indians (AL), 1916–1926; Washington Senators (AL), 1927; Philadelphia Athletics (AL), 1928.

Season 67, by Earl Webb, Boston Red Sox (AL), in 1931.

Game Four, by many players in both leagues.

Triples

Career 312, by Sam Crawford, Cincinnati Reds (NL), 1899–1902; Detroit Tigers (AL), 1903–17.

Season 36, by Owen Wilson, Pittsburgh Pirates (NL), in 1912.

Game Four, by two players: George A. Strief, Philadelphia Athletics (American Association) on June 25, 1885; William Joyce, New York Giants (NL) on May 18, 1897. The modern-day record for both leagues is three, achieved by several players.

Home Runs

Career 755, by Hank Aaron, Milwaukee/Atlanta Braves (NL), 1954–74; Milwaukee Brewers (AL), 1975–76. Aaron hit his record dingers in 12,364 at-bats.

Season 61, Roger Maris, New York Yankees (AL), in 1961.

Game Four, by 12 players: Bobby Lowe, Boston (NL), May 30, 1894; Ed Delahanty, Philadelphia Phillies (NL), July 13, 1896; Lou Gehrig, New York Yankees (AL), June 3, 1932; Chuck Klein, Philadelphia Phillies (NL), July 10, 1936; Pat Seerey, Chicago White Sox (AL), July 18, 1948; Gil Hodges, Brooklyn Dodgers (NL), August 31, 1950; Joe Adcock, Milwaukee Braves (NL), July 31, 1954; Rocky Colavito, Cleveland Indians (AL), June 10, 1959; Willie Mays, San Francisco Giants (NL), April 30, 1961; Mike Schmidt, Philadelphia Phillies (NL), April 17, 1976; Bob Horner, Atlanta Braves (NL), July 6, 1986; and Mark Whiten, St. Louis Cardinals (NL), September 7, 1993. Klein, Schmidt and Seerey matched the record in extra-inning games.

1996 was baseball's year of the home run, with a record 4,962 dingers knocked out of the ballyards. A record 16 players hit 40 or more home runs during the season, including (left to right) Mark McGwire, Brady Anderson, Todd Hundley, and Jay Buhner.
(Doug Pensinger/Allsport; Otto Greule/Allsport; Al Bello/Allsport; Otto Greule/Allsport)

Junior's League

The baseball world knows him best as "Junior," but there is nothing minor about Ken Griffey Jr.'s impact on major league baseball. The 27-year-old Seattle Mariners centerfielder is widely regarded as baseball's best player and has already earned a place in the record books. In 1995 he became the third ball player to hit a home run in eight consecutive games. His entry to the majors, however, was a record in itself.

His father, Ken Griffey Sr., was playing for the Cincinnati Reds at the time, and so they became the first father-and-son duo to play in the majors. Later they would team together in Seattle, becoming the first father and son to play together on the same team.

Not surprisingly, "Junior" lists his father as his greatest influence. "My dad always said, 'Don't be a one-dimensional player.' He stressed that to me. He said some guys can hit but can't play defense. He said work on all aspects of your game." Adds Griffey: "That's what I try to do."

His father's advice was also invaluable to Griffey during his home run streak: "The more home runs I hit, the more my father said, 'Just take one pitch that you can hit, and try and hit it out." The duo were both patrolling the Mariners outfield during the streak. Playing together was only an advantage for Junior. "He batted second, I batted third. He treated me like a player, not a son." Adds Junior, "When we were in the locker room, I was a player, I wasn't his son. But when we were at home, then I was his son."

Otto Greule/Allsport

Junior also tips his cap to his father for the baseball "family firsts" that they share. "It was tougher for him than it was for me because he had to do all the hard work," says Griffey. Proudly Junior points out: "He had to stay here (at Seattle), taking the pay cuts, just keeping his foot in the door to allow us to play together. A lot of people are proud, and they say 'I'm worth this much' and they overprice themselves out of the game." The center fielder also notes that lunchtime bore special dividends during their time together on the Mariners. "It was fun. He treated me for lunch every day, you know, those fatherly things. He was 'Mr. Provider.' "

Only just entering his prime years as a baseball player, Griffey has not set himself any particular targets. "I always try to improve on what I did the year before," the all-star says. "I don't set goals like 30 or 40 home runs." Adds Griffey, "I just want to add on to what I have. If I have two hits in a game, I want to get a third. If I have three stolen bases, I want a fourth and so on."

Junior is also multi-dimensional off the field. He likes to read Stephen King novels and is a partner in the All Star Cafe restaurant chain. He and his wife are building a house in Florida that Griffey helped design. His dream is to one day get a degree in architecture. "I've accomplished my dreams by being able to play baseball. I would like to help other people attain their dreams by building their houses," he says.

Grand Slams

Career 23, by Lou Gehrig, New York Yankees (AL), 1923–39.

Season Six, by Don Mattingly, New York Yankees (AL), in 1987.

Game Two, by eight players: Tony Lazzeri, New York Yankees (AL), May 24, 1936; Jim Tabor, Boston Red Sox (AL), July 4, 1939; Rudy York, Boston Red Sox (AL), July 27, 1946; Jim Gentile, Baltimore Orioles (AL), May 9, 1961; Tony Cloninger, Atlanta Braves (NL), July 3, 1966; Jim Northrup, Detroit Tigers (AL), June 24, 1968; Frank Robinson, Baltimore Orioles (AL), June 26, 1970; and Robin Ventura, Chicago White Sox (AL), September 4, 1995. Cloninger is the only player from the National League to achieve this feat, and he was a pitcher.

Runs Batted In

Career 2,297, by Hank Aaron, Milwaukee/Atlanta Braves (NL), 1954–74; Milwaukee Brewers (AL), 1975–76.

Season 190, by Hack Wilson, Chicago Cubs (NL), in 1930.

Game 12, by two players: Jim Bottomley, St. Louis Cardinals (NL), on September 16, 1924; and Mark Whiten, St. Louis Cardinals (NL), on September 7, 1993.

Runs Scored

Career 2,245, by Ty Cobb, Detroit Tigers (AL), 1905–26; Philadelphia Athletics (AL), 1927–28.

Season 196, by Billy Hamilton, Philadelphia Phillies (NL), in 1894. The modern-day record is 177 runs, scored by Babe Ruth, New York Yankees (AL), in 1921.

Game Seven, by Guy Hecker, Louisville Colonels (American Association), on August 15, 1886. The modern-day record is six runs scored, achieved by 12 players, 10 in the National League and two in the American League.

Total Bases

Career 6,856, by Hank Aaron, Milwaukee/Atlanta Braves (NL), 1954–74; Milwaukee Brewers (AL),

1975–76. Aaron's record includes 2,294 singles, 624 doubles, 98 triples and 755 home runs.

Season 457, by Babe Ruth, New York Yankees (AL) in 1921. Ruth's total comprised 85 singles, 44 doubles, 16 triples and 59 home runs.

Game 18, by Joe Adcock, Milwaukee Braves (NL) on July 31, 1954. Adcock hit four home runs and a double.

Walks

Career 2,056, by Babe Ruth, Boston Red Sox (AL), 1914–19; New York Yankees (AL), 1920–34; Boston Braves (NL), 1935.

Season 170, by Babe Ruth, New York Yankees (AL) in 1923.

Strikeouts

Career 2,597, by Reggie Jackson, Kansas City/Oakland Athletics (AL), 1967–75, 1987; Baltimore Orioles (AL), 1976; New York Yankees (AL), 1977–81; California Angels (AL), 1982–86.

Season 189, by Bobby Bonds, San Francisco Giants (NL), in 1970.

Hit by Pitch

Career 267, by Don Baylor, Baltimore Orioles (AL), 1970–75; Oakland Athletics (AL), 1976, 1988; California Angels (AL), 1977–82; New York Yankees (AL), 1983–85; Boston Red Sox (AL), 1986–87; Minnesota Twins (AL), 1987.

Season 50, by Ron Hunt, Montreal Expos (NL), 1971.

Consecutive Batting Records

Hits in a row 12, by two players: Pinky Higgins, Boston Red Sox (AL), over four games, June 19–21, 1938; and Walt (Moose) Dropo, Detroit Tigers (AL), over three games, July 14–15, 1952.

Games batted safely 56, by Joe DiMaggio, New York Yankees (AL), May 15 through July 16, 1941. During the streak, DiMaggio gained 91 hits in 223 at-bats: 56 singles, 16 doubles, 4 triples and 15 home runs.

Home runs in a row Four, by four players: Bobby Lowe, Boston (NL), May 30, 1894; Lou Gehrig, New York Yankees (AL), June 3, 1932; Rocky Colavito, Cleveland Indians (AL), June 10, 1959; and Mike Schmidt, Philadelphia Phillies (NL), April 17, 1976.

Games hitting home runs Eight, by three players: Dale Long, Pittsburgh Pirates (NL), May 19–28, 1956; Don Mattingly, New York Yankees (AL), July 8–18, 1987; Ken Griffey, Jr., Seattle Mariners (AL), July 20–28, 1993.

Walks in a row Seven, by four players: Billy Rogell, Detroit Tigers (AL), August 17–19, 1938; Mel Ott, New York Giants (NL), June 16–18, 1943; Eddie Stanky, New York Giants (NL), August 29–30, 1950; Jose Canseco, Oakland Athletics (AL), August 4–5, 1994.

Games receiving a walk 22, by Roy Cullenbine, Detroit Tigers (AL), July 2 through July 22, 1947.

PITCHING RECORDS

Games Played

Career 1,070, by Hoyt Wilhelm, New York Giants (NL), 1952–56; St. Louis Cardinals (NL), 1957; Cleveland Indians (AL), 1957–58; Baltimore Orioles (AL), 1958–62; Chicago White Sox (AL), 1963–68; California Angels (AL), 1969; Atlanta Braves (NL), 1969–70; Chicago Cubs (NL), 1970; Atlanta Braves (NL), 1971; Los Angeles Dodgers (NL), 1971–72.

Season 106, by Mike Marshall, Los Angeles Dodgers (NL), in 1974.

Victories

Career 511, by Cy Young, Cleveland Spiders (NL), 1890–98; St. Louis Cardinals (NL), 1899–1900; Boston Red Sox (AL), 1901–08; Cleveland Indians (AL), 1909–11; Boston Braves (NL), 1911.

Season 60, by "Old Hoss" Radbourn, Providence Grays (NL), in 1884. The modern-day record is 41, by Jack Chesbro, New York Yankees (AL), in 1904.

Losses

Career 315, by Cy Young, Cleveland Spiders (NL), 1890–98; St. Louis Cardinals (NL), 1899–1900; Boston

Roger Clemens tied his own mark for most strikeouts in a game (20) on September 18, 1996.
(Doug Pensinger/Allsport)

Red Sox (AL), 1901–08; Cleveland Indians (AL), 1909–11; Boston Braves (NL), 1911.

Season 48, by John Coleman, Philadelphia Phillies (NL), in 1883. The modern-day record is 29, by Vic Willis, Boston Braves (NL), in 1905.

Earned Run Average (ERA)

Career (min. 2,000 innings) 1.82, by Ed Walsh, Chicago White Sox (AL), 1904–16; Boston Braves (NL), 1917.

Widest differential (min. 200 innings)
In 1994, Greg Maddux (Atlanta Braves, NL) had an ERA of 1.56, 2.56 below the league's overall average.

Innings Pitched

Career 7,356, by Cy Young, Cleveland Spiders (NL), 1890–98; St. Louis Cardinals (NL), 1899–1900; Boston

Red Sox (AL), 1901–08; Cleveland Indians (AL), 1909–11; Boston Braves (NL), 1911.

Season 680, by Will White, Cincinnati Reds (NL), in 1879. The modern-day record is 464, by Ed Walsh, Chicago White Sox (AL), in 1908.

Complete Games

Career 749, by Cy Young, Cleveland Spiders (NL), 1890–98; St. Louis Cardinals (NL), 1899–1900; Boston Red Sox (AL), 1901–08; Cleveland Indians (AL), 1909–11; Boston Braves (NL), 1911. The modern-day record is 531, by Walter Johnson, Washington Senators (AL), 1907–27.

Season 75, by Will White, Cincinnati Reds (NL) in 1879. The modern-day record is 48, by Jack Chesbro, New York Yankees (AL), in 1904.

Shutouts

Career 110, by Walter Johnson, Washington Senators (AL), 1907–27.

Season 16, by two pitchers: George Bradley, St. Louis (NL), in 1876; and Grover Alexander, Philadelphia Phillies (NL), in 1916.

Strikeouts

Career 5,714, by Nolan Ryan, New York Mets (NL), 1966–71; California Angels (AL), 1972–79; Houston Astros (NL), 1980–88; Texas Rangers (AL), 1989–93.

Season 513, by Matt Kilroy, Baltimore (American Association), in 1886. The modern-day record is 383, by Nolan Ryan, California Angels (AL), in 1973.

Game (extra innings) 21, by Tom Cheney, Washington Senators (AL), on September 12, 1962 in a 16-inning game.

Game (nine innings) 20, twice, by Roger Clemens, Boston Red Sox (AL), on April 29, 1986 and on September 18, 1996.

Walks

Career 2,795, by Nolan Ryan, New York Mets (NL), 1966–71; California Angels (AL), 1972–79; Houston Astros (NL), 1980–88; Texas Rangers (AL), 1989–93.

Season 289, by Amos Rusie, New York Giants (NL), in 1890. The modern-day record is 208, by Bob Feller, Cleveland Indians (AL), in 1938.

Game 16, by two pitchers: Bruno Haas, Philadelphia Athletics (AL), on June 23, 1915 in a nine-inning game; Tom Byrne, St. Louis Browns (AL) on August 22, 1951 in a 13-inning game.

Saves

Career 473, by Lee Smith, Chicago Cubs (NL), 1980–87; Boston Red Sox (AL), 1988–90; St. Louis Cardinals (NL), 1990–93; New York Yankees (AL), 1993; the Baltimore Orioles (AL), 1994; California Angels (AL), 1995–96; Cincinnati Reds (NL), 1996.

Season 57, by Bobby Thigpen, Chicago White Sox (AL), in 1990.

No-Hitters

On September 4, 1991, baseball's Committee for Statistical Accuracy defined a no-hit game as "one in which a pitcher or pitchers complete a game of nine innings or more without allowing a hit." All previously considered no-hit games that did not fit into this definition—such as rain-shortened games; eight-inning, complete game no-hitters hurled by losing pitchers; and games in which hits were recorded in the tenth inning or later—would be considered "notable achievements," not no-hitters.

The first officially recognized no-hitter was pitched by Joe Borden for Philadelphia of the National Association vs. Chicago on July 28, 1875. The most no-hitters pitched in one season is seven, in both 1990 and 1991.

Career Seven, by Nolan Ryan: California Angels vs. Kansas City Royals (3–0), May 15, 1973; California Angels vs. Detroit Tigers (6–0), July 15, 1973; California Angels vs. Minnesota Twins (4–0), September 28, 1974; California Angels vs. Baltimore Orioles (1–0), June 1, 1975; Houston Astros vs. Los Angeles Dodgers (5–0), September 26, 1981; Texas Rangers vs. Oakland Athletics (5–0), June 11, 1990; and Texas Rangers vs. Toronto Blue Jays (3–0), May 1, 1991.

Season Two, by four players: Johnny Vander Meer, Cincinnati Reds (NL), 1938; Allie Reynolds, New York Yankees (AL), 1951; Virgil Trucks, Detroit Tigers (AL) 1952; and Nolan Ryan, California Angels (AL), 1973.

Perfect Games

In a perfect game, no batter reaches base during a complete game of at least nine innings.

The first officially recognized perfect game was hurled by John Richmond on June 12, 1880 for Worcester vs. Cleveland in a National League game. Through the 1996 season there have been 15 perfect games pitched: Richmond (see above); John Ward, Providence vs. Buffalo (NL), June 17, 1880; Cy Young, Boston Red Sox vs. Philadelphia Athletics (AL), May 5, 1904; Addie Joss, Cleveland Indians vs. Chicago White Sox (AL), October 2, 1908; Ernie Shore, Boston Red Sox vs. Washington Senators (AL), June 23, 1917; Charlie Robertson, Chicago White Sox vs. Detroit Tigers (AL), April 30, 1922; Don Larsen, New York Yankees vs. Brooklyn Dodgers (World Series game), October 8, 1956; Jim Bunning, Philadelphia Phillies vs. New York Mets (NL), June 21, 1964; Sandy Koufax, Los Angeles Dodgers vs. Chicago Cubs (NL), September 9, 1965; Catfish Hunter, Oakland Athletics vs. Minnesota Twins (AL), May 8, 1968; Len Barker, Cleveland Indians vs. Toronto Blue Jays (AL), May 15, 1981; Mike Witt, California Angels vs. Texas Rangers (AL), September 30, 1984; Tom Browning, Cincinnati Reds vs. Los Angeles Dodgers (NL), September 16, 1988; Dennis Martinez, Montreal Expos vs. Los Angeles Dodgers (NL), July 28, 1991; and Kenny Rogers, Texas Rangers (AL) vs. California Angels (AL), July 29, 1994.

Consecutive Pitching Records

Games won 24, by Carl Hubbell, New York Giants (NL), 16 in 1936 and eight in 1937.

Starting assignments 595, by Nolan Ryan, from July 30, 1974 through 1993, for three teams: California Angels (AL), Houston Astros (NL), and Texas Rangers (AL).

Scoreless innings 59, by Orel Hershiser, Los Angeles Dodgers (NL), from sixth inning, August 30 through tenth inning, September 28, 1988.

No-hitters Two, by Johnny Vander Meer, Cincinnati Reds (NL), on June 11 and June 15, 1938.

Shutouts Six, by Don Drysdale, Los Angeles Dodgers (NL), May 14 through June 4, 1968.

Strikeouts 10, by Tom Seaver, New York Mets (NL) on April 22, 1970.

BASERUNNING

Stolen Bases

Career 1,186, by Rickey Henderson, Oakland Athletics (AL), 1979–84, 1989–94; New York Yankees (AL), 1985–89; Toronto Blue Jays (AL), 1993; Oakland Athletics (AL), 1994–95; San Diego Padres (NL), 1996.

Season 130, by Rickey Henderson, Oakland Athletics (AL), in 1982.

Game Seven, by two players: George Gore, Chicago Cubs (NL), on June 25, 1881; Billy Hamilton, Philadelphia Phillies (NL), on August 31, 1894. The modern-day record is six, by three players: Eddie Collins, Philadelphia Athletics (AL), on September 11, 1912; Otis Nixon, Atlanta Braves (NL), on June 17, 1991; Eric Young, Colorado Rockies (NL), on June 30, 1996.

40/40 Club Two players have stolen at least 40 bases and hit at least 40 home runs in one season: Jose Canseco, Oakland Athletics (AL), 40 stolen bases and 42 home runs, 1988; and Barry Bonds, San Francisco Giants (NL), 40 stolen bases and 42 home runs, 1996.

MANAGERS

Most games managed 7,755, by Connie Mack, Pittsburgh Pirates (NL), 1894–96; Philadelphia Athletics (AL), 1901–50. Mack's career record was 3,731 wins, 3,948 losses, 75 ties and one no-decision.

Most wins 3,731, by Connie Mack, Pittsburgh Pirates (NL), 1894–96; Philadelphia Athletics (AL), 1901–50.

Most losses 3,948, by Connie Mack, Pittsburgh Pirates (NL), 1894–96; Philadelphia Athletics (AL), 1901–50.

Highest winning percentage .615, by Joe McCarthy, Chicago Cubs (NL), 1926–30; New York Yankees (AL), 1931–46; Boston Red Sox (AL), 1948–50. McCarthy's career record was 2,125 wins, 1,333 losses, 26 ties and three no-decisions.

MISCELLANEOUS

Father and son On August 31, 1990, Ken Griffey Sr. and Ken Griffey, Jr., of the Seattle Mariners (AL), became the first father and son to play for the same

Yankees skipper Joe Torre waited longer than any other player and/or manager to reach the World Series, 4,268 games. The wait proved worthwhile with Torre's Yankees coming from behind to win the 1996 World Series.
(Doug Pensinger/Allsport)

major league team at the same time. In 1989 the Griffeys had been the first father/son combination to play in the major leagues at the same time. Griffey Sr. played for the Cincinnati Reds (NL) during that season.

Father, son and grandson There are two three-generation families in Major League history. On August 19, 1992, Bret Boone made his major league debut for the Seattle Mariners (AL), making the Boone family the first three-generation family. Boone's father Bob Boone played 18 seasons in the majors, 1972–89, and his grandfather Ray Boone played from 1948 to 1960. On May 5, 1995 David Bell made his Major League debut for the Cleveland Indians (AL), making the Bell family the second three-generation family. David's father, Buddy Bell, played 18 seasons in the majors, 1972–89, and his grandfather, Gus Bell, played 15 seasons, 1950–64.

Youngest player The youngest major league player of all time was the Cincinnati Reds (NL) pitcher Joe Nuxhall, who played one game in June 1944, at age

15 years 314 days. He did not play again in the National League until 1952.

Oldest player Satchel Paige pitched for the Kansas City A's (AL) at age 59 years 80 days on September 25, 1965.

Shortest and tallest players The shortest major league player was Eddie Gaedel, a 3-foot-7-inch, 65-pound midget, who pinch-hit for the St. Louis Browns (AL) vs. the Detroit Tigers (AL) on August 19, 1951. Wearing number 1/8, the batter with the smallest-ever major league strike zone walked on four pitches. Following the game, major league rules were hastily rewritten to prevent any recurrence. The tallest major leaguers of all time are two 6-foot-10-inch pitchers: Randy Johnson, who played in his first game for the Montreal Expos (NL) on September 15, 1988; and Eric Hillman, who debuted for the New York Mets (NL) on May 18, 1992.

Record attendances The all-time season record for attendance for both leagues is 70,256,459, set in 1993 (33,332,603 for the 14-team American League, and 36,923,856 for the 14-team National League). The American League and National League totals were both league records. The record for home-team attendance is held by the Colorado Rockies (NL) at 4,483,350 in 1993. The American League record is held by the Toronto Blue Jays at 4,057,947 in 1993.

Shortest game The New York Giants (NL) beat the Philadelphia Phillies (NL), 6–1, in nine innings in 51 minutes on September 28, 1919.

Longest games The Brooklyn Dodgers (NL) and the Boston Braves (NL) played to a 1–1 tie after 26 innings on May 1, 1920. The Chicago White Sox (AL) played the longest ballgame in elapsed time—8 hours 6 minutes—before beating the Milwaukee Brewers, 7–6, in the 25th inning on May 9, 1984 in Chicago. The game started on a Tuesday night and was tied at 3–3 when the 1 A.M. curfew caused suspension until Wednesday night.

The actual longest game was a minor league game in 1981 that lasted 33 innings. At the end of nine innings the score was tied, 1–1, with the Rochester (NY) Red Wings battling the home team Pawtucket (R.I.) Red Sox. At the end of 32 innings the score was still 2–2, when the game was suspended. Two months later, play was resumed, and 18 minutes later, Pawtucket scored one run and won.

Most Valuable Player Award (MVP)

There have been three different MVP Awards in baseball: the Chalmers Award (1911–14), the League Award (1922–29), and the Baseball Writers' Association of America Award (1931–present).

CHALMERS AWARD (1911–14)

National League

Year	Player	Team
1911	Wildfire Schulte (OF)	Chicago Cubs
1912	Larry Doyle (2B)	New York Giants
1913	Jake Daubert (1B)	Brooklyn Dodgers
1914	Johnny Evers (2B)	Boston Braves

American League

Year	Player	Team
1911	Ty Cobb (OF)	Detroit Tigers
1912	Tris Speaker (OF)	Boston Red Sox
1913	Walter Johnson (P)	Washington Senators
1914	Eddie Collins (2B)	Philadelphia A's

LEAGUE AWARD (1922–29)

National League

Year	Player	Team
1922	no selection	
1923	no selection	
1924	Dazzy Vance (P)	Brooklyn Dodgers
1925	Rogers Hornsby (2B)	St. Louis Cardinals
1926	Bob O'Farrell (C)	St. Louis Cardinals
1927	Paul Waner (OF)	Pittsburgh Pirates
1928	Jim Bottomley (1B)	St. Louis Cardinals
1929	Rogers Hornsby (2B)	Chicago Cubs

American League

Year	Player	Team
1922	George Sisler (1B)	St. Louis Browns
1923	Babe Ruth (OF)	New York Yankees
1924	Walter Johnson (P)	Washington Senators
1925	Roger Peckinpaugh (SS)	Washington Senators
1926	George Burns (1B)	Cleveland Indians
1927	Lou Gehrig (1B)	New York Yankees
1928	Mickey Cochrane (C)	Philadelphia A's
1929	no selection	

BASEBALL WRITERS' AWARD (1931–96)

Most wins

Three, by eight players: Jimmie Foxx, Philadelphia Athletics (AL), 1932–33, 1938; Joe DiMaggio, New York Yankees (AL), 1939, 1941, 1947; Stan Musial, St. Louis Cardinals (NL), 1943, 1946, 1948; Roy Campanella, Brooklyn Dodgers (NL), 1951, 1953, 1955; Yogi Berra, New York Yankees (AL), 1951, 1954–55; Mickey Mantle, New York Yankees (AL), 1956–57, 1962; Mike Schmidt, Philadelphia Phillies (NL), 1980–81, 1986; and Barry Bonds, Pittsburgh Pirates (NL),1990, 1992, San Francisco Giants (NL), 1993.

Wins, both leagues

Frank Robinson, Cincinnati Reds (NL), in 1961; Baltimore Orioles (AL), in 1966.

National League

Year	Player	Team	Year	Player	Team
1931	Frankie Frisch (2B)	St. Louis Cardinals	1945	Phil Cavarretta (1B)	Chicago Cubs
1932	Chuck Klein (OF)	Philadelphia Phillies	1946	Stan Musial (1B–OF)	St. Louis Cardinals
1933	Carl Hubbell (P)	New York Giants	1947	Bob Elliott (3B)	Boston Braves
1934	Dizzy Dean (P)	St. Louis Cardinals	1948	Stan Musial (OF)	St. Louis Cardinals
1935	Gabby Hartnett (C)	Chicago Cubs	1949	Jackie Robinson (2B)	Brooklyn Dodgers
1936	Carl Hubbell (P)	New York Giants	1950	Jim Konstanty (P)	Philadelphia Phillies
1937	Joe Medwick (OF)	St. Louis Cardinals	1951	Roy Campanella (C)	Brooklyn Dodgers
1938	Ernie Lombardi (C)	Cincinnati Reds	1952	Hank Sauer (OF)	Chicago Cubs
1939	Bucky Walters (P)	Cincinnati Reds	1953	Roy Campanella (C)	Brooklyn Dodgers
1940	Frank McCormick (1B)	Cincinnati Reds	1954	Willie Mays (OF)	New York Giants
1941	Dolf Camilli (1B)	Brooklyn Dodgers	1955	Roy Campanella (C)	Brooklyn Dodgers
1942	Mort Cooper (P)	St. Louis Cardinals	1956	Don Newcombe (P)	Brooklyn Dodgers
1943	Stan Musial (OF)	St. Louis Cardinals	1957	Hank Aaron (OF)	Milwaukee Braves
1944	Marty Marion (SS)	St. Louis Cardinals	1958	Ernie Banks (SS)	Chicago Cubs

Most Valuable Player Award (MVP) (continued)

National League (continued)

Year	Player	Team
1959	Ernie Banks (SS)	Chicago Cubs
1960	Dick Groat (SS)	Pittsburgh Pirates
1961	Frank Robinson (OF)	Cincinnati Reds
1962	Maury Wills (SS)	Los Angeles Dodgers
1963	Sandy Koufax (P)	Los Angeles Dodgers
1964	Ken Boyer (3B)	St. Louis Cardinals
1965	Willie Mays (OF)	San Francisco Giants
1966	Roberto Clemente (OF)	Pittsburgh Pirates
1967	Orlando Cepeda (1B)	St. Louis Cardinals
1968	Bob Gibson (P)	St. Louis Cardinals
1969	Willie McCovey (1B)	San Francisco Giants
1970	Johnny Bench (C)	Cincinnati Reds
1971	Joe Torre (3B)	St. Louis Cardinals
1972	Johnny Bench (C)	Cincinnati Reds
1973	Pete Rose (OF)	Cincinnati Reds
1974	Steve Garvey (1B)	Los Angeles Dodgers
1975	Joe Morgan (2B)	Cincinnati Reds
1976	Joe Morgan (2B)	Cincinnati Reds
1977	George Foster (OF)	Cincinnati Reds
1978	Dave Parker (OF)	Pittsburgh Pirates
1979	Willie Stargell (1B*)	Pittsburgh Pirates
	Keith Hernandez (1B*)	St. Louis Cardinals
1980	Mike Schmidt (3B)	Philadelphia Phillies
1981	Mike Schmidt (3B)	Philadelphia Phillies
1982	Dale Murphy (OF)	Atlanta Braves
1983	Dale Murphy (OF)	Atlanta Braves
1984	Ryne Sandberg (2B)	Chicago Cubs
1985	Willie McGee (OF)	St. Louis Cardinals
1986	Mike Schmidt (3B)	Philadelphia Phillies
1987	Andre Dawson (OF)	Chicago Cubs
1988	Kirk Gibson (OF)	Los Angeles Dodgers
1989	Kevin Mitchell (OF)	San Francisco Giants
1990	Barry Bonds (OF)	Pittsburgh Pirates
1991	Terry Pendleton (3B)	Atlanta Braves
1992	Barry Bonds (OF)	Pittsburgh Pirates
1993	Barry Bonds (OF)	San Francisco Giants
1994	Jeff Bagwell (1B)	Houston Astros
1995	Barry Larkin (SS)	Cincinnati Reds
1996	Ken Caminiti (3B)	San Diego Padres

* tied vote

American League

Year	Player	Team
1931	Lefty Grove (P)	Philadelphia A's
1932	Jimmie Foxx (1B)	Philadelphia A's
1933	Jimmie Foxx (1B)	Philadelphia A's
1934	Mickey Cochrane (C)	Detroit Tigers
1935	Hank Greenberg (1B)	Detroit Tigers
1936	Lou Gehrig (1B)	New York Yankees
1937	Charlie Gehringer (2B)	Detroit Tigers
1938	Jimmie Foxx (1B)	Boston Red Sox
1939	Joe DiMaggio (OF)	New York Yankees
1940	Hank Greenberg (OF)	Detroit Tigers
1941	Joe DiMaggio (OF)	New York Yankees
1942	Joe Gordon (2B)	New York Yankees
1943	Spud Chandler (P)	New York Yankees
1944	Hal Newhouser (P)	Detroit Tigers
1945	Hal Newhouser (P)	Detroit Tigers
1946	Ted Williams (OF)	Boston Red Sox
1947	Joe DiMaggio (OF)	New York Yankees
1948	Lou Boudreau (SS)	Cleveland Indians
1949	Ted Williams (OF)	Boston Red Sox
1950	Phil Rizzuto (SS)	New York Yankees
1951	Yogi Berra (C)	New York Yankees
1952	Bobby Shantz (P)	Philadelphia A's
1953	Al Rosen (3B)	Cleveland Indians
1954	Yogi Berra (C)	New York Yankees
1955	Yogi Berra (C)	New York Yankees
1956	Mickey Mantle (OF)	New York Yankees
1957	Mickey Mantle (OF)	New York Yankees
1958	Jackie Jensen (OF)	Boston Red Sox
1959	Nellie Fox (2B)	Chicago White Sox
1960	Roger Maris (OF)	New York Yankees
1961	Roger Maris (OF)	New York Yankees
1962	Mickey Mantle (OF)	New York Yankees
1963	Elston Howard (C)	New York Yankees
1964	Brooks Robinson (3B)	Baltimore Orioles
1965	Zoilo Versalles (SS)	Minnesota Twins
1966	Frank Robinson (OF)	Baltimore Orioles
1967	Carl Yastrzemski (OF)	Boston Red Sox
1968	Denny McLain (P)	Detroit Tigers
1969	Harmon Killebrew (1B–3B)	Minnesota Twins
1970	Boog Powell (1B)	Baltimore Orioles
1971	Vida Blue (P)	Oakland A's
1972	Dick Allen (1B)	Chicago White Sox
1973	Reggie Jackson (OF)	Oakland A's
1974	Jeff Burroughs (OF)	Texas Rangers
1975	Fred Lynn (OF)	Boston Red Sox
1976	Thurman Munson (C)	New York Yankees
1977	Rod Carew (1B)	Minnesota Twins
1978	Jim Rice (OF–DH)	Boston Red Sox
1979	Don Baylor (OF–DH)	California Angels
1980	George Brett (3B)	Kansas City Royals
1981	Rollie Fingers (P)	Milwaukee Brewers
1982	Robin Yount (SS)	Milwaukee Brewers
1983	Cal Ripken Jr. (SS)	Baltimore Orioles
1984	Willie Hernandez (P)	Detroit Tigers
1985	Don Mattingly (1B)	New York Yankees
1986	Roger Clemens (P)	Boston Red Sox
1987	George Bell (OF)	Toronto Blue Jays
1988	Jose Canseco (OF)	Oakland A's
1989	Robin Yount (OF)	Milwaukee Brewers
1990	Rickey Henderson (OF)	Oakland A's
1991	Cal Ripken Jr. (SS)	Baltimore Orioles
1992	Dennis Eckersley (P)	Oakland A's
1993	Frank Thomas (1B)	Chicago White Sox
1994	Frank Thomas (1B)	Chicago White Sox
1995	Mo Vaughn (1B)	Boston Red Sox
1996	Juan Gonzalez (OF)	Texas Rangers

Cy Young Award Winners
Inaugurated in 1956, this award is given to the best pitcher in baseball as judged by the Baseball Writers' Association of America. Since 1967, separate awards have been given to the best pitcher in each league.

Most wins
Four, by two players: Steve Carlton, Philadelphia Phillies, 1972, 1977, 1980, 1982; and Greg Maddux, Chicago Cubs, 1992, Atlanta Braves, 1993-95.

Most consecutive wins
Greg Maddux is the only pitcher in baseball history to win the Cy Young Award four times in a row: Chicago Cubs (NL), 1992; Atlanta Braves (NL), 1993, 1994 and 1995.

Wins, both leagues
The only pitcher to win the Cy Young Award in both leagues is Gaylord Perry: Cleveland Indians (AL), 1972; San Diego Padres (NL), 1978.

Year	Pitcher	Team	Year	Pitcher	Team
1956	Don Newcombe	Brooklyn Dodgers (NL)	1962	Don Drysdale	Los Angeles Dodgers (NL)
1957	Warren Spahn	Milwaukee Braves (NL)	1963	Sandy Koufax	Los Angeles Dodgers (NL)
1958	Bob Turley	New York Yankees (AL)	1964	Dean Chance	Los Angeles Angels (AL)
1959	Early Wynn	Chicago White Sox (AL)	1965	Sandy Koufax	Los Angeles Dodgers (NL)
1960	Vernon Law	Pittsburgh Pirates (NL)	1966	Sandy Koufax	Los Angeles Dodgers (NL)
1961	Whitey Ford	New York Yankees (AL)			

National League

Year	Pitcher	Team	Year	Pitcher	Team
1967	Mike McCormick	San Francisco Giants	1982	Steve Carlton	Philadelphia Phillies
1968	Bob Gibson	St. Louis Cardinals	1983	John Denny	Philadelphia Phillies
1969	Tom Seaver	New York Mets	1984	Rick Sutcliffe	Chicago Cubs
1970	Bob Gibson	St. Louis Cardinals	1985	Dwight Gooden	New York Mets
1971	Ferguson Jenkins	Chicago Cubs	1986	Mike Scott	Houston Astros
1972	Steve Carlton	Philadelphia Phillies	1987	Steve Bedrosian	Philadelphia Phillies
1973	Tom Seaver	New York Mets	1988	Orel Hershiser	Los Angeles Dodgers
1974	Mike Marshall	Los Angeles Dodgers	1989	Mark Davis	San Diego Padres
1975	Tom Seaver	New York Mets	1990	Doug Drabek	Pittsburgh Pirates
1976	Randy Jones	San Diego Padres	1991	Tom Glavine	Atlanta Braves
1977	Steve Carlton	Philadelphia Phillies	1992	Greg Maddux	Chicago Cubs
1978	Gaylord Perry	San Diego Padres	1993	Greg Maddux	Atlanta Braves
1979	Bruce Sutter	Chicago Cubs	1994	Greg Maddux	Atlanta Braves
1980	Steve Carlton	Philadelphia Phillies	1995	Greg Maddux	Atlanta Braves
1981	Fernando Valenzuela	Los Angeles Dodgers	1996	John Smoltz	Atlanta Braves

Cy Young Award Winners (continued)

American League

Year	Pitcher	Team
1967	Jim Lonborg	Boston Red Sox
1968	Denny McLain	Detroit Tigers
1969*	Mike Cuellar	Baltimore Orioles
	Denny McLain	Detroit Tigers
1970	Jim Perry	Minnesota Twins
1971	Vida Blue	Oakland Athletics
1972	Gaylord Perry	Cleveland Indians
1973	Jim Palmer	Baltimore Orioles
1974	"Catfish" Hunter	Oakland Athletics
1975	Jim Palmer	Baltimore Orioles
1976	Jim Palmer	Baltimore Orioles
1977	Sparky Lyle	New York Yankees
1978	Ron Guidry	New York Yankees
1979	Mike Flanagan	Baltimore Orioles
1980	Steve Stone	Baltimore Orioles
1981	Rollie Fingers	Milwaukee Brewers
1982	Pete Vukovich	Milwaukee Brewers
1983	LaMarr Hoyt	Chicago White Sox
1984	Willie Hernandez	Detroit Tigers
1985	Bret Saberhagen	Kansas City Royals
1986	Roger Clemens	Boston Red Sox
1987	Roger Clemens	Boston Red
1988	Frank Viola	Minnesota Twins
1989	Bret Saberhagen	Kansas City Royals
1990	Bob Welch	Oakland Athletics
1991	Roger Clemens	Boston Red Sox
1992	Dennis Eckersley	Oakland Athletics
1993	Jack McDowell	Chicago White Sox
1994	David Cone	Kansas City Royals
1995	Randy Johnson	Seattle Mariners
1996	Pat Hentgen	Toronto Blue Jays

*Tied vote

The 1996 Cy Young Award winners were John Smoltz (left) and Pat Hentgen.
(Otto Greule/Allsport; Rick Stewart/Allsport)

Rookie of the Year

The Rookie of the Year Award is voted on by the Baseball Writers Association and was first presented in 1947. In 1947 and 1948 only one award was given for both leagues.

MVP winner (Baseball Writers' Award):

The only Rookie of the Year to win the MVP was Fred Lynn (Boston Red Sox, 1975).

Ties:

Ties have only occurred twice, once in each league. In the National League, Butch Metzger (San Dieto Padres) and Pat Zachry (Cincinnati Reds) tied in 1976. In the American League, John Castino (Minnesota Twins) and Alfredo Griffin (Toronto Blue Jays) tied in 1979.

Youngest Rookie of the Year:

19—Dwight Gooden, New York Mets, 1984.

Oldest Rookie of the Year:

Four players are tied at 28—Jackie Robinson, Brooklyn Dodgers, 1947; Sam Jethroe, Boston Braves, 1950; Joe Black, Brooklyn Dodgers, 1952; and Jack Sanford, Philadelphia Phillies, 1957.

Most Rookie of the Year honors by a team:

16—Los Angeles Dodgers, 1947, 1949, 1952, 1953, 1960, 1965, 1969, 1979–82, 1992–96.

Most consecutive Rookie of the Year honors by a team:

5—Los Angeles Dodgers, 1992–96.

American League and National League Combined

Year	Player	Team
1947	Jackie Robinson (1B)	Brooklyn Dodgers (NL)
1948	Alvin Dark (SS)	Boston Braves (NL)

National League

Year	Player	Team
1949	Don Newcombe (P)	Brooklyn Dodgers
1950	Sam Jethroe (OF)	Boston Braves
1951	Willie Mays (OF)	New York Giants
1952	Joe Black (P)	Brooklyn Dodgers
1953	Jim Gilliam (2B)	Brooklyn Dodgers
1954	Wally Moon (OF)	St. Louis Cardinals
1955	Bill Virdon (OF)	St. Louis Cardinals
1956	Frank Robinson (OF)	Cincinnati Reds
1957	Jack Sanford (P)	Philadelphia Phillies
1958	Orlando Cepeda (1B)	San Francisco Giants
1959	Willie McCovey (1B)	San Francisco Giants
1960	Frank Howard (OF)	Los Angeles Dodgers
1961	Billy Williams (OF)	Chicago Cubs
1962	Ken Hubbs (2B)	Chicago Cubs
1963	Pete Rose (2B)	Cincinnati Reds
1964	Richie Allen (3B)	Philadelphia Phillies
1965	Jim Lefebvre (2B)	Los Angeles Dodgers
1966	Tommy Helms (3B)	Cincinnati Reds
1967	Tom Seaver (P)	New York Mets
1968	Johnny Bench (C)	Cincinnati Reds
1969	Ted Sizemore (2B)	Los Angeles Dodgers
1970	Carl Morton (P)	Montreal Expos
1971	Earl Williams (C)	Atlanta Braves
1972	Jon Matlack (P)	New York Mets
1973	Gary Matthews (OF)	San Francisco Giants
1974	Bake McBride (OF)	St. Louis Cardinals
1975	John Montefusco (P)	San Francisco Giants
1976*	Butch Metzger (P) Pat Zachry (P)	San Diego Padres Cincinnati Reds
1977	Andre Dawson (OF)	Montreal Expos
1978	Bob Horner (3B)	Atlanta Braves
1979	Rick Sutcliffe (P)	Los Angeles Dodgers
1980	Steve Howe (P)	Los Angeles Dodgers
1981	Fernando Valenzuela (P)	Los Angeles Dodgers
1982	Steve Sax (2B)	Los Angeles Dodgers
1983	Darryl Strawberry (OF)	New York Mets
1984	Dwight Gooden (P)	New York Mets
1985	Vince Coleman (OF)	St. Louis Cardinals
1986	Todd Worrell (P)	St. Louis Cardinals
1987	Benito Santiago (C)	San Diego Padres
1988	Chris Sabo (3B)	Cincinnati Reds
1989	Jerome Walton (OF)	Chicago Cubs
1990	David Justice (OF)	Atlanta Braves
1991	Jeff Bagwell (1B)	Houston Astros
1992	Eric Karros (1B)	Los Angeles Dodgers
1993	Mike Piazza (C)	Los Angeles Dodgers
1994	Raul Mondesi (OF)	Los Angeles Dodgers
1995	Hideo Nomo (P)	Los Angeles Dodgers
1996	Todd Hollandsworth (OF)	Los Angeles Dodgers

* tied vote

Rookie of the Year (continued)

American League

Year	Player	Team
1949	Roy Sievers (OF)	St. Louis Cardinals
1950	Walt Dropo (1B)	Boston Red Sox
1951	Gil McDougald (3B)	New York Yankees
1952	Harry Byrd (P)	Philadelphia Athletics
1953	Harvey Kuenn (SS)	Detroit Tigers
1954	Bob Grim (P)	New York Yankees
1955	Herb Score (P)	Cleveland Indians
1956	Luis Aparicio (SS)	Chicago White Sox
1957	Tony Kubek (OF–INF)	New York Yankees
1958	Albie Pearson (OF)	Washington Senators
1959	Bob Allison (OF)	Washington Senators
1960	Ron Hansen (SS)	Baltimore Orioles
1961	Don Schwall (P)	Boston Red Sox
1962	Tom Tresh (SS–OF)	New York Yankees
1963	Gary Peters (P)	Chicago White Sox
1964	Tony Oliva (OF)	Minnesota Twins
1965	Curt Blefary (OF)	Baltimore Orioles
1966	Tommy Agee (OF)	Chicago White Sox
1967	Rod Carew (2B)	Minnesota Twins
1968	Stan Bahnsen (P)	New York Yankees
1969	Lou Piniella (OF)	Kansas City Royals
1970	Thurman Munson (C)	New York Yankees
1971	Chris Chambliss (1B)	Cleveland Indians
1972	Carlton Fisk (C)	Boston Red Sox
1973	Al Bumbry (OF)	Baltimore Orioles
1974	Mike Hargrove (1B)	Texas Rangers
1975	Fred Lynn (OF)	Boston Red Sox
1976	Mark Fidrych (P)	Detroit Tigers
1977	Eddie Murray (1B–DH)	Baltimore Orioles
1978	Lou Whitaker (2B)	Detroit Tigers
1979*	John Castino (3B)	Minnesota Twins
	Alfredo Griffin (SS)	Toronto Blue Jays
1980	Joe Charboneau (DH–OF)	Cleveland Indians
1981	Dave Righetti (P)	New York Yankees
1982	Cal Ripken Jr. (SS)	Baltimore Orioles
1983	Ron Kittle (OF)	Chicago White Sox
1984	Alvin Davis (1B)	Seattle Mariners
1985	Ozzie Guillen (SS)	Chicago White Sox
1986	Jose Canseco (OF)	Oakland Athletics
1987	Mark McGwire (1B)	Oakland Athletics
1988	Walt Weiss (SS)	Oakland Athletics
1989	Greg Olson (P)	Baltimore Orioles
1990	Sandy Alomar Jr. (C)	Cleveland Indians
1991	Chuck Knoblauch (2B)	Minnesota Twins
1992	Pat Listach (SS)	Milwaukee Brewers
1993	Tim Salmon (DH)	California Angels
1994	Robert Hamelin (1B)	Kansas City Royals
1995	Marty Cordova (OF)	Minnesota Twins
1996	Derek Jeter (SS)	New York Yankees

* tied vote

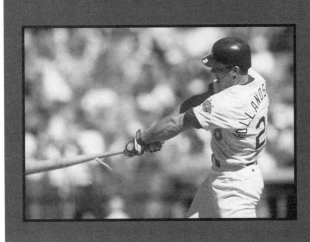

The 1996 Rookies of the Year were Todd Hollandsworth (left) and Derek Jeter.
(Stephen Dunn/Allsport; Al Bello/Allsport)

LEAGUE CHAMPIONSHIP SERIES RECORDS

Games Played

Most series played   11, by Reggie Jackson, Oaklad Athletics (AL), 1971–75; New York Yankees (AL), 1977–78, 1980–81; California Angels (AL), 1982, 1986.

Most games played   45, by Reggie Jackson, Oakland Athletics (AL), 1971–75; New York Yankees (AL), 1977–78, 1980–81; California Angels (AL), 1982, 1986.

Hitting Records (Career)

Batting average (minimum 50 at-bats)
.392, by Devon White, California Angels (AL), 1986, Toronto Blue Jays (AL), 1991–93. White collected 29 hits in 74 at-bats in 21 games.

Hits   45, by Pete Rose, Cincinnati Reds (NL), 1970, 1972–73, 1975–76; Philadelphia Phillies (NL), 1980, 1983.

Home runs   Nine, by George Brett, Kansas City Royals (AL), 1976–78, 1980, 1984–85.

Runs batted in (RBIs)   21, by Steve Garvey, Los Angeles Dodgers (NL), 1974, 1977–78, 1981; San Diego Padres (NL), 1984.

Runs scored   22, by George Brett, Kansas City Royals (AL), 1976–78, 1980, 1984–85.

Walks   23, by Joe Morgan, Cincinnati Reds (NL), 1972–73, 1975–76, 1979; Houston Astros (NL), 1980; Philadelphia Phillies (NL), 1983.

Stolen bases   16, by Rickey Henderson, Oakland Athletics (AL), 1981, 1989–90, 1992; Toronto Blue Jays (AL), 1993.

Pitching Records (Career)

Most series pitched   Eight, by Bob Welch, Los Angeles Dodgers (NL), 1978, 1981, 1983, 1985; Oakland Athletics (AL), 1988–90, 1992.

Most games pitched   20, by Rick Honeycutt, Los Angeles Dodgers (NL), 1983, 1985; Oakland Athletics (AL), 1988–90 and 1992; St. Louis Cardinals, 1996.

Wins   Eight, by Dave Stewart, Oakland Athletics (AL), 1988–90, 1992; Toronto Blue Jays (AL), 1993.

Losses   Seven, by Jerry Reuss, Pittsburgh Pirates (NL), 1974–75; Los Angeles Dodgers (NL), 1981, 1983, 1985.

Innings pitched   75, by Dave Stewart, Oakland Athletics (AL), 1988–90 and 1992; Toronto Blue Jays (AL), 1993.

Complete games   Five, by Jim Palmer, Baltimore Orioles (AL), 1969–71, 1973–74, 1979.

Strikeouts   58, by John Smoltz, Atlanta Braves (NL), 1991–93, 1995–96.

Saves   11, by Dennis Eckersley, Chicago Cubs (NL), 1984; Oakland Athletics (AL), 1988–90, 1992; St. Louis Cardinals (NL), 1996.

Terry Pendleton has played in a record 38 NLCS games.
(Jonathan Daniel/Allsport)

League Championship Series

League Championship Series (LCS) playoffs began in 1969 when the American and National Leagues expanded to 12 teams each and created two divisions, East and West. To determine the respective league pennant winners, the division winners played a best-of-five-games series, which was expanded to best-of-seven in 1985.

National League

Year	Winner		Year	Winner
1969	New York Mets (East)		1983	Philadelphia Phillies (East)
1970	Cincinnati Reds (West)		1984	San Diego Padres (West)
1971	Pittsburgh Pirates (East)		1985	St. Louis Cardinals (East)
1972	Cincinnati Reds (West)		1986	New York Mets (East)
1973	New York Mets (East)		1987	St. Louis Cardinals (East)
1974	Los Angeles Dodgers (West)		1988	Los Angeles Dodgers (West)
1975	Cincinnati Reds (West)		1989	San Francisco Giants (West)
1976	Cincinnati Reds (West)		1990	Cincinnati Reds (West)
1977	Los Angeles Dodgers (West)		1991	Atlanta Braves (West)
1978	Los Angeles Dodgers (West)		1992	Atlanta Braves (West)
1979	Pittsburgh Pirates (East)		1993	Philadelphia Phillies (East)
1980	Philadelphia Phillies (East)		1994	*canceled*
1981	Los Angeles Dodgers (West)		1995	Atlanta Braves (East)
1982	St. Louis Cardinals (East)		1996	Atlanta Braves (East)

American League

Year	Winner		Year	Winner
1969	Baltimore Orioles (East)		1983	Baltimore Orioles (East)
1970	Baltimore Orioles (East)		1984	Detroit Tigers (East)
1971	Baltimore Orioles (East)		1985	Kansas City Royals (West)
1972	Oakland A's (West)		1986	Boston Red Sox (East)
1973	Oakland A's (West)		1987	Minnesota Twins (West)
1974	Oakland A's (West)		1988	Oakland A's (West)
1975	Boston Red Sox (East)		1989	Oakland A's (West)
1976	New York Yankees (East)		1990	Oakland A's (West)
1977	New York Yankees (East)		1991	Minnesota Twins (West)
1978	New York Yankees (East)		1992	Toronto Blue Jays (East)
1979	Baltimore Orioles (East)		1993	Toronto Blue Jays (East)
1980	Kansas City Royals (West)		1994	*canceled*
1981	New York Yankees (East)		1995	Cleveland Indians (Central)
1982	Milwaukee Brewers (East)		1996	New York Yankees (East)

WORLD SERIES

Origins

Played annually between the champions of the National League and the American League, the World Series was first staged unofficially in 1903, and officially from 1905 on.

On October 20, 1992 the Toronto Blue Jays hosted the first World Series game played outside the United States. The Blue Jays won the 1992 Series, thus becoming the first non-U.S. team to win the fall classic.

TEAM RECORDS

Most wins 23, by the New York Yankees (AL), 1923, 1927–28, 1932, 1936–39, 1941, 1943, 1947, 1949–53, 1956, 1958, 1961–62, 1977–78, 1996.

Most appearances 34, by the New York Yankees (AL), 1921–23, 1926–28, 1932, 1936–39, 1941–43, 1947, 1949–53, 1955–58, 1960–64, 1976–78, 1981, 1996.

INDIVIDUAL RECORDS

Most Valuable Player Award The World Series MVP award has been won a record two times by three players: Sandy Koufax, Los Angeles Dodgers (NL), 1963 and 1965; Bob Gibson, St. Louis Cardinals (NL), 1964 and 1967; and Reggie Jackson, Oakland Athletics (AL), 1973, New York Yankees (AL), 1977.

Games Played

Most series 14, by Yogi Berra, New York Yankees (AL), 1947, 1949–53, 1955–58, 1960–63.

Most series (pitcher) 11, by Whitey Ford, New York Yankees (AL), 1950, 1953, 1955–58, 1960–64.

Most games 75, by Yogi Berra, New York Yankees (AL), 1947, 1949–53, 1955–58, 1960–63.

Most games (pitcher) 22, by Whitey Ford, New York Yankees (AL), 1950, 1953, 1955–58, 1960–64.

HITTING RECORDS

Batting Average

Career (min. 20 games) .391, by Lou Brock, St. Louis Cardinals (NL), 1964, 1967–68. Brock collected 34 hits in 87 at-bats over 21 games.

Series (min. four games) .750, by Billy Hatcher, Cincinnati Reds (NL), in 1990. Hatcher collected nine hits in 12 at-bats in four games.

Hits

Career 71, by Yogi Berra, New York Yankees (AL), 1947–63. In 259 at-bats, Berra hit 12 home runs, 10 doubles and 49 singles.

Series 13, by three players: Bobby Richardson, New York Yankees, (AL), in 1960; Lou Brock, St. Louis Cardinals (NL), in 1968; Marty Barrett, Boston Red Sox (AL), in 1986.

Home Runs

Career 18, by Mickey Mantle, New York Yankees (AL), 1951–53, 1955–58, 1960–64. Mantle hit his record 18 homers in 230 at-bats in 65 games.

Series Five, by Reggie Jackson, New York Yankees (AL), in 1977.

Game Three, by two players: Babe Ruth, New York Yankees (AL), who did it twice: on October 6, 1926 vs. St. Louis Cardinals, and on October 9, 1928 vs. St. Louis Cardinals; and Reggie Jackson, New York Yankees (AL), on October 18, 1977 vs. Los Angeles Dodgers.

Runs Batted in (RBIs)

Career 40, by Mickey Mantle, New York Yankees (AL), 1951–53, 1955–58, 1960–64.

Series 12, by Bobby Richardson, New York Yankees (AL), in 1960.

Game Six, by Bobby Richardson, New York Yankees (AL), on October 8, 1960 vs. Pittsburgh Pirates.

Andruw Jones' long blast over the fence in Game One of the '96 World Series made him the youngest player ever to hit a home run in the Fall Classic.
(Doug Pensinger/Allsport)

PITCHING RECORDS

Perfect game The only perfect game in World Series history was hurled by Don Larsen, New York Yankees (AL), on October 8, 1956 vs. Brooklyn Dodgers.

Wins

Career 10, by Whitey Ford, New York Yankees (AL), in 11 series, 1950–64. Ford's career record was 10 wins, 8 losses in 22 games.

Series Three, by 12 pitchers. Only two pitchers have won three games in a five-game series: Christy Mathewson, New York Giants (NL) in 1905; Jack Coombs, Philadelphia Athletics (AL) in 1910.

Strikeouts

Career 94, by Whitey Ford, New York Yankees (AL), in 11 series, 1950–64.

Series 35, by Bob Gibson, St. Louis Cardinals (NL) in 1968, from seven games.

Game 17, by Bob Gibson, St. Louis Cardinals (NL), on October 2, 1968 vs. Detroit Tigers.

Innings Pitched

Career 146, by Whitey Ford, New York Yankees (AL), in 11 series, 1950, 1953, 1955–58, 1960–64.

Series 44, by Deacon Phillippe, Pittsburgh Pirates (NL), in 1903 in an eight-game series.

Game 14, by Babe Ruth, Boston Red Sox (AL), on October 9, 1916 v . Brooklyn Dodgers.

Saves

Career Six, by Rollie Fingers, Oakland Athletics (AL), 1972–74.

Series Four, by John Wetteland, New York Yankees (AL), in 1996 in a six-game series.

MANAGERS

Most series 10, by Casey Stengel, New York Yankees (AL), 1949–53, 1955–58, 1960. Stengel's record was seven wins, three losses.

Most wins Seven, by two managers: Joe McCarthy, New York Yankees (AL), 1932, 1936–39, 1941, 1943; and Casey Stengel, New York Yankees (AL), 1949–53, 1956, 1958.

Most losses Six, by John McGraw, New York Giants (NL), 1911–13, 1917, 1923–24.

Wins, both leagues The only manager to lead a team from each league to a World Series title is Sparky Anderson, who skippered the Cincinnati Reds (NL) to championships in 1975–76, and the Detroit Tigers (AL) in 1984.

World Series

Year	Winner	Loser	Series
1903	Boston Pilgrims (AL)	Pittsburgh Pirates (NL)	5–3
1904	*no series*		
1905	New York Giants (NL)	Philadelphia A's (AL)	4–1
1906	Chicago White Sox (AL)	Chicago Cubs (NL)	4–2
1907	Chicago Cubs (NL)	Detroit Tigers (AL)	4–0–1
1908	Chicago Cubs (NL)	Detroit Tigers (AL)	4–1
1909	Pittsburgh Pirates (NL)	Detroit Tigers (AL)	4–3
1910	Philadelphia A's (AL)	Chicago Cubs (NL)	4–1
1911	Philadelphia A's (AL)	New York Giants (NL)	4–2
1912	Boston Red Sox (AL)	New York Giants (NL)	4–3–1*
1913	Philadelphia A's (AL)	New York Giants (NL)	4–1
1914	Boston Braves (NL)	Philadelphia A's (AL)	4–0
1915	Boston Red Sox (AL)	Philadelphia Phillies (NL)	4–1
1916	Boston Red Sox (AL)	Brooklyn Robins (NL)	4–1
1917	Chicago White Sox (AL)	New York Giants (NL)	4–2
1918	Boston Red Sox (AL)	Chicago Cubs (NL)	4–2
1919	Cincinnati Reds (NL)	Chicago White Sox (AL)	5–3
1920	Cleveland Indians (AL)	Brooklyn Robins (NL)	5–2
1921	New York Giants (NL)	New York Yankees (AL)	5–3
1922	New York Giants (NL)	New York Yankees (AL)	4–0–1*
1923	New York Yankees (AL)	New York Giants (NL)	4–2
1924	Washington Senators (AL)	New York Giants (NL)	4–3
1925	Pittsburgh Pirates (NL)	Washington Senators (AL)	4–3
1926	St. Louis Cardinals(NL)	New York Yankees (AL)	4–3
1927	New York Yankees (AL)	Pittsburgh Pirates (NL)	4–0
1928	New York Yankees (AL)	St. Louis Cardinals (NL)	4–0
1929	Philadelphia A's (AL)	Chicago Cubs (NL)	4–1
1930	Philadelphia A's (AL)	St. Louis Cardinals (NL)	4–2
1931	St. Louis Cardinals (NL)	Philadelphia A's (AL)	4–3
1932	New York Yankees (AL)	Chicago Cubs (NL)	4–0
1933	New York Giants (NL)	Washington Senators (AL)	4–1
1934	St. Louis Cardinals (NL)	Detroit Tigers (AL)	4–3
1935	Detroit Tigers (AL)	Chicago Cubs (NL)	4–2
1936	New York Yankees (AL)	New York Giants (NL)	4–2
1937	New York Yankees (AL)	New York Giants (NL)	4–1
1938	New York Yankees (AL)	Chicago Cubs (NL)	4–0
1939	New York Yankees (AL)	Cincinnati Reds (NL)	4–0
1940	Cincinnati Reds (NL)	Detroit Tigers (AL)	4–3
1941	New York Yankees (AL)	Brooklyn Dodgers (NL)	4–1
1942	St. Louis Cardinals (NL)	New York Yankees (AL)	4–1
1943	New York Yankees (AL)	St. Louis Cardinals (NL)	4–1
1944	St. Louis Cardinals (NL)	St. Louis Browns (AL)	4–2
1945	Detroit Tigers (AL)	Chicago Cubs (NL)	4–3

* Tied game

World Series (continued)

Year	Winner	Loser	Series
1946	St. Louis Cardinals (NL)	Boston Red Sox (AL)	4–3
1947	New York Yankees (AL)	Brooklyn Dodgers (NL)	4–3
1948	Cleveland Indians (AL)	Boston Braves (NL)	4–2
1949	New York Yankees (AL)	Brooklyn Dodgers (NL)	4–1
1950	New York Yankees (AL)	Philadelphia Phillies (NL)	4–0
1951	New York Yankees (AL)	New York Giants (NL)	4–2
1952	New York Yankees (AL)	Brooklyn Dodgers (NL)	4–3
1953	New York Yankees (AL)	Brooklyn Dodgers (NL)	4–2
1954	New York Giants (NL)	Cleveland Indians (AL)	4–0
1955	Brooklyn Dodgers (NL)	New York Yankees (AL)	4–3
1956	New York Yankees (AL)	Brooklyn Dodgers (NL)	4–3
1957	Milwaukee Braves (NL)	New York Yankees (AL)	4–3
1958	New York Yankees (AL)	Milwaukee Braves (NL)	4–3
1959	Los Angeles Dodgers (NL)	Chicago White Sox (AL)	4–2
1960	Pittsburgh Pirates (NL)	New York Yankees (AL)	4–3
1961	New York Yankees (AL)	Cincinnati Reds (NL)	4–1
1962	New York Yankees (AL)	San Francisco Giants (NL)	4–3
1963	Los Angeles Dodgers (NL)	New York Yankees (AL)	4–0
1964	St. Louis Cardinals (NL)	New York Yankees (AL)	4–3
1965	Los Angeles Dodgers (NL)	Minnesota Twins (AL)	4–3
1966	Baltimore Orioles (AL)	Los Angeles Dodgers (NL)	4–0
1967	St. Louis Cardinals (NL)	Boston Red Sox (AL)	4–3
1968	Detroit Tigers (AL)	St. Louis Cardinals (NL)	4–3
1969	New York Mets (NL)	Baltimore Orioles (AL)	4–1
1970	Baltimore Orioles (AL)	Cincinnati Reds (NL)	4–1
1971	Pittsburgh Pirates (NL)	Baltimore Orioles (AL)	4–3
1972	Oakland A's (AL)	Cincinnati Reds (NL)	4–3
1973	Oakland A's (AL)	New York Mets (NL)	4–3
1974	Oakland A's (AL)	Los Angeles Dodgers (NL)	4–1
1975	Cincinnati Reds (NL)	Boston Red Sox (AL)	4–3
1976	Cincinnati Reds (NL)	New York Yankees (AL)	4–0
1977	New York Yankees (AL)	Los Angeles Dodgers (NL)	4–2
1978	New York Yankees (AL)	Los Angeles Dodgers (NL)	4–2
1979	Pittsburgh Pirates(NL)	Baltimore Orioles (AL)	4–3
1980	Philadelphia Phillies (NL)	Kansas City Royals (AL)	4–2
1981	Los Angeles Dodgers (NL)	New York Yankees (AL)	4–2
1982	St. Louis Cardinals (NL)	Milwaukee Brewers (AL)	4–3
1983	Baltimore Orioles (AL)	Philadelphia Phillies (NL)	4–1
1984	Detroit Tigers (AL)	San Diego Padres (NL)	4–1
1985	Kansas City Royals (AL)	St. Louis Cardinals (NL)	4–3

World Series (continued)

Year	Winner	Loser	Series
1986	New York Mets (NL)	Boston Red Sox (AL)	4–3
1987	Minnesota Twins (AL)	St. Louis Cardinals (NL)	4–3
1988	Los Angeles Dodgers (NL)	Oakland A's (AL)	4–1
1989	Oakland A's (AL)	San Francisco Giants (NL)	4–0
1990	Cincinnati Reds (NL)	Oakland A's (AL)	4–0
1991	Minnesota Twins (AL)	Atlanta Braves (NL)	4–3
1992	Toronto Blue Jays (AL)	Atlanta Braves (NL)	4–2
1993	Toronto Blue Jays (AL)	Philadelphia Phillies (NL)	4–2
1994	*canceled*		
1995	Atlanta Braves (NL)	Cleveland Indians (AL)	4–2
1996	New York Yankees (AL)	Atlanta Braves (NL)	4–2

The New York Yankees celebrate their 1996 World Series win in the traditional manner.
(Doug Pensinger/Allsport)

The Zantac Kid

Dubbed the "Zantac Kid," John Wetteland is a pharmacist's dream: full pitch counts, a liberal sprinkling of walks, and runners hovering on the bases cause an inordinate amount of indigestion for coaches, teammates and fans. The cure, however, is Wetteland himself. His blazing fastball and sharp curveball anchored the New York Yankees 1996 World Series triumph and garnered him the Series' MVP award.

The reliever's season resembled his pitching style. By mid-season he had broken Lee Smith's record for consecutive saves, then pulled a groin muscle and landed on the disabled list in August. As the Yankees' lead in the AL East slipped, Wetteland came back to the team to help clinch the pennant. The ace "closer" went on to save a record four games in the World Series, leading the Bronx Bombers to their record 23rd World Series championship.

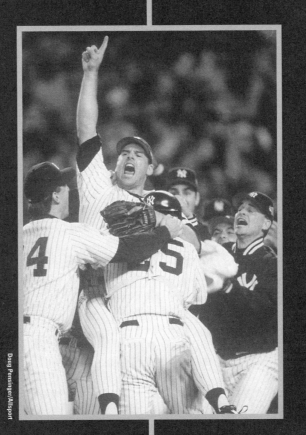

Doug Pensinger/Allsport

For a man of such accomplishment, Wetteland is extraordinarily modest. "I never pitch for personal records," he says. "I don't pitch to get on All-Star teams. The most important thing is that the team comes in the clubhouse after a game in the win column." Wetteland views his records as a team accomplishment. "The closer has to be put into the position to save a game 24 consecutive times." Adds the reliever, "I was just fortunate to be put in that position."

Wetteland is an avid hockey fan and his hobbies include roller blading and playing hockey in the off-season. The pitcher also enjoys snowboarding and mountain biking. Some players would worry about the potential for serious injury from such activities, but not Wetteland. "I'm more worried about not living," he declares. "People say, 'Aren't you afraid of getting hurt?' and I say, 'You've got to live.'"

One area where Wetteland does advise caution is to young pitchers, concerning their pitch selection. "Don't throw curveballs, sliders or anything like that until you are at least 16 years old," he says. Known for his wicked curveball, Wetteland says he never tried the pitch until his late teens. "You see so many kids growing up throwing all of these trick pitches and at 22 years old they can't bend their arm straight and they can't throw as hard."

The Zantac Kid has no use for his medical namesake when pitching. "What is important to know as a closer is that you are the last line of defense. There isn't anyone who is going to come in and clean up your mess."

Wetteland concludes, "I never look at the long term because I know this is a day-to-day thing. If you don't win today, there isn't tomorrow. It takes that kind of mentality in baseball, especially in the 'pen."

COLLEGE BASEBALL

Origins

Various forms of college baseball have been played throughout the 20th century; however, the NCAA did not organize a championship until 1947 and did not begin to keep statistical records until 1957.

NCAA DIVISION I

Hitting Records (Career)

Home runs 100, by Pete Incaviglia, Oklahoma State, 1983–85.

Hits 418, by Phil Stephenson, Wichita State, 1979–82.

Pitching Records (Career)

Wins 51, by Don Heinkel, Wichita State, 1979–82.

Strikeouts 602, by John Powell, Auburn University, 1990–94.

COLLEGE WORLD SERIES

The first College World Series was played in 1947 in Kalamazoo, Mich. The University of California at Berkeley defeated Yale University in a best-of-three-game series, 2–0. In 1949 the series format was changed to a championship game. Since 1950 the College World Series has been played at Rosenblatt Stadium, Omaha, NE.

Most championships The most wins is 11, by Southern Cal., in 1948, 1958, 1961, 1963, 1968, 1970–74 and 1978.

Hitting Records (Career)

Home runs Five, by J. D. Drew, Florida State University, 1995–96.

Hits 23, by Keith Moreland, Texas, 1973–75.

Pitching Records (Career)

Wins Four, by nine players: Bruce Gardner, Southern Cal., 1958, 1960; Steve Arlin, Ohio State, 1965–66; Bert Hooten, Texas at Austin, 1969–70; Steve Rogers, Tulsa, 1969, 1971; Russ McQueen, Southern Cal., 1972–73; Mark Bull, Southern Cal., 1973–74; Greg Swindell, Texas, 1984–85; Kevin Sheary, Miami (FL), 1984–85; Greg Brummett, Wichita State, 1988–89.

Strikeouts 64, by Carl Thomas, Arizona, 1954–56.

College World Series

Year	Winner				
1947	California	1963	Southern Cal.	1980	Arizona
1948	Southern Cal.	1964	Minnesota	1981	Arizona State
1949	Texas	1965	Arizona State	1982	Miami (FL)
1950	Texas	1966	Ohio State	1983	Texas
1951	Oklahoma	1967	Arizona State	1984	Cal. State Fullerton
1952	Holy Cross	1968	Southern Cal.	1985	Miami (FL)
1953	Michigan	1969	Arizona State	1986	Arizona
1954	Missouri	1970	Southern Cal.	1987	Stanford
1955	Wake Forest	1971	Southern Cal.	1988	Stanford
1956	Minnesota	1972	Southern Cal.	1989	Wichita State
1957	California	1973	Southern Cal.	1990	Georgia
1958	Southern Cal.	1974	Southern Cal.	1991	Louisiana State
1959	Oklahoma State	1975	Texas	1992	Pepperdine
1960	Minnesota	1976	Arizona	1993	Louisiana State
1961	Southern Cal.	1977	Arizona St.	1994	Oklahoma
1962	Michigan	1978	Southern Cal.	1995	Cal. State Fullerton
		1979	Cal. State Fullerton	1996	LSU

Little League Baseball World Championship

Year	Winner
1947	Maynard, PA
1948	Lock Haven, PA
1949	Hammonton, NJ
1950	Houston, TX
1951	Stamford, CT
1952	Norwalk, CT
1953	Birmingham, AL
1954	Schenectady, NY
1955	Morrisville, PA
1956	Rosewell Lions Hondo, NM
1957	Monterrey, Mexico
1958	Monterrey, Mexico
1959	Hamtramck, MI
1960	Levittown, PA
1961	El Cajon, CA
1962	San Jose, CA
1963	Granada Hills, CA
1964	Staten Island, NY
1965	Windsor Locks, CT
1966	Houston, TX
1967	Tokyo, Japan
1968	Wakayama, Japan
1969	Taipei, Taiwan
1970	Wayne, NJ
1971	Tainan, Taiwan
1972	Taipei, Taiwan
1973	Tainan City, Taiwan
1974	Kao Hsiung, Taiwan
1975	Lakewood, NJ
1976	Chofu, Japan
1977	Li-Teh, Taiwan
1978	Pin-Kuang, Taiwan
1979	Pu-Tzu Town, Taiwan
1980	Long Kuong, Taiwan
1981	Tai-Ping, Taiwan
1982	Kirkland, WA
1983	Marietta, GA
1984	Seoul, South Korea
1985	Seoul, South Korea
1986	Tainan Park, Taiwan
1987	Hua Lian, Taiwan
1988	Tai Ping, Taiwan
1989	Trumbull, CT
1990	San-Hua, Taiwan
1991	Hsi Nan, Tai Chung, Taiwan
1992	Long Beach, CA *
1993	Long Beach, CA
1994	Latin America, Maracaibo, Venezuela
1995	Far East, Tainan, Chinese Taiwan
1996	Far East Team, Kao-Hsuing City, Chinese Taiwan

*Zamboanga City, Philippines won the game but was subsequently disqualified for fielding overage players. The game was declared a forfeit.

Taiwan's 1996 Little League World Series triumph was the tiny island's record 17th triumph in the event.
(Al Bello/Allsport)

BASKETBALL

Origins

Basketball was invented by Canadian-born Dr. James Naismith at the Training School of the International YMCA College in Springfield, MA in mid-December 1891. The first game played under modified rules was on January 20, 1892. The International Amateur Basketball Federation (FIBA) was founded in 1932; it has now dropped the word Amateur from its title.

NATIONAL BASKETBALL ASSOCIATION (NBA)

Origins

The Amateur Athletic Union (AAU) organized the first national tournament in the United States in 1897. The first professional league was the National Basketball League (NBL), founded in 1898, but this league lasted only two seasons. The American Basketball League was formed in 1925, but declined, and the NBL was refounded in 1937. This organization merged with the Basketball Association of America in 1949 to form the National Basketball Association (NBA).

NBA TEAM RECORDS

Scoring

Most points (one team)   186, by the Detroit Pistons, defeating the Denver Nuggets, 186–184, at Denver, on December 13, 1983 after three overtimes.

Most points, regulation (one team)   173, by two teams: Boston Celtic vs. Minneapolis Lakers (139 points), at Boston, on February 27, 1959; Phoenix Suns vs. Denver Nuggets (143 points), at Phoenix, on November 10, 1990.

Highest-scoring game (aggregate)   370 points, Detroit Pistons defeated the Denver Nuggets, 186–184, at Denver, on December 13, 1983 after three overtimes.

Highest-scoring game (aggregate), regulation   320 points, Golden State Warriors defeated the Denver Nuggets, 162–158, at Denver, on November 2, 1990.

Lowest-scoring game (aggregate)   37 points, Fort Wayne Pistons defeated the Minneapolis Lakers, 19–18, at Minneapolis, on November 22, 1950.

Greatest margin of victory   68 points, by the Cleveland Cavaliers, defeating the Miami Heat, 148–80, on December 17, 1991.

Wins and Losses

Most wins (season)   72, by the Chicago Bulls in 1995–96.

Most consecutive wins   33, by the Los Angeles Lakers. The Lakers' streak began with a 110–106 victory over the Baltimore Bullets on November 5, 1971 in Los Angeles, and ended on January 9, 1972 when they were beaten 120–104 by the Milwaukee Bucks in Milwaukee.

Most losses (season)   73, by the Philadelphia 76ers in 1972–73.

NBA players get bigger, stronger and faster—and younger as well. In December 1996, Portland's Jermaine O'Neal (left) became the NBA's youngest-ever player.
(AP Photo/Rich Pedroncelli)

Most consecutive losses 24, by the Cleveland Cavaliers. The Cavs' undesirable roll started on March 19, 1982 when they lost to the Milwaukee Bucks, 119–97, in Milwaukee, and ended on November 10, 1982 when they defeated the Golden State Warriors 132–120 in overtime on November 10, 1982. During the streak the Cavs lost the last 19 games of the 1981–82 season, and the first five of the 1982–83 season.

INDIVIDUAL RECORDS (GENERAL)

Youngest player The youngest NBA player was Jermaine O'Neal, who made his debut for the Portland Trail Blazers on December 5, 1996 at 18 years 53 days.

Oldest player The oldest NBA player is Robert Parish. On February 24, 1997, he played for the Chicago Bulls at age 43 years 177 days.

Tallest basketball player Gheorghe Muresan, 7 feet 7 inches, is the tallest player in NBA history. He made his pro debut for the Washington Bullets in 1994.

Consecutive Records (Individual)

Games played 906, by Randy Smith, from February 18, 1972 to March 13, 1983. During his streak, Smith played for the Buffalo Braves, San Diego Clippers (twice), Cleveland Cavaliers, and New York Knicks.

Games scoring 50 · points Seven, by Wilt Chamberlain, Philadelphia Warriors, December 16–29, 1961.

Games scoring 10 · points 787, by Kareem Abdul-Jabbar, Los Angeles Lakers, from December 4, 1977 through December 2, 1987.

Free throws 97, by Micheal Williams, Minnesota Timberwolves, from March 24 through November 9, 1993.

Free throws (game) 23, by Dominique Wilkins, Atlanta Hawks, on December 8, 1992.

The Romanian giant Gheorghe Muresan is the NBA's tallest player ever, at 7 feet 7 inches tall.
(David Leah/Allsport)

COACHES

Most wins 1,050, by Lenny Wilkens, as of February 26, 1997. Wilkens coached the Seattle SuperSonics (1969–72), the Portland Trail Blazers (1974–76), the Seattle SuperSonics (1977–85), the Cleveland Cavaliers (1986–93) and the Atlanta Hawks (1994–97).

Most wins (playoffs) Pat Riley has won a record 137 playoff games, 102 with the Los Angeles Lakers (1981–90) and 35 with the New York Knicks (1992–95).

Highest winning percentage .736, by Phil Jackson, Chicago Bulls, 1989–February 26, 1997. Jackson's record is 463 wins, 166 losses.

Most games 1,938, by Bill Fitch, Cleveland Cavaliers, 1970–79; Boston Celtics, 1979–83; Houston Rockets, 1983–88; New Jersey Nets, 1989–92; Los Angeles Clippers, 1994–97. Fitch's career totals were 914 wins, 1,024 losses as of February 26, 1997.

Dream Coach

An NBA legend himself, Lenny Wilkens was most influenced by one of baseball's greatest heroes. "I really looked up to Jackie Robinson," says Wilkens. "I went to Ebbits Field a lot. He never made excuses for himself. No matter what was said or done, he never let anyone discourage him from what his goal was. He had great dedication, and no one worked harder than him. I always thought those were great characteristics." Those same characteristics are evident in Wilkens, and are the foundation for his stellar career in the NBA as a player and record-breaking coach.

By current NBA standards, Wilkens, at 6' 1", was a relatively diminutive point guard, but as the first coach to amass 1,000 wins in the NBA, Wilkens is firmly established as a giant in the coaching ranks. The New York native, however, wasn't sure that he wanted to coach: "I just never thought about coaching. If you didn't plan on it, you didn't think about." In fact, prior to joining the coaching ranks, the Providence College graduate had spent three off-seasons working in the sales and marketing division of Monsanto, the chemicals company.

Job stability is not usually associated with the NBA coaching profession, making Wilkens' achievement all the more remarkable. Wilkens stresses that teaching is the key to coaching success and thus longevity: "You have to have the ability to teach young players so that they can grow and develop. You have to be consistent. Players must know what is expected of them." Adds the coach, "Today, players come out of college early, and in some cases right out of high school. They lack experience in the game, and so it's even more important than ever that coaches know how to teach."

Wilkens has seen a tremendous transformation in the NBA during his four-decade association with the league. "The players are much bigger and there are more great athletes than at any other time." But the coach observes: "Although there is great athleticism I don't think the players are necessarily smarter. I don't think the players understand the game as well as players did in my time." Wilkens sees the best change in the game as the introduction of the 3-point shot: "A great addition to the league," says the coach.

Last summer Wilkens coached the U.S. "Dream Team" at the 1996 Olympics. Wilkens rates the gold medal win as the highlight of his career, even better than his NBA title with the Seattle SuperSonics: "A championship is great, but here [the Olympics] you are representing your country on the world stage. It was an incredible feeling." The coach strongly supports the participation of NBA players in the Olympics. "Players for other countries play professional ball when they are not playing for their country," he observes.

Wilkens is still motivated to win another NBA title, but ultimately he is a teacher, and it's life lessons that he feels are the most important. "If you want to impact your future you have to arm yourself with all the power that knowledge gives. The only way to do that is through education." Adds Wilkens, "I always hope that when I meet people I impact them in a positive way that helps them impact other people in a positive way."

Doug Pensinger/Allsport

NBA Individual Records

		Player(s)	Team(s)	Date(s)
Games Played				
Season	88	Walt Bellamy	New York Knicks, Detroit Pistons	1968–69
Career	1,595	Robert Parish	Golden StateWarriors, Boston Celtics, Charlotte Hornets, Chicago Bulls	1976–97*
Points				
Game	100	Wilt Chamberlain	Philadelphia Warriors vs. New York Knicks	March 2, 1962
Season	4,029	Wilt Chamberlain	Philadelphia Warriors	1961–62
Career	38,387	Kareem Abdul-Jabbar	Milwaukee Bucks, Los Angeles Lakers	1969–89
Field Goals				
Game	36	Wilt Chamberlain	Philadelphia Warriors vs. New York Knicks	March 2, 1962
Season	1,597	Wilt Chamberlain	Philadelphia Warriors	1961–62
Career	15,837	Kareem Abdul-Jabbar	Milwaukee Bucks, Los Angeles Lakers	1969–89
Three-Point Field Goal				
Game	11	Dennis Scott	Orlando Magic vs. Atlanta Hawks	April 18, 1996
Season	267	Dennis Scott	Orlando Magic	1995–96
Career	1,396	Dale Ellis	Dallas Mavericks, SeattleSuperSonics, Milwaukee Bucks, San Antonio Spurs, Denver Nuggets	1983–97*
Free Throws				
Game	28	Wilt Chamberlain	Philadelphia Warriors vs. New York Knicks	March 2, 1962
		Adrian Dantley	Utah Jazz vs. Houston Rockets	January 4, 1984
Season	840	Jerry West	Los Angeles Lakers	1965–66
Career	8,531	Moses Malone	Buffalo Braves, Houston Rockets, Philadelphia 76ers, Washington Bullets, Atlanta Hawks, Milwaukee Bucks, Philadelphia 76ers, San Antonio Spurs	1976–95
Assists				
Game	30	Scott Skiles	Orlando Magic vs. Denver Nuggets	December 30, 1990
Season	1,164	John Stockton	Utah Jazz	1990-91
Career	11,880	John Stockton	Utah Jazz	1984-97*
Rebounds				
Game	55	Wilt Chamberlain	Philadelphia Warriors vs. Boston Celtics	November 24, 1960
Season	2,149	Wilt Chamberlain	Philadelphia Warriors	1960–61
Career	23,924	Wilt Chamberlain	Philadelphia/San Francisco Warriors, Philadelphia 76ers, Los Angeles Lakers	1959–73

* As of February 24, 1997.

NBA Individual Records (continued)

		Player(s)	Team(s)	Date(s)
Steals				
Game	11	Larry Kenon	San Antonio Spurs vs. Kansas City Kings	December 26, 1976
Season	301	Alvin Robertson	San Antonio Spurs	1985–86
Career	2,475	John Stockton	Utah Jazz	1984–97*
Blocked Shots +				
Game	17	Elmore Smith	Los Angeles Lakers vs. Portland Trail Blazers October 28,	1973
Season	456	Mark Eaton	Utah Jazz	1984–85
Career	3,310	Hakeem Olajuwon	Houston Rockets	1984–97*
Personal Fouls				
Game	8	Don Otten	Tri-Cities vs. Sheboygan	November 24, 1949
Season	386	Darryl Dawkins	New Jersey Nets	1983–84
Career	4,657	Kareem Abdul-Jabbar	Milwaukee Bucks, Los Angeles Lakers	1969–89
Disqualifications ++				
Season	26	Don Meineke	Fort Wayne Pistons	1952–53
Career	127	Vern Mikkelsen	Minneapolis Lakers	1950–59

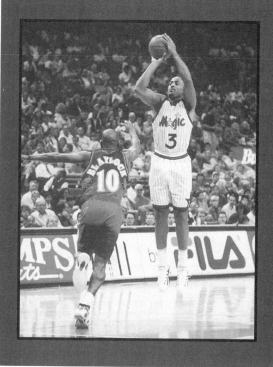

* As of February 24, 1997.

\+ Compiled since 1973–74 season.

\++ From January 7, 1978 through the 1994–95 season, Moses Malone (Houston Rockets, Philadelphia 76ers, Washington Bullets, Atlanta Hawks, Milwaukee Bucks, Philadelphia 76ers, San Antoni Spurs) played 1,212 consecutive games without fouling out.

Dennis Scott holds NBA marks for most three-pointers made in a game in a season.
(Allsport)

NBA Most Valuable Player Award

The Maurice Podoloff Trophy was instituted in 1956 to be awarded to the NBA's most valuable player. From 1956 to 1980 the award was decided by a vote of eligible NBA players; since 1980 the winner has been decided by a vote of eligible writers and broadcasters.

Most wins

Six, by Kareem Abdul-Jabbar, Milwaukee Bucks, 1971–72, 1974; Los Angeles Lakers, 1976–77, 1980.

Year	Player	Team
1956	Bob Pettit	St. Louis Hawks
1957	Bob Cousy	Boston Celtics
1958	Bill Russell	Boston Celtics
1959	Bob Pettit	St. Louis Hawks
1960	Wilt Chamberlain	Philadelphia Warriors
1961	Bill Russell	Boston Celtics
1962	Bill Russell	Boston Celtics
1963	Bill Russell	Boston Celtics
1964	Oscar Robertson	Cincinnati Royals
1965	Bill Russell	Boston Celtics
1966	Wilt Chamberlain	Philadelphia 76ers
1967	Wilt Chamberlain	Philadelphia 76ers
1968	Wilt Chamberlain	Philadelphia 76ers
1969	Wes Unseld	Baltimore Bullets
1970	Willis Reed	New York Knicks
1971	Kareem Abdul-Jabbar	Milwaukee Bucks
1972	Kareem Abdul-Jabbar	Milwaukee Bucks
1973	Dave Cowens	Boston Celtics
1974	Kareem Abdul-Jabbar	Milwaukee Bucks
1975	Bob McAdoo	Buffalo Braves
1976	Kareem Abdul-Jabbar	Los Angeles Lakers
1977	Kareem Abdul-Jabbar	Los Angeles Lakers
1978	Bill Walton	Portland Trail Blazers
1979	Moses Malone	Houston Rockets
1980	Kareem Abdul-Jabbar	Los Angeles Lakers
1981	Julius Erving	Philadelphia 76ers
1982	Moses Malone	Houston Rockets
1983	Moses Malone	Philadelphia 76ers
1984	Larry Bird	Boston Celtics
1985	Larry Bird	Boston Celtics
1986	Larry Bird	Boston Celtics
1987	Magic Johnson	Los Angeles Lakers
1988	Michael Jordan	Chicago Bulls
1989	Magic Johnson	Los Angeles Lakers
1990	Magic Johnson	Los Angeles Lakers
1991	Michael Jordan	Chicago Bulls
1992	Michael Jordan	Chicago Bulls
1993	Charles Barkley	Phoenix Suns
1994	Hakeem Olajuwon	Houston Rockets
1995	David Robinson	San Antonio Spurs
1996	Michael Jordan	Chicago Bulls

Charles Barkley was named league MVP in 1993.
(Doug Pensinger/Allsport)

NBA CHAMPIONSHIPS

The NBA recognizes the 1946–47 season as its first championship; however, at that time the league was known as the Basketball Association of America (BAA).

Most titles   16, by the Boston Celtics, 1957, 1959–66, 1968–69, 1974, 1976, 1981, 1984, 1986.

Consecutive titles   Eight, by the Boston Celtics, 1959–66.

Most titles (coach)   Nine, by Red Auerbach, Boston Celtics, 1957, 1959–66.

NBA FINALS

Individual Records (Game)

Most minutes played   62, by Kevin Johnson, Phoenix Suns vs. Chicago Bulls on June 13, 1993. The game went to three overtimes.

Most points scored   61, by Elgin Baylor, Los Angeles Lakers vs. Boston Celtics on April 14, 1962 in Boston.

Most field goals made   22, by two players: Elgin Baylor, Los Angeles Lakers vs. Boston Celtics on April 14, 1962 in Boston; Rick Barry, San Francisco Warriors vs. Philadelphia 76ers on April 18, 1967 in San Francisco.

Most free throws made   19, by Bob Pettit, St. Louis Hawks vs. Boston Celtics on April 9, 1958 in Boston.

Most rebounds   40, by Bill Russell, Boston Celtics, who has performed this feat twice: vs. St. Louis Hawks on March 29, 1960; vs. Los Angeles Lakers on April 18, 1962, in an overtime game.

Most assists   21, by Magic Johnson, Los Angeles Lakers vs. Boston Celtics on June 3, 1984.

Most steals   Seven, by Robert Horry, Houston Rockets vs. Orlando Magic, June 9, 1995.

Most blocked shots   Eight, by two players: Bill Walton, Portland Trail Blazers vs. Philadelphia 76ers, June 5, 1977; Hakeem Olajuwon, Houston Rockets vs. Boston Celtics, June 5, 1986.

Team Records (Game)

Most points (one team)   148, by the Boston Celtics vs. Los Angeles Lakers (114 points) on May 27, 1985.

Highest-scoring game (aggregate)   276 points, Philadelphia 76ers defeated the San Francisco Warriors, 141–135, in overtime, on April 14, 1967.

Highest-scoring game, regulation (aggregate)   263 points, Los Angeles Lakers defeated the Boston Celtics, 141–122, on June 4, 1987.

Greatest margin of victory   35 points, Washington Bullets shot down the Seattle SuperSonics, 117-82, on June 4, 1978.

Three players hold the mark for most blocked shots in an NBA Finals game: Bill Walton, Hakeem Olajuwon (below right), and Patrick Ewing (below left).
(Allsport)

NBA Playoff Records

		Player(s)	Team(s)	Date(s)
Points				
Game	63	Michael Jordan	Chicago Bulls vs. Boston Celtics	April 20, 1986 (2 OT)
	61	Elgin Baylor	Los Angeles Lakers vs. Boston Celtics	April 14, 1962
Series	284	Elgin Baylor	Los Angeles Lakers vs. Boston Celtics	1962
Career	5,762	Kareem Abdul-Jabbar	Milwaukee Bucks, Los Angeles Lakers	1969–89
Field Goals				
Game	24	Wilt Chamberlain	Philadelphia Warriors vs. Syracuse Nationals	March 14,1960
		John Havlicek	Boston Celtics vs. Atlanta Hawks	April 1, 1973
		Michael Jordan	Chicago Bulls vs. Cleveland Cavaliers	May 1, 1988
Series	113	Wilt Chamberlain	San Francisco Warriors vs. St. Louis	1964
Career	2,356	Kareem Abdul-Jabbar	Milwaukee Bucks, Los Angeles Lakers	1970–89
Free Throws				
Game	30	Bob Cousy	Boston Celtics vs. Syracuse Nationals	March 21, 1953 (4 OT)
	23	Michael Jordan	Chiacgo Bulls vs. New York Knicks	May 14,1989
Series	86	Jerry West	Los Angeles Lakers vs. Baltimore Bullets	1965
Career	1,213	Jerry West	Los Angeles Lakers	1960–74
Assists				
Game	24	Magic Johnson	Los Angeles Lakers vs. Phoenix Suns	May 15, 1984
		John Stockton	Utah Jazz vs. Los Angeles Lakers	May 17, 1988
Series	115	John Stockton	Utah Jazz vs. Los Angeles Lakers	1988
Career	2,346	Magic Johnson	Los Angeles Lakers	1979–91, 1995–96
Rebounds				
Game	41	Wilt Chamberlain	Philadelphia 76ers vs. Boston Celtics	April 5, 1967
Series	220	Wilt Chamberlain	Philadelphia 76ers vs. Boston Celtics	1965
Career	4,104	Bill Russell	Boston Celtics	1956–69
Steals				
Game	8	Rick Barry	Golden State Warriors vs. Seattle SuperSonics	April 14, 1975
		Lionel Hollins	Portland Trail Blazers vs. Los Angeles Lakers	May 8, 1977
		Maurice Cheeks	Philadelphia 76ers vs. New Jersey Nets	April 11, 1979
		Craig Hodges	Milwaukee Bucks vs. Philadelphia 76ers	May 9, 1986
		Tim Hardaway	Golden State Warriors vs. Los Angeles Lakers	May 8, 1991
		Tim Hardaway	Golden State Warriors vs. Seattle SuperSonics	April 30, 1992
		Mookie Blaylock	Atlanta Hawks vs. Indiana Pacers	April 29, 1996
Series	28	John Stockton	Utah Jazz vs. Los Angeles Lakers	1988
Career	358	Magic Johnson	Los Angeles Lakers	1979–91, 1995–96

Source: NBA

NBA Championship Finals

Year	Winner	Loser	Series
1947	Philadelphia Warriors	Chicago Stags	4–1
1948	Baltimore Bullets	Philadelphia Warriors	4–2
1949	Minneapolis Lakers	Washington Capitols	4–2
1950	Minneapolis Lakers	Syracuse Nationals	4–2
1951	Rochester Royals	New York Knicks	4–3
1952	Minneapolis Lakers	New York Knicks	4–3
1953	Minneapolis Lakers	New York Knicks	4–1
1954	Minneapolis Lakers	Syracuse Nationals	4–3
1955	Syracuse Nationals	Fort Wayne Pistons	4–3
1956	Philadelphia Warriors	Fort Wayne Pistons	4–1
1957	Boston Celtics	St. Louis Hawks	4–3
1958	St. Louis Hawks	Boston Celtics	4–2
1959	Boston Celtics	Minneapolis Lakers	4–0
1960	Boston Celtics	St. Louis Hawks	4–3
1961	Boston Celtics	St. Louis Hawks	4–1
1962	Boston Celtics	Los Angeles Lakers	4–3
1963	Boston Celtics	Los Angeles Lakers	4–2
1964	Boston Celtics	San Francisco Warriors	4–1
1965	Boston Celtics	Los Angeles Lakers	4–1
1966	Boston Celtics	Los Angeles Lakers	4–3
1967	Philadelphia 76ers	San Francisco Warriors	4–2
1968	Boston Celtics	Los Angeles Lakers	4–2
1969	Boston Celtics	Los Angeles Lakers	4–3
1970	New York Knicks	Los Angeles Lakers	4–3
1971	Milwaukee Bucks	Baltimore Bullets	4–0
1972	Los Angeles Lakers	New York Knicks	4–1
1973	New York Knicks	Los Angeles Lakers	4–1
1974	Boston Celtics	Milwaukee Bucks	4–3
1975	Golden State Warriors	Washington Bullets	4–0
1976	Boston Celtics	Phoenix Suns	4–2
1977	Portland Trail Blazers	Philadelphia 76ers	4–2
1978	Washington Bullets	Seattle SuperSonics	4–3

NBA Championship Finals (continued)

1979	Seattle SuperSonics	Washington Bullets	4–1
1980	Los Angeles Lakers	Philadelphia 76ers	4–2
1981	Boston Celtics	Houston Rockets	4–2
1982	Los Angeles Lakers	Philadelphia 76ers	4–2
1983	Philadelphia 76ers	Los Angeles Lakers	4–0
1984	Boston Celtics	Los Angeles Lakers	4–3
1985	Los Angeles Lakers	Boston Celtics	4–2
1986	Boston Celtics	Houston Rockets	4–2
1987	Los Angeles Lakers	Boston Celtics	4–2
1988	Los Angeles Lakers	Detroit Pistons	4–3
1989	Detroit Pistons	Los Angeles Lakers	4–0
1990	Detroit Pistons	Portland Trail Blazers	4–1
1991	Chicago Bulls	Los Angeles Lakers	4–1
1992	Chicago Bulls	Portland Trail Blazers	4–2
1993	Chicago Bulls	Phoenix Suns	4–2
1994	Houston Rockets	New York Knicks	4–3
1995	Houston Rockets	Orlando Magic	4–0
1996	Chicago Bulls	Seattle Supersonics	4–2

The Chicago Bulls' NBA dynasty was reestablished in 1996. The team won a record 72 regular-season games and defeated the Seattle Supersonics to gain its fourth NBA title in six years.
(Barry Gossage/NBA/Allsport; Jonathan Daniel/ Allsport)

NCAA (MEN)

The National Collegiate Athletic Association (NCAA) has compiled statistics for its men's basketball competitions since the 1937–38 season. NCAA men's basketball is classified by three divisions: I, II and III.

INDIVIDUAL RECORDS (ALL DIVISIONS)

Points Scored

Game 113, by Clarence "Bevo" Francis, Rio Grande (Division II), vs. Hillsdale on February 2, 1954.

Season 1,381, by Pete Maravich, Louisiana State (Division I) in 1970. Pistol Pete hit 522 field goals and 337 free throws in 31 games.

Career 4,045, by Travis Grant, Kentucky State (Division II), 1969–72.

Field Goals Made

Game 41, by Frank Selvy, Furman (Division I), vs. Newberry on February 13, 1954. Selvy amassed his record total from 66 attempts.

Season 539, by Travis Grant, Kentucky State (Division II) in 1972. Grant's season record was gained from 869 attempts.

Career 1,760, by Travis Grant, Kentucky State (Division II), 1969–72. Grant achieved his career record from 2,759 attempts.

Assists

Game 26, by Robert James, Kean (Division III), vs. New Jersey Tech on March 11, 1989.

Season 406, by Mark Wade, UNLV (Division I) in 1987. Wade played in 38 games.

Career 1,076, by Bobby Hurley, Duke (Division I), 1990–93. During his record-setting career Hurley played in 140 games.

Rebounds

Game 51, by Bill Chambers, William & Mary (Division I), vs. Virginia on February 14, 1953.

Season 799, by Elmore Smith, Kentucky State (Division II) in 1971. Smith played in 33 games.

Career 2,334, by Jim Smith, Steubenville (Division II), 1955–58. Smith amassed his record total from 112 games.

NCAA TEAM RECORDS (DIVISION I)

Most points scored (one team) 186, by Loyola Marymount (CA) vs. U.S. International (140 points), on January 5, 1991.

Highest-scoring game (aggregate) 331 points, Loyola Marymount (CA) defeating U.S. International, 181–150, on January 31, 1989.

Fewest points scored (team) Six, by two teams: Temple vs. Tennessee (11 points), on December 15, 1973; Arkansas State vs. Kentucky (75 points), on January 8, 1945.

Lowest-scoring game (aggregate) 17 points, Tennessee defeating Temple, 11–6, on December 15, 1973.

Widest margin of victory 97 points, Southern-Baton Rouge defeating Patten, 154–57, on November 26, 1993.

Greatest deficit overcome 32 points, Duke defeating Tulane, 74–72, on December 30, 1950, after trailing 22–54 with two minutes left in the first half.

Most wins (season) 37, by two teams: Duke in 1986 (37 wins, 3 losses); UNLV in 1987 (37 wins, 2 losses).

Most losses (season) 28, by Prairie View in 1992 (0 wins, 28 losses).

Consecutive Records (Individual, Division I)

Games scoring 10 · points 115, by Lionel Simmons, La Salle, 1987–90.

Games scoring 50 · points Three, by Pete Maravich, Louisiana State, February 10 to February 15, 1969.

NCAA Division I Men's Records

		Player(s)	Team(s)	Date(s)
Points				
Game	100	Frank Selvy	Furman vs. Newberry	February 13, 1954
	72	Kevin Bradshaw	U.S. International vs. Loyola-Marymount	January 5, 1991*
Season	1,381	Pete Maravich	Louisiana State	1970
Career	3,667	Pete Maravich	Lousiana State	1968–70
Field Goals				
Game	41	Frank Selvy	Furman vs. Newberry	February 13, 1954
Season	522	Pete Maravich	Lousiana State	1970
Career	1,387	Pete Maravich	Lousiana State	1968–70
Three-point Field Goals				
Game	15	Keith Veney	Marshall vs. Morehead State	December 14, 1996
Season	158	Darren Fitzgerald	Butler	1987
Career	401	Doug Day	Radford	1990–93
Free Throws				
Game	30	Pete Maravich	Louisiana State vs. Oregon State	December 22, 1969
Season	355	Frank Selvy	Furman	1954
Career	905	Dickie Hemric	Wake Forest	1952–55
Assists				
Game	22	Tony Fairly	Baptist CS vs. Armstrong State	February 9, 1987
		Avery Johnson	Southern–B.R. vs. Texas Southern	January 25, 1988
		Sherman Douglas	Syracuse vs. Providence	January 28, 1989
Season	406	Mark Wade	UNLV	1987
Career	1,076	Bobby Hurley	Duke	1990–93
Rebounds				
Game	51	Bill Chambers	William & Mary vs. Virginia	February 14, 1953
Season	734	Walt Dukes	Seton Hall	1953
Career	2,201	Tom Gola	La Salle	1952–55
Blocked Shots				
Game	14	David Robinson	Navy vs. N.C.–Wilmington	January 4, 1986
		Shawn Bradley	BYU vs. Eastern Kentucky	December 7, 1990
Season	207	David Robinson	Navy	1986
Career	453	Alonzo Mourning	Georgetown	1989–92
Steals				
Game	13	Mookie Blaylock	Oklahoma vs. Centenary	December 12, 1987
		Mookie Blaylock	Oklahoma vs. Loyola-Marymount	December 17, 1988
Season	150	Mookie Blaylock	Oklahoma	1988
Career	376	Eric Murdock	Providence	1988–91

* Game between two Division I teams

Source: NCAA

Field goals   25, by Ray Voelkel, American, over nine games from November 24 through December 16, 1978.

Field goals (game)   16, by Doug Grayson, Kent vs. North Carolina on December 6, 1967.

Three-point field goals   15, by Todd Leslie, Northwestern, over four games from December 15 through December 28, 1990.

Three-point field goals (game)   11, by Gary Bossert, Niagara vs. Siena, January 7, 1987.

Free throws   64, by Joe Dykstra, Western Illinois, over eight games, December 1, 1981 through January 4, 1982.

Free throws (game)   24, by Arlen Clark, Oklahoma State vs. Colorado, March 7, 1959.

Consecutive Records (Team, Division I)

Wins (regular season)   76, by UCLA, from January 30, 1971 through January 17, 1974. The streak was ended on January 19, 1974 when the Bruins were defeated by Notre Dame, 71–70.

Wins (regular season and layoffs) 88, by UCLA, from January 30, 1971 through January 17, 1974.

Losses   37, by Citadel, from January 16, 1954 through December 12, 1955.

Winning seasons   49, by UCLA, 1949–97.

Coaches (Division I)

Most wins   879, by Dean Smith, North Carolina, 1962–97.

Highest winning percentage   .822, by Adolph Rupp, Kentucky, 1931–52, 1954–72. Rupp's career record was 876 wins, 190 losses.

Most games   1,105, by Henry Iba, Northwest Missouri State, 1930–33; Colorado, 1934; Oklahoma State, 1935–70. Iba's career record was 767 wins, 338 losses.

Most years   48, by Phog Allen, Baker, 1906–08; Kansas, 1908–09; Haskell, 1909, Central Missouri State, 1913–19, Kansas, 1920–56.

NCAA CHAMPIONSHIP TOURNAMENT

The NCAA finals were first contested in 1939 at Northwestern University, Evanston, IL. The University of Oregon, University of Oklahoma, Villanova University and Ohio State University were the first "final four." Oregon defeated Ohio State 46–33 to win the first NCAA title.

Most wins (team)   11, by UCLA, 1964–65, 1967–73, 1975, 1995.

Most wins (coach)   10, by John Wooden, UCLA, 1967–73, 1975.

Championship Game Records (Individual, 1939-97)

Most points   44, by Bill Walton, UCLA vs. Memphis State in 1973.

Most field goals   21, by Bill Walton, UCLA vs. Memphis State in 1973.

Most rebounds   27, by Bill Russell, San Francisco vs. Iowa in 1956.

Most assists   11, by Rumeal Robinson, Michigan vs. Seton Hall, 1989.

The UCLA Bruins have won a record 11 NCAA titles. The team (below) celebrates its 1995 title win.
(Stephen Dunn/Allsport)

NCAA Division I Men's Champions

Year	Winner	Runner-Up	Score
1939	Oregon	Ohio State	46–33
1940	Indiana	Kansas	60–42
1941	Wisconsin	Washington State	39–34
1942	Stanford	Dartmouth	53–38
1943	Wyoming	Georgetown	46–34
1944	Utah	Dartmouth	42–40+
1945	Oklahoma State	NYU	49–45
1946	Oklahoma State	North Carolina	43–40
1947	Holy Cross	Oklahoma	58–47
1948	Kentucky	Baylor	58–42
1949	Kentucky	Oklahoma State	46–36
1950	CCNY	Bradley	71–68
1951	Kentucky	Kansas State	68–58
1952	Kansas	St. John's	80–63
1953	Indiana	Kansas	69–68
1954	LaSalle	Bradley	92–76
1955	San Francisco	LaSalle	77–63
1956	San Francisco	Iowa	83–71
1957	North Carolina	Kansas	54–53++
1958	Kentucky	Seattle	84–72
1959	California	West Virginia	71–70
1960	Ohio State	California	75–55
1961	Cincinnati	Ohio State	70–65+
1962	Cincinnati	Ohio State	71–59
1963	Loyola (IL)	Cincinnati	60–58+
1964	UCLA	Duke	98–83
1965	UCLA	Michigan	91–80
1966	UTEP	Kentucky	72–65
1967	UCLA	Dayton	79–64
1968	UCLA	North Carolina	78–55
1969	UCLA	Purdue	92–72
1970	UCLA	Jacksonville	80–69
1971	UCLA	Villanova*	68–62
1972	UCLA	Florida State	81–76
1973	UCLA	Memphis State	87–66
1974	N. Carolina State	Marquette	76–64
1975	UCLA	Kentucky	92–85
1976	Indiana	Michigan	86–68
1977	Marquette	North Carolina	67–59
1978	Kentucky	Duke	94–88
1979	Michigan State	Indiana State	75–64
1980	Louisville	UCLA*	59–54
1981	Indiana	North Carolina	63–50
1982	North Carolina	Georgetown	63–62
1983	N. Carolina State	Houston	54–52
1984	Georgetown	Houston	84–75
1985	Villanova	Georgetown	66–64
1986	Louisville	Duke	72–69
1987	Indiana	Syracuse	74–73
1988	Kansas	Oklahoma	83–79
1989	Michigan	Seton Hall	80–79+
1990	UNLV	Duke	103–73
1991	Duke	Kansas	72–65
1992	Duke	Michigan	71–51
1993	North Carolina	Michigan	77–71
1994	Arkansas	Duke	76–72
1995	UCLA	Arkansas	89–78
1996	Kentucky	Syracuse	76–67
1997	Arizona	Kentucky	84–79+

* These teams were disqualified by the NCAA for rules violations uncovered following the completion of the tournament.

+ Overtime

++ Triple overtime

During the 1997 NCAA Tournament, North Carolina's Dean Smith set the all-time coaching mark for victories.
(AP Photo/Steve Helber)

NCAA (WOMEN)

Origins

Senda Berenson and Clara Baer are generally credited as the pioneers of women's basketball. In 1892, Berenson, a physical education instructor at Smith College, adapted James Naismith's rules of basketball to create a "divided-court" version, which required the players to remain in their assigned sections of the court, making the game less physically demanding and thus, presumably, more suitable for women. Clara Baer introduced women's basketball to Sophie Newcomb Memorial College in her native New Orleans, LA, in 1893. Baer also adapted the style of Naismith's game, and published her own set of rules in 1895; these became known as the Newcomb College rules.

The game spread rapidly in the late 19th century, with the first women's collegiate game being played between California and Stanford on April 4, 1896. Women's basketball was unable to sustain its growth in the 20th century, however, due to controversy over whether it was safe for women to play the game. It was not until after World War II that attitudes changed and women's basketball began to organize itself on a national level and bring its rules into line with the men's game.

In 1969, Carol Eckman, coach at West Chester University, PA, organized the first national invitation tournament. Under the auspices of the Association for Intercollegiate Athletics for Women (AIAW) the national tournament was expanded, and in 1982 the NCAA was invited to take over the tournament.

NCAA INDIVIDUAL RECORDS (DIVISIONS I, II, III)

Points Scored

Game 67, by Jackie Givens, Fort Valley State (Division II), vs. Knoxville on February 22, 1991. Givens hit 19 field goals, six three-point field goals, and 11 free throws.

Season 1,075, by Jackie Givens, Fort Valley State (Division II), in 1991. Givens' record-setting season consisted of 249 field goals, 120 three-point field goals, and 217 free throws in 28 games.

Career 3,171, by Jeannie Demers, Buena Vista (Division III), 1983–87. Demers' career totals are 1,386 field goals and 399 free throws in 105 games.

Field Goals Made

Game 28, by Ann Gilbert, Oberlin (Division III), vs. Allegheny on February 6, 1991.

Season 392, by Barbara Kennedy, Clemson (Division I) in 1982. Kennedy set her record total from 760 attempts.

Career 1,386, by Jeannie Demers, Buena Vista (Division III), 1984–87. Demers made her record total from 2,838 attempts.

Assists

Game 24, by Joanna Bernabei, West Liberty State (Division II) vs. West Virginia State, February 8, 1997.

Season 355, by Suzie McConnell, Penn State (Division I), in 1987.

Career 1,307, by Suzie McConnell, Penn State (Division I), 1984–88.

Rebounds

Game 40, by Deborah Temple, Delta State (Division I), vs. Alabama–Birmingham, on February 14, 1983.

Season 635, by Francine Perry, Quinnipiac (Division II), in 1982.

Career 1,887, by Wanda Ford, Drake (Division I), 1983–86.

NCAA TEAM RECORDS (DIVISION I)

Most points scored (one team) 149, by Long Beach State vs. San Jose State (69 points), on February 16, 1987.

Highest-scoring game (aggregate) 243 points, Virginia defeating North Carolina State, 123–120, after three overtimes on January 12, 1991.

NCAA Division I Women's Records

		Player(s)	Team(s)	Date(s)
Points				
Game	60	Cindy Brown	Long Beach State vs. San Jose State	February 16, 1987
Season	974	Cindy Brown	Long Beach State	1987
Career	3,122	Patricia Hoskins	Mississippi Valley	1985–89
Field Goals				
Game	27	Lorri Bauman	Drake vs. Southwest Missouri State	January 6, 1984
Season	392	Barbara Kennedy	Clemson	1982
Career	1,259	Joyce Walker	Louisiana State	1981–84
Free Throws				
Game	23	Shaunda Greene	Washington vs. Illinois	November 30, 1991
Season	275	Lorri Bauman	Drake	1982
Career	907	Lorri Bauman	Drake	1981–84
Assists				
Game	23	Michelle Burden	Kent vs. Ball State	February 6, 1991
Season	355	Suzie McConnell	Penn State	1987
Career	1,307	Suzie McConnell	Penn State	1984–88
Rebounds				
Game	40	Deborah Temple	Delta State vs. Alabama–Birmingham	February 14, 1983
Season	534	Wanda Ford	Drake	1985
Career	1,887	Wanda Ford	Drake	1983–86
Blocked Shots				
Game	15	Amy Lundquist	Loyola (Cal.) vs. Western Illinois	December 20, 1992
Season	151	Michelle Wilson	Texas Southern	1989
Career	428	Genia Miller	Cal. St. Fullerton	1987–91
Steals				
Game	14	Natalie White	Florida A&M vs. South Alabama	December 13, 1991
	14	Heidi Caruso	Lafayette vs. Kansas St.	December 5, 1992
	14	Stephanie Wine	Marshall vs. Western Carolina	January 23, 1995
	14	Keisha Anderson	Wisconsin vs. Cleveland State	February 11, 1996
Season	191	Natalie White	Florida A&M	1995
Career	624	Natalie White	Florida A&M	1991–95

Source: NCAA

Fewest points scored (one team) 12, by Bennett vs. North Carolina A&T (85 points), on November 21, 1990.

Lowest-scoring game (aggregate) 72 points, Virginia defeating San Diego State, 38–34, on December 29, 1981.

Most wins (season) 35, by four teams: Texas, 1982; Louisiana Tech., 1982; Tennessee, 1989; Connecticut, 1995.

Most losses (season) 28, by Charleston Southern in 1991.

Coaches (Division I)

Most wins 694, by Jody Conradt, Texas, 1970– February 24, 1997.

Highest winning percentage .863, by Leon Barmore, Louisiana Tech. His career record from 1983 through the 1995–96 season is 397 wins, 63 losses.

NCAA CHAMPIONSHIP TOURNAMENT

The NCAA instituted a women's basketball championship in 1982.

Most wins (team) Five, by Tennessee, 1987, 1989, 1991 and 1996–97.

Most wins (coach) Five, by Pat Summitt. Summitt coached Tennessee to all five NCAA titles.

Championship Game Records (Individual)

Most points 47, by Sheryl Swoopes, Texas Tech vs. Ohio State in 1993.

Most field goals 16, by Sheryl Swoopes, Texas Tech vs. Ohio State, in 1993.

Most rebounds 23, by Charlotte Smith, North Carolina vs. Louisiana Tech, in 1994.

Most assists 10, by two players: Kamie Ethridge, Texas vs. Southern Cal, in 1986; Melissa McCray, Tennessee vs. Auburn, in 1989.

NCAA Women's Championship

Year	Winner	Runner-Up	Score
1982	Louisiana Tech.	Cheyney	76–62
1983	Southern Cal.	Louisiana Tech.	69–67
1984	Southern Cal.	Tennessee	72–61
1985	Old Dominion	Georgia	70–65
1986	Texas	Southern Cal.	97–81
1987	Tennessee	Louisiana Tech.	67–44
1988	Louisiana Tech.	Auburn	56–54
1989	Tennessee	Auburn	76–60
1990	Stanford	Auburn	88–81
1991	Tennessee	Virginia	70–67*
1992	Stanford	Western Kentucky	78–62
1993	Texas Tech.	Ohio State	84–82
1994	North Carolina	Louisiana Tech.	60–59
1995	Connecticut	Tennessee	70–64
1996	Tennessee	Georgia	83–65
1997	Tennessee	Old Dominion	68–59

*Overtime

The University of Tennessee Lady Vol's won a record fifth NCAA basketball title in 1997.
(Matthew Stockman/Allsport)

Triple Gold Guard

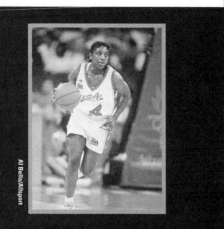

Al Bello/Allsport

Teresa Edwards bounced her first basketball at age 10. Twenty-two years and three Olympic gold medals later, she's still going strong.

Perseverance and hard work are what make Edwards the winningest basketball Olympian in history. She won her first Olympic gold medal in the 1984 games and from then on winning became a bug for her. "I loved playing so much, I wanted more—so I just kept coming back. The healthier I stayed, the more I wanted to play," she enthuses.

Out of the many sports Edwards played when she was a kid, basketball was the one she decided to stick with. "It was the one I truly excelled at and got the most out of mentally," she says.

Although taller than the average woman, Edwards is only 5'11"—not giant for a basketball player. "I was never taller than anyone else when I was young. I was tall for a guard," she recalls. "So it's good that I had those skills, but that was the only advantage I had."

Her career in basketball began to heat up when she made the team in junior high school, she recalls. After that, high school led her right into the Nationals. "I tried out for my first National tournament when I was a junior in high school, and I made the team," Edwards remembers happily. "When I decided to try out for the Olympic team, I was at the University of Georgia and I had a big talk with my coach about it. I just went out and did it."

After winning the gold in '84, Edwards went on to win golds in 1988 and 1996 and a bronze in 1992. "If anyone wants to be the best, they have to have that in mind at all times. Always try your hardest and that's when you excel beyond your wildest dreams," Edwards explains. "Your abilities can always go beyond your body."

OLYMPIC GAMES

The men's basketball competition was introduced at the Berlin Olympics in 1936. In April 1989, the International Olympic Committee voted to allow professional players to compete in the Games. The women's basketball competition was introduced at the Montreal Olympics in 1976.

Most gold medals (men) The United States has won 11 gold medals in Olympic basketball competition: 1936, 1948, 1952, 1956, 1960, 1964, 1968, 1976, 1984, 1992 and 1996.

Most gold medals (women) In the women's basketball tournament the gold medal has been won three times by two teams: the USSR/Unified Teams in 1976, 1980 and 1992; and the United States in 1984, 1988 and 1996.

⟹ Fantastic Feats

Basketball-spinning On July 18, 1994, Bruce Crevier balanced and spun 18 balls across his body.

Dribbling (24 hours) Jamie Borges (U.S.) dribbled a basketball a distance of 85.25 miles in 24 hours on September 7–8, 1995.

Longest goal (men) Christopher Eddy scored a field goal measured at 90 feet 2 3/4 inches for Fairview High School in Erie, PA on February 25, 1989.

Longest goal (women) Nikki Fierstos scored a field goal of approximately 79 feet on January 2, 1993 at Huntington North High School, Huntington, IN.

Most valuable basket Don Calhoun, a spectator randomly picked from the stands at a Chicago Bulls home game on April 14, 1993, sank a basket from the opposite foul line—a distance of 75 feet—and won $1 million.

Vertical dunk height Joey Johnson of San Pedro, CA successfully dunked a basketball at a rim height of 11 feet 7 inches at the One-on-One Collegiate Challenge on June 25, 1990 at Trump Plaza Hotel and Casino in Atlantic City, New Jersey.

BIATHLON

The biathlon is a composite test of cross-country skiing and rifle marksmanship. Competitors ski over a prepared course carrying a small-bore rifle; at designated ranges the skiers stop and complete the shooting assignment for the race. Time penalties are assessed for missed shots; the winner of the event is the one with the fastest time.

Origins

The sport reflects one of the earliest techniques of human survival; rock carvings in Roedoey, Norway dating to 3000 B.C. seem to depict hunters stalking their prey on skis. Biathlon as a modern sport evolved from military ski patrol maneuvers, which tested the soldier's ability as a fast skier and accurate marksman. In 1958 the *Union Internationale de Pentathlon Moderne et Biathlon* (UIPMB) was formed as the international governing body of biathlon and modern pentathlon. Biathlon was included in the Olympic Games for the first time in 1960; women's biathlon was added in 1992.

United States The 1960 Olympic Games in Squaw Valley, CA introduced biathlon to this country. National championships were first held in 1965. The current governing body of the sport is the United States Biathlon Association, founded in 1980 and based in Burlington, VT.

Olympic Games

"Military patrol," the forerunner to biathlon, was included in the Games of 1924, 1928, 1936 and 1948. Biathlon was included in the Winter Games for the first time in Squaw Valley, CA in 1960. Women's events were included for the first time at the 1992 Games in Albertville, France.

Most gold medals Aleksandr Tikhonov (USSR) won four gold medals as a member of the Soviet relay team that won the 4 x 7.5 km races in 1968, 1972, 1976 and 1980. Magnar Solberg (Norway) and Franz-Peter Rotsch (East Germany) have both won two gold medals in individual events. Solberg won the 20 km in 1968 and 1972; Rotsch won the 10 km and 20 km in 1988.

Anfisa Reztsova (Unified Team/Russia) and Myriam Bedard (Canada) have both won two gold medals. Reztsova won the 7.5 km event in 1992 and was a member of the winning team in the 4 x 7.5 km relay race in 1994. Bedard won a women's record two gold medals in individual events, the 7.5 km and 15 km events, in 1994.

Most medals Aleksandr Tikhonov has won a record five medals in Olympic competition. In addition to his four gold medals (see above), he won the silver medal in the 20 km in 1968.

World Championships

First held in 1958 for men and in 1984 for women, the world championships are an annual event. In Olympic years, the Games are considered the world championships; therefore, records in this section include results from the Games.

Most titles (overall) Aleksandr Tikhonov (USSR) has won 14 world titles: 10 in the 4 x 7.5 km relay, 1968–74, 1976–77 and 1980; four individual events, 10 km in 1977 and 20 km in 1969–70 and 1973. In women's events, Kaya Parve (USSR) has won a record six gold medals: four in the 3 x 5km relay, 1984–86, 1988; two individual titles, the 5 km in 1986 and the 10 km in 1985.

Most titles (individual) Frank Ullrich (East Germany) won a record six individual titles: the 10 km in 1978–81 and the 20 km in 1982–83. The most women's individual titles is three, by Anne-Elinor Elvebakk (Norway): the 10 km in 1988 and the 7.5 km in 1989–90.

United States National Championships

In this competition, first held in 1965 in Rosendale, NY, men's events have been staged annually. Women's events were included in 1985.

Most titles Lyle Nelson has won seven national championships: five in the 10 km, 1976, 1979, 1981, 1985 and 1987; two in the 20 km, 1977 and 1985. Anna Sonnerup holds the women's record with five titles: two in the 10 km, 1986–87; two in the 15 km, 1989 and 1991; and one in the 7.5 km in 1989.

Two Disciplines, Two Golds

Pascal Rondeau/Allsport

In an event where concentration and endurance are just as important as strength and speed, two gold medals seems like an exceptional feat for anybody.

The biathlon is an Olympic event that combines cross-country skiing with rifle shooting. Myriam Bedard has taken hold of this record, grabbing the gold in the 7.5 km and 15 km events in the 1994 Olympics.

"Breaking this record is something exceptional—something that doesn't happen at every Olympics," Bedard exclaims. "Especially in the biathlon where anything can happen with the snow and the shooting. So when you set a record like this, you feel it's something you might never get to do again unless all conditions are perfect. It's something special."

"I started the biathlon in the Army Cadets, at the age of 15. They introduced me by accident. I wasn't interested in the actual sport—I didn't know at that time it was an Olympic sport," she recalls. "I was just doing it because I liked it. By the time I found out it was an Olympic sport, I was already the Canadian champion. That's how I decided to go further. At the 1992 Olympic games I won a bronze medal."

The biathlon isn't an easy sport to get into, explains Bedard. Either you absolutely love it, or you don't do it. "It's very hard to practice. Going to shoot every day is rough as well as roller-skiing in the summer—you have to go far away where's there's no cars. Nothing's very accessible. It's not like you just go down to the swimming pool at the end of the street. What drives me the most is the passion I have for the sport. That's why I do it. After one week, I think many people might quit," she adds thoughtfully.

As for how to get into this strenuous sport as a young person, Bedard believes the starting age of the biathlon should be higher than most conventional sports.

"Kids shouldn't get into this sport before the age of 13 or 14 because carrying a rifle is dangerous. Before that, they could just learn cross-country and how to shoot an air rifle—which isn't a live rifle," she says. "If a child is interested in the sport, they could get into it, but not in exactly the same way. Carrying a rifle is something that needs to be done by a responsible person. I wasn't by myself with my own rifle until I was 17—not before that."

BOBSLED AND LUGE

BOBSLED

Origins

The earliest known sled is dated to c. 6500 B.C. and was found in Heinola, Finland. There are references to sled racing in Norwegian folklore dating from the 15th century. The first tracks built for sled racing were constructed in the mid-18th century in St. Petersburg, Russia. The modern sport of bobsled dates to the late 19th century, when British enthusiasts organized competitions in Switzerland. The first run built for bobsled racing was constructed in St. Moritz, Switzerland in 1902. The *Fédération Internationale de Bobsleigh et Tobogganing* (FIBT) was founded in 1923 and is the world governing body of bobsled racing.

United States The United States Bobsled & Skeleton Federation was founded in 1941 and is still the governing body for the sport in this country.

Olympic Games

A four-man bob competition was included in the first Winter Games in 1924 in Chamonix, France. Bobsled events have been included in every Games except 1960, when the Squaw Valley organizing committee refused to build a bobsled track.

Four-man bob Switzerland has won a record five Olympic titles: 1924, 1936, 1956, 1972 and 1988.

Two-man bob Switzerland has won a record four Olympic titles: 1948, 1980, 1992 and 1994.

Most gold medals Meinhard Nehmer and Bernhard Germeshausen (both East Germany) have both won a record three gold medals. They were both members of the 1976 two-man and four-man winning crews and the 1980 four-man winning crews.

Most medals Eugenio Monti (Italy) has won six medals: two gold, two silver and two bronze, 1956–68.

World Championships

A world championship staged independently of the Olympic Games was first held in 1930 for four-man bob, and from 1931 for two-man bob. In Olympic years the Games are considered the world championship; therefore, records in this section include the Games of 1924 and 1928.

Four-man bob Switzerland has won the world title a record 20 times: 1924, 1936, 1939, 1947, 1954–57, 1971–73, 1975, 1982–83, 1986–90 and 1993.

Two-man bob Italy has won the world title 14 times: 1954, 1956–63, 1966, 1968–69, 1971 and 1975.

Most titles Eugenio Monti (Italy) has won 11 bobsled world championships: eight in the two-man, 1957–61, 1963, 1966 and 1968; three in the four-man, 1960–61 and 1968.

LUGE

In luge the rider adopts a supine as opposed to a sitting position.

Origins

The first international luge race took place in 1883. Organized by the hotel keepers of Davos, Switzerland to promote their town, the race attracted 21 entrants from seven countries, including the United States. The course was 2 1/2 miles, from St. Wolfgang to Klosters. The FIBT governed luge racing until 1957, when the *Fédération Internationale de Luge* (FIL) was formed.

United States The United States has participated in all Olympic luge events since the sport was sanctioned for the 1964 Games, but there was no organized governing body for the sport in this country until 1979, when the United States Luge Association was formed. There are two luge runs in the United States that are accredited for international competition: one in Lake Placid, NY and one in Park City, UT.

Olympic Games

One-man skeleton races were included in the 1928 and 1948 Games; however, in skeleton races riders race face down rather than lying on their backs as in luge. Luge was included in the Games for the first time in 1964 in Innsbruck, Austria.

Most gold medals Thomas Kohler, Hans Rinn, Norbert Hahn and Steffi Martin-Walter (all East Germany) and George Hackl (West Germany; Germany) have each won two Olympic titles: Kohler won the single-seater in 1964 and the two-seater in 1968; Rinn and Hahn won the two-seater in 1976 and 1980; Martin-Walter won the women's single-seater in 1984 and 1988; Hackl won the single-seater in 1992 and 1996.

United States No American luger has won a medal at the Olympic Games. In the skeleton sled races held in 1928 and 1948, the United States won one gold and two silvers out of six races. Jennison Heaton was the winner of the 1928 single skeleton sled event.

World Championships

First held in 1955, the world championships have been staged biennially since 1981. In Olympic years the Games are considered the world championships; therefore, records in this section include results from the Games.

Most titles Thomas Kohler and Hans Rinn (both East Germany) have both won six world titles: Kohler won the single-seater in 1962, 1964 and 1966–67, and the two-seater in 1967–68; Rinn won the single-seater in 1973 and 1977, and the two-seater in 1976–77 and 1980 (two world championships were held in 1980, with Rinn winning each time). Margit Schumann (East Germany) holds the women's mark with five world titles, 1973–77.

United States National Championships

This competition was inaugurated in 1974.

Most titles Frank Masley has won a record six men's championships: 1979, 1981–83 and 1987–88. Cammy Myler has won a record six women's titles, 1985, 1989, 1991–93, and 1996.

The fastest speed on a luge is 85.38 mph.
(Shaun Botterill/Allsport)

BOWLING

Origins

The ancient German game of nine-pins (*Heidenwerfen* — "knock down pagans") was exported to the United States in the early 17th century. In 1841, the Connecticut state legislature prohibited the game, and other states followed. Eventually a tenth pin was added to evade the ban. The first body to standardize rules was the American Bowling Congress (ABC), established in New York City on September 9, 1895.

PROFESSIONAL BOWLERS ASSOCIATION (PBA)

The PBA was founded in 1958 by Eddie Elias and is based in Akron, OH.

Tournament of Champions

In this tournament, inaugurated in 1965, the most wins is three, by Mike Durbin in 1972, 1982 and 1984.

Most titles (career)   Earl Anthony of Dublin, CA has won a career record 41 PBA titles, 1970–83.

Most titles (season)   The record number of titles won in one PBA season is eight, by Mark Roth of North Arlington, NJ, in 1978.

Triple Crown

The United States Open, the PBA National Championship and the Tournament of Champions make up the Triple Crown of men's professional bowling. No bowler has won all three titles in the same year, and only four have managed to win all three during a career. The first bowler to accumulate the three legs of the triple crown was Billy Hardwick: National Championship (1963); Tournament of Champions (1965); U.S. Open (1969). Hardwick's feat was matched by Johnny Petraglia: Tournament of Champions (1971); U.S. Open (1977); National (1980); by Pete Weber: Tournament of Champions (1987); U.S. Open (1988 and 1991); National (1989); and by Mike Aulby: National (1985); U.S. Open (1989); Tournament of Champions (1995).

U.S. Open

In this tournament, inaugurated in 1942, the most wins is four, by two bowlers: Don Carter in 1953–54 and 1957–58, and Dick Weber in 1962–63 and 1965–66.

PBA National Championship

In this contest, inaugurated in 1960, the most wins is six, by Earl Anthony in 1973–75 and 1981–83.

Perfect Games

A total of 210 perfect (300 score) games were bowled in PBA tournaments in 1993, the most ever for one year.

Most perfect games (career)   Since 1977, when the PBA began to keep statistics on perfect games, Wayne Webb has bowled 35 in tournament play.

PBA Tour Scoring Records

Games	Score	Bowler	Site	Year
6	1,635	Norm Duke	Peoria, IL	1994
8	2,165	Billy Hardwick	Tokyo, Japan	1968
12	3,083	Mike Aulby	Baltimore, MD	1996
16	4,019	John Mazza	Las Vegas, NV	1996
18	4,696	Norm Duke	Peoria, IL	1994
24	6,019	Pete Weber	Las Vegas, NV	1996

Source: PBA Tour

Most perfect games (season) Three bowlers have bowled eight perfect games in one season: Kelly Coffman, 1994; Dave D'Entremont, 1995; and Eric Forkel, 1995.

Perfect games (tournament)
Two bowlers have bowled four perfect games in one tournament: Walter Ray Williams Jr., Mechanicsburg, PA, 1993; and Dave D'Entremont, Peoria, IL, 1995.

Highest earnings
Walter Ray Williams Jr. has won a career record $1,874,349 in PBA competitions through March 8, 1997. Mike Aulby of Indianapolis, IN set a single-season earnings mark of $298,237 in 1989.

LADIES PRO-FESSIONAL BOWLERS TOUR (LPBT)

Founded in 1981, the LPBT is currently based in Rockford, IL.

Most titles (career)
Lisa Wagner has won 30 tournaments in her 18-year career, 1980–97.

Most titles (season) Patty Costello won a season record seven tournaments in 1976.

Perfect Games

Most bowled (career) Tish Johnson has bowled an LPBT-approved record 38 perfect games.

Walter Ray Williams Jr. may lay claim to the title of perfect bowler, as he holds PBA Tour perfect game marks in several categories.
(Courtesy of PBA Tour)

Most bowled (season) The most perfect games in a season is seven, by Tish Johnson in 1993.

Highest earnings
Aleta Fill won a career record $821,462 in prize money through December 31, 1996. She also had the season high record in 1994, with $126,325 in earnings.

AMERICAN BOWLING CONGRESS (ABC)

Scoring Records

Highest individual score (three games) The highest individual score for three games is 900, by Jeremy Sonnenfeld in Lincoln, NE, February 2, 1997.

Highest team score (one game)
The all-time ABC-sanctioned two-man single-game record is 600, held jointly by five teams: John Cotta and Steve Larson, May 1, 1981 in Manteca, CA; Jeff Mraz and Dave Roney, November 8, 1987 in Canton, OH; William Gruner and Dave Conway, February 27, 1990 in Oceanside, CA; Scott Williams and Willie Hammar, June 7, 1990 in Utica, NY; Darrell Guertin and George Tignor, February 20, 1993 in Rutland, VT.

Highest team score (three games) The highest three-game team score is 3,868, by Hurst Bowling Supplies, of Luzerne, PA on February 23, 1994.

Highest season average The highest season average attained in sanctioned competition is 247.89, by Jeff Phipps of Salem, OR, in the 1992–93 season.

Juniors Brentt Arcement, at age 16, bowled a three-game series of 888, the highest ever bowled in a league or tournament sanctioned by the Young American Bowling Alliance, which is the national organization serving junior bowlers (age 21 and under). The highest score by a girl is 824 by Cindy Shipman of Endicott, NY during the 1985–86 season.

Consecutive strikes The record for consecutive strikes in sanctioned play is 33, by two bowlers: John Pezzin in Toledo, OH on March 4, 1976, and Fred Dusseau in Yuma, AZ, on March 3, 1992.

Perfect Games

Most bowled (career) The highest number of sanctioned 300 games is 52, by Mike Whalin of Cincinnati, OH.

Oldest The oldest person to bowl a perfect game is Jerry Whelman of Port St. Lucie, FL. He performed the feat at St. Lucie Lanes on April 15, 1992 when aged 81 years old.

Youngest The youngest person to bowl a perfect game is Scott Owsley of Fontana, CA, on March 26, 1994, aged 10 years 9 months 6 days.

Consecutive Two perfect games were rolled back to back twice by three bowlers: Al Spotts of West Reading, PA, on March 14, 1982 and again on February 1, 1985; Jerry Wright of Idaho Falls, ID, on January 9, 1992 and again on February 26, 1992; and Steve Gehringer of Reading, PA, on October 3, 1991 and again on February 7, 1992.

WOMEN'S INTERNATIONAL BOWLING CONGRESS (WIBC)

Scoring Records

Highest individual score (three games) The highest individual score for three games is 865, by Anne Marie Duggan in Edmond, OK, on July 18, 1993.

Highest team score (one game) Pamela Beach and Cindy Fry bowled the all-time two-woman single-game highest score of 578 in Lansing, MI, on November 21, 1992.

Highest team score (three games) The highest three-game team score is 3,446, by Drug Package Inc. of St. Louis, MO, on January 5, 1993.

"Mr. 900," Jeremy Sonnenfeld, stunned the bowling world in February 1997 when he bowled three straight perfect games.
(AP Photo/Lincoln Journal Star, Ian Doremus)

Perfect Games

Most bowled (career) The highest number of WIBC-sanctioned perfect games (300) is 21, by Jeanne Naccarato.

Oldest The oldest woman to bowl a perfect game is Evelyn Culbert of Austin, MN. She performed the feat at Eden Lanes, Austin, MN, on April 4, 1993 when aged 66 years old.

Bowled, lowest average Of all the women who have rolled a perfect game, the one with the lowest average was Diane Ponza of Santa Cruz, CA, who had a 112 average in the 1977–78 season.

⇒ Fantastic Feats

Consecutive spares and splits Mabel Henry of Winchester, KY had 30 consecutive spares in the 1986–87 season.

Shirley Tophigh of Las Vegas, NV holds the record of rolling 14 consecutive splits, in the 1968–69 season.

Highest score in 24 hours A team of six scored 242,665 at Dover Bowl, Dover, DE on March 18–19, 1995. During this attempt a member of the team, Richard Ranshaw, set an individual record of 51,064.

Highest season average The highest season average attained in sanctioned WIBC competition is 234, by Elizabeth Johnson of Niagara Falls, NY in the 1993–94 season.

Consecutive strikes Jeanne Naccarato bowled a record 40 consecutive strikes on November 23, 1986 in Sodon, OH.

BOXING

The nationality of the competitors in this section is U.S. unless stated otherwise.

Origins

Boxing with gloves is depicted on a fresco from the Isle of Thera, Greece that has been dated to 1520 B.C. The earliest prize-ring code of rules was formulated in England in 1743 by the champion pugilist Jack Broughton, who reigned from 1734 to 1750. In 1867, boxing came under the Queensberry Rules, formulated for John Sholto Douglas, 8th Marquess of Queensberry.

Longest fights The longest recorded fight with gloves was between Andy Bowen and Jack Burke in New Orleans, LA on April 6–7, 1893. It lasted 110 rounds, 7 hours 19 minutes and was declared a no contest (later changed to a draw).

The longest bare-knuckle fight was 6 hours 15 minutes between James Kelly and Jack Smith in Fiery Creek, Dalesford, Victoria, Australia on December 3, 1855.

Shortest fights The shortest fight on record appears to be one in a Golden Gloves tournament in Minneapolis, MN on November 4, 1947, when Mike Collins floored Pat Brownson with the first punch and the contest was stopped, without a count, four seconds after the bell.

The World Boxing Council reports that the shortest fight in professional boxing occurred on June 19, 1991, when Paul Rees (Australia) scored a technical knockout over Charlie Hansen (Australia) in five seconds in a junior-middleweight bout in Brisbane, Australia.

The shortest world title fight was 20 seconds, when Gerald McClellan beat Jay Bell in a WBC middleweight bout in Bayamon, Puerto Rico on August 7, 1993.

Most fights without loss Of boxers with complete records, Packey McFarland had 97 fights (five draws) from 1905 to 1915 without a defeat.

Consecutive wins Pedro Carrasco (Spain) won 83 consecutive fights, April 22, 1964–September 3, 1970.

Most knockouts The greatest number of finishes classified as "knockouts" in a career is 145 (129 in professional bouts), by Archie Moore, 1936–63.

Consecutive knockouts The record for consecutive knockouts is 44, by Lamar Clark, 1958–1960.

Evander Holyfield's shock defeat of heavyweight champion Mike Tyson in November 1996 made Holyfield the second boxer to regain the heavyweight title twice.
(Jed Jacobsohn/Allsport)

Most knock-downs in a title fight Vic Toweel (South Africa) floored Danny O'Sullivan (Great Britain) 14 times in 10 rounds to win the bantamweight bout on December 2, 1950 in Johannesburg, South Africa.

HEAVYWEIGHT DIVISION

Longest reign Joe Louis was champion for 11 years 252 days, from June 22, 1937, when he knocked out James J. Braddock in the eighth round in Chicago, IL, until announcing his retirement on March 1, 1949. During his reign, Louis defended his title a record 25 times.

Most recaptures Two boxers have regained the heavyweight championship twice: Muhammad Ali and Evander Holyfield. Ali first won the title on February 25, 1964, defeating Sonny Liston. He defeated George Foreman on October 30, 1974, having been stripped of the title by the world boxing authorities on April 28, 1967. He won the WBA title from Leon Spinks on September 15, 1978, having previously lost to him on February 15, 1978. Holyfield won the title on October 20, 1990, defeating James "Buster" Douglas. He regained the WBA and IBF titles from Riddick Bowe on November 6, 1993, having lost to him previously on November 13, 1992. After losing to Michael Moorer on April 22, 1994, Holyfield regained the WBA title on November 9, 1996, when he beat Mike Tyson.

Undefeated Rocky Marciano is the only world champion at any weight to have won every fight of his entire professional career (1947–56); 43 of his 49 fights were by knockouts or stoppages.

Oldest champion The oldest heavyweight boxing champion was George Foreman, at 45 years 287 days old. He knocked out former WBA/IBF champion Michael Moorer in the tenth round on November 5, 1994. Foreman was Moorer's senior by 19 years, and he outweighed him by 28 pounds. It had been 21 years since Foreman lost the crown; he defeated Joe Frazier for the title in 1973, but lost it the following year to Muhammad Ali. Foreman defended the IBF version on April 22, 1995 at 46 years 104 days when he knocked out Axel Schulz.

Youngest champion Mike Tyson was 20 years 144 days when he beat Trevor Berbick to win the WBC title in Las Vegas, NV on November 22, 1986. He added the WBA title when he beat James "Bone-crusher" Smith on March 7, 1987 at 20 years 249 days. He became the youngest undisputed champion on August 1, 1987 when he defeated Tony Tucker for the IBF title at 21 years 59 days.

Lightest champion Bob Fitzsimmons (Great Britain) weighed 167 pounds when he won the title by knocking out James J. Corbett in Carson City, NV on March 17, 1897.

Heaviest champion Primo Carnera (Italy) weighed in at 270 pounds for the defense of his title vs. Tommy Loughran on March 1, 1934. Carnera won a unanimous point decision.

Quickest knockout The quickest knockout in a heavyweight title fight was 55 seconds, by James J. Jeffries over Jack Finnegan in Detroit, MI on April 6, 1900.

WORLD CHAMPIONS (Any Weight)

Longest reign Joe Louis's heavyweight duration record of 11 years 252 days stands for all divisions.

Most recaptures The only boxer to win a world title five times at one weight is Sugar Ray Robinson, who beat Carmen Basilio in Chicago Stadium, Chicago, IL on March 25, 1958 to regain the world middleweight title for the fourth time.

Greatest weight difference Primo Carnera (Italy) outweighed his opponent, Tommy Loughran, by 86 pounds (270 pounds to 184 pounds) when they fought for the heavyweight title on March 1, 1934 in Miami, FL. Surprisingly, the bout went the distance, with Carnera winning on points.

AMATEUR

Olympic Games

Boxing contests were included in the ancient games, and were first included in the modern Games in 1904.

Most gold medals Two boxers have won three gold medals: Laszlo Papp (Hungary) won the middleweight title in 1948, and the light middleweight in 1952 and 1956; Teofilo Stevenson (Cuba) won the heavyweight division in 1972, 1976 and 1980. The only man to win two titles at the same Games was Oliver L. Kirk, who won both the bantamweight and featherweight titles in 1904. It should be noted that Kirk only had to fight one bout in each class.

World Championships

The world championships were first staged in 1974, and are held quadrennially.

Most titles Félix Savon (Cuba) has won a record five world titles. Savon won the heavyweight division in 1986, 1989, 1991, and 91 kg in 1993 and 1995.

CANOEING

Origins

The most influential pioneer of canoeing as a sport was John MacGregor, a British attorney, who founded the Canoe Club in Surrey, England in 1866. The sport's world governing body is the International Canoe Federation, founded in 1924.

United States The New York Canoe Club, founded in Staten Island, NY in 1871, is the oldest in the United States. The American Canoe Association was formed on August 3, 1880.

OLYMPIC GAMES

Canoeing was first included in the Olympic Games as a demonstration sport in 1924. At the 1936 Games, canoeing was included as an official Olympic sport for the first time.

Most gold medals Gert Fredriksson (Sweden) won a record six Olympic gold medals: 1,000 meter Kayak Singles (K1), 1948, 1952 and 1956; 10,000 meter K1, 1948 and 1956; 1,000 meter Kayak Pairs (K2), 1960.

In women's competition, Birgit Schmidt (née Fischer; East Germany/Germany) has won five golds: 500 meter K1, 1980 and 1992; 500 meter K2, 1988; 500 meter K4, 1988 and 1996.

WORLD CHAMPIONSHIPS

In Olympic years, the Games also serve as the world championship.

Most titles Birgit Schmidt (East Germany/Germany) has won a record 26 titles, 1979–96. The men's record is 13, by three canoeists: Gert Fredriksson (Sweden), 1948–60; Rudiger Helm (East Germany), 1976–83; and Ivan Patzaichin (Romania), 1968–84.

UNITED STATES NATIONAL CHAMPIONSHIPS

Most titles Marcia Smoke won 35 national titles, 1962–81. The men's record is 33, by Ernest Riedel, 1930–48.

CRICKET

Origins

Cricket originated in England in the Middle Ages. It is impossible to pinpoint its exact origin; however, historians believe that the modern game developed in the mid-16th century. The Marylebone Cricket Club (MCC) was founded in 1787 and, until 1968, was the world governing body for the sport. The International Cricket Conference (ICC) is responsible for international (Test) cricket, while the MCC remains responsible for the laws of cricket.

INTERNATIONAL (TEST) CRICKET

Test match cricket is the highest level of the sport. The Test-playing nations are Australia, England, India, New Zealand, Pakistan, South Africa, Sri Lanka, the West Indies and Zimbabwe. Test matches are generally played over five days. The result is decided by which team scores the most runs in two full innings (one inning sees all 11 members of a team come to bat; their opponents must achieve 10 outs to end the inning). If, at the end of the allotted time period, one or either team has not completed two full innings, the game is declared a tie. The first Test match was played at Melbourne, Australia on March 15–19, 1877 between Australia and England.

TEST MATCH RECORDS (TEAM)

Most runs (innings) England scored 903 runs (for 7 declared) vs. Australia at The Oval, London on August 20, 22 and 23, 1938.

Most runs (total aggregate) In a 10-day match played March 3–14, 1939 in Durban, South Africa, England and South Africa scored 1,981 runs. South Africa scored 530 runs in the first innings and 481 in the second. England scored 316 runs in the first innings and 654 for 5 in the second. The record for a five-day match (standard for current Test matches) is 1,764 runs, Australia (533, 339 for 9) vs. West Indies (276, 616) in Adelaide, Australia on January 24–29, 1969. Both games ended in stalemate and were declared ties as time ran out.

Fewest runs (innings) New Zealand scored 26 runs vs. England in Auckland on March 28, 1955.

Fewest runs (two innings) South Africa scored a combined 81 runs (36, 45) vs. Australia in Melbourne, Australia on February 12–15, 1932. Australia scored 153 runs and won the match by an inning and 72 runs.

Greatest margin of victory England defeated Australia by an inning and 579 runs at The Oval on August 20–24, 1938. Australia scored 201 in its first innings and 123 in the second. In each innings they played with only nine players, two short of a full team.

Tied score matches There have been two tied score matches (both teams' aggregate scores the same at the end of play on the final day) in Test cricket history: Australia vs. West Indies in Brisbane, Australia, December 9–14, 1960; India vs. Australia, in Madras, India, September 18–22, 1986.

Pakistan's Wasim Akram has taken more wickets in one-day cricket internationals than any other bowler.
Shaun Botterill/Allsport

TEST MATCH RECORDS (INDIVIDUAL)

Most runs (game) 375 not out, by Brian Lara, West Indies vs. England in St. Johns, Antigua on April 16–18, 1994.

Most runs (career) 11,174 runs, by Allan Border, Australia, 1978–94. Border has played in 156 Tests for an average of 50.56 runs.

Highest average (career) 99.94 runs, by Donald Bradman, Australia, 1928–48. The "Don" played in 52 Tests, scoring 6,996 runs.

Most wickets (game) 19, by Jim Laker for England vs. Australia at Old Trafford, Manchester, England, July 27–31, 1956.

Most wickets (career) 434, by Kapil Dev Nikhanj, India. Kapil had played in 131 Tests, 1978–94.

NATIONAL CRICKET CHAMPIONSHIPS

Australia The premier event in Australia is the Sheffield Shield, an interstate competition contested since 1891–94. New South Wales has won the title a record 42 times.

England The major championship in England is the County Championship, an intercounty competition officially recognized since 1890. Yorkshire has won the title a record 30 times.

India The Ranji Trophy is India's premier cricket competition. Established in 1934 in memory of K. S. Ranjitsinhji, it is contested on a zonal basis, culminating in a playoff competition. Bombay has won the tournament a record 30 times.

New Zealand Since 1975, the major championship in New Zealand has been the Shell Trophy. Otago, Wellington and Auckland have each won the competition four times.

Pakistan Pakistan's national championship is the Quaid-e-Azam Trophy, established in 1953. Karachi has won the trophy a record eight times.

South Africa The Currie Cup, donated by Sir Donald Currie, was first contested in 1889. Transvaal has won the competition a record 28 times.

West Indies The Red Stripe Cup, established in 1966, is the premier prize played for by the association of Caribbean islands (plus Guyana) that form the West Indies Cricket League. Barbados has won the competition a record 13 times.

CROSS-COUNTRY RUNNING

Origins

The earliest recorded international cross-country race took place on March 20, 1898 between England and France. The race was staged at Ville d'Avray, near Paris, France over a course 9 miles 18 yards long.

World Championships

The first international cross-country championships were staged in Glasgow, Scotland on March 28, 1903. Since 1973 the event has been an official world championship organized by the International Amateur Athletic Federation.

Most titles   England has won the men's team event a record 45 times, 1903–14, 1920–21, 1924–25, 1930–38, 1951, 1953–55, 1958–60, 1962, 1964–72, 1976, 1979–80. The women's competition has been won eight times by two countries: United States, 1968–69, 1975, 1979, 1983–85, 1987; USSR, 1976–77, 1980–82, 1988–90.

Most titles (individual)   Two women have won five titles: Doris Brown (U.S.), 1967–71, and Grete Waitz (Norway), 1978–81 and 1983. John Ngugi (Kenya) has won the men's title a record five times, 1986–89 and 1992.

United States National Championships

This competition was first staged in 1890 for men, and in 1972 for women.

Most titles   Lynn Jennings has won the women's event nine times, 1985, 1987–93 and 1996. Pat Porter has won the men's event eight times, 1982-89.

NCAA Championships

The first NCAA cross-country championship was held in 1938, and was open only to men's teams. A women's event was not staged until 1981.

Most titles (team)   In men's competition, two teams have won the team title a record eight times:

Kenyan runners have dominated the Cross-Country World Championships in recent years. Paul Tergat continued his nation's tradition by winning the 1996 title.
(Tertius Pickard/Allsport)

Michigan State, 1939, 1948–49, 1952, 1955–56, 1958–59; and Arkansas, 1984, 1986–87, 1990–93, 1995.

Most titles (individuals)   Three athletes have won the men's individual title three times: Gerry Lindgren (Washington State), 1966–67 and 1969; Steve Prefontaine (Oregon), 1970–71 and 1973; Henry Rono (Washington State), 1976–77 and 1979.

Most titles (team)   In women's competition, Villanova has won the team title six times, 1989–94.

Most titles (individual)   Three runners have won the title twice: Betty Springs (North Carolina State), 1981 and 1983; Sonia O'Sullivan (Villanova), 1990 and 1991; Carole Zajac (Villanova), 1992–93.

CURLING

Origins

The traditional home of curling is Scotland; some historians, however, believe that the sport originated in the Netherlands in the 15th century. The earliest recorded club is the Muthill Curling Club, Tayside, Scotland, formed in 1739, which produced the first known written rules of the game on November 17, 1739. The Grand (later Royal) Caledonian Curling Club was founded in 1838 and was the international governing body of the sport until 1966, when the International Curling Federation was formed; this was renamed the World Curling Federation in 1991.

United States and Canada Scottish immigrants introduced curling to North America in the 18th century. The earliest known club was the Royal Montreal Curling Club, founded in 1807. The first international game was between Canada and the United States in 1884—the inaugural Gordon International Medal series. In 1832, Orchard Lake (MI) Curling Club, the first in the United States, was formed. The oldest club in continuous existence in the U.S. is the Milwaukee (WI) Curling Club, formed c. 1850. Regional curling associations governed the sport in the U.S. until 1947, when the United States Women's Curling Association was formed, followed in 1958 by the Men's Curling Association. The United States Curling Association was formed in 1986 and is the current governing body for the sport. In Canada, the Dominion Curling Association was formed in 1935, renamed the Canadian Curling Association in 1968.

Olympic Games

Curling, a demonstration sport at the Olympic Games of 1924, 1932, 1988 and 1992, will be a full-medal sport in 1998.

World Championships

These annual championships were first held in 1959. Women's competition was introduced in 1979.

Most titles (men) Canada has dominated this event, winning 24 titles: 1959–64, 1966, 1968–72, 1980, 1982–83, 1985 87, 1989–90, and 1993–96. Ernie Richardson (Canada) has been a winning skip a record four times, 1959–60, 1962–63.

Most titles (women) Canada has won nine championships, in 1980, 1984–87, 1989, 1993–94, and 1996. Three women have been skips of two winning teams: Djordy Nordby (Norway), 1990–91; Sandra Peterson (Canada), 1993–94; and Elisabet Gustafson (née Johanssen; Sweden), 1992 and 1995.

United States National Championships

A men's tournament was first held in 1957. A women's event was introduced in 1977.

Men Bud Somerville of the Superior (WI) Curling Club has been the skip on five championship teams, in 1965, 1968–69, 1974 and 1981.

Women In this competition, Nancy Langley of the Granite Curling Club, Seattle, WA has been the skip of a record four championship teams: 1979, 1981, 1983 and 1988.

The Labatt Brier
(formerly the MacDonald Brier 1927-79)

The Brier is the Canadian men's curling championship. The competition was first held at the Granite Club, Toronto in 1927. Sponsored by Macdonald Tobacco Inc., it had been known as the Macdonald Brier; since 1980 Labatt Brewery has sponsored the event.

Most titles The most wins is 25, by Manitoba (1928–32, 1934, 1936, 1938, 1940, 1942, 1947, 1949, 1952–53, 1956, 1965, 1970–72, 1979, 1981, 1984, 1992 and 1995–96). Ernie Richardson (Saskatchewan) has been winning skip a record four times (1959–60 and 1962–63).

Perfect game Stu Beagle, of Calgary, Alberta, played a perfect game (48 points) against Nova Scotia in the Canadian Championships (Brier) in Fort William (now Thunder Bay), Ontario on March 8, 1960. Andrew McQuiston skipped the Scotland team to a perfect game vs. Switzerland at the Uniroyal Junior Men's World Championship at Kitchener, Ontario, Canada in 1980. Bernice Fekete, of Edmonton, Alberta, Canada, skipped her rink to two consecutive eight-enders on the same ice at the Derrick Club, Edmonton on January 10 and February 6, 1973.

Two eight-enders in one bonspiel were scored at the Parry Sound Curling Club, Ontario, Canada from January 6-8, 1983.

CYCLING

Origins

The forerunner of the bicycle, the *celerifere*, was demonstrated in the garden of the Palais Royale, Paris, France in 1791. The velocipede, the first practical pedal-propelled vehicle, was built in March 1861 by Pierre Michaux and his son Ernest and demonstrated in Paris. The first velocipede race occurred on May 31, 1868 at the Parc St. Cloud, Paris, over a distance of 1.24 miles. The first international organization was the International Cyclist Association (ICA), founded in 1892, which launched the first world championships in 1893. The current governing body, the *Union Cycliste Internationale* (UCI), was founded in 1900.

OLYMPIC GAMES

Cycling was included in the first modern Games held in 1896, and has been part of every Games since, with the exception of 1904. Women's events were first staged in 1984.

Most gold medals   Four men have won three gold medals: Paul Masson (France), 1,000 meter time-trial, 1,000 meter sprint, 10,000 meter track in 1896;

Francesco Verri (Italy), 1,000 meter time-trial, 1,000 meter sprint, 5,000 meter track in 1906; Robert Charpentier (France), individual road race, team road race, 4,000 meter team pursuit in 1936; Daniel Morelon (France), 1,000 meter sprint in 1968 and 1972, 2,000 meter tandem in 1968.

Most medals   Daniel Morelon (France) won five Olympic medals: three gold (see above); one silver, 1,000 meter sprint, 1972; one bronze, 1,000 meter sprint, 1964.

WORLD CHAMPIONSHIPS

World championships are contested annually. They were first staged for amateurs in 1893 and for professionals in 1895.

Most titles (one event)   The most wins in a single event is 10, by Koichi Nakano (Japan), professional sprint 1977–86. The most wins in a men's amateur event is seven, by two cyclists: Daniel Morelon (France), sprint, 1966–67, 1969–71, 1973, 1975; and Leon Meredith (Great Britain), 100 kilometer motor-paced, 1904–05, 1907–09, 1911 and 1913. The most women's titles is 11, by Jeannie Longo (France), individual pursuit, 1986 and 1988–89; road

Transcontinental Cycling Records

Event	Rider(s)	Start/Finish	Days: Hrs: Min	Av. mph	Year
Men's Records (United States Crossing)					
Solo (time)	Michael Secrest	HB–NYC	7:23:16	15.24	1990
Solo (av. mph)	Pete Penseyres	HB–AC	8:09:47	15.40	1986
Tandem	Lon Haldeman and Pete Penseyres	HB–AC	7:14:15	15.97	1987
Men's Records (Canada Crossing)					
Solo	William Narasnek	Van–Hal	13:09:06	11.68	1991
Women's Records (United States Crossing)					
Solo	Seana Hogan	Irv–Sav	9:04:02	13.21	1995
Tandem	Estelle Grey and Cheryl Marek	SM–NYC	10:22:48	11.32	1984

HB: Huntington Beach, CA; NYC: New York City; AC: Atlantic City, NJ; Van: Vancouver; Hal: Halifax, Nova Scotia; CM: Costa Mesa, CA; SM: Santa Monica, CA; Irv: Irvine, CA; Sav: Savannah, GA.

Source: Ultra Marathon Cycling Association (UMCA)

In winning the individual pursuit Olympic gold medal, Italian cyclist Andrea Collinelli set a new world record for the 4,000 m. (Bruno Bade/Vandystadt/Allsport)

race, 1985–87, 1989 and 1995; points race, 1989; and individual time trial, 1995–96.

United States The most world titles won by a U.S. cyclist is six, in women's 3 kilometer pursuit by Rebecca Twigg, 1982, 1984–85, 1987, 1993 and 1995. The most successful man has been Greg LeMond, winner of the individual road race in 1983 and 1989.

UNITED STATES NATIONAL CHAMPIONSHIPS

National cycling championships have been held annually since 1899. Women's events were first included in 1937.

Most titles Rebecca Twigg has won 18 titles: seven individual pursuit (1981–82, 1984, 1986, 1992, 1995–96); three 1-kilometer time trial (1984, 1986, 1995); three individual time trial (1982, 1993–94); one road race (1983); one match sprint (1984); one points race (1984); and two criterium (1991, 1993). Leonard Nitz has won a men's record 16 titles: five pursuit (1976 and 1980–83); eight team pursuit (1980–84, 1986 and 1988–89); two 1-kilometer time-trial (1982 and 1984); one criterium (1986).

TOUR DE FRANCE

First staged in 1903, the Tour meanders throughout France and sometimes neighboring countries over a four-week period.

Most wins Four riders have each won the event five times: Jacques Anquetil (France), 1957, 1961–64; Eddy Merckx (Belgium), 1969–72, 1974; Bernard Hinault (France), 1978–79, 1981–82, 1985; Miguel Indurain (Spain), 1991–95.

Longest race The 1926 race was 3,569 miles long.

Closest race The closest race ever was in 1989, when, after 2,030 miles over 23 days (July 1–23), Greg LeMond (U.S.), who completed the Tour in 87 hours 38 minutes 35 seconds, beat Laurent Fignon (France) in Paris by only 8 seconds.

Fastest speed The fastest average speed was 24.547 mph, by Miguel Indurain (Spain) in 1992.

Longest stage The longest-ever stage was the 486 kilometers (302 miles) from Les Sables d'Olonne to Bayonne in 1919.

Most participants The most participants was 210 starters in 1986.

The dominant rider in women's cycling history, France's Jeannie Longo-Ciprelli finally won her first Olympic title at the 1996 Atlanta Games.
(Bruno Bade/Vandystadt/Allsport)

Tour de France Champions

Year	Winner	Country
1903	Maurice Garin	France
1904	Henri Cornet	France
1905	Louis Trousselier	France
1906	Rene Pottier	France
1907	Lucien Petit-Breton	France
1908	Lucien Petit-Breton	France
1909	Francois Faber	Luxembourg
1910	Octave Lapize	France
1911	Gustave Garrigou	France
1912	Odile Defraye	Belgium
1913	Philippe Thys	Belgium
1914	Philippe Thys	Belgium
1915	*not held*	
1916	*not held*	
1917	*not held*	
1918	*not held*	
1919	Firmin Labot	Belgium
1920	Philippe Thys	Belgium
1921	Leon Scieur	Belgium
1922	Firmin Labot	Belgium
1923	Henri Pelissier	France
1924	Ottavio Bottecchia	Italy
1925	Ottavio Bottecchia	Italy
1926	Lucien Buysse	Belgium
1927	Nicholas Frantz	Luxembourg
1928	Nicholas Frantz	Luxembourg
1929	Maurice Dewaele	Belgium
1930	Andre Leducq	France
1931	Antonin Magne	France
1932	Andre Leducq	France
1933	Georges Speicher	France
1934	Antonin Magne	France
1935	Romain Maes	Belgium
1936	Sylvere Maes	Belgium
1937	Roger Lapebie	France
1938	Gino Bartali	Italy
1939	Sylvere Maes	Belgium
1940	*not held*	

Year	Winner	Country
1941	*not held*	
1942	*not held*	
1943	*not held*	
1944	*not held*	
1945	*not held*	
1946	Jean Lazarides	France
1947	Jean Robic	France
1948	Gino Bartali	Italy
1949	Fausto Coppi	Italy
1950	Ferdinand Kubler	Switzerland
1951	Hugo Koblet	Switzerland
1952	Fausto Coppi	Italy
1953	Louison Bobet	France
1954	Louison Bobet	France
1955	Louison Bobet	France
1956	Roger Walkowiak	France
1957	Jacques Anquetil	France
1958	Charly Gaul	Luxembourg
1959	Federico Bahamontes	Spain
1960	Gastone Nencini	Italy
1961	Jacques Anquetil	France
1962	Jacques Anquetil	France
1963	Jacques Anquetil	France
1964	Jacques Anquetil	France
1965	Felice Gimondi	Italy
1966	Lucien Aimar	France
1967	Roger Pingeon	France
1968	Jan Janssen	Netherlands
1969	Eddy Merckx	Belgium
1970	Eddy Merckx	Belgium
1971	Eddy Merckx	Belgium
1972	Eddy Merckx	Belgium
1973	Luis Ocana	Spain
1974	Eddy Merckx	Belgium
1975	Bernard Thevenet	France
1976	Lucien van Impe	Belgium
1977	Bernard Thevenet	France
1978	Bernard Hinault	France
1979	Bernard Hinault	France

Tour de France Champions (continued)

1980	Joop Zoetemilk	Netherlands
1981	Bernard Hinault	France
1982	Bernard Hinault	France
1983	Laurent Fignon	France
1984	Laurent Fignon	France
1985	Bernard Hinault	France
1986	Greg LeMond	U.S.
1987	Stephen Roche	Ireland
1988	Pedro Delgado	Spain
1989	Greg LeMond	U.S.
1990	Greg LeMond	U.S.
1991	Miguel Indurain	Spain
1992	Miguel Indurain	Spain
1993	Miguel Indurain	Spain
1994	Miguel Indurain	Spain
1995	Miguel Indurain	Spain
1996	Bjarne Riis	Denmark

Denmark's Bjarne Riis won the 1996 Tour de France, snapping Miguel Indurain's five-year winning streak.
(Phil Cole/Allsport)

Most finishers A record 151 riders finished the 1988 race.

Most races Joop Zoetemilk (Netherlands) participated in a record 16 tours, 1970–86. He won the race in 1980 and finished second a record six times.

Most stage wins Eddy Merckx (Belgium) won a record 35 individual stages in just seven races, 1969–75.

United States Greg LeMond became the first American winner in 1986; he returned from serious injury to win again in 1989 and 1990.

RACE ACROSS AMERICA
Origins

An annual nonstop transcontinental crossing of the United States from west to east, the Race Across AMerica was first staged in 1982. A women's division was introduced in 1984. The start and finish lines have varied, but currently the race starts in Irvine, CA, and finishes in Savannah, GA. The race must travel a minimum distance of 2,900 miles.

Most wins Seana Hogan has won four women's titles, in 1992–93 and 1994–95. Rob Kish has won three men's titles, in 1992 and 1994–95.

DIVING

Origins

Diving as an organized sport traces its roots to the gymnastics movement that developed in Germany and Sweden in the 17th century. During the summer, gymnasts would train at the beach, and acrobatic techniques would be performed over water as a safety measure. From this activity the sport of diving developed. The world governing body for diving is the *Fédération Internationale de Natation Amateur* (FINA), founded in 1980. FINA is also the governing body for swimming, water polo and synchronized swimming.

United States Ernst Bransten and Mike Peppe are considered the two main pioneers of diving in the United States. Bransten, a Swede, came to the United States following World War I. He introduced Swedish training methods and diving techniques, which revolutionized the sport in this country. Peppe's highly successful program at Ohio State University, 1931–63, produced several Olympic medalists and helped promote the sport here.

Olympic Games

Men's diving events were introduced at the 1904 Games, and women's events in 1912.

Most gold medals Two divers have won four gold medals: Pat McCormick (U.S.), who won both the

China's Fu Mingxia won both springboard and platform events at the 1996 Olympic Games.
(Doug Pensinger/Allsport)

women's springboard and the platform events in 1952 and 1956; and Greg Louganis (U.S.), who performed the platform/springboard double in 1984 and 1988.

Most medals Two divers have won five medals: Klaus Dibiasi (Italy), three golds, platform in 1968, 1972 and 1976, and two silver, platform in 1964 and springboard in 1968; and Greg Louganis, four golds (see above) and one silver, platform in 1976.

World Championships

Diving events were included in the first world aquatic championships staged in 1973.

Most titles Greg Louganis (U.S.) won a record five world titles—platform in 1978 and the platform/springboard double in 1982 and 1986. Philip Boggs (U.S.) is the only diver to win three gold medals at one event, springboard, in 1973, 1975 and 1978.

United States National Championships

The Amateur Athletic Union (AAU) organized the first national diving championships in 1909. Since 1981, United States Diving has been the governing body of the sport in this country, and thus responsible for the national championships.

Most titles Greg Louganis has won a record 47 national titles: 17, one-meter springboard; 17, three-meter springboard; 13, platform. In women's competition, Cynthia Potter has won a record 28 titles.

EQUESTRIAN SPORTS

Origins

Evidence of horseback riding dates from a Persian engraving dated c. 3000 B.C. The three separate equestrian competitions recognized at the Olympic level are show jumping, the three-day event and dressage. The earliest known show jumping competition was in Ireland, when the Royal Dublin Society held its first "Horse Show" on April 15, 1864. Dressage competition derived from the exercises taught at 16th-century Italian and French horsemanship academies, while the three-day event developed from cavalry endurance rides. The world governing body for all three disciplines is the *Fédération Equestre Internationale* (FEI), founded in Brussels, Belgium in 1921.

Olympic Games

In the ancient games, chariot races featured horses, and later riding contests were included. Show jumping was included in the 1900 Games; the three-day event and dressage disciplines were not added until 1912. In 1956 the equestrian events were held in Stockholm, Sweden, separate from the main Games in Melbourne, Australia, because of strict Australian quarantine laws.

Most medals (all events)   Germany has dominated the equestrian events, winning 68 medals overall: 31 gold, 17 silver and 20 bronze.

SHOW JUMPING

Olympic Games

Most gold medals (rider)   Hans-Gunther Winkler (West Germany) has won five titles, 1956, 1960, 1964 and 1972 in the team competition, and the individual championship in 1956. The only rider to win two individual titles is Pierre Jonqueres d'Oriola (France), in 1952 and 1964.

Most gold medals (horse)   The most successful horse is Halla, ridden by Hans-Gunther Winkler during his individual and team wins in 1956, and during the team win in 1960.

Ulrich Kirchoff rode Jus de Pomme to the 1996 Olympic gold medal. Kirchoff was the fourth rider to win the individual title with two clear rounds.
(AP Photo/John Bazemore)

Most medals   Hans-Gunther Winkler has won a record seven medals: five gold (see above), one silver and one bronze in the team competition in 1976 and 1968.

United States   Two American riders have won the individual event: Bill Steinkraus in 1968, and Joe Fargis in 1984. The United States won the team event in 1984.

World Championships

The men's world championship was inaugurated in 1953. In 1965, 1970 and 1974 separate women's championships were held. An integrated championship was first held in 1978 and is now held every four years.

Most titles Two riders share the record for most men's championships with two victories: Hans-Gunther Winkler (West Germany), 1954–55, and Raimondo d'Inzeo (Italy), 1956 and 1960. The women's title was won twice by Janou Tissot (née Lefebvre) of France, in 1970 and 1974. No rider has won the integrated competition more than once.

THREE-DAY EVENT

Olympic Games

Most gold medals
Charles Pahud de Mortanges (Netherlands) has won four gold medals—the individual title in 1928 and 1932, and the team event in 1924 and 1928. Mark Todd (New Zealand) is the only other rider to have won the individual title twice, in 1984 and 1988.

Most medals (rider) Charles Pahud de Mortanges has won five medals: four gold (see above) and one silver in the 1932 team event.

Most gold medals (horse) Marcroix was ridden by Charles Pahud de Mortanges in three of his four medal rounds, 1928–32.

United States The most medals won for the U.S. is six, by J. Michael Plumb: team gold, 1976 and 1984, and four silver medals, team 1964, 1968 and 1972, and individual 1976. Tad Coffin is the only U.S. rider to have won both team and individual gold medals, in 1976.

World Championship

First held in 1966, the event is held quadrenially and is open to both men and women.

Most titles (rider) Two riders have won three world titles: Bruce Davidson (U.S.), individual title in 1974 and 1978, team title in 1974; and Virginia Leng (Great Britain), individual 1986 and team in 1982 and 1986. Davidson is the only rider to have won two individual championships.

Most titles (country) Great Britain has won the team title a record three times, 1970, 1982 and 1986. The United States won the team event in 1974.

DRESSAGE

Olympic Games

Most gold medals (rider) Reiner Klimke (West Germany) has won six gold medals: one individual in 1984, and five team in 1964, 1968, 1976, 1984 and 1988. Henri St. Cyr (Sweden) is the only rider to have won two individual titles, in 1952 and 1956. Two riders have won the individual title on two occasions: Henri St. Cyr (Sweden), 1952 and 1956; and Nicole Uphoff (Germany), 1988 and 1992.

Most gold medals (horse) Rembrandt was ridden by Nicole Uphoff in all four of her medal-winning rounds—two individual titles and two team titles, both in 1988 and 1992.

Most medals Reiner Klimke won eight medals: six gold (see above), and two bronze in the individual event in 1968 and 1976.

United States The United States has never won a gold medal in dressage. In the team event the United States has won one silver, 1948, and four bronze, in 1932, 1976, 1992 and 1996. Hiram Tuttle is the only rider to have won an individual medal, earning the bronze in 1932.

World Championships

This competition was instituted in 1966.

Most titles (country) West Germany has won a record six times: 1966, 1974, 1978, 1982, 1986 and 1990.

Most titles (rider) Reiner Klimke (West Germany) is the only rider to have won two individual titles, on Mehmed in 1974 and on Ahlerich in 1982.

POLO

The object of the game is to score in the opponent's goals, the goalposts being eight yards wide, with the team scoring the most goals winning the game. Each side fields a team of four players; the game is played over six periods of seven minutes' duration each. A period is known as a chukka, and players must change their mount after each chukka.

**The 1996 German Olympic dressage
champions on the medal podium
in Atlanta.**
(Jamie Squire/Allsport)

Origins

Polo originated in Central Asia, possibly as early as
3100 B.C., in the state of Manipur. The name is derived
from the Tibetan word *pulu*. The modern era began
in India in the 1850s when British army officers were
introduced to the game. The Cachar Club, Assam, India
was founded in 1859, and is believed to be the first
polo club of the modern era. The game was introduced
in England in 1869. The world governing body, the
Hurlingham Polo Association, was founded in London,
England in 1874 and drew up the laws of the game
in 1875.

United States Polo was introduced to the U.S. by
James Gordon Bennett in 1876, when he arranged for
the first indoor game at Dickel's Riding Academy, NY.
The first game played outdoors was held on May 13,
1876 at the Jerome Park Racetrack in Westchester
County, NY. The oldest existing polo club in the United
States is Meadowbrook Polo Club, Jericho, NY,
founded in 1879. The United States Polo Association
was formed on March 21, 1890.

United States Open Polo Championship

The U.S. Open was first staged in 1904 and is an
annual event.

Most wins The Meadow Brook Club, Westbury, NY
has won the U.S. Open 28 times: 1916, 1920,
1923–41, 1946–51, and 1953.

Highest score The highest aggregate number of
goals scored in an international match is 30, when
Argentina beat the U.S. 21–9 at the Meadow Brook
Club, Westbury, NY in September 1936.

Highest handicap Polo players are assigned
handicaps based on their skill, with a 10 handicap
being the highest level of play. Only 56 players have
been awarded the 10-goal handicap.

40-goal games There have only been three games
staged between two 40-goal handicap teams. These
games were staged in Argentina in 1975, the United
States in 1990 and Australia in 1991.

EXTREME SPORTS

Bungee jumping is thought to have originated 1,500 years ago in the South Pacific. The longest bungee cord measured 820 feet long and was used by Gregory Riffi in a jump from a helicopter above the Loire Valley, France in February 1992.
(Thierry Martinez/Vandystadt/Allsport)

Hang Gliding

Origins

In the 11th century the monk Eilmer is reported to have flown from the 60-foot tower of Malmesbury Abbey, Wiltshire, England. The earliest modern pioneer was Otto Lilienthal (Germany), with about 2,500 flights in gliders of his own construction between 1891 and 1896. In the 1950s, Professor Francis Rogallo of the National Space Agency developed a flexible "wing" from his space capsule reentry research.

World Records

The *Fédération Aéronautique Internationale* recognizes world records for flexible-wing, rigid-wing, and multiplace flexible-wing.

United States

The United States Hang Gliding Association (USHGA), located in Colorado Springs, CO, is the national governing body for the sport. Founded in 1971 as the Southern California Hang Gliding Association (SCHGA), it became the USGA in 1973.

Flexible Wing–Single Place Distance Records (Men)

Straight line   Larry Tudor (U.S.) piloted a Ram-Air 154 for a straight-line distance of 307.696 miles from Rock Springs, WY to Stoneham, CO on June 30, 1994.

Single turnpoint   Larry Tudor (U.S.) piloted his Ram-Air 154 a single turnpoint (dogleg) record 307.773 miles from Rock Springs, WY to Stoneham, CO on June 30, 1994.

Triangular course   James Lee Jr. (U.S.) piloted a Willis Wing HPAT 158 for a triangular course record 121.79 miles over Wild Horse Mesa, CO on July 4, 1991.

Out and return   The out and return goal distance record is 192.818 miles, set by two pilots on the same day, July 26, 1988, over Lone Pine, CA: Larry Tudor, Wills Wing HPAT 158; Geoffrey Loyns (Great Britain), Enterprise Wings.

Altitude gain Larry Tudor set a height gain record of 14,250.69 feet flying a G2-155 over Horseshoe Meadows, CA on August 4, 1985.

Flexible Wing–Single Place Distance Records (Women)

Straight line Kari Castle (U.S.) piloted a Wills Wing AT 145 a straight-line distance of 208.63 miles over Lone Pine, CA on July 22, 1991.

Single turnpoint Kari Castle piloted a Pacific Airwave Magic Kiss a single-turnpoint distance of 181.47 miles over Hobbs, NM on July 1, 1990.

Triangular course Judy Leden (Great Britain) flew a triangular course record 70.173 miles over Austria on June 22, 1991.

Out and return The out and return goal distance record is 81.99 miles, set by Tover Buas-Hansen (Norway), piloting an International Axis over Owens Valley, CA on July 6, 1989.

Altitude gain The record for height gain is 13,025 feet by Judy Leden (Great Britain), flying over Kuruman, South Africa on December 1, 1992.

British hang glider Judy Leden holds several hang gliding records, including record altitude gain by a woman at 13,025 feet.
(Tony Larkin/Rex Features)

Rigid Wing–Single Place Distance Records (Men)

Straight line The straight-line distance record is 139.07 miles, set by William Reynolds (U.S), piloting a Wills Wing over Lone Pine, CA on June 27, 1988.

Out and return The out and return goal distance is 47.46 miles, set by Randy Bergum (U.S.), piloting an Easy Riser over Big Pine, CA on July 12, 1988.

Altitude gain Rainer Scholl (South Africa) set an altitude gain record of 12,532.80 feet on May 8, 1985.

Flexible Wing–Multiplace Distance Records (Men)

Straight line The straight line distance record is 100.60 miles, set by Larry Tudor and Eri Fujita, flying a Comet II-185 on July 12, 1985.

Out and return The out and return goal distance record is 81.99 miles, set by Kevin and Tom Klinefelter (U.S.) on July 6, 1989.

Altitude gain Tom and Kevin Klinefelter set an altitude record of 10,997.30 feet on July 6, 1989 over Bishop Airport, CA flying a Moyes Delta Glider.

Inline Skating
(Rollerblading)

Origins

The roots of inline skating (often referred to as "rollerblading" or "blading") can be traced to Belgian Joseph Merlin's 18th-century invention, the roller skate. In 1823, 40 years prior to James Plimpton's patent of the four-wheeled roller skate, Englishman Robert John Tyers created the first inline skate—then called a "rolite"—by positioning five wheels in a row on the bottom of the skate. The idea was ridiculed until 1980, when Scott and Brennan Olsen took the concept of the five-wheel skate and applied it to an ice hockey boot,

thereby creating the modern inline skate (then called the "Ultimate Street Skate"). In 1986, five-wheel skates called "skeelers" began to see usage in the Netherlands. Today, inline skates have revolutionized speed skating because they are dramatically faster than conventional skates; they are now preferred by millions of professional and amateur rollerbladers world-wide. Related sports such as roller hockey and roller basketball continue to increase in popularity.

In the United States, the leading organization for roller blading is the Atlanta-based International Inline Skating Association (IISA). The United States Amateur Confederation of Roller Skating (USACRS) also governs amateur competitions. Inline skates were first allowed in international competition in 1992.

WORLD CHAMPIONSHIPS

The United States has dominated the sport thus far. Derek Parra (Dover, DE) was the overall world track champion in 1993 and the overall individual road champion for 1994. No woman inline skater has won more than one overall title.

Speed records In the 1994 Championships in Gujan Mestras, France, Derek Parra broke two records: the 1,500 meter, 2 minutes 4.26 seconds; and the 42k marathon, 1 hour 4 minutes 27.986 seconds.

The greatest distance skated in 24 hours is 283.07 miles; the fastest time for the classic distance of 1,500 meters is 2:04.26.
(©Mike Powell/Allsport USA)

Inline Skating World Records

Skater (Country)	Distance	Place	Date
One Hour (Track)			
Haico Bauma (Netherlands)	22.11 miles	Groningen, Netherlands	August 16, 1994
One Hour (Road)			
Eddy Matzger (U.S.)	21.64 miles	Long Beach, CA	February 2, 1991
Six Hours (Road)			
Jonathan Seutter (U.S.)	91.35 miles	Long Beach, CA	February 2, 1991
Twelve Hours (Road)			
Jonathan Seutter (U.S.)	177.63 miles	Long Beach, CA	February 2, 1991
Twenty-four Hours (Road)			
Kimberly Ames (U.S.)	283.07 miles	Portland, OR	October 2, 1994

Source: International Inline Skating Association

Mountain bike racing is the first of the extreme sports to gain official Olympic recognition. The men's cross-country event was won by Bart Jan Brentjens of the Netherlands; the women's was won by Paola Pezzo of Italy.
(Clive Mason/Allsport)

Mountaineering developed as a sport following the conquest of Mont Blanc, the highest point in Europe.
(Didier Givois/Vandystadt)

Mountaineering

Origins

In 1786 two Swiss climbers, Michel Paccard and Jacques Balmat, reached the summit of Mont Blanc, the highest mountain in Europe at 15,771 feet. Their feat is generally regarded as the beginning of the sport of mountain climbing. During the second half of the nineteenth century climbers scaled all the major mountains of the world except those of the Himalayas range. In the 20th century climbers turned their attention to the Himalayas, site of the world's 14 tallest mountains. The first expedition to attempt to climb Mount Everest, the world's tallest mountain, was staged in 1922. In 1953 Edmund Hillary (New Zealand) and Tenzig Norgay, a Sherpa native, gained Everest's summit, creating headlines around the world.

Mount Everest

Most conquests Ang Rita Sherpa (Nepal) has scaled Mount Everest (29,029 feet) eight times, 1983–85, 1987–88, 1990, 1992–93. On each occasion Ang reached the summit without the use of bottled oxygen.

Most climbers The greatest number of climbers to reach the summit from one expedition is 20 members of the Mount Everest International Peace Climb. The team led by James Whittaker (U.S.), comprised a group of Chinese, American and Russian climbers, who reached Everest's peak between May 7–10, 1990.

Most in one day 40 climbers (32 men and 8 women) reached the summit of Everest on May 12, 1992. The climbers were members of nine separate expeditions. The nationalities represented were: Australia, Canada, Finland, Great Britain, India, Lithuania, Nepal, New Zealand, Russia and the United States.

Sea level to summit Timothy Macartney-Snape (Australia) is the only person to traverse Mt. Everest's entire altitude from sea level to summit. He set off on foot from the Bay of Bengal near Calcutta, India on February 5, 1990. He reached the summit on May 11, having walked approximately 745 miles.

Oldest The oldest person to climb Everest is Ramon Blanco (Spain). He was 60 years old when he reached the summit on October 7, 1993.

⟫ Fantastic Feats

Most summits Reinhold Messner is the only climber to have scaled all 14 of the world's mountains above 26,250 feet. On each occasion he gained the summit without the use of bottled oxygen.

Oldest mountain climber Ichijirou Araya (Japan) climbed Mount Fuji, Japan, at the age of 100 years 258 days on August 5, 1994.

Highest bivouac Four Nepalese climbers bivouacked at more than 28,870 feet on Mount Everest as they descended from the summit on the night of April 23, 1990. The occupants of the world's greatest "room with a view" were Ang Rita Sherpa, Ang Kami Sherpa, Pasang Norbu Sherpa and Top Bahadur Khatri.

Building climb The longest climb on the vertical face of a building occurred on May 25, 1981, when Daniel Goodwin climbed up the outside of Sears Tower in Chicago, IL. His 1,454 feet climb was achieved using suction cups and metal clips for support.

Rope slide The greatest distance traveled down a rope slide is 5,730 feet by Lance Corporal Peter Baldwin (Great Britain) and Stu Leggett (Canada). The journey from the top of Mount Gibraltar, near Calgary, Canada to level ground on August 31, 1994. Speeds during portions of the descent topped the 100-mph mark.

Orienteering

Orienteering combines cross-country running with compass and map navigation. The object of the sport is to navigate across a set course in the fastest time using a topographical map and a compass. The course contains designated locations called controls, which the runner must find and identify on a punch card that is handed to the official timer at the end of the race.

Origins

Orienteering can be traced to Scandinavia at the turn of the 20th century. Major Ernst Killander (Sweden) is regarded as the father of the sport, having organized the first large race in Saltsjobaden, Sweden in 1919. The Swedish federation, *Svenska Orienteringsforbundet*, was founded in 1936. The International Orienteering Federation was established in 1961.

United States Orienteering was introduced to the U.S. in the 1940s. The first U.S. Orienteering Championships were held on October 17, 1970. The U.S. Orienteering Federation was founded in 1971.

World Championships

The world championships were first held in 1966 in Fiskars, Finland, and are held biennially.

Most titles (relay) The men's relay has been won a record seven times by Norway: 1970, 1978, 1981, 1983, 1985, 1987, and 1989. Sweden has won the women's relay 10 times—1966, 1970, 1974, 1976, 1981, 1983, 1985, 1989, 1991, 1993.

Most titles (individual) Three women's individual titles have been won by Annichen Kringstad (Sweden), in 1981, 1983 and 1985. The men's title has been won twice by four men: Age Hadler (Norway), in 1966 and 1972; Egil Johansen (Norway), in 1976 and 1978; Oyvin Thon (Norway), in 1979 and 1981; Jörgen Mårtensson (Sweden), in 1991 and 1995.

United States National Championships

The annual nationals were first held in October 1970.

Most titles Sharon Crawford, New England Orienteering Club, has won a record 11 overall women's titles: 1977–82, 1984–87, and 1989. Mikell Platt, Rocky Mountain Orienteering Club, has won eight men's titles, 1986, 1988–93, and 1996.

Skateboarding

Origins

A combination of surfing and roller skating, skateboarding gained attention in the early 1970's. The first World Championship of skateboarding took place in 1966, but it is only in recent years that a defined sport has developed.

⇒ Fantastic Feats

Distance Eleftherios Argiropoulos covered 271.3 miles in 36 hours 33 minutes 17 seconds in Ekali, Greece on November 4–5, 1993.

Fastest speed (prone) The fastest speed recorded on a skateboard is 78.37 mph by Roger Hickey (US), on a course near Los Angeles, CA on March 15, 1990.

Fastest speed (standing) The stand-up record is 55.43 mph, achieved by Roger Hickey, in San Demas, CA on July 3, 1990.

Highest jump The high jump record is 5 feet 5 3/4 inches by Trevor Baxter (England), in Grenoble, France on September 14, 1982.

Longest jump At the World Professional Championships in Long Beach, CA on September 25, 1977, Tony Alva jumped over 17 barrels for a distance of 17 feet.

Street luge is a popular offshoot of skateboarding. A featured event in ESPN's X-Games, the sport is so new that there is no governing body to accredit records.
(Simon Bruty/Allsport)

FENCING

Origins

Evidence of swordsmanship can be traced back to Egypt c. 1360 B.C. Fencing, "fighting with sticks," gained popularity as a sport in Europe in the 16th century.

The modern foil, a light court sword, was introduced in France in the mid-17th century; in the late 19th century, the fencing "arsenal" was expanded to include the épée, a heavier dueling weapon, and the saber, a light cutting sword.

The *Fédération Internationale d'Escrime* (FIE), the world governing body, was founded in Paris, France in 1913. The first European championships were held in 1921 and were expanded into world championships in 1935.

Olympic Games

Fencing was included in the first Olympic Games of the modern era at Athens in 1896, and is one of only four sports to be featured in every Olympiad.

Most gold medals Aladar Gerevich (Hungary) has won a record seven gold medals, all in saber: individual, 1948; team, 1932, 1936, 1948, 1952, 1956 and 1960. In individual events, two fencers have won three titles: Ramon Fonst (Cuba), épée, 1900 and 1904, and foil, 1904; Nedo Nadi (Italy), foil, 1912 and 1920, and saber, 1920. The most golds won by a woman is four, by Yelena Novikova (née Belova; USSR), all in foil: individual, 1968; team, 1968, 1972 and 1976.

Most medals Edoardo Mangiarotti (Italy) has won a record 13 medals in fencing: six gold, five silver and two bronze in foil and épée events from 1936 to 1960.

United States Albertson Van Zo Post is the only American to have won an Olympic title. He won the single sticks competition and teamed with two Cubans to win the team foil title in 1904. In overall competition the United States has won 19 medals (both Cuba and the United States are credited with a gold medal for the 1904 team foil): two gold, six silver and 11 bronze—all in men's events.

World Championships

The first world championships were staged in Paris, France in 1937. Foil, épée and saber events were held for men and just foil for women. In 1989, women's épée was added. The tournament is staged annually.

Most titles The greatest number of individual world titles won is five, by Aleksandr Romankov (USSR), at foil, 1974, 1977, 1979, 1982 and 1983. Five women foilists have won three world titles: Hélène Mayer (Germany), 1929, 1931 and 1937; Ilona Schacherer-Elek (Hungary), 1934–35, 1951; Ellen Müller-Preis (Austria), 1947, 1949–50; Cornelia Hanisch (West Germany), 1979, 1981 and 1985; and Anja Fichtel (West Germany), 1986, 1988 and 1990.

United States National Championships

Most titles The most U.S. titles won at one weapon is 17 at saber, by Norman Armitage, 10 indoor events in 1930, 1934–36, 1939–43 and 1945; and seven outdoor events, 1929–30, 1932–33, 1935 and 1939–40. The women's record is 10 at foil, by Janice Romary, 1950–51, 1956–57, 1960–61, 1964–66, 1968.

The most individual foil championships won is eight, by Michael Marx in 1977, 1979, 1982, 1985–87, 1990 and 1993. Leo Nunes won the most épée championships, with eight: six indoor events, 1917, 1922, 1924, 1926, 1928 and 1932; and two outdoor events, 1921 and 1925. Vincent Bradford won a record number of women's épée championships with four in 1982–84 and 1986.

NCAA Championship Division I (Team)

A men's championship was first staged in 1941. A women's championship was not introduced until 1982. In 1990 these two tournaments were replaced by a combined team event. In the now-defunct separate events, New York University won the men's title 12 times, 1947–76; and Wayne State (MI), won the women's event three times, 1982, 1988–89.

Most wins Penn State has won the most championships, with four titles: 1990–91 and 1995–96.

Most titles (fencer) The most titles won in a career is four, by Michael Lofton, New York University, with four victories in saber, 1984–87; and by Olga Kalinovskaya, Penn State, with four victories in foil, 1993–96.

FIELD HOCKEY

Origins

Hitting a ball with a stick is a game that dates back to the origins of the human race. Bas-reliefs and frescoes discovered in Egypt and Greece depict hockey-like games. The birthplace of modern hockey is Great Britain, where the first definitive code of rules was established in 1886. The *Fédération Internationale de Hockey* (FIH), the world governing body, was founded on January 7, 1924.

United States The sport was introduced to this country in 1901 by a British teacher, Constance M. K. Applebee, who later founded the United States Field Hockey Association (USFHA), the governing body for women, in 1928. The governing body for men was also founded in 1928, by Henry Greer. The two organizations merged in 1993 under the USFHA banner.

Olympic Games

Field hockey was added to the Olympic Games in 1908 and became a permanent feature in 1928; a women's tournament was added in 1980.

Most gold medals (team) In the men's competition, India has won eight gold medals: 1928, 1932, 1936, 1948, 1952, 1956, 1964 and 1980. In the women's competition, no team has won the event more than once.

United States The United States has never won either the men's or women's events; the best result has been a bronze in 1932 (men), and in 1984 (women).

Most international appearances Alison Ramsay has made a record 257 international appearances, 150 for Scotland and 107 for Great Britain, 1982–95.

United States Barbara Marois made a U.S. record 155 appearances, 1986–96.

NCAA Division I (Women)

The women's championship was inaugurated in 1981.

Most titles Old Dominion has won the most championships, with seven titles: 1982–84, 1988 and 1990–92.

Australia's women captured the field hockey gold medal at the 1996 Atlanta Games.
(Mike Powell/Allsport)

SCORING RECORDS

Highest score The highest score in an international game was India's 24–1 defeat of the United States in Los Angeles, CA, in the 1932 Olympic Games. In women's competition, England hammered France 23–0 in Merton, England on February 3, 1923.

Most goals Paul Litjens (Netherlands) holds the record for most goals by one player in international play. He scored 267 goals in 177 games.

Fastest goal The fastest goal scored in an international game was netted only seven seconds after the bully by John French for England vs. West Germany in Nottingham, England on April 25, 1971.

FIGURE SKATING

Origins

The earliest reference to ice skating is in Scandinavian literature dating to the second century A.D. Jackson Haines, a New Yorker, is regarded as the pioneer of the modern concept of figure skating, a composite of skating and dancing. Although his ideas were not initially favored in the United States, Haines moved to Europe in the mid-1860s, where his "International Style of Figure Skating" was warmly received and promoted. The first artificial rink was opened in London, England on January 7, 1876. The world governing body is the International Skating Union (ISU), founded in 1892. The sport functioned informally in the United States until 1921, when the United States Figure Skating Association (USFSA) was formed to oversee skating in this country— a role it still performs.

Olympic Games

Figure skating was first included in the 1908 Summer Games in London, and has been featured in every Games since 1920. Uniquely, both men's and women's events have been included in the Games from the first introduction of the sport.

Most gold medals Three skaters have won three gold medals: Gillis Grafstrom (Sweden) in 1920, 1924 and 1928; Sonja Henie (Norway) in 1928, 1932 and 1936; Irina Rodnina (USSR), with two different partners, in the pairs in 1972, 1976 and 1980.

Fourteen-year-old Tara Lipinski stunned the skating world by winning the 1997 World Figure Skating title, becoming the youngest-ever champion.
(Doug Pensinger/Allsport)

United States Dick Button is the only American skater to win two gold medals, in 1948 and 1952. American skaters have won the men's title six times and the women's five. No American team has won either the pairs or dance titles.

World Championships

This competition was first staged in 1896.

Most titles (individual) The greatest number of men's individual world figure skating titles is 10, by Ulrich Salchow (Sweden), in 1901–05 and 1907–11. The women's record (instituted 1906) is also 10 individual titles, by Sonja Henie (Norway) between 1927 and 1936.

Most titles (pairs) Irina Rodnina (USSR) has won 10 pairs titles (instituted 1908), four with Aleksey Ulanov, 1969–72, and six with her husband, Aleksandr Zaitsev, 1973–78.

Most titles (ice dance) The most ice dance titles (instituted 1952) won is six, by Lyudmila Pakhomova and her husband, Aleksandr Gorshkov (USSR), 1970–74 and 1976.

United States Dick Button won five world titles, 1948–52. Five women's world titles were won by Carol Heise, 1956–60.

United States National Championships

The U.S. championships were first held in 1914.

Most titles The most titles won by an individual is nine, by Maribel Y. Vinson, 1928–33 and 1935–37. She also won six pairs titles, and her aggregate of 15 titles is equaled by Therese Blanchard (née Weld), who won six individual and nine pairs titles between 1914 and 1927. The men's individual record is seven, by Roger Turner, 1928–34, and by Dick Button, 1946–52.

Highest Marks The highest tally of maximum six marks awarded in an international championship was 29, to Jayne Torvill and Christopher Dean (Great Britain) in the World Ice Dance Championships in Ottawa, Canada on March 22–24, 1984. They previously gained a perfect set of nine sixes for artistic presentation in the free dance at the 1983 World Championships inHelsinki, Finland and at the 1984 Winter Olympic Games in Sarajevo, Yugoslavia. In their career, Torvill and Dean received a record total of 136 sixes. The highest tally by a soloist is seven, by Donald Jackson (Canada) in the World Men's Championship in Prague, Czechoslovakia, 1962; and by Midori Ito (Japan) in the World Ladies' Championships in Paris, France in 1989.

⠿➡ **Fantastic Feats**

Barrel jumping In Terrebonne, Quebec, Canada, Yvon Jolin cleared 18 barrels on January 25, 1981. The distance of 29 feet 5 inches was a record for a jumper wearing ice skates.

Canada's Elvis Stojko won the 1997 World Championship. His long program included the first quadruple jump performed by a skater in winning the world title.
(AP Photo/Paul Chiasson)

FOOTBALL

Origins

On November 6, 1869, Princeton and Rutgers staged what is generally regarded as the first intercollegiate football game in New Brunswick, NJ. In October 1873 the Intercollegiate Football Association (Columbia, Princeton, Rutgers and Yale) was formed with the purpose of standardizing rules. At this point football was a modified version of soccer. The first significant move toward today's style of play came when Harvard played McGill University in a series of three challenge matches, starting in May 1874, under modified rugby rules. Walter Camp is credited with organizing the basic format of the current game. Between 1880 and 1906, Camp sponsored the concepts of scrimmage lines, 11-man teams, reduction in field size, downs and yards to gain and a new scoring system.

NATIONAL FOOTBALL LEAGUE (NFL)

Origins

William (Pudge) Heffelfinger became the first professional player on November 12, 1892, when he was paid $500 by the Allegheny Athletic Association (AAA) to play for them against the Pittsburgh Athletic Club (PAC). In 1893, PAC signed one of its players, believed to have been Grant Dibert, to the first known professional contract. The first game to be played with admitted professionals participating was played in Latrobe, PA, on August 31, 1895, with Latrobe YMCA defeating the Jeanette Athletic Club 12–0. Professional leagues existed in Pennsylvania and Ohio at the turn of the 20th century; however, the major breakthrough for professional football was the formation of the

Cowboys kicker Chris Boniol tied the NFL mark for most field goals in a game when he kicked seven in a Monday night game vs. the Green Bay Packers on November 18, 1996.
(Al Bello/Allsport)

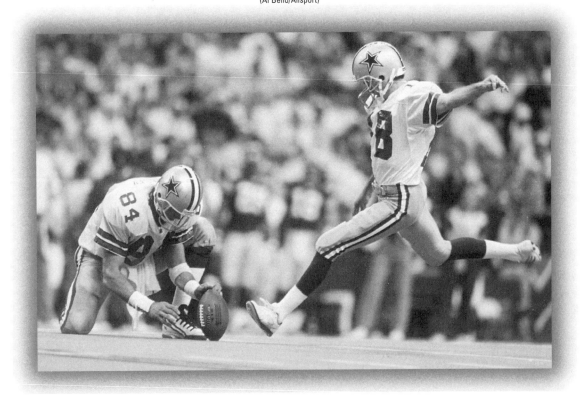

American Professional Football Association (APFA), founded in Canton, OH on September 17, 1920. Reorganized a number of times, the APFA was renamed the National Football League (NFL) on June 24, 1922. Since 1922, several rival leagues have challenged the NFL, the most significant being the All-America Football Conference (AAFL) and the American Football League (AFL). The AAFL began play in 1946 but after four seasons merged with the NFL for the 1950 season. The AFL challenge was stronger and more acrimonious. Formed in 1959, it had its inaugural season in 1960. The AFL–NFL "war" was halted on June 4, 1966 with an agreement to merge the leagues. The leagues finally merged for the 1970 season, but an AFL–NFL championship game, the Super Bowl, was first played in January 1967.

INDIVIDUAL RECORDS

Endurance

Most games played (career) George Blanda played in a record 340 games in a record 26 seasons in the NFL, for the Chicago Bears (1949, 1950–58), the Baltimore Colts (1950), the Houston Oilers (1960–66), and the Oakland Raiders (1967–75).

Most consecutive games played Jim Marshall played 282 consecutive games, 1960–79, for two teams: the Cleveland Browns, 1960, and the Minnesota Vikings, 1961–79.

Longest Plays

Run from scrimmage Tony Dorsett, Dallas Cowboys, ran through the Minnesota Vikings defense for a 99-yard touchdown on January 3, 1983.

Pass completion The longest pass completion, all for touchdowns, is 99 yards, performed by eight quarterbacks: Frank Filchock (to Andy Farkas), Washington Redskins vs. Pittsburgh Steelers, October 15, 1939; George Izo (to Bobby Mitchell), Washington Redskins vs. Cleveland Browns, September 15, 1963; Karl Sweetan (to Pat Studstill), Detroit Lions vs. Baltimore Colts, October 16, 1966; Sonny Jurgensen (to Gerry Allen), Washington Redskins vs. Chicago Bears, September 15, 1968; Jim Plunkett (to Cliff Branch), Los Angeles Raiders vs. Washington Redskins, October 2, 1983; Ron Jaworski (to Mike Quick), Philadelphia Eagles vs. Atlanta Falcons, November 10, 1985; Stan

Lions receiver Herman Moore holds the NFL record for most receptions in a season.
(Andy Lyons/Allsport)

Humphries (to Tony Martin), San Diego Chargers vs. Seattle Seahawks, September 18, 1994; Brett Favre (to Robert Brooks), Green Bay Packers vs. Chicago Bears, September 11, 1995.

Field goal The longest was 63 yards, by Tom Dempsey, New Orleans Saints vs. Detroit Lions, on November 8, 1970.

Punt Steve O'Neal, New York Jets, boomed a 98-yard punt on September 21, 1969 vs. Denver Broncos.

Interception return The longest interception return for a touchdown is 104 yards, by James Willis and Troy Vincent, both of the Philadelphia Eagles, vs. Dallas Cowboys, November 3, 1996. Willis returned the ball 14 yards, then lateraled the ball to Vincent, who returned it for the remaining 90 yards.

Kickoff return Three players share the record for a kickoff return at 106 yards: Al Carmichael, Green Bay Packers vs. Chicago Bears, October 7, 1956; Noland Smith, Kansas City Chiefs vs. Denver Broncos, December 17, 1967; and Roy Green, St. Louis Cardinals vs. Dallas Cowboys, October 21, 1979. All three players scored touchdowns.

Punt return The longest punt return in an NFL regular-season game is 103 yards by Robert Bailey, Los Angeles Rams vs. New Orleans Saints on October 23, 1994.

Snap To It!

On October 19, 1996, Nick Lowery kicked his 374th field goal, surpassing the NFL all-time mark of Hall of Famer Jan Stenerud. "It was overwhelming. I never experienced anything like it," says Lowery. "All of us want to achieve something special in life. The setting of a record and being the best at anything is meaningful." Adds the kicker, "It may be my record but it's been achieved with the help of the players I've played with over the years."

Yet when Lowery started out in the National Football League kicking records seemed as far off as the goal posts on a 60-yard attempt. The Dartmouth graduate was not drafted when he left college, and he was cut 11 times by eight different teams before finally joining the Kansas City Chiefs in 1980. There he replaced Stenerud, the man whose record he was destined to break and who had been his idol.

Lowery's kicking career was the legacy of his father, a foreign service officer. Born in Munich, (West) Germany, Lowery spent his childhood in Germany, England and the United States. "Kicking was something that came naturally to me," says Lowery. "We lived in England from '65 to '67 and in Germany from '67 to '69. In England, I played soccer all day, before school, after school, during recess, at lunch time. You got

the feeling that the ball was attached to your foot. The rhythm of kicking is instinctive."

A master of technique, Lowery takes an intellectual approach to his profession. "What I try to do is prepare and practice each week as if the game is going to come down to me," explains the kicking ace. "My position is a mental as well as physical one. The kicker has to concentrate, execute and perform in a matter of seconds. It takes 1.3 seconds for the ball to be snapped, put on the ground and kicked. It is a unique challenge." Lowery's preparation includes visualizing game situations and a lot of physical exercise. "I lift weights, run sprints and do lots of stretching."

"You should do anything that helps your sense of balance," Lowery advises aspiring athletes. He suggests that young kickers enroll in karate or ballet classes. He also recommends reading *The Inner Game of Tennis* by Timothy Gallwey. "This is the best introductory book on the mental side of sports that I have ever read," says the kicker.

At age 40, Lowery is geriatric in NFL terms, but he is not ready to retire. "I always motivate myself by choosing a new record to shoot for. My next goal is to be the first kicker to get 400 field goals." Then Lowery will take aim at the ultimate benchmark. "I want to break George Blanda's career record for points," he says.

Rick Stewart/Allsport

Kickoff return yardage (game) Tyrone Hughes, New Orleans Saints, combined punt and kickoff returns for a record total 347 yards against the Los Angeles Rams on October 23, 1994. In the same game, Hughes also set the mark for kickoff return yardage with 304.

Missed field goal return Al Nelson, Philadelphia Eagles, returned a Dallas Cowboys missed field goal

101 yards for a touchdown on September 26, 1971.

Punt return Robert Bailey, Los Angeles Rams, returned a punt 103 yards for a touchdown against the New Orleans Saints on October 23, 1994.

Fumble return Jack Tatum, Oakland Raiders, returned a Green Bay Packers fumble 104 yards for a touchdown on September 24, 1972.

NFL Individual Records

		Player(s)	Team(s)	Date(s)
POINTS SCORED				
Game	40	Ernie Nevers	Chicago Cardinals vs. Chicago Bears	November 18, 1929
Season	176	Paul Hornung	Green Bay Packers	1960
Career	2,002	George Blanda	Chicago Bears, Baltimore Colts, Houston Oilers, Oakland Raiders	1949–75
TOUCHDOWNS SCORED				
Game	6	Ernie Nevers	Chicago Cardinals vs. Chicago Bears	November 28, 1929
		Dub Jones	Cleveland Browns vs. Chicago Bears	November 25, 1951
		Gale Sayers	Chicago Bears vs. San Francisco 49ers	December 12, 1965
Season	25	Emmitt Smith	Dallas Cowboys	1995
Career	165	Jerry Rice	San Francisco 49ers	1985–96

PASSING

Yards Gained

Game	554	Norm Van Brocklin	Los Angeles Rams vs. New York Yankees	September 28, 1951
Season	5,084	Dan Marino	Miami Dolphins	1984
Career	51,636	Dan Marino	Miami Dolphins	1983–96

Completions

Game	45	Drew Bledsoe	New England Patriots vs. Minnesota Vikings	November 13, 1994*
Season	404	Warren Moon	Houston Oilers	1991
Career	4,134	Dan Marino	Miami Dolphins	1983–96

Attempts

Game	68	George Blanda	Houston Oilers vs. Buffalo Bills	November 1, 1964
Season	655	Warren Moon	Houston Oilers	1991
Career	6,904	Dan Marino	Miami Dolphins	1983–96

Touchdowns Thrown

Game	7	Sid Luckman	Chicago Bears vs. New York Giants	November 14, 1943
		Adrian Burk	Philadelphia Eagles vs. Washington Redskins	October 17, 1954
		George Blanda	Houston Oilers vs. New York Titans	November 19, 1961
		Y. A. Tittle	New York Giants vs. Washington Redskins	October 28, 1962
		Joe Kapp	Minnesota Vikings vs. Baltimore Colts	September 28, 1969
Season	48	Dan Marino	Miami Dolphins	1984
Career	369	Dan Marino	Miami Dolphins	1983–96

Average Yards Gained

Game (min. 20 attempts)	18.58	Sammy Baugh	Washington Redskins vs. Boston Yanks (24–446)	October 31, 1948
Season (qualifiers)	11.17	Tommy O'Connell	Cleveland Browns (110–1,229)	1957
Career (min. 1,500 attempts)	8.63	Otto Graham	Cleveland Browns (1,565–13,499)	1950–55

* Overtime

NFL Individual Records (continued)

PASS RECEIVING		Player(s)	Team(s)	Date(s)
Receptions				
Game	18	Tom Fears	Los Angeles Rams vs. Green Bay Packers	December 3, 1950
Season	123	Herman Moore	Detroit Lions	1995
Career	1,050	Jerry Rice	San Francisco 49ers	1985–96
Yards Gained				
Game	336	Willie Anderson	Los Angeles Rams vs. New Orleans Saints	November 26,1989*
Season	1,846	Jerry Rice	San Francisco 49ers	1995
Career	16,377	Jerry Rice	San Francisco 49ers	1985–96
Touchdown Receptions				
Game	5	Bob Shaw	Chicago Cardinals vs. Baltimore Colts	October 2, 1950
		Kellen Winslow	San Diego Chargers vs. Oakland Raiders	November 22, 1981
		Jerry Rice	San Francisco 49ers vs. Atlanta Falcons	October 14, 1990
Season	22	Jerry Rice	San Francisco 49ers	1987
Career	154	Jerry Rice	San Francisco 49ers	1985–96
Average Yards Gained				
Game (min. 3 catches)	60.67	Bill Groman	Houston Oilers vs. Denver Broncos (3–182)	November 20, 1960
		Homer Jones	New York Giants vs. Washington Redskins (3–182)	December 12, 1965
Season (min. 24 catches)	32.58	Don Currivan	Boston Yanks (24–782)	1947
Career (min. 200 catches)	22.26	Homer Jones	New York Giants, Cleveland Browns (224–4,986)	1964–70
RUSHING				
Yards Gained				
Game	275	Walter Payton	Chicago Bears vs. Minnesota Vikings	November 20, 1977
Season	2,105	Eric Dickerson	Los Angeles Rams	1984
Career	16,726	Walter Payton	Chicago Bears	1975–87

*Overtime

During the 1996 NFL season, Marcus Allen (above) set the career rushing record for most touchdowns. 49ers great Jerry Rice (right) extended his NFL marks for receptions, yards gained and touchdowns.
(Stephen Dunn/Allsport)

NFL Individual Records (continued)

		Player(s)	Team(s)	Date(s)
Attempts				
Game	45	Jamie Morris	Washington Redskins vs. Cincinnati Bengals	December 17, 1988*
Season	407	James Wilder	Tampa Bay Buccaneers	1984
Career	3,838	Walter Payton	Chicago Bears	1975–87
Touchdowns Scored				
Game	6	Ernie Nevers	Chicago Cardinals vs. Chicago Bears	November 28, 1929
Season	25	Emmitt Smith	Dallas Cowboys	1995
Career	112	Marcus Allen	Los Angeles Raiders, Kansas City Chiefs	1982–96
Average Yards Gained				
Game (min. 10 attempts)	17.09	Marion Mottley	Cleveland Browns vs. Pittsburgh Steelers (11–88)	October 29, 1950
Season (qualifiers)	8.44	Beattie Feathers	Chicago Bears (119–1,004)	1934
Career (min. 750 attempts)	5.22	Jim Brown	Cleveland Browns (2,359–12,312)	1957–65
INTERCEPTIONS				
Game	4	16 players have achieved this feat.		
Season	14	Dick Lane	Los Angeles Rams	1952
Career	81	Paul Krause	Washington Redskins, Minnesota Vikings	1964–79
Interceptions Returned for Touchdowns				
Game	2	18 players have achieved this feat.		
Season	4	Ken Houston	Houston Oilers	1971
		Jim Kearney	Kansas City Chiefs	1972
		Eric Allen	Philadelphia Eagles	1993
Career	9	Ken Houston	Houston Oilers, Washington Redskins	1967–80
SACKS (compiled since 1982)				
Game	7	Derrick Thomas	Kansas City vs. Seattle Seahawks	November 11, 1990
Season	22	Mark Gastineau	New York Jets	1984
Career	165.5	Reggie White	Philadelphia Eagles, Green Bay Packers	1985–96
KICKING				
Field Goals				
Game	7	Jim Bakken	St. Louis Cardinals vs. Pittsburgh Steelers	September 24, 1967
		Rich Karlis	Minnesota Vikings vs. Los Angeles Rams	November 5, 1989*
		Chris Boniol	Dallas Cowboys vs. Green Bay Packers	November 18, 1996
Season	37	John Kasay	North Carolina Panthers	1996
Career	383	Nick Lowery	New England Patriots, Kansas City Chiefs, New York Jets	1978, 1980–96
Highest Percentage				
Game	100.00	This has been achieved by many kickers. The most field goals kicked with no misses is 7, by two players: Rich Karlis, Minnesota Vikings vs. Los Angeles Rams on November 5, 1989 in an overtime game; and Chris Boniol, Dallas Cowboys vs. Green Bay Packers on November 18, 1996.		
Season (qualifiers)	100.00	Tony Zendejas	Los Angeles Rams (17–17)	1991
Career (min. 100 field goals)	81.3	Doug Pelfrey	New England Patriots, Kansas City Chiefs, Cincinnati Bengals (104–128)	1993–96
		Travis Williams	Green Bay Packers, Los Angeles Rams	1967–71

*Overtime

NFL Individual Records (continued)

		Player(s)	Team(s)	Date(s)
KICKING				
Field Goals 50 or More Yards				
Game	3	Morten Andersen	Atlanta Falcons vs. New Orleans Saints	December 10, 1995
Season	8	Morten Andersen	Atlanta Falcons	1995
Career	31	Morten Andersen	New Orleans Saints, Atlanta Falcons	1982–96
Points After Touchdown (PATs)				
Game	9	Pat Harder	Chicago Cardinals vs. New York Giants	October 17, 1948
		Bob Waterfield	Los Angeles Rams vs. Baltimore Colts	October 22, 1950
		Charlie Gogolak	Washington Redskins vs. New York Giants	November 27, 1966
Season	66	Uwe von Schamann	Miami Dolphins	1984
Career	943	George Blanda	Chicago Bears, Baltimore Colts, Houston Oilers, Oakland Raiders	1949–75
PUNTING				
Punts				
Game	15	John Teltschik	Philadelphia Eagles vs. New York Giants	December 6, 1987*
Season	114	Bob Parsons	Chicago Bears	1981
Career	1,154	Dave Jennings	New York Giants, New York Jets	1974–87
Average Yards Gained				
Game (min. 4 punts)	61.75	Bob Cifers	Detroit Lions vs. Chicago Bears (4–247)	November 24, 1946
Season (qualifiers)	51.40	Sammy Baugh	Washington Redskins (35–1,799)	1940
Career (min. 250 punts)	45.10	Sammy Baugh	Washington Redskins (338–15,245)	1937–52
SPECIAL TEAMS				
Punt Returns for Touchdowns				
Game	2	Jack Christiansen	Detroit Lions vs. Los Angeles Rams	October 14, 1951
		Jack Christiansen	Detroit Lions vs. Green Bay Packers	November 22, 1951
		Dick Christy	New York Titans vs. Denver Broncos	September 24, 1961
		Rick Upchurch	Denver Broncos vs. Cleveland Browns	September 26, 1976
		LeRoy Irvin	Los Angeles Rams vs. Atlanta Falcons	October 11, 1981
		Vai Sikahema	St. Louis Cardinals vs. Tampa Bay Buccaneers	December 21, 1986
		Todd Kinchen	Los Angeles Rams vs. Atlanta Falcons	December 27, 1992
		Eric Metcalf	Cleveland Browns vs. Pittsburgh Steelers	October 24, 1993
Season	4	Jack Christiansen	¡Detroit Lions	1951
		Rick Upchurch	Denver Broncos	1976
Career	8	Jack Christiansen	Detroit Lions	1951–58
		Rick Upchurch	Denver Broncos	1975–83
Kickoff Returns for Touchdowns				
Game	2	Timmy Brown	Philadelphia Eagles vs. Dallas Cowboys	November 6, 1966
		Travis Williams	Green Bay Packers vs. Cleveland Browns	November 12, 1967
		Ron Brown	Los Angeles Rams vs. Green Bay Packers	November 24, 1985
		Tyrone Hughes	New Orleans Saints vs. Los Angeles Rams	October 23, 1994
Season	4	Travis Williams	Green Bay Packers	1967
		Cecil Turner	Chicago Bears	1970
Career	6	Ollie Matson	Chicago Cardinals, Los Angeles Rams, Detroit Lions, Philadelphia Eagles	1952–64
		Gale Sayers	Chicago Bears	1965–71
		Travis Williams	Green Bay Packers, Los Angeles Rams	1967–71
		Mel Gray	New Orleans Saints, Detroit Lions, Houston Oilers	1986–96

Source: NFL

STREAKS

Scoring (games)   206, Morten Andersen, New Orleans Saints, 1982–94; Atlanta Falcons, 1995–96.

Scoring touchdowns (games)   18, Lenny Moore, Baltimore Colts, 1963–65.

Points after touchdown, consecutive kicked   234, Tommy Davis, San Francisco 49ers, 1959–65.

Field goals, consecutive kicked   31, Fuad Reveiz, Minnesota Vikings, 1994–95.

Field goals (games)   31, Fred Cox, Minnesota Vikings, 1968–70.

100+ yards rushing (games)   11, Marcus Allen, Los Angeles Raiders, 1985–86.

Touchdown passes (games)   47, Johnny Unitas, Baltimore Colts, 1956–60.

Touchdown rushes (games)   13, by two players: John Riggins, Washington Redskins, 1982–83; George Rogers, Washington Redskins, 1985–86.

Touchdown receptions (games)   13, Jerry Rice, San Francisco 49ers, 1986–87.

Passes completed (consecutive)   22, Joe Montana, San Francisco 49ers vs. Cleveland Browns, November 29, 1987 (5); vs. Green Bay Packers, December 6, 1987 (17).

Pass receptions (games)   183, by Art Monk, Washington Redskins, 1980–93; New York Jets, 1994; and Philadelphia Eagles, 1995.

TEAM RECORDS

Most consecutive games won   The Chicago Bears won 17 straight regular-season games, 1933–34.

Most consecutive games unbeaten   The Canton Bulldogs played 25 regular-season games without a defeat, covering the 1921–23 seasons. The Bulldogs won 22 games and tied three.

Most games won in a season   Two teams have compiled 15-win seasons: the San Francisco 49ers in 1984, and the Chicago Bears in 1985.

Perfect season   The only team to win all its games in one season was the 1972 Miami Dolphins. The Dolphins won 14 regular-season games and then won three playoff games, including Super Bowl VII.

Most consecutive games lost   This most undesirable of records is held by the Tampa Bay Buccaneers, who lost 26 straight games, 1976–77.

Most games lost in a season   Five teams hold the dubious honor of having lost 15 games in one season: the New Orleans Saints in 1980, the Dallas Cowboys in 1989, the New England Patriots in 1990, the Indianapolis Colts in 1991, and the New York Jets in 1996.

Most points scored, game   The Washington Redskins scored 72 points vs. the New York Giants on November 27, 1966 to set the single-game NFL regular-season record for most points scored by one team.

Highest aggregate score   On November 27, 1966, the Washington Redskins defeated the New York Giants 72–41 in Washington, D.C. The Redskins' total was an NFL record for most points (see above).

Largest deficit overcome   On January 3, 1993, the Buffalo Bills, playing at home in the AFC Wild Card game, trailed the Houston Oilers 35–3 with 28 minutes remaining. The Bills rallied to score 35 unanswered points and take the lead with 3:08 left. The Bills eventually won the game in overtime, overcoming a deficit of 32 points—the largest in NFL history.

Largest trade in NFL history   Based on the number of players and/or draft choices involved, the largest trade in NFL history is 15, which has happened twice. On March 26, 1953 the Baltimore Colts and the Cleveland Browns exchanged 15 players; and on January 28, 1971, the Washington Redskins and the Los Angeles Rams completed the transfer of seven players and eight draft choices.

COACHES

Most seasons   40, George Halas, Decatur/Chicago Staleys/Chicago Bears: 1920–29, 1933–42, 1946–55, 1958–67.

Most wins (including playoffs)   347, by Don Shula, Baltimore Colts, 1963–69; Miami Dolphins, 1970–95.

NFL CHAMPIONSHIP

The first NFL championship was awarded in 1920 to the Akron Pros, as the team with the best record. From 1920 to 1931, the championship was based on regular-season records. The first championship game was played in 1932.

In 1966, the National Football League (NFL) and the American Football League (AFL) agreed to merge their competing leagues to form an expanded NFL. Regular-season play did not begin until 1970, but the two leagues agreed to stage an annual AFL–NFL world championship game beginning in January 1967. The proposed championship game was dubbed the Super Bowl, and in 1969 the NFL officially recognized the title.

Most NFL titles The Green Bay Packers have won 12 NFL championships: 1929–31, 1936, 1939, 1944, 1961–62, 1965, and Super Bowls I, II and XXXI (1966, 1967 and 1996 seasons).

THE SUPER BOWL

Super Bowl I was played on January 15, 1967, with the Green Bay Packers (NFL) defeating the Kansas City Chiefs (AFL), 35–10.

Most wins Two teams have won five Super Bowls. The San Francisco 49ers won Super Bowls XVI, XIX, XXIII, XXIV and XXIX. The Dallas Cowboys won Super Bowls VI, XII, XXVII, XXVIII and XXX.

Consecutive wins Five teams have won Super Bowls in successive years: the Green Bay Packers, I and II; the Miami Dolphins, VII and VIII; the Pittsburgh Steelers (twice), IX and X, and XIII and XIV; the San Francisco 49ers, XXIII and XXIV; and the Dallas Cowboys, XXVII and XXVIII.

Most appearances The Dallas Cowboys have played in eight Super Bowls: V, VI, X, XII, XIII, XXVII, XXVIII and XXX. The Cowboys have won five games and lost three.

Scoring Records

Most points scored The San Francisco 49ers scored 55 points vs. the Denver Broncos in Super Bowl XXIV.

Highest aggregate score The highest aggregate score is 75 points, set when the San Francisco 49ers beat the San Diego Chargers 49–26 in Super Bowl XXIX.

NFL CHAMPIONS (1920–1965)

Year	Winner	Loser	Score
1920	Akron Pros		
1921	Chicago Staleys		
1922	Canton Bulldogs		
1923	Canton Bulldogs		
1924	Cleveland Bulldogs		
1925	Chicago Cardinals		
1926	Frankford Yellowjackets		
1927	New York Giants		
1928	Providence Steam Roller		
1929	Green Bay Packers		
1930	Green Bay Packers		
1931	Green Bay Packers		
1932	Chicago Bears	Portsmouth Spartans	9–0
1933	Chicago Bears	New York Giants	23–21
1934	New York Giants	Chicago Bears	30–13
1935	Detroit Lions	New York Giants	26–7
1936	Green Bay Packers	Boston Redskins	21–6
1937	Washington Redskins	Chicago Bears	28–21
1938	New York Giants	Green Bay Packers	23–17
1939	Green Bay Packers	New York Giants	27–0
1940	Chicago Bears	Washington Redskins	73–0
1941	Chicago Bears	New York Giants	37–9
1942	Washington Redskins	Chicago Bears	14–6
1943	Chicago Bears	Washington Redskins	41–21
1944	Green Bay Packers	New York Giants	14–7
1945	Cleveland Rams	Washington Redskins	15–14
1946	Chicago Bears	New York Giants	24–14
1947	Chicago Cardinals	Philadelphia Eagles	28–21
1948	Philadelphia Eagles	Chicago Cardinals	7–0
1949	Philadelphia Eagles	Los Angeles Rams	14–0
1950	Cleveland Browns	Los Angeles Rams	30–28
1951	Los Angeles Rams	Cleveland Browns	24–17
1952	Detroit Lions	Cleveland Browns	17–7
1953	Detroit Lions	Cleveland Browns	17–16
1954	Cleveland Browns	Detroit Lions	56–10
1955	Cleveland Browns	Los Angeles Rams	38–14
1956	New York Giants	Chicago Bears	47–7
1957	Detroit Lions	Cleveland Browns	59–14
1958	Baltimore Colts	New York Giants	23–17*
1959	Baltimore Colts	New York Giants	31–16
1960	Philadelphia Eagles	Green Bay Packers	17–13
1961	Green Bay Packers	New York Giants	37–0
1962	Green Bay Packers	New York Giants	16–7
1963	Chicago Bears	New York Giants	14–10
1964	Cleveland Browns	Baltimore Colts	27–0
1965	Green Bay Packers	Cleveland Browns	23–12

*Overtime

SUPER BOWL RESULTS

Bowl	Date	Winner	Loser	Score	Site
I	Jan. 15, 1967	Green Bay Packers	Kansas City Chiefs	35–10	Los Angeles, Calif.
II	Jan. 14, 1968	Green Bay Packers	Oakland Raiders	33–14	Miami, FL
III	Jan. 12, 1969	New York Jets	Baltimore Colts	16–7	Miami, Fla.
IV	Jan. 11, 1970	Kansas City Chiefs	Minnesota Vikings	23–7	New Orleans, La.
V	Jan. 17, 1971	Baltimore Colts	Dallas Cowboys	16–13	Miami, Fla.
VI	Jan. 16, 1972	Dallas Cowboys	Miami Dolphins	24–3	New Orleans, La.
VII	Jan. 14, 1973	Miami Dolphins	Washington Redskins	14–7	Los Angeles, Calif.
VIII	Jan. 13, 1974	Miami Dolphins	Minnesota Vikings	24–7	Houston, Tex.
IX	Jan. 12, 1975	Pittsburgh Steelers	Minnesota Vikings	16–6	New Orleans, La.
X	Jan. 18, 1976	Pittsburgh Steelers	Dallas Cowboys	21–17	Miami, Fla.
XI	Jan. 9, 1977	Oakland Raiders	Minnesota Vikings	32–14	Pasadena, Calif.
XII	Jan. 15, 1978	Dallas Cowboys	Denver Broncos	27–10	New Orleans, La.
XIII	Jan. 21, 1979	Pittsburgh Steelers	Dallas Cowboys	35–31	Miami, Fla.
XIV	Jan. 20, 1980	Pittsburgh Steelers	Los Angeles Rams	31–19	Pasadena, Calif.
XV	Jan. 25, 1981	Oakland Raiders	Philadelphia Eagles	27–10	New Orleans, La.
XVI	Jan. 24, 1982	San Francisco 49ers	Cincinnati Bengals	26–21	Pontiac, Mich.
XVII	Jan. 30, 1983	Washington Redskins	Miami Dolphins	27–17	Pasadena, Calif.
XVIII	Jan. 22, 1984	Los Angeles Raiders	Washington Redskins	38–9	Tampa, Fla.
XIX	Jan. 20, 1985	San Francisco 49ers	Miami Dolphins	38–16	Stanford, Calif.
XX	Jan. 26, 1986	Chicago Bears	New England Patriots	46–10	New Orleans, La.
XXI	Jan. 25, 1987	New York Giants	Denver Broncos	39–20	Pasadena, Calif.
XXII	Jan. 31, 1988	Washington Redskins	Denver Broncos	42–10	San Diego, Calif.
XXIII	Jan. 22, 1989	San Francisco 49ers	Cincinnati Bengals	20–16	Miami, Fla.
XXIV	Jan. 28, 1990	San Francisco 49ers	Denver Broncos	55–10	New Orleans, La.
XXV	Jan. 27, 1991	New York Giants	Buffalo Bills	20–19	Tampa, Fla.
XXVI	Jan. 25, 1992	Washington Redskins	Buffalo Bills	37–24	Minneapolis, Minn.
XXVII	Jan. 31, 1993	Dallas Cowboys	Buffalo Bills	52–17	Pasadena, Calif.
XXVIII	Jan. 30, 1994	Dallas Cowboys	Buffalo Bills	30–13	Atlanta, Ga.
XXIX	Jan. 29, 1995	San Francisco 49ers	San Diego Chargers	49–26	Miami, Fla.
XXX	Jan. 28, 1996	Dallas Cowboys	Pittsburgh Steelers	27–17	Tempe, AZ
XXXI	Jan. 26, 1997	Green Bay Packers	New England Patriots	35–21	New Orleans, LA

Desmond Howard's record 99-yard kickoff return sealed the Green Bay Packers' Super Bowl XXXI victory.
(Stephen Dunn/Allsport)

SUPER BOWL RECORDS

		Player(s)	Team(s)	Super Bowl
POINTS SCORED				
Game	18	Roger Craig	San Francisco 49ers	XIX
		Jerry Rice	San Francisco 49ers	XXIV, XXIX
		Ricky Watters	San Francisco 49ers	XXIX
Career	42	Jerry Rice	San Francisco 49ers	XXIII, XXIV, XXIX
TOUCHDOWNS SCORED				
Game	3	Roger Craig	San Francisco 49ers	XIX
		Jerry Rice	San Francisco 49ers	XXIV, XXIX
		Ricky Watters	San Francisco 49ers	XXIX
Career	7	Jerry Rice	San Francisco 49ers	XXIII, XXIV, XXIX
PASSING				
Yards Gained				
Game	357	Joe Montana	San Francisco 49ers	XXIII
Career	1,142	Joe Montana	San Francisco 49ers	XVI, XIX, XXIII, XXIV
Completions				
Game	31	Jim Kelly	Buffalo Bills	XXVIII
Career	83	Joe Montana	San Francisco 49ers	XVI, XIX, XXIII, XXIV
Touchdowns Thrown				
Game	6	Steve Young	San Francisco 49ers	XXIX
Career	11	Joe Montana	San Francisco 49ers	XVI, XIX, XXIII, XXIV
Highest Completion Percentage				
Game (min. 20 attempts)	88.0	Phil Simms	New York Giants (22–25)	XXI
Career (min. 40 attempts)	70.0	Troy Aikman	Dallas Cowboys (56–80)	XXVII, XXVIII, XXX
PASS RECEIVING				
Receptions				
Game	11	Dan Ross	Cincinnati Bengals	XVI
		Jerry Rice	San Francisco 49ers	XXIII
Career	28	Jerry Rice	San Francisco 49ers	XXIII, XXIV, XXIX
Yards Gained				
Game	215	Jerry Rice	San Francisco 49ers	XXIII
Career	512	Jerry Rice	San Francisco 49ers	XXIII, XXIV, XXIX
Touchdown Receptions				
Game	3	Jerry Rice	San Francisco 49ers	XXIV, XXIX
Career	7	Jerry Rice	San Francisco 49ers	XXIII, XXIV, XXIX
RUSHING				
Yards Gained				
Game	204	Timmy Smith	Washington Redskins	XXII
Career	354	Franco Harris	Pittsburgh Steelers	IX, X, XIII, XIV

SUPER BOWL RECORDS (continued)

		Player(s)	Team(s)	Super Bowl
RUSHING				
Touchdowns Scored				
Game	2	This feat has been achieved 11 times. Emmitt Smith (Dallas Cowboys) is the only player to have done it twice.		
Career	5	Emmitt Smith	Dallas Cowboys	XXVII, XXVIII, XXX
INTERCEPTIONS				
Game	3	Rod Martin	Oakland Raiders	XV
Career	3	Chuck Howley	Dallas Cowboys	V, VI
		Rod Martin	Oakland/Los Angeles Raiders	XV, XVIII
		Larry Brown	Dallas Cowboys	XXVII, XXVIII, XXX
FIELD GOALS KICKED				
Game	4	Don Chandler	Green Bay Packers	II
		Ray Wersching	San Francisco 49ers	XVI
Career	5	Ray Wersching	San Francisco 49ers	XVI, XIX
LONGEST PLAYS				
Run from Scrimmage	74 yards	Marcus Allen	Los Angeles Raiders	XVIII
Pass Completion	81 yards	Brett Favre	(to Antonio Freeman) Green Bay Packers	XXXI
Field Goal	54 yards	Steve Christie	Buffalo Bills	XXVIII
Kickoff Return	99 yards	Desmond Howard	Green Bay Packers	XXXI
Punt	63 yards	Lee Johnson	Cincinnati Bengals	XXIII

Source: NFL

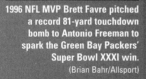

1996 NFL MVP Brett Favre pitched a record 81-yard touchdown bomb to Antonio Freeman to spark the Green Bay Packers' Super Bowl XXXI win.
(Brian Bahr/Allsport)

Greatest margin of victory The greatest margin of victory is 45 points, set by the San Francisco 49ers when they defeated the Denver Broncos 55–10 in Super Bowl XXIV.

Most MVP awards Joe Montana, quarterback of the San Francisco 49ers, has been voted the Super Bowl MVP on a record three occasions, XVI, XIX and XXIV.

Coaches

Most wins Chuck Noll led the Pittsburgh Steelers to four Super Bowl titles, IX, X, XIII and XIV.

Most appearances Don Shula has been the head coach of six Super Bowl teams: the Baltimore Colts, III; the Miami Dolphins, VI, VII, VIII, XVII and XIX. He won two games and lost four.

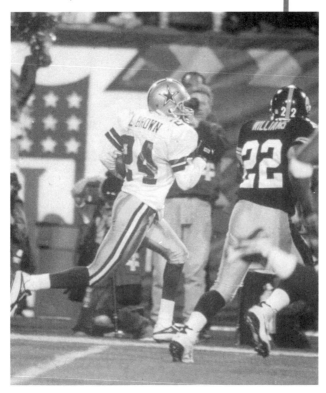

Larry Brown's two interception touchdown returns sealed Dallas's Super Bowl XXX win; the Cowboys' fifth title tied the all-time mark.
(Mike Powell/Allsport)

COLLEGE FOOTBALL (NCAA)

Origins

At the turn of the 20th century, football's popularity was rising rapidly; however, with the increased participation came a rise in serious injuries and even some deaths. Many institutions, alarmed at the violent nature of the game, called for controls to be established.

In December 1905, 13 universities, led by Chancellor Henry M. MacCracken of New York University, outlined a plan to establish an organization to standardize playing rules. On December 28, the Intercollegiate Athletic Association of the United States (IAAUS) was founded in New York City with 62 charter members. The IAAUS was officially constituted on March 31, 1906, and was renamed the National Collegiate Athletic Association (NCAA) in 1910.

The NCAA first began to keep statistics on football in 1937, and the records in this section date from that time. In 1973, the NCAA introduced a new classification system creating Divisions I, II, and III to identify levels of college play. In 1978, Division I was subdivided into I-A and I-AA.

INDIVIDUAL RECORDS

CAREER RECORDS (ALL DIVISIONS)

Points Scored

Game Four players have scored 48 points in an NCAA game: Junior Wolf, Panhandle State (Div. II), November 8, 1958 vs. St. Mary's (Kans.); Paul Zaeske, North Park (Div. II), October 12, 1968 vs. North Central; Howard Griffith, Illinois (Div I-A), September 22, 1990 vs. Southern Illinois; and Carey Bender, Coe College (Div. III), November 12, 1994 vs. Beloit.

NCAA Division I-A Records

SCORING		Player(s)	Team(s)	Date(s)
Points Scored				
Game	48	Howard Griffith	Illinois vs. Southern Illinois (8 TDs)	September 22, 1990
Season	234	Barry Sanders	Oklahoma State (39 TDs)	1988
Career	423	Roman Anderson	Houston (70 FGs, 213 PATs)	1988–91
Touchdowns Scored				
Game	8	Howard Griffith	Illinois vs. Southern Illinois (all rushing)	September 22, 1990
Season	39	Barry Sanders	Oklahoma State	1988
Career	65	Anthony Thompson	Indiana (64 rushing, 1 reception)	1986–89
2-Point Conversions				
Game	6	Jim Pilot	New Mexico State vs. Hardin-Simmons	November 25, 1961
Season		Pat McCarthy	Holy Cross	1960
		Jim Pilot	New Mexico State	1961
		Howard Twilley	Tulsa	1964
Career	13	Pat McCarthy	Holy Cross	1960–62
PASSING				
Touchdown Passes				
Game	11	David Klingler	Houston vs. Eastern Washington	November 17, 1990
Season	54	David Klingler	Houston	1990
Career	121	Ty Detmer	BYU	1988–91
Yards Gained				
Game	716	David Klingler	Houston vs. Arizona State	December 1, 1990
Season	5,188	Ty Detmer	BYU	1990
Career	15,031	Ty Detmer	BYU	1988–91
Completions				
Game	55	Rusty LaRue	Wake Forest vs. Duke	October 28, 1995
Season	374	David Klingler	Houston	1990
Career	958	Ty Detmer	BYU	1988–91
Attempts				
Game	79	Matt Vogler	TCU vs. Houston	November 3, 1990
Season	643	David Klingler	Houston	1990
Career	1,530	Ty Detmer	BYU	1988–91
Average Yards Gained per Attempt				
Game (min. 40 attempts)	14.07	John Walsh	BYU vs. Utah State (44 for 619 yards)	October 30, 1993
Season (min. 400 attempts)	11.07	Ty Detmer	BYU (412 for 4,560 yards)	1989
Career (min. 1,000 attempts)	9.82	Ty Detmer	BYU (1,530 for 15,031 yards)	1988–91

NCAA Division I-A Records (continued)

The fewest number of games taken to gain 1,000 yards in a season is five, a feat achieved by seven players. Among them are Troy Davis (Iowa State; below) and Byron Hanspard (Texas Tech; right).
(Stephen Dunn/Allsport; Robert Seale/Allsport)

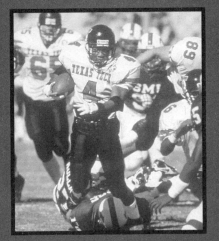

PASS RECEIVING		Player(s)	Team(s)	Date(s)
Touchdown Receptions				
Game	6	Tim Delaney	San Diego State vs. New Mexico State	November 15, 1969
Season	22	Manny Hazard	Houston	1989
Career	43	Aaron Turner	Pacific (Cal.)	1989–92
Receptions				
Game	23	Randy Gatewood	UNLV vs. Idaho	September 17, 1994
Season	142	Manny Hazard	Houston	1989
Career	266	Aaron Turner	Pacific (Cal.)	1989–92
Yards Gained				
Game	363	Randy Gatewood	UNLV vs. Idaho	September 17, 1994
Season	1,854	Alex Van Dyke	Nevada	1995
Career	4,518	Marcus Harris	Wyoming	1993–96
Average Yards Gained per Reception				
Game (min. 5 catches)	52.6	Alexander Wright	Auburn vs. Pacific (5 for 263 yards)	September 9,1989
Season (min. 50 catches)	24.4	Henry Ellard	Fresno State (62 for 1,510 yards)	1982
Career (min. 105 catches)	22.0	Herman Moore	Virginia (114 for 2,504 yards)	1988–90

Season The most points scored in one season is 234, by Barry Sanders, Oklahoma State (Div. I-A) in 1988, all from touchdowns, 37 rushing and two receptions.

Career The career record for most points scored is 528, by Carey Bender, Coe College (Div. III), 1991–94. Bender scored 86 touchdowns, 70 rushing, 16 receptions and 12 extra points.

Rushing (Yards Gained)

Game A.J. Pittorino, Hartwick (Div. III) rushed for an NCAA single-game record 443 yards vs. Waynesburg on November 2, 1996.

Season The most yards gained in a season is 2,628, by Barry Sanders, Oklahoma State (Div. I-A), in 1988. Sanders played in 11 games and carried the ball 344 times for an average gain of 7.64 yards per carry.

Career The career record for most yards gained is 6,320, by Johnny Bailey, Texas A&M–Kingsville (Div. II), 1986–89. Bailey carried the ball 885 times for an average gain of 7.14 yards per carry.

Passing (Yards Gained)

Game David Klingler, Houston (Div. I-A) threw for an NCAA single-game record 716 yards vs. Arizona State on December 2, 1990.

Season The single-season NCAA mark is held by Ty Detmer, BYU, who threw for 5,188 yards in 1990.

Career The career passing record is 15,031 yards, set by Ty Detmer, BYU (Div. I-A), 1988–91.

Receiving (Yards Gained)

Game The most yards gained from pass receptions in a single game is 370, by two players: Barry Wagner, Alabama A&M (Div. II), vs. Clark Atlanta on November 4, 1989; Michael Lerch, Princeton (Div. 1-AA), vs. Brown on October 12, 1991.

Season The single-season NCAA record is 1,876 yards, by Chris George, Glenville State (Div. II). George caught 117 passes for an average gain of 16.03 yards.

Career The all-time NCAA mark is held by Jerry Rice, Mississippi Valley (Div. I-AA), 1981–84. He gained 4,693 yards on 301 catches (also an NCAA career record), for an average gain of 15.6 yards.

Field Goals (Most Made)

Game Goran Lingmerth, Northern Arizona (Div. I-AA) booted 8 out of 8 field goals vs. Idaho on October 25, 1986. The distances were 39, 18, 20, 33, 46, 27, 22 and 35 yards each.

Season The most kicks made in one season is 29, by John Lee, UCLA (Div. I-A) from 33 attempts in 1984.

Career The NCAA all-time career record is 80, by Jeff Jaeger, Washington (Div. I-A) from 99 attempts, 1983–86.

Longest Plays (Division I-A)

Run from scrimmage 99 yards, by four players: Gale Sayers (Kansas vs. Nebraska), 1963; Max Anderson (Arizona State vs. Wyoming), 1967; Ralph Thompson (West Texas State vs. Wichita State), 1970; Kelsey Finch (Tennessee vs. Florida), 1977.

Pass completion 99 yards, on nine occasions, performed by eight players (Terry Peel and Robert Ford did it twice): Fred Owens (to Jack Ford), Portland vs. St. Mary's, CA, 1947; Bo Burris (to Warren McVea), Houston vs. Washington State, 1966; Colin Clapton (to Eddie Jenkins), Holy Cross vs. Boston U, 1970; Terry Peel (to Robert Ford), Houston vs. Syracuse, 1970; Terry Peel (to Robert Ford), Houston vs. San Diego State, 1972; Cris Collingsworth (to Derrick Gaffney), Florida vs. Rice, 1977; Scott Ankrom (to James Maness), TCU vs. Rice, 1984; Gino Torretta (to Horace Copeland), Miami vs. Arkansas, 1991; John Paci (to Thomas Lewis), Indiana vs. Penn State, 1993.

Field goal 67 yards, by three players: Russell Erxleben (Texas vs. Rice), 1977; Steve Little (Arkansas vs. Texas), 1977; Joe Williams (Wichita State vs. Southern Illinois), 1978.

Punt 99 yards, by Pat Brady, Nevada-Reno vs. Loyola Marymount in 1950.

NCAA Division I-A Records

		Player(s)	Team(s)	Date(s)
RUSHING				
Yards Gained				
Game	396	Tony Sands	Kansas vs. Missouri	November 23, 1991
Season	2,628	Barry Sanders	Oklahoma State	1988
Career	6,082	Tony Dorsett	Pittsburgh	1973–76
Attempts				
Game	58	Tony Sands	Kansas vs. Missouri	November 23, 1991
Season	403	Marcus Allen	Southern Cal.	1981
Career	1,215	Steve Bartalo	Colorado State	1983–86
Average Yards Gained per Attempt				
Game (min. 15 rushes)	21.40	Tony Jeffery	TCU vs. Tulane (16 for 343 yards)	September 13, 1986
Season (min. 250 rushes)	7.81	Mike Rozier	Nebraska (275 for 2,148 yards)	1983
Career (min. 600 rushes)	7.16	Mike Rozier	Nebraska (668 for 4,780 yards)	1981–83
Touchdowns Scored				
Game	8	Howard Griffith	Illinois vs. Southern Illinois	September 22, 1990
Season	37	Barry Sanders	Oklahoma State	1988
Career	64	Anthony Thompson	Indiana	1986–89
TOTAL OFFENSE (RUSHING PLUS PASSING)				
Yards Gained				
Game	732	David Klingler	Houston vs. Arizona State (716 passing, 16 rushing)	December 2, 1990
Season	5,221	David Klingler	Houston (81 rushing, 5,140 passing)	1990
Career	14,665	Ty Detmer	BYU (-366 rushing, 15,031 passing)	988–91
Interceptions				
Game	5	Lee Cook	Oklahoma State vs. Detroit	November 28, 1942
		Walt Pastuszak	Brown vs. Rhode Island	October 8, 1949
		Byron Beaver	Houston vs. Baylor	September 22, 1962
		Dan Rebsch	Miami (Ohio) vs. Western Michigan	November 4, 1972
Season	14	Al Worley	Washington	1968
Career	29	Al Brosky	Illinois	1950–52

During the 1996 season, Wyoming's Marcus Harris set the NCAA Division I-A mark for career yards gained by a receiver.
(Todd Warshaw/Allsport)

NCAA Division I-A Records

Wake Forest QB Rusty LaRue holds the NCAA Division I-A for most pass completions in a game.
(Doug Pensinger/Allsport)

		Player(s)	Team(s)	Date(s)
KICKING				
Field Goals Kicked				
Game	7	Mike Prindle	Western Michigan vs. Marshall	September 29, 1984
		Dale Klein	Nebraska vs. Missouri	October 19, 1985
Season	29	John Lee	UCLA	1984
Career	80	Jeff Jaeger	Washington	1983–86
Points Scored				
Game	24	Mike Prindle	Western Michigan vs. Marshall (7 Fgs, PATSs)	September 29, 1984
Season	131	Roman Anderson	Houston (22 FGS, 65 PATs)	1989
Career	423	Roman Anderson	Houston (70 FGS, 213 PATs)	1988–91
Points After Touchdown (PATs)				
Game	13	Terry Leiweke	Houston vs. Tulsa	November 23, 1968
		Derek Mahoney	Fresno State vs. New Mexico	October 5, 1991
Season	71	Bart Edmiston	Florida	1995
Career	216	Derek Mahoney	Fresno State	1990–93
PUNTING				
Most Punts				
Game	36	Charlie Calhoun	Texas Tech vs. Centenary	November 11, 1939
Season	101	Jim Bailey	Virginia Military	1969
Career	320	Cameron Young	TCU	1976–79
Average Yards Gained				
Game (min. 5 punts)	60.4	Lee Johnson	BYU vs. Wyoming (5 for 302 yds)	October 8, 1983
Season (min. 50 punts)	48.4	Todd Sauerbrun	West Virginia (72 for 3,486)	1994
Career (min. 200 punts)	44.7	Ray Guy	Southern Mississippi (200 for 8,934)	1970–72
Yards Gained				
Game	1,318	Charlie Calhoun	Texas Tech vs. Centenary	November 11, 1939
Season	4,138	Johnny Pingel	Michigan State	1938
Career	12,947	Cameron Young	TCU	1976–79

Source: NCAA

CONSECUTIVE RECORDS

Regular Season (Individual–Division I-A)

Scoring touchdowns (games) 23, by Bill Burnett, Arkansas. Burnett amassed 47 touchdowns during his 23-game streak, which ran from October 5, 1968 to October 31, 1970.

Touchdown passes (games) 35, Ty Detmer, BYU, September 7, 1989–November 23, 1991.

Touchdown passes (consecutive) 6, by Brooks Dawson, UTEP vs. New Mexico, October 28, 1967. Dawson completed his first 6 passes for touchdowns, which must rank as the greatest start to a game ever.

Passes completed 23, shared by two players: Rob Johnson, Southern Cal, 1994 (completed last 15 attempts vs. Arizona, November 12, and first eight attempts vs. UCLA, November 19); Scott Milanovich, Maryland, 1994 (completed last four attempts vs. Tulane, October 29, and first 19 attempts vs. North Carolina State, November 5). The most passes completed consecutively in one game is 22, by Chuck Long, Iowa vs. Indiana, October 27, 1984.

100 yards+ rushing (games) 31, by Archie Griffin, Ohio State, September 15, 1973–November 22, 1975.

200 yards+ rushing (games) 5, shared by two players: Marcus Allen, Southern CA, 1981; Barry Sanders, Oklahoma State, 1988.

Touchdown receptions (games) 12, by two players: Desmond Howard, Michigan, 1990–91; Aaron Turner, Pacific (CA), 1990–91.

Pass receptions (caught for touchdowns)
6, by two players: Carlos Carson, Louisiana State, 1977. Carson scored touchdowns on his last five receptions vs. Rice on September 24, 1977, and from his first reception vs. Florida on October 1, 1977 (amazingly, these were the first six receptions of his collegiate career) and Gerald Armstrong, Nebraska, 1992. Armstrong caught six touchdown passes over five games, September 5–November 7.

Pass receptions (games) 46, by Carl Winston, New Mexico, 1990–93.

Field goals (consecutive) 30, by Chuck Nelson, Washington, 1981–82. Nelson converted his last five kicks of the season vs. Southern Cal. on November 14, 1981, and then booted the first 25 of the 1982 season, missing an attempt vs. Washington State on November 20, 1982.

Field goals (games) 19, shared by two players: Larry Roach, Oklahoma State (1983–84); Gary Gussman, Miami (Ohio) (1986–87).

Team Records (Division I-A)

Most wins Michigan has won 764 games out of 1,054 played, 1879–1996.

Highest winning percentage The highest winning percentage in college football history is .759 by Notre Dame. The Fighting Irish have won 746, lost 222 and tied 42 out of 1,010 games played, 1887–1996.

Longest winning streak The longest winning streak in Division I-A football, including bowl games, is 47 games by Oklahoma, 1953–57. Oklahoma's streak was stopped on November 16, 1957, when Notre Dame defeated them 7–0 in Norman.

Longest home winning streak 58, by Miami (Florida). The Hurricanes defeated all visitors from 1985 to 1994.

Longest undefeated streak Including bowl games, Washington played 63 games, 1907–17, without losing a game. California ended the streak with a 27–0 victory on November 3, 1917. Washington's record during the streak was 59 wins and 4 ties.

Longest losing streak The most consecutive losses in Division I-A football is 34 games, by Northwestern. This undesirable streak started on September 22, 1979 and was finally snapped three years later on September 25, 1982 when Northern Illinois succumbed to the Wildcats 31–6.

Most points scored Wyoming crushed Northern Colorado 103–0 on November 5, 1949 to set the Division I-A mark for most points scored by one team in a single game. The Cowboys scored 15 touchdowns and converted 13 PATs.

Highest-scoring game The most points scored in a Division I-A game is 124, when Oklahoma defeated Colorado 82–42 on October 4, 1980.

Highest-scoring tie game BYU and San Diego State played a 52–52 tie on November 16, 1991.

NCAA Division I-A National Champions (1936–1996)

Year	Team	Record	Year	Team	Record
1936	Minnesota	7–1–0	1968	Ohio State	10–0–0
1937	Pittsburgh	9–0–1	1969	Texas	11–0–0
1938	TCU	11–0–0	1970	Nebraska (AP)	11–0–1
1939	Texas A&M	11–0–0		Texas (UPI)	10–1–0
1940	Minnesota	8–0–0	1971	Nebraska	13–0–0
1941	Minnesota	8–0–0	1972	Southern Cal.	12–0–0
1942	Ohio State	9–1–0	1973	Notre Dame (AP)	11–0–0
1943	Notre Dame	9–1–0		Alabama (UPI)	11–1–0
1944	Army	9–0–0	1974	Oklahoma (AP)	11–0–0
1945	Army	9–0–0		Southern Cal. (UPI)	10–1–1
1946	Notre Dame	8–0–1	1975	Oklahoma	11–1–0
1947	Notre Dame	9–0–0	1976	Pittsburgh	12–0–0
1948	Michigan	9–0–0	1977	Notre Dame	11–1–0
1949	Notre Dame	10–0–0	1978	Alabama (AP)	11–1–0
1950	Oklahoma	10–1–0		Southern Cal. (UPI)	12–1–0
1951	Tennessee	10–0–0	1979	Alabama	12–0–0
1952	Michigan State	9–0–0	1980	Georgia	12–0–0
1953	Maryland	10–1–0	1981	Clemson	12–0–0
1954	Ohio State (AP)	10–0–0	1982	Penn State	11–1–0
	UCLA (UPI)	9–0–0	1983	Miami, Fla.	11–1–0
1955	Oklahoma	11–0–0	1984	BYU	13–0–0
1956	Oklahoma	10–0–0	1985	Oklahoma	11–1–0
1957	Auburn (AP)	10–0–0	1986	Penn State	12–0–0
	Ohio State (UPI)	9–1–0	1987	Miami, Fla.	12–0–0
1958	LSU	11–0–0	1988	Notre Dame	12–0–0
1959	Syracuse	11–0–0	1989	Miami, Fla.	11–1–0
1960	Minnesota	8–2–0	1990	Colorado (AP)	11–1–1
1961	Alabama	11–0–0		Georgia Tech (UPI)	11–0–1
1962	Southern Cal.	11–0–0	1991	Miami, Fla. (AP)	12–0–0
1963	Texas	11–0–0		Washington (UPI)	12–0–0
1964	Alabama	10–1–0	1992	Alabama	13–0–0
1965	Alabama (AP)	9–1–1	1993	Florida State	12–1–0
	Michigan State (UPI)	10–1–0	1994	Nebraska	13–0–0
1966	Notre Dame	9–0–1	1995	Nebraska	12–0–0
1967	Southern Cal.	10–1–0	1996	Florida	12–1–0

BOWL GAMES

The oldest college bowl game is the Rose Bowl. It was first played on January 1, 1902 at Tournament Park, Pasadena, CA, where Michigan defeated Stanford 49–0. The other three bowl games that make up the "big four" are the Orange Bowl, initiated in 1935; the Sugar Bowl, 1935; and the Cotton Bowl, 1937.

Rose Bowl

In the first game, played on January 1, 1902, Michigan blanked Stanford 49–0.

Most wins Southern Cal. has won the Rose Bowl 20 times: 1923, 1930, 1932–33, 1939–40, 1944–45, 1953, 1963, 1968, 1970, 1973, 1975, 1977, 1979–80, 1985, 1990, 1996.

Most appearances Southern Cal. has played in the Rose Bowl 28 times, with 20 wins and 8 losses.

Orange Bowl

In the first game, played on January 1, 1935, Bucknell shut out Miami (Florida) 26–0.

Most wins Oklahoma has won the Orange Bowl 11 times: 1954, 1956, 1958159, 1968, 1976, 1979–81, 1986–87.

Most appearances Oklahoma and Nebraska have each played in the Orange Bowl 16 times, Oklahoma with a record of 11 wins and 5 losses and Nebraska with 7 wins and 9 losses.

Sugar Bowl

In the first game, played on January 1, 1935, Tulane defeated Temple 20–14.

Most wins Alabama has won the Sugar Bowl eight times: 1962, 1964, 1967, 1975, 1978–80, 1993.

Most appearances Alabama has played in the Sugar Bowl 12 times, with a record of 8 wins and 4 losses.

Cotton Bowl

In the first game, played on January 1, 1937, Texas Christian defeated Marquette 16–6.

Most wins Texas has won the Cotton Bowl nine times: 1943, 1946, 1953, 1962, 1964, 1969–70, 1973, 1982.

Most appearances Texas has played in the Cotton Bowl 19 times, with a record of 9 wins, 9 losses and 1 tie.

Bowl Game Records

Alabama, Georgia, Georgia Tech, Notre Dame and Penn State are the only five teams to have won each of the "big four" bowl games.

Most wins Alabama has won a record 28 bowl games: Sugar Bowl, eight times, 1962, 1964, 1967, 1975, 1978–80, 1992; Rose Bowl, four times, 1926, 1931, 1935, 1946; Orange Bowl, four times, 1943, 1953, 1963, 1966; Sun Bowl (now John Hancock Bowl), three times, 1983, 1986, 1988; Cotton Bowl, twice, 1942, 1981; Liberty Bowl, twice, 1976, 1982; Aloha Bowl, once, 1985; Blockbuster Bowl, once, 1991; Gator Bowl, once, 1993; Florida Citrus Bowl, once, 1995; Outback Bowl, once, 1997.

The most storied team in college football, Notre Dame has the highest winning percentage in Division I-A football.
(Brian Bahr/Allsport)

Heisman Trophy Winners

Year	Player	Team	Year	Player	Team
1935	Jay Berwanger	Chicago	1979	Charles White	Southern Cal.
1936	Larry Kelley	Yale	1980	George Rogers	South Carolina
1937	Clint Frank	Yale	1981	Marcus Allen	Southern Cal.
1938	Davey O'Brien	TCU	1982	Herschel Walker	Georgia
1939	Nile Kinnick	Iowa	1983	Mike Rozier	Nebraska
1940	Tom Harmon	Michigan	1984	Doug Flutie	Boston College
1941	Bruce Smith	Minnesota	1985	Bo Jackson	Auburn
1942	Frank Sinkwich	Georgia	1986	Vinny Testaverde	Miami, Fla.
1943	Angelo Bertelli	Notre Dame	1987	Tim Brown	Notre Dame
1944	Les Horvath	Ohio State	1988	Barry Sanders	Oklahoma State
1945	Doc Blanchard	Army	1989	Andre Ware	Houston
1946	Glenn Davis	Army	1990	Ty Detmer	BYU
1947	Johnny Lujack	Notre Dame	1991	Desmond Howard	Michigan
1948	Doak Walker	SMU	1992	Gino Torretta	Miami, FL
1949	Leon Hart	Notre Dame	1993	Charlie Ward	Florida State
1950	Vic Janowicz	Ohio State	1994	Rashaan Salaam	Colorado
1951	Dick Kazmaier	Princeton	1995	Eddie George	Ohio State
1952	Billy Vessels	Oklahoma	1996	Danny Wuerffel	Florida
1953	Johnny Lattner	Notre Dame			
1954	Alan Ameche	Wisconsin			
1955	Howard Cassady	Ohio State			
1956	Paul Hornung	Notre Dame			
1957	John David Crow	Texas A&M			
1958	Pete Dawkins	Army			
1959	Billy Cannon	LSU			
1960	Joe Bellino	Navy			
1961	Ernie Davis	Syracuse			
1962	Terry Baker	Oregon State			
1963	Roger Staubach	Navy			
1964	John Huarte	Notre Dame			
1965	Mike Garrett	Southern Cal.			
1966	Steve Spurrier	Florida			
1967	Gary Beban	UCLA			
1968	O. J. Simpson	Southern Cal.			
1969	Steve Owens	Oklahoma			
1970	Jim Plunkett	Stanford			
1971	Pat Sullivan	Auburn			
1972	Johnny Rodgers	Nebraska			
1973	John Cappelletti	Penn State			
1974	Archie Griffin	Ohio State			
1975	Archie Griffin	Ohio State			
1976	Tony Dorsett	Pittsburgh			
1977	Earl Campbell	Texas			
1978	Billy Sims	Oklahoma			

In 1996, Danny Wuerffel led Florida to a national championship and gained the Heisman Trophy.
(Andy Lyons/Allsport)

Consecutive seasons Florida State won a bowl game for 11 consecutive seasons: Gator Bowl, 1985; All-American Bowl, 1986; Fiesta Bowl, 1988; Sugar Bowl, 1989; Fiesta Bowl, 1990; Blockbuster Bowl, 1990; Cotton Bowl, 1992; Orange Bowl, 1993–94; Sugar Bowl, 1995; Orange Bowl, 1996.

Bowl game appearances Alabama has played in 48 bowl games.

Coaches

Wins (Division I-A) In Division I-A competition, Paul "Bear" Bryant has won more games than any other coach, with 323 victories over 38 years. Bryant coached four teams: Maryland, 1945 (6–2–1); Kentucky, 1946–53 (60–23–5); Texas A&M, 1954–57 (25–14–2); and Alabama, 1958–82 (232–46–9). His completed record was 323 wins–85 losses–17 ties, for a .780 winning percentage.

Wins (all divisions) In overall NCAA competition, Eddie Robinson, Grambling (Division I-AA) holds the mark for most victories with 405.

Highest winning percentage (Division I-A) The highest winning percentage in Division I-A competition is .881, held by Knute Rockne of Notre Dame. Rockne coached the Irish from 1918 to 1930, for a record of 105 wins–112 losses–15 ties.

Attendances

Single game It has been estimated that crowds of 120,000 were present for two Notre Dame games played at Soldier Field, Chicago, IL: vs. Southern Cal. (November 26, 1927); vs. Navy (October 13, 1928). Attendance records have been kept by the NCAA since 1948. The highest official crowd for a regular-season NCAA game was 107,608 Volunteers fans at Neyland Football Stadium, Knoxville, TN on September 21, 1996 for the Tennessee vs. Florida game.

Bowl game The record attendance for a bowl game is 106,869 people at the 1973 Rose Bowl, where Southern Cal. defeated Ohio State 42–17.

Season average The highest average attendance for home games is 106,217 for the six games played by Michigan in 1994.

CANADIAN FOOTBALL LEAGUE (CFL)

Origins

The earliest recorded football game in Canada was an intramural contest between students of the University of Toronto on November 9, 1861. As with football in the U.S., the development of the game in Canada dates from a contest between two universities— McGill and Harvard, played in May 1874.

Canadian football differs in many ways from its counterpart in the U.S. The major distinctions are the number of players (CFL–12, NFL–11); size of field (CFL–110 yards x 65 yards, NFL–100 yards x 53 yards); number of downs (CFL–3, NFL–4); and a completely different system for scoring and penalties.

The current CFL comprises nine teams in two divisions, the Western and Eastern. The divisional playoff champions meet in the Grey Cup to decide the CFL champion.

TEAM RECORDS

Longest winning streak The Calgary Stampeders won 22 consecutive games between August 25, 1948 and October 22, 1949 to set the CFL mark.

Longest winless streak The Hamilton Tiger-Cats hold the dubious distinction of being the CFL's most unsuccessful team, amassing a 20-game winless streak (0–19–1), from September 28, 1948 to September 2, 1950.

Highest-scoring game The Toronto Argonauts defeated the B.C. Lions 68–43 on September 1, 1990 to set a CFL combined score record of 111 points.

Highest score by one team The Montreal Alouettes rolled over the Hamilton Tiger-Cats 82–14 on October 20, 1956 to set the CFL highest-score mark.

Most points in a season The Edmonton Eskimos tallied 32 points in the 1989 season. The team's season record was 16 wins and two losses.

CFL Individual Records

		Player(s)	Team(s)	Date(s)
Games Played				
Most	336	Lui Passaglia	B.C. Lions	1976–96
Consecutive	293	Bob Cameron	Winnipeg Blue Bombers	1980–96
Points Scored				
Game	36	Bob McNamara	Winnipeg Blue Bombers vs. B.C. Lions	October 13,1956
Season	236	Lance Chomyc	Toronto Argonauts	1991
Career	3,316	Lui Passaglia	B.C. Lions	1976–96
Touchdowns Scored				
Game	6	Eddie James	Winnipegs vs. Winnipeg St. Jonns	September 28, 1932
		Bob McNamara	Winnipeg Blue Bombers vs. B.C. Lions	October 13, 1956
Season	22	Cory Philpot	B.C. Lions	1995
Career	137	George Reed	Saskatchewan Roughriders	1963–75

PASSING

		Player(s)	Team(s)	Date(s)
Yards Gained				
Game	713	Matt Dunigan	Edmonton Eskimos vs. Winnipeg Blue Bombers	July 14, 1994
Season	6,619	Doug Flutie	B.C. Lions	1991
Career	50,535	Ron Lancaster	Ottawa Roughriders/Saskatchewan Roughriders	1960–78
Touchdowns Thrown				
Game	8	Joe Zuger	Hamilton Tiger-Cats	October 15, 1962
Season	48	Doug Flutie	Calgary Stampeders	1994
Career	333	Ron Lancaster	Ottawa/Saskatchewan Roughriders	1960–78
Completions				
Game	41	Dieter Brock	Winnipeg Blue Bombers vs. Ottawa Roughrider	October 3, 1981
		Kent Austin	Saskatchewan Roughriders vs. Toronto Argonauts	October 31, 1993
Season	466	Doug Flutie	B.C. Lions	1991
Career	3,384	Ron Lancaster	Ottawa Roughriders/Saskatchewan Roughriders	1960–78

PASS RECEIVING

		Player(s)	Team(s)	Date(s)
Receptions				
Game	16	Terry Greer	Toronto Argonauts vs. Ottawa Roughrider	August 19, 1983
		Brian Wiggins	Calgary Stampeders vs. Saskatchewan Roughriders	October 23, 1993
Season	126	Allen Pitts	Calgary Stampeders	1994
Career	830	Ray Elgaard	Saskatchewan Roughriders	1983–96
Yards Gained				
Game	338	Hal Patterson	Montreal Alouettes vs. Hamilton Tiger-Cats	September 29, 1956
Season	2,036	Allen Pitts	Calgary Stempeders	1984
Career	13,198	Ray Elgaard	Saskatchewan Roughriders	1983–96

CFL Individual Records (continued)

		Player(s)	Team(s)	Date(s)
RUSHING				
Touchdown Receptions				
Game	5	Ernie Pitts	Winnipeg Blue Bombers vs. Saskatchewan Roughriders	August 29,1959
Season	21	Allen Pitts	Calgary Stampeders	1994
Career	97	Brian Kelly	Edmonton Eskimos	1979–87
Yards Gained				
Game	287	Ron Stewart	Ottawa Roughriders vs. Montreal Alouettes	October 10, 1960
Season	1,972	Mike Pringle	Baltimore	1994
Career	16,116	George Reed	Saskatchewan Roughriders	1963–75
Touchdowns Scored				
Game	5	Earl Lunsford	Calgary Stampeders vs. Edmonton Eskimos	September 3, 1962
		Martin Patton	Shreveport Pirates vs. Winnipeg Blue Bombers	August 5, 1995
Season	18	Gerry James	Winnipeg Blue Bombers	1957
		Jim Germany	Edmonton Eskimos	1981
Career	134	George Reed	Saskatchewan Roughriders	1963–75
Longest Plays (Yards)				
Rushing	109	George Dixon	Montreal Alouettes	September 2, 1963
		Willie Fleming	B.C. Lions	October 17, 1964
Pass Completion	109	Sam Etcheverry to Hal Patterson	Montreal Alouettes	September 22, 1956
		Jerry Keeling to Terry Evanshen	Calgary Stampeders	September 27, 1966
Field Goal	60	Dave Ridgway	Saskatchewan Roughriders	September 6, 1987
Punt	108	Zenon Andrusyshyn	Toronto Argonauts	October 23, 1977

Source: CFL

THE GREY CUP

In 1909, Lord Earl Grey, the governor general of Canada, donated a trophy that was to be awarded to the Canadian Rugby Football champion. The competition for the Grey Cup evolved during the first half of the 20th century from an open competition for amateurs, college teams and hybrid rugby teams to the championship of the professional Canadian Football League that was formed in 1958.

Most wins 13, Toronto Argonauts: 1914, 1921, 1933, 1937–38, 1945–47, 1950, 1952, 1983, 1991, 1996.

Most consecutive wins 5, Edmonton Eskimos: 1978–83.

Grey Cup Results

Year	Winner
1909	University of Toronto
1910	University of Toronto
1911	University of Toronto
1912	Hamilton Alerts
1913	Hamilton Tigers
1914	Toronto Argonauts
1915	Hamilton Tigers
1916	*not held*
1917	*not held*
1918	*not held*
1919	*not held*
1920	University of Toronto
1921	Toronto Argonauts
1922	Queen's University
1923	Queen's University
1924	Queen's University
1925	Ottawa Senators
1926	Ottawa Senators
1927	Toronto Balmy Beach
1928	Hamilton Tigers
1929	Hamilton Tigers
1930	Toronto Balmy Beach
1931	Montreal AAA Winged Wheelers
1932	Hamilton Tigers
1933	Toronto Argonauts
1934	Sarnia Imperials
1935	Winnipegs
1936	Sarnia Imperials
1937	Toronto Argonauts
1938	Toronto Argonauts
1939	Winnipeg Blue Bombers
1940 (November)	Ottawa Rough Riders
1940 (December)	Ottawa Rough Riders
1941	Winnipeg Blue Bombers
1942	Toronto Hurricanes
1943	Hamilton Flying Wildcats
1944	St. Hyacinthe-Donnacona Navy
1945	Toronto Argonauts
1946	Toronto Argonauts
1947	Toronto Argonauts
1948	Calgary Stampeders
1949	Montreal Alouettes
1950	Toronto Argonauts
1951	Ottawa Rough Riders
1952	Toronto Argonauts
1953	Hamilton Tiger-Cats
1954	Edmonton Eskimos
1955	Edmonton Eskimos
1956	Edmonton Eskimos
1957	Hamilton Tiger-Cats
1958	Winnipeg Blue Bombers
1959	Winnipeg Blue Bombers
1960	Ottawa Senators
1961	Winnipeg Blue Bombers
1962	Winnipeg Blue Bombers
1963	Hamilton Tiger-Cats
1964	B.C. Lions
1965	Hamilton Tiger-Cats
1966	Saskatchewan Roughriders
1967	Hamilton Tiger-Cats
1968	Ottawa Rough Riders
1969	Ottawa Rough Riders
1970	Montreal Alouettes
1971	Calgary Stampeders
1972	Hamilton Tiger-Cats
1973	Ottawa Rough Riders
1974	Montreal Alouettes
1975	Edmonton Eskimos
1976	Ottawa Rough Riders
1977	Montreal Alouettes
1978	Edmonton Eskimos
1979	Edmonton Eskimos
1980	Edmonton Eskimos
1981	Edmonton Eskimos
1982	Edmonton Eskimos
1983	Toronto Argonauts
1984	Winnipeg Blue Bombers
1985	B.C. Lions
1986	Hamilton Tiger-Cats
1987	Edmonton Eskimos
1988	Winnipeg Blue Bombers
1989	Saskatchewan Roughriders
1990	Winnipeg Blue Bombers
1991	Toronto Argonauts
1992	Calgary Stampeders
1993	Edmonton Eskimos
1994	B.C. Lions
1995	Baltimore Stallions
1996	Toronto Argonauts

CFL record-holder Doug Flutie led the Toronto Argonauts to the 1996 Grey Cup title.
(Toronto Argonauts/John Sokolowski)

GAMES AND PASTIMES

BOWLS

Origins

The game of bowls can be traced back to 13th-century England. The Chesterfield Bowling Club claims that its "green" dates to 1294. The earliest documented bowling club is Southampton Town Bowling, which was formed in 1299. The rules of the modern game were framed in 1848–49 by a group of Scottish bowlers, headed by William W. Mitchell.

World Championships (Outdoor)

The first world championship was staged in 1966.

Most titles (singles)   David Bryant (England) has won a record three singles titles, 1966, 1980 and 1988. Elsie Wilke (New Zealand) holds the women's record with two wins, 1969 and 1974.

Most titles (Overall)   David Bryant (England) has won six world titles: three individual (see above), two team titles, 1980 and 1988, and the triples, 1980. Three women have won three titles: Merle Richardson (Australia) fours, 1977, singles and pairs, 1985;

The team of David Bryant (right) and Tony Allcock has won six World Indoor Bowls titles.
(Gary M. Prior/Allsport)

Dorothy Roche (Australia) triples, 1985 and 1988, fours, 1988; Margaret Johnston (Ireland), singles, 1992, pairs 1988 and 1992.

Most titles (team)   Scotland has won the team trophy, known as the Leonard Trophy, a record four times, 1972, 1984, 1992 and 1996.

World Championships (Indoor)

The first indoor world championships were staged in 1979.

Most titles (singles)   Two men have won three singles titles: David Bryant (England), 1979–81; and Richard Corsie (England), 1989, 1991 and 1993.

Most titles (pairs)   The team of David Bryant and Tony Allock (England) have won a record six pairs titles, 1986-87, 1989-92.

CROQUET

Origins

It is believed that croquet developed from the French game *jeu de mail*. A game resembling croquet was played in Ireland in the 1830s and introduced to England 20 years later. Although croquet was played in the United States for a number of years, a national body was not established until the formation of the United States Croquet Association (USCA) in 1976. The first United States championship was played in 1977.

World Championships

The first World Championships were held at the Hurlington Club in Great Britain in 1989. Robert Fulford (Great Britain) has won four times: 1990, 1992–94.

USCA National Championships

J. Archie Peck has won the singles title a record four times (1977, 1979–80, 1982). Ted Prentis has won the doubles title four times with three different partners (1978, 1980–81, 1988). The teams of J. Archie Peck and Jack Osborn (1977–79); Ted Prentis and Ned Prentis (1980–81); Dana Dribben and Ray Bell (1985–86); Reid Fleming and Debbie Cornelius (1990–91); and John Phaneuf and Karl Mabee (1994–96) have each won the doubles title twice. The New York Croquet Club has won a record five National Club Championships (1980–81, 1983, 1986, 1988).

DARTS

Origins

Darts, or dartes (heavily weighted 10-inch throwing arrows) were first used for self-defense in Ireland in the 16th century. The Pilgrims played darts for recreation aboard the Mayflower in 1620. The modern game dates to 1896, when Brian Gamlin of Bury, England devised the present board numbering system. The first recorded score of 180, the maximum with three darts, was by John Reader at the Highbury Tavern, Sussex, England in 1902.

World Championship

This competition was instituted in 1978.

Most titles Eric Bristow of England has won the title a record five times (1980–81, 1984–86).

SCORING RECORDS (HIGHEST SCORES)

10-Hour Scores

Individual The pair of Jon Archer and Neil Rankin (Great Britain) scored 465,919, retrieving their own darts, at the Royal Oak, Cossington, England on November 17, 1990.

Bulls Jim Damore (U.S.) hit 1,321 bulls in 10 hours at the Parkside Pub, Chicago IL on June 29, 1996.

24-Hour Scores

Individual Kenny Fellowes (Great Britain) scored 567,145 points at The Prince of Wales, Cashes Green, England on September 28–29, 1996.

Team (8-man) The Broken Hill Darts Club of New South Wales, Australia scored 1,722,249 points in 24 hours from September 28–29, 1985.

Team (8-woman) A team representing the Lord Clyde of Leyton, England scored 744,439 points on October 13–14, 1990.

Bulls and 25s (8-man team) An eight-member team hit 526,750 bulls and 25s at the George Inn, in Morden, England on July 1–2, 1994.

FISHING

Largest single catch The largest officially ratified fish ever caught on a rod was a great white shark (*Carcharodon carcharias*) weighing 2,664 pounds and measuring 16 feet 10 inches long, caught on a 130-lb test line by Alf Dean at Denial Bay, near Ceduna, South Australia on April 21, 1959.

In June 1978, a great white shark measuring 20 feet 4 inches in length and weighing more than 5,000 pounds was harpooned and landed by fishermen in the harbor of San Miguel, Azores.

Casting The longest freshwater cast ratified under ICF (International Casting Federation) rules is 574 feet 2 inches, by Walter Kummerow (West Germany), for the Bait Distance Double-Handed 30 g event held in Lenzerheide, Switzerland in the 1968 championships.

At the currently contested weight of 17.7 g, the longest Double-Handed cast is 457 feet 1/2 inch by Kevin Carriero (U.S.) in Toronto, Canada on July 24, 1984.

The longest Fly Distance Double-Handed cast is 319 feet 1 inch by Wolfgang Feige (West Germany) in Toronto, Canada on July 23, 1984.

World Championship (Freshwater)

The first freshwater world championships were held in 1957. The event is staged annually.

Most wins (team) France has won the team event 13 times, 1959, 1963–64, 1966, 1968, 1972, 1974–75, 1978–79, 1981, 1990 and 1995.

Most wins (individual) Two men have won the individual title three times: Robert Tesse (France), 1959–60 and 1965; and Bob Nudd (Great Britain), 1990–91 and 1994.

World Championship (Fly Fishing)

First staged in 1981, this event is held annually.

Most wins (team) Italy has won the team event five times, 1982–84, 1986 and 1992.

Most wins (individual) Brian Leadbetter (Great Britain) has won two titles, in 1987 and 1991.

All-Tackle Class World Records—Freshwater and Saltwater

A selection of records ratified by the International Game Fish Association to January 1, 1996.

Species	Weight	Caught By	Location	Date
Barracuda, great	85 lb 0 oz	John W. Helfrich	Republic of Kiribati	April 11, 1992
Bass, kelp	14 lb 7 oz	Thomas Murphy	Newport Beach, CA	October 22, 1993
Bass, largemouth	22 lb 4 oz	George W. Perry	Montgomery Lake, GA	June 2, 1932
Bass, smallmouth	10 lb 14 oz	John T. Gorman	Dale Hollow Lake, TN	April 24, 1969
Bass, striped	78 lb 8 oz	Albert Reynolds	Atlantic City, NJ	September 21, 1982
Bluefish	31 lb12 oz	James M. Hussey	Hatteras, NC	January 30, 1972
Carp, common	75 lb 11 oz	Leo van der Gugten	France	May 21,1987
Carp, grass	65 lb 14 oz	Todd Brewer	Horseshoe Lake, AR	April 28, 1995
Catfish, blue	109 lb 4 oz	George A. Lijewski	Moncks Corner, SC	March 14, 1991
Chub, Bermuda	12 lb 7 oz	Judy Cornetta	Fort Pierce Inlet, FL	October 3, 1994
Cod, Atlantic	98 lb 12 oz	Alphonse Bielevich	Isle of Shoals, NH	June 8, 1969
Conger	133 lb 4 oz	Vic Evans	Berry Head, England	June 5, 1995
Eel, American	9 lb 4 oz	Jeff Pennick	Cape May, NJ	October 9, 1995
Flounder, summer	22 lb 7 oz	Charles Nappi	Montauk, NY	September 15,1975
Goldfish	6lb 10 oz	Florentino M. Abena	Lake Hodges, CA	April 17, 1996
Grouper, black	113 lb 6 oz	Donald Bone	Dry Tortugas, FL	January 27, 1990
Haddock	11 lb 11 oz	Jim Mailea	Ogunquit, ME	September 12, 1991
Halibut, Atlantic	255 lb 4 oz	Sonny Manley	Gloucester, MA	July 28, 1989
Halibut, Pacific	459 lb 0 oz	Jack Tragis	Dutch Harbor, AK	June 11, 1996
Houndfish	14 lb 0 oz	Deborah Dunaway	Costa Rica	July 18, 1992
Marlin, black	1,560 lb 0 oz	Alfred C. Glassell Jr.	Peru	Aug. 4, 1953
Marlin, blue (Atlantic)	1,402 lb 2 oz	Roberto A. Amorim	Brazil	February 29, 1992
Marlin, blue (Pacific)	1,376 lb 0 oz	Jay W. de Beaubien	Kona, HI	May 31, 1982
Perch, Nile	191 lb 8 oz	Andy Davison	Kenya	September 5, 1991
Pike, northern	55 lb 1 oz	Lothar Louis	Germany	Oct. 16, 1986
Piranha, black	6 lb 15 oz	Alejandro Mata	Venezuela	February 27, 1995
Ray, black	82 lb 10 oz	Peter Blondell	Australia	January 20, 1993
Sailfish, Atlantic	141 lb 1 oz	Alfredo de Sousa Nevis	Angola	February 19, 1994
Sailfish, Pacific	221 lb 0 oz	C.W. Stewart	Ecuador	February 12, 1947
Salmon, Atlantic	79 lb 2 oz	Henrik Henriksen	Norway	1928
Salmon, chinook	97 lb 4 oz	Les Anderson	Kenai River, AK	May 17, 1985
Salmon, pink	13 lb 1 oz	Ray Higaki	Canada	September 23, 1992
Shad, American	11 lb 4 oz	Bob Thibodo	S. Hadley, MA	May 19, 1986
Shark, blue	454 lb 0 oz	Peter Bergin	Martha's Vineyard, MA	July 19, 1996
Shark, Greenland	1,708 lb 9 oz	Terje Nordtvedt	Norway	Oct. 18, 1987
Shark, great hammerhead	991 lb 0 oz	Allen Ogle	Sarasota, FL	May 30, 1982
Shark, shortfin mako	1,115 lb 0 oz	Patrick Guillanton	Mauritius	November 16, 1988
Shark, tiger	1,780 lb 0 oz	Walter Maxwell	Cherry Grove, SC	June 14, 1964
Shark, white	2,664 lb 0 oz	Alfred Dean	Australia	April 21, 1959
Snapper, red	50 lb 4 oz	Capt. Doc Kennedy	Gulf of Mexico, LA	June 23, 1996
Stingray, southern	239 lb 0 oz	Davey Wright	Padre Island, TX	October 10, 1992
Sturgeon, lake	168 lb 0 oz	Edward Paszkowski	Ontario, Canada	May 29, 1982
Sturgeon, white	468 lb 0 oz	Joey Pallotta III	Benica, CA	July 9, 1983
Swordfish	1,182 lb 0 oz	L. Marron	Chile	May 7, 1953
Tarpon	283 lb 4 oz	Yvon Victor Sebag	Sierra Leone	April 16, 1991
Trout, brook	14 lb 8 oz	Dr. W. J. Cook	Ontario, Canada	July, 1916
Trout, rainbow	42 lb 2 oz	David Robert White	Bell Island, AK	June 22, 1970
Tuna, bluefin	1,496 lb 0 oz	Ken Fraser	Nova Scotia, Canada	October 26, 1979

The largest Pacific halibut was landed in Dutch Harbor, AK on June 11, 1996.
(International Game Fish Association)

FOOTBAG

A footbag (also sometimes known by the brand names Hacky Sack® or Sipa Sipa) is a small, pliable, pellet-filled ball-like object with little or no bounce. The goal of the game is to keep the footbag in the air for the longest possible time. Both the time and the number of consecutive kicks are recorded.

Origins

The sport of footbag was invented by Mike Marshall and John Stalberger (U.S.) in 1972. The governing body for the sport is the World Footbag Association, based in Steamboat Springs, CO.

Consecutive Records

Open singles   51,155 kicks by Ted Martin (U.S.) on May 29, 1993 in Mount Prospect, IL. Martin kept the footbag aloft for 7 hours 1 minute 37 seconds.

Women's singles   20,717 kicks by Tricia George (U.S.) on September 21, 1996 in Golden, CO. George kept the footbag aloft for 5 hours 15 minutes 18 seconds.

Open doubles   123,456 kicks by Gary Lautt and Tricia George (both U.S.) on November 12, 1995 in Chico, CA. The pair kept the footbag aloft for 19 hours 38 minutes 20 seconds.

Women's doubles   34,543 kicks by Constance Constable and Tricia George (both U.S.) on February 18, 1995. The pair kept the footbag aloft for 5 hours 38 minutes 22 seconds.

⫸ Fantastic Feats

Largest footbag circle   The largest continuous circle of people playing footbag was 932. This gathering was staged at St. Patrick High School, Chicago, IL on May 3, 1996.

FRISBEE (FLYING DISC THROWING)

Origins

The design of a carved plastic flying disc was patented in the United States by Fred Morrison in 1948. Wham-O Inc. of San Gabriel, CA bought Morrison's patent and trademarked the name Frisbee in 1958. In 1968 Wham-O helped form the International Frisbee Association (IFA). The IFA folded in 1982 and it wasn't until 1986 that the World Flying Disc Federation was formed to organize and standardize rules for the sport.

Flying Disc Records

Distance thrown   Scott Stokely (U.S.) set the flying disc distance record at 656 feet 2 inches on May 14, 1995 in Fort Collins, CO. The women's record is 447 feet 3 inches by Anni Kreml (U.S.) on August 27, 1994 in Fort Collins, CO.

Throw, run, catch   Hiroshi Oshima (Japan) set the throw, run, catch distance record at 303 feet 11 inches on July 20, 1988 in San Francisco, CA. The women's record is 196 feet 11 inches by Judy Horowitz (U.S.) on June 29, 1985 in La Mirada, CA.

Time aloft   The record for maximum time aloft is 16.72 seconds, by Don Cain (U.S.) on May 26, 1984 in Philadelphia, PA. The women's record is 11.81 seconds, by Amy Bekken (U.S.) on August 1, 1991.

24-hour distance (pairs)   Conrad Damon and Pete Fust (both U.S.) threw a Frisbee 367.94 miles on April 24–25, 1993 in San Marino, CA. The women's record is 115.65 miles by Jo Cahow and Amy Berard (both U.S.) on December 30-31, 1979 in Pasadena, CA.

HORSESHOE PITCHING

Origins

Historians claim that a variation of horseshoe pitching was first played by Roman soldiers to relieve the monotony of guard duty. Horseshoes was introduced to North America by the first settlers, and every town had its own horseshoe competitions. The modern sport of horseshoes dates to the formation of the National Horseshoe Pitcher's Association (NHPA) in 1914.

World Championships

First held in 1909, the tournament was staged intermittently until 1946; since then it has been an annual event.

Most titles (men)   Ted Allen (U.S.) has won 10 world titles: 1933–35, 1940, 1946, 1953, 1955–57, 1959.

Most titles (women)   Vicki Winston (née Chappelle) has won a record 10 women's titles: 1956, 1958–59, 1961, 1963, 1966–67, 1969, 1975 and 1981.

Perfect game   A perfect game consists of amassing 40 points throwing only ringers. In world championship play only three pitchers have thrown perfect games: Guy Zimmerman (U.S.) in 1948; Elmer Hohl (Canada) in 1968; and Jim Walters (U.S.) in 1993. Hohl extended past his perfect game for a total of 56 consecutive ringers, a championship record.

POOL

Origins

Pool traces its ancestry to the English game of billiards. The original form of pool in the United States was known as pyramid pool, with the object being to pocket eight out of the 15 balls on the table. From this game, "61-pool" evolved: each of the 15 balls was worth points equal to its numerical value; the first player to score 61 points was the winner. In 1878 the first world championship was staged under the rules of 61-pool. In 1910, Jerome Keogh suggested that the rules be adjusted to make the game faster and more attractive; he proposed that the last ball be left free on the table to be used as a target on the next rack; the result was 14.1 continuous pool (also known as American straight pool). The game of 14.1 was adopted as the championship form of pool from 1912 onwards. In 1990 the World Pool Billiard Association inaugurated the nine-ball world championship.

14.1 Continuous Pool World Championships

The first official world championship was held in April 1912 and was won by Edward Ralph (U.S.).

Most titles   Two players have won six world titles: Ralph Greenleaf (U.S.) and Willie Mosconi (U.S.). Greenleaf won the title six times and defended it 13 times, 1919–37. Between 1941 and 1956, Mosconi also won the title six times and defended it 13 times.

Longest consecutive run The longest consecutive run in 14.1 recognized by the Billiard Congress of America (BCA) is 526 balls, by Willie Mosconi in March 1954 during an exhibition in Springfield, OH Michael Eufemia is reported to have pocketed 625 balls at Logan's Billiard Academy in Brooklyn, NY on February 2, 1960; however, this run has never been ratified by the BCA.

Nine-Ball Pool World Championship

In this competition, inaugurated in 1990, Earl Strickland (U.S.) has won the men's title twice, 1990–91. Robin Bell (U.S.) has won the women's title twice, 1990–91.

SNOOKER

Origins

Neville Chamberlain, a British army officer, is credited with inventing the game in Jubbulpore, India in 1875. Snooker is a hybrid of pool and pyramids. The name snooker comes from the term coined for new recruits at the Woolwich Military Academy and was Chamberlain's label for anyone who lost at his game.

In 1990, Stephen Hendry became the world's youngest snooker world champion. He has dominated the sport ever since, winning six world titles.
(Anton Want/Allsport)

World Professional Championships

This competition was first organized in 1927.

Most titles Joe Davis (England) won the world title on the first 15 occasions it was contested, from 1927 to 1940 and in 1946; this still stands as the all-time record for victories. In the Amateur Championships, the most wins is two—by Gary Owen (England), 1963 and 1966; Ray Edmonds (England), 1972 and 1974; and Paul Mifsud (Malta), 1985–86. Allison Fisher (Great Britain) has won seven World Championships, 1985–86, 1988–89, and 1991–93. Maureen Bayton (née Barrett) won a record eight Women's Amateur Championships between 1954 and 1968, as well as seven at billiards.

Maximum break More than 200 male players have scored the 147 "maximum break." The highest break by a woman is 137, by Stacey Hilliard (Great Britain), in Aylesbury, Great Britain on February 23, 1992.

TUG-OF-WAR

Origins

Tug-of-War, a trial of strength and skill involving two teams of eight pulling against each other on opposite ends of a long, thick rope, gained its name in England in the 19th century. The actual test of strength that the sport is based on dates to antiquity.

Olympic Games

Tug-of-War was an Olympic event from 1900–20.

Most wins Great Britain won the event twice, 1908 and 1920.

World Championships

A men's tournament was first staged in 1975 and a women's was added in 1986.

Most wins (men) England has won 15 titles in all weight classes, 1975–90.

Most wins (women) Sweden has won nine titles: 520 kg, 1986, 1988, 1990, 1994; 560 kg, 1986, 1988, 1990, 1992, 1994.

GOLF

The nationality of the competitors in this section is U.S. unless stated otherwise.

Origins

There is evidence that a game resembling golf was played in Holland in the Middle Ages. Scotland, however, is generally regarded as the home of the modern game. The oldest club of which there is written evidence is the Honourable Company of Edinburgh Golfers, Scotland, founded in 1744.

United States There are claims that golf was played in this country as early as the 18th century in North Carolina and Virginia. The oldest recognized club in North America is the Royal Montreal Golf Club, Canada, formed on November 4, 1873. Two clubs claim to be the first established in the U.S.: the Foxberg Golf Club, Clarion County, PA (1887), and St. Andrews Golf Club of Yonkers, NY (1888).

The United States Golf Association (USGA) was founded in 1894 as the governing body of golf in the United States.

Masters Champions

Year	Champion	Year	Champion
1934	Horton Smith	1966	Jack Nicklaus
1935	Gene Sarazen	1967	Gay Brewer
1936	Horton Smith	1968	Bob Goalby
1937	Byron Nelson	1969	George Archer
1938	Henry Picard	1970	Billy Casper
1939	Ralph Guldahl	1971	Charles Coody
1940	Jimmy Demaret	1972	Jack Nicklaus
1941	Craig Wood	1973	Tommy Aaron
1942	Byron Nelson	1974	Gary Player
1943	*not held*	1975	Jack Nicklaus
1944	*not held*	1976	Raymond Floyd
1945	*not held*	1977	Tom Watson
1946	Herman Keiser	1978	Gary Player
1947	Jimmy Demaret	1979	Fuzzy Zoeller
1948	Claude Harmon	1980	Seve Ballesteros [2]
1949	Sam Snead	1981	Tom Watson
1950	Jimmy Demaret	1982	Craig Stadler
1951	Ben Hogan	1983	Seve Ballesteros
1952	Sam Snead	1984	Ben Crenshaw
1953	Ben Hogan	1985	Bernhard Langer [3]
1954	Sam Snead	1986	Jack Nicklaus
1955	Cary Middlecoff	1987	Larry Mize
1956	Jack Burke Jr.	1988	Sandy Lyle [4]
1957	Doug Ford	1989	Nick Faldo [4]
1958	Arnold Palmer	1990	Nick Faldo
1959	Art Wall Jr.	1991	Ian Woosnam [4]
1960	Arnold Palmer	1992	Fred Couples
1961	Gary Player [1]	1993	Bernhard Langer
1962	Arnold Palmer	1994	José Maria Olazabal [2]
1963	Jack Nicklaus	1995	Ben Crenshaw
1964	Arnold Palmer	1996	Nick Faldo [4]
1965	Jack Nicklaus	1997	Tiger Woods

1—South Africa
2—Spain
3—Germany
4—Great Britain

THE MAJORS

Grand Slam

In 1930, Bobby Jones won the U.S. and British Open Championships and the U.S. and British Amateur Championships. This feat was christened the "Grand Slam". In 1960, the professional Grand Slam (the Masters, U.S. Open, British Open, and Professional Golfers Association [PGA] Championships) gained recognition when Arnold Palmer won the first two legs, the Masters and the U.S. Open. However, he did not complete the set of titles, and the Grand Slam has still not been attained. Ben Hogan came the closest in 1951, when he won the first three legs but did not return to the United States from Great Britain in time for the PGA Championship.

Most grand slam titles   Jack Nicklaus has won the most majors, with 18 professional titles (six Masters, four U.S. Opens, three British Opens, five PGA Championships).

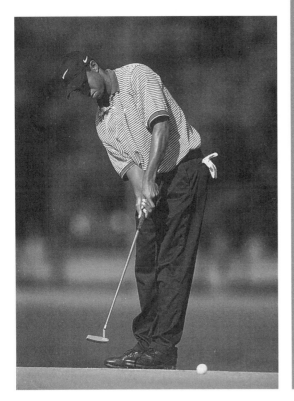

The Masters

Inaugurated in 1934, this event is held annually at the 6,980-yard Augusta National Golf Club in Augusta, GA.

Most wins   Jack Nicklaus has won the coveted green jacket a record six times (1963, 1965–66, 1972, 1975, 1986).

Consecutive wins   Jack Nicklaus (1965–66) and Nick Faldo (1989–90) are the only two players to have won back-to-back Masters.

Lowest 18-hole total (any round)   63, by two players: Nick Price (Zimbabwe) in 1986; and Greg Norman (Australia) in 1996.

Lowest 72-hole total   270, by Tiger Woods (70, 66, 65, 69) in 1997.

Largest margin of victory   12, by Tiger Woods in 1997. Woods' victory also set the mark for the widest margin of victory at a Major played in the United States, topping the 11-stroke margin set by Willie Smith at the 1899 U.S. Open.

Oldest champion   46 years 81 days, Jack Nicklaus (1986).

Youngest champion   21 years 104 days, Tiger Woods, 1997.

The outstanding record-breaking performance of 1997 was achieved by Tiger Woods at the 1997 Masters. He not only became the youngest champion and set the low 72-hole total, but also won the tournament by a breathtaking 12 strokes.
(J. D. Cuban/Allsport)

U.S. Open Champions

Year	Champion
1895	Horace Rawlins
1896	James Foulis
1897	Joe Lloyd
1898	Fred Herd
1899	Willie Smith
1900	Harry Vardon [1]
1901	Willie Anderson
1902	Laurie Auchterlonie
1903	Willie Anderson
1904	Willie Anderson
1905	Willie Anderson
1906	Alex Smith
1907	Alex Ross
1908	Fred McLeod
1909	George Sargent
1910	Alex Smith
1911	John McDermott
1912	John McDermott
1913	Francis Ouimet
1914	Walter Hagen
1915	Jerome Travers
1916	Charles Evans Jr.
1917	not held
1918	not held
1919	Walter Hagen
1920	Edward Ray [1]
1921	Jim Barnes
1922	Gene Sarazen
1923	Bobby Jones
1924	Cyril Walker
1925	Willie MacFarlane
1926	Bobby Jones
1927	Tommy Armour
1928	Johnny Farrell
1929	Bobby Jones
1930	Bobby Jones
1931	Billy Burke
1932	Gene Sarazen
1933	Johnny Goodman
1934	Olin Dutra
1935	Sam Parks Jr.
1936	Tony Manero
1937	Ralph Guldahl
1938	Ralph Guldahl
1939	Byron Nelson
1940	Lawson Little
1941	Craig Wood
1942	not held
1943	not held
1944	not held
1945	not held
1946	Lloyd Mangrum
1947	Lew Worsham
1948	Ben Hogan
1949	Cary Middlecoff
1950	Ben Hogan
1951	Ben Hogan
1952	Julius Boros
1953	Ben Hogan
1954	Ed Furgol
1955	Jack Fleck
1956	Cary Middlecoff
1957	Dick Mayer
1958	Tommy Bolt
1959	Billy Casper
1960	Arnold Palmer
1961	Gene Littler
1962	Jack Nicklaus
1963	Julius Boros
1964	Ken Venturi
1965	Gary Player [2]
1966	Billy Casper
1967	Jack Nicklaus
1968	Lee Trevino
1969	Orville Moody
1970	Tony Jacklin [1]
1971	Lee Trevino
1972	Jack Nicklaus
1973	Johnny Miller
1974	Hale Irwin
1975	Lou Graham
1976	Jerry Pate
1977	Hubert Green
1978	Andy North
1979	Hale Irwin
1980	Jack Nicklaus
1981	David Graham [3]
1982	Tom Watson
1983	Larry Nelson
1984	Fuzzy Zoeller
1985	Andy North
1986	Raymond Floyd
1987	Scott Simpson
1988	Curtis Strange
1989	Curtis Strange
1990	Hale Irwin
1991	Payne Stewart
1992	Tom Kite
1993	Lee Janzen
1994	Ernie Els [2]
1995	Corey Pavin
1996	Steve Jones

1—Great Britain
2—South Africa
3—Australia

The United States Open

Inaugurated in 1895, this event is held on a different course each year. The Open was expanded from a three-day, 36-hole Saturday finish to four days of 18 holes of play in 1965.

Most wins Four players have won the title four times: Willie Anderson (1901, 1903–05); Bobby Jones (1923, 1926, 1929–30); Ben Hogan (1948, 1950–51, 1953); Jack Nicklaus (1962, 1967, 1972, 1980).

Most consecutive wins Three, by Willie Anderson (1903–05).

Lowest 18-hole total (any round) 63, by three players: Johnny Miller at Oakmont Country Club, PA, on June 17, 1973; Jack Nicklaus and Tom Weiskopf at Baltusrol Country Club, Springfield, NJ, June 12, 1980.

Lowest 72-hole total 272, by two players: Jack Nicklaus (63, 71, 70, 68), at Baltusrol Country Club, Springfield, NJ, in 1980; and Lee Janzen (67, 67, 69, 69), also at Baltusrol, in 1993.

Oldest champion 45 years 15 days, Hale Irwin (1990).

Youngest champion 19 years 317 days, John J. McDermott (1911).

British Open Champions

Year	Champion	Year	Champion	Year	Champion
1860	Willie Park Sr. [1]	1886	David Brown [1]	1913	John H. Taylor
1861	Tom Morris Sr. [1]	1887	Willie Park Jr. [1]	1914	Harry Vardon
1862	Tom Morris Sr.	1888	Jack Burns [1]	1915	*not held*
1863	Willie Park Sr.	1889	Willie Park Jr.	1916	*not held*
1864	Tom Morris Sr.	1890	John Ball [1]	1917	*not held*
1865	Andrew Strath [1]	1891	Hugh Kirkaldy [1]	1918	*not held*
1866	Willie Park Sr.	1892	Harold H. Hilton [1]	1919	*not held*
1867	Tom Morris Sr.	1893	William Auchterlonie [1]	1920	George Duncan [1]
1868	Tom Morris Jr. [1]	1894	John H. Taylor [1]	1921	Jock Hutchinson
1869	Tom Morris Jr.	1895	John H. Taylor	1922	Walter Hagen
1870	Tom Morris Jr.	1896	Harry Vardon [1]	1923	Arthur Havers [1]
1871	*not held*	1897	Harold H. Hilton	1924	Walter Hagen
1872	Tom Morris Jr.	1898	Harry Vardon	1925	Jim Barnes
1873	Tom Kidd [1]	1899	Harry Vardon	1926	Bobby Jones
1874	Mungo Park [1]	1900	John H. Taylor	1927	Bobby Jones
1875	Willie Park Sr.	1901	James Braid [1]	1928	Walter Hagen
1876	Bob Martin [1]	1902	Sandy Herd [1]	1929	Walter Hagen
1877	Jamie Anderson [1]	1903	Harry Vardon	1930	Bobby Jones
1878	Jamie Anderson	1904	Jack White [1]	1931	Tommy Armour
1879	Jamie Anderson	1905	James Braid	1932	Gene Sarazen
1880	Robert Ferguson [1]	1906	James Braid	1933	Densmore Shute
1881	Robert Ferguson	1907	Arnaud Massy [2]	1934	Henry Cotton [1]
1882	Robert Ferguson	1908	James Braid	1935	Alfred Perry [1]
1883	Willie Fernie [1]	1909	John H. Taylor	1936	Alfred Padgham [1]
1884	Jack Simpson [1]	1910	James Braid	1937	Henry Cotton
1885	Bob Martin [1]	1911	Harry Vardon		
		1912	Edward Ray [1]		

1—Great Britain
2—France

British Open Champions (continued)

Year	Champion		Year	Champion
1938	Reg Whitcombe [1]		1970	Jack Nicklaus
1939	Dick Burton [1]		1971	Lee Trevino
1940	*not held*		1972	Lee Trevino
1941	*not held*		1973	Tom Weiskopf
1942	*not held*		1974	Gary Player
1943	*not held*		1975	Tom Watson
1944	*not held*		1976	Johnny Miller
1945	*not held*		1977	Tom Watson
1946	Sam Snead		1978	Jack Nicklaus
1947	Fred Daly [1]		1979	Seve Ballesteros [7]
1948	Henry Cotton		1980	Tom Watson
1949	Bobby Locke [3]		1981	Bill Rogers
1950	Bobby Locke		1982	Tom Watson
1951	Max Faulkner [1]		1983	Tom Watson
1952	Bobby Locke		1984	Seve Ballesteros
1953	Ben Hogan		1985	Sandy Lyle [1]
1954	Peter Thomson [4]		1986	Greg Norman [4]
1955	Peter Thomson		1987	Nick Faldo [1]
1956	Peter Thomson		1988	Seve Ballesteros
1957	Bobby Locke		1989	Mark Calcavecchia
1958	Peter Thomson		1990	Nick Faldo
1959	Gary Player [3]		1991	Ian Baker-Finch [4]
1960	Kel Nagle [4]		1992	Nick Faldo
1961	Arnold Palmer		1993	Greg Norman
1962	Arnold Palmer		1994	Nick Price [8]
1963	Bob Charles [5]		1995	John Daly
1964	Tony Lema		1996	Tom Lehman
1965	Peter Thomson			
1966	Jack Nicklaus			
1967	Roberto de Vicenzo [6]			
1968	Gary Player			
1969	Tony Jacklin [1]			

1—Great Britain
2—France
3—South Africa
4—Australia
5—New Zealand
6—Argentina
7—Spain
8—Zimbabwe

The British Open

In this event, inaugurated in 1860, the first dozen tournaments were staged at Prestwick, Scotland. Since 1873, the locations have varied, but all venues are coastal links courses.

Most wins Harry Vardon won a record six titles, in 1896, 1898–99, 1903, 1911, 1914.

Most consecutive wins Four, by Tom Morris Jr. (1868–70, 1872; the event was not held in 1871).

Lowest 18-hole total (any round) 63, by seven players: Mark Hayes at Turnberry, Scotland, on July 7, 1977; Isao Aoki (Japan) at Muirfield, Scotland, on July 19, 1980; Greg Norman (Australia) at Turnberry, Scotland, on July 18, 1986; Paul Broadhurst (Great Britain) at St. Andrews, Scotland, on July 21, 1990; Jodie Mudd at Royal Birkdale, England, on July 21, 1991; Nick Faldo (Great Britain) on July 16, 1993 at Royal St. Georges; and Payne Stewart on July 18, 1993 at Royal St. Georges.

Lowest 72-hole total 267 (66, 68, 69, 64) by Greg Norman (Australia) at Royal St. George's, England in 1993.

Oldest champion 46 years 99 days, Tom Morris Sr. (Great Britain) (1867).

Youngest champion 17 years 249 days, Tom Morris Jr. (Great Britain) (1868).

PGA Champions

Year	Champion	Year	Champion
1916	Jim Barnes	1958	Dow Finsterwald
1917	*not held*	1959	Bob Rosburg
1918	*not held*	1960	Jay Herbert
1919	Jim Barnes	1961	Jerry Barber
1920	Jock Hutchinson	1962	Gary Player [1]
1921	Walter Hagen	1963	Jack Nicklaus
1922	Gene Sarazen	1964	Bobby Nichols
1923	Gene Sarazen	1965	Dave Marr
1924	Walter Hagen	1966	Al Geiberger
1925	Walter Hagen	1967	Don January
1926	Walter Hagen	1968	Julius Boros
1927	Walter Hagen	1969	Raymond Floyd
1928	Leo Diegel	1970	Dave Stockton
1929	Leo Diegel	1971	Jack Nicklaus
1930	Tommy Armour	1972	Gary Player [1]
1931	Tom Creavy	1973	Jack Nicklaus
1932	Olin Dutra	1974	Lee Trevino
1933	Gene Sarazen	1975	Jack Nicklaus
1934	Paul Runyan	1976	Dave Stockton
1935	Johnny Revolta	1977	Lanny Wadkins
1936	Densmore Shute	1978	John Mahaffey
1937	Densmore Shute	1979	David Graham [2]
1938	Paul Runyan	1980	Jack Nicklaus
1939	Henry Picard	1981	Larry Nelson
1940	Byron Nelson	1982	Raymond Floyd
1941	Vic Chezzi	1983	Hal Sutton
1942	Sam Snead	1984	Lee Trevino
1943	*not held*	1985	Hubert Green
1944	Bob Hamilton	1986	Bob Tway
1945	Byron Nelson	1987	Larry Nelson
1946	Ben Hogan	1988	Jeff Sluman
1947	Jim Ferrier	1989	Payne Stewart
1948	Ben Hogan	1990	Wayne Grady [2]
1949	Sam Snead	1991	John Daly
1950	Chandler Harper	1992	Nick Price [3]
1951	Sam Snead	1993	Paul Azinger
1952	Jim Turnesa	1994	Ernie Els [1]
1953	Walter Burkemo	1995	Steve Elkington [2]
1954	Chick Harbert	1996	Mark Brooks
1955	Doug Ford		
1956	Jack Burke Jr.		
1957	Lionel Hebert		

1—South Africa
2—Australia
3—Zimbabwe

The Professional Golfers Association (PGA) Championship

Inaugurated in 1916, the tournament was originally a match-play event, but switched to a 72-hole stroke-play event in 1958.

Most wins Two players have won the title five times: Walter Hagen (1921, 1924–27); and Jack Nicklaus (1963, 1971, 1973, 1975, 1980).

Most consecutive wins Four, by Walter Hagen (1924–27).

Lowest 18-hole total (any round) 63, by six players: Bruce Crampton (Australia) at Firestone Country Club, Akron, OH, in 1975; Ray Floyd at Southern Hills, Tulsa, OK, in 1982; Gary Player (South Africa) at Shoalcreek Country Club, Birmingham, AL in 1984; Vijay Singh (Fiji) at the Inverness Club, Toledo, OH in 1993; Michael Bradley and Brad Faxon at Riviera Country Club, Pacific Palisades, CA in 1995.

Lowest 72-hole total 267, by Steve Elkington (Australia) (68, 67, 68, 64) and by Colin Montgomerie (Great Britain) (68, 67, 67, 65) at the Riviera Country Club, Pacific Palisades, CA in 1995. Elkington defeated Montgomerie in a playoff.

Oldest champion 48 years 140 days, Julius Boros (1968).

Youngest champion 20 years 173 days, Gene Sarazen (1922).

PGA TOUR RECORDS

Most wins (season) Byron Nelson won a record 18 tournaments in 1945.

Most wins (career) Sam Snead won 81 official PGA tour events from 1936–65.

Most consecutive wins 11, Byron Nelson, 1945.

Most wins (same event) Sam Snead won the Greater Greensboro Open eight times to set the individual tournament win mark. His victories came in 1938, 1946, 1949–50, 1955–56, 1960, 1965.

Most consecutive wins (same event) Four, by Walter Hagen, PGA Championship, 1924–27.

Oldest winner 52 years 10 months, Sam Snead, 1965 Greater Greensboro Open.

Youngest winner 19 years 10 months, Johnny McDermott, 1911 U.S. Open.

Widest winning margin 16 strokes, by two players: Joe Kirkwood Sr., 1924, Corpus Christi Open; and Bobby Locke (South Africa), 1948 Chicago Victory National Championship.

Lowest Scores

Nine holes 27, by two players: Mike Souchak at the Brackenridge Park Golf Course, San Antonio, TX, on the back nine of the first round of the 1955 Texas Open; Andy North at the En-Joie Golf Club, Endicott, NY, on the back nine of the first round of the 1975 B.C. Open.

PGA Tour player of the year Tom Lehman won his first major, the British Open, and set a new tour earnings mark in 1996.
(Stephen Munday/Allsport)

18 holes 59, by two players: Al Geiberger at the Colonial Country Club, Memphis, TN, during the second round of the 1977 Danny Thomas Memphis Classic; Chip Beck at the Sunrise Golf Club, Las Vegas, NV, during the third round of the 1991 Las Vegas Invitational.

36 holes 125, by four players: Gay Brewer at the Pensacola Country Club, Pensacola, FL, during the second and third rounds of the 1967 Pensacola Open; Ron Streck at the Oak Hills Country Club, San Antonio, TX, during the third and fourth rounds of the 1978 Texas Open; Blaine McCallister at the Oakwood Country Club, Coal Valley, IL, during the second and third rounds of the 1988 Hardee's Golf Classic; John Cook at the Tournament Players Club at Southwind, Germantown, TN during the second and third rounds of the 1996 FedEx St. Jude Classic.

54 holes 189, by two players: Chandler Harper at the Brackenridge Park Golf Course, San Antonio, TX, during the last three rounds of the 1954 Texas Open; and John Cook at the Tournament Players Club at Southwind, Germantown, TN during the first three rounds of the 1996 FedEx St. Jude Classic.

72 holes 257, by Mike Souchak at the Brackenridge Park Golf Course, San Antonio, TX, at the 1955 Texas Open.

90 holes 325, by Tom Kite at four courses, La Quinta, CA, at the 1993 Bob Hope Chrysler Classic.

Most shots under par 35, by Tom Kite at the 90-hole 1993 Bob Hope Chrysler Classic. The most shots under par in a 72-hole tournament is 27, shared by two players: Mike Souchak, at the 1955 Texas Open; and Ben Hogan, at the 1945 Portland Invitational.

Highest Earnings

Season Tom Lehman, $1,780,159 in 1996.

Career As of February 9, 1997 Greg Norman (Australia) had career earnings of $10,484,065.

Most times leading money winner Eight, Jack Nicklaus, 1964–65, 1967, 1971–73, 1975–76.

Slammin' Sammy

Long before Tiger Woods made his name, or for that matter Arnold Palmer, the PGA Tour was dominated by a long hitter: Sam Snead. Now in his mid-80's, the Hot Springs, VA native still holds several PGA Tour records, including all-time wins (81) and the oldest player to win a tourney. Snead still loves to play golf, and is still willing to pass along his knowledge of the game.

"The number one thing in golf is to be a good putter. People don't practice the short game enough as they should, pitching, chipping and putting," admonishes Snead. The golfing legend pinpoints the grip as the largest factor separating the pro from the hacker. "Eighty-five percent of all amateur players who don't play well, it's because of their grip. It's either too weak or too strong." Counsels Snead, "Go to a competent pro and get the fundamentals starting with the grip."

During his long association with the game, Snead has seen many changes. "The scores are better now because the golf courses are manicured so well. Today you don't get a bad lie unless you get in a divot hole." Quips Snead, "The fairways are as good as the greens that I putted on."

Snead earned the sobriquet "Slammin' Sammy" for his monstrously long drives. His length was achieved in the era of wood-headed clubs. New technology in golf has helped the modern pro. "The players hit a drive and it seems to run forever. Golf has improved like automobiles and other machinery."

J. D. Cuban/Allsport

But Snead observes, "In Bobby Jones's day, golf courses were 6,200 to 6,300 yards and today they run up to 7,100 yards."

The biggest change between Snead's era and the modern tour is in lifestyle and prize money. "We had to drive everywhere we went. There were no 'courtesy cars.' Golfers traveled together, two or three in a car," says Snead. In 1946, Snead won the British Open and won $600. "It cost me $2,000 to play," laughs Snead. "I said, 'Is this my tipping money? I can get that much for a putting lesson.' "

Despite Snead's counsel to practice putting, some hackers just can't resist "hitting for show." He advises, "To be a long hitter, you have to be able to turn on the backswing. A lot of people make the mistake of having their legs too far apart. You can't do anything with the legs too far apart."

The Hall of Famer cautions, "The best golfers are swingers, not hitters. In 1950, I didn't try to outdrive anybody. I stayed within 85 percent of my power, and worked the ball left or right." That year Snead won 11 tournaments and topped the money list for the second consecutive year. "I went 96 rounds and averaged 69.23 a round that year," notes Snead. That average secured the old master the Vardon Trophy and still stands as the PGA Tour non-adjusted season record.

SENIOR PGA TOUR

The Senior PGA tour was established in 1982. Players 50 years and older are eligible to compete on the tour.

Most wins 27, by Lee Trevino (1990–97).

Most wins (season) Nine, by Peter Thomson (Australia), 1985.

Most consecutive wins Four, by Chi Chi Rodriguez in 1987.

Senior Tour/Regular Tour win Ray Floyd (U.S.) is the only player to win a Senior Tour event and a PGA Tour event in the same year. He won the Doral Open PGA event in March 1992 and the GTE Northern in September 1992.

Highest earnings (season) $1,627,890, Jim Colbert, in 1996.

Highest earnings (career) As of February 9, 1997 Bob Charles (New Zealand) had career earnings of $6,754,066.

PGA EUROPEAN TOUR

Most wins (career) 54, by Severiano Ballesteros (Spain), 1976–96.

Highest earnings (season) £1,220,540, by Nick Faldo (Great Britain) in 1992.

Highest earnings (career) £5,364,718 (as of February 17, 1997) by Bernhard Langer (Germany), 1976–97.

Ryder Cup

A biennial match-play competition between professional representative teams of the United States and Europe (Great Britain and Ireland prior to 1979), this event was launched in 1927. The U.S. leads the series 23–6, with two ties.

Most individual wins Arnold Palmer has won the most matches in Ryder Cup competition with 22 victories out of 32 played.

Most selections The most contests played is 10, by two players: Christy O'Connor Sr. (Great Britain and Ireland), 1955–73; and Nick Faldo (Great Britain and Ireland/Europe), 1977–95. The record in the United States is eight, held by three players: Billy Casper, 1961–75; Ray Floyd, 1969–93; and Lanny Wadkins, 1977–93.

U.S. Open Champions

Year	Champion
1946	Patty Berg
1947	Betty Jameson
1948	Babe Zaharias
1949	Louise Suggs
1950	Babe Zaharias
1951	Betsy Rawls
1952	Louise Suggs
1953	Betsy Rawls
1954	Babe Zaharias
1955	Fay Crocker
1956	Kathy Cornelius
1957	Betsy Rawls
1958	Mickey Wright
1959	Mickey Wright
1960	Betsy Rawls
1961	Mickey Wright
1962	Murle Lindstrom
1963	Mary Mills
1964	Mickey Wright
1965	Carol Mann
1966	Sandra Spuzich
1967	Catherine Lacoste [1]
1968	Susie Berning
1969	Donna Caponi
1970	Donna Caponi
1971	JoAnne Carner
1972	Susie Berning
1973	Susie Berning
1974	Sandra Haynie
1975	Sandra Palmer
1976	JoAnne Carner
1977	Hollis Stacy
1978	Hollis Stacy
1979	Jerilyn Britz
1980	Amy Alcott
1981	Pat Bradley
1982	Janet Anderson
1983	Jan Stephenson
1984	Hollis Stacy
1985	Kathy Baker
1986	Jane Geddes
1987	Laura Davies [2]
1988	Liselotte Neumann [3]
1989	Betsy King
1990	Betsy King
1991	Meg Mallon
1992	Patty Sheehan
1993	Laurie Merten
1994	Patty Sheehan
1995	Annika Sorenstam [3]
1996	Annika Sorenstam

1—France
2—Great Britain
3—Sweden

LPGA RECORDS

THE MAJORS

Grand Slam

A Grand Slam in ladies' professional golf has been recognized since 1955. From 1955–66, the United States Open, Ladies Professional Golf Association (LPGA) Championship, Western Open and Titleholders Championship served as the "majors." From 1967–82 the Grand Slam events changed, as first the Western Open (1967) and then the Titleholders Championship (1972) were discontinued. Since 1983, the U.S. Open, LPGA Championship, du Maurier Classic and Nabisco Dinah Shore have comprised the Grand Slam events.

Most grand slam titles Patty Berg has won the most majors, with 15 titles (one U.S. Open, seven Titleholders, seven Western Open).

The United States Open

In this competition, inaugurated in 1946, the first event was a match-play tournament; however, since 1947, the 72-hole stroke-play format has been used.

Most wins Two players have won the title four times: Betsy Rawls (1951, 1953, 1957, 1960); Mickey Wright (1958–59, 1961, 1964).

Most consecutive wins Two, by six players: Mickey Wright, 1958–59; Donna Caponi, 1969–70; Susie Berning, 1972–73; Hollis Stacy, 1977–78; Betsy King, 1989–90; Annika Sorenstam (Sweden), 1995–96.

Lowest 18-hole total 63, by Helen Alfredsson (Sweden) at Indianwood Golf and Country Club, Lake Orion, MI in 1994.

Lowest 72-hole total 277, by Liselotte Neumann (Sweden) at Baltimore (MD) Country Club in 1988.

Oldest champion 40 years 11 months, Fay Croker, 1955.

Youngest champion 22 years 5 days, Catherine Lacoste (France), 1967.

LPGA Championship

This event was inaugurated in 1955; from 1987 to 1993, it was called the Mazda LPGA Championship. Since 1993 it has been called the McDonald's LPGA Championship.

Most wins Mickey Wright has won the LPGA a record four times: 1958, 1960–61, 1963.

Most consecutive wins Two, by two players: Mickey Wright (1960–61); Patty Sheehan (1983–84).

Lowest 18-hole total 63, by Patty Sheehan at the Jack Nicklaus Golf Course, Kings Island, OH, in 1984.

Lowest 72-hole total 267, by Betsy King at the Bethesda (MD) Country Club in 1992.

Sweden's Annika Sorenstam successfully defended her U.S. Open title in 1996.
(J. D. Cuban/Allsport)

Nabisco Dinah Shore

Inaugurated in 1972, this event was formerly called the Colgate-Dinah Shore (1972–82). The event was designated a "major" in 1983. Mission Hills Country Club, Rancho Mirage, CA is the permanent site.

Most wins   Three, by two players: Amy Alcott (1983, 1988 and 1991); Betsy King (1987, 1990 and 1997).

Most consecutive wins   Two, by Sandra Post (1978–79).

Lowest 18-hole total   64, by two players: Nancy Lopez in 1981; Sally Little in 1982.

Lowest 72-hole total   273, by Amy Alcott in 1991.

Du Maurier Classic

Inaugurated in 1973, this event was formerly known as La Canadienne (1973) and the Peter Jackson Classic (1974–82). Granted "major" status in 1979, the tournament is held annually at different sites in Canada.

Most wins   Pat Bradley has won this event a record three times, 1980, 1985–86.

Most consecutive wins   Two, by Pat Bradley (1985–86).

Lowest 18-hole total   64, by three players: Jo-Anne Carner at St. George's Country Club, Toronto in 1978; Jane Geddes at Beaconsfield Country Club, Montreal in 1985; Dawn Coe-Jones at London (Ontario) Hunt and Country Club in 1993.

Lowest 72-hole total   272, by Jody Rosenthal at Islesmere Golf Course, Laval, Quebec in 1987.

LPGA TOUR RECORDS

Origins

In 1944, three women golfers, Hope Seignious, Betty Hicks and Ellen Griffin, launched the Women's Professional Golf Association (WPGA). By 1947 the WPGA was unable to sustain the tour at the level that was hoped, and it seemed certain that women's professional golf would fade away. However, Wilson Sporting Goods stepped in, overhauled the tour and called it the Ladies Professional Golf Association. In 1950, the LPGA received its official charter.

Most wins (career)   88, by Kathy Whitworth, 1959–91.

Most wins (season)   13, by Mickey Wright, in 1963.

Most consecutive wins (scheduled events)
Four, by two players: Mickey Wright, on two occasions, 1962, 1963; Kathy Whitworth, 1969.

Aussie rookie Karrie Webb took the LPGA Tour by storm in her first season on tour. She topped the 1996 earnings table, setting a new tour earnings record in the process.
(Otto Greule/Allsport)

Vicki Fergon is one of four players who share the LPGA tour low 18, at 62.
(Ken Levine/Allsport)

Most consecutive wins (in events participated in)
Five, by Nancy Lopez between May and June 1978.

Most wins (same event) Seven, by Patty Berg, who won two tournaments, the Titleholders Championship and the Western Open, both now defunct, on seven occasions during her illustrious career. She won the Titleholders in 1937–39, 1948, 1953, 1955, 1957; and the Western in 1941, 1943, 1948, 1951, 1955, 1957–58.

Oldest winner 46 years 5 months 9 days, JoAnne Carner at the 1985 Safeco Classic.

Youngest winner 18 years 14 days, Marlene Hagge at the 1952 Sarasota Open.

Widest margin of victory 14 strokes, by two players: Louise Suggs in the 1949 U.S. Open; Cindy Mackey in the 1986 Mastercard International.

Highest Earnings

Season $1,002,000, by Karrie Webb (Australia), 1996.

Career As of March 31, 1997 Betsy King had earned $5,730,407.

Most times leading money winner Eight, Kathy Whitworth, 1965–68, 1970–73.

Lowest Scores

Nine holes 28, by five players: Mary Beth Zimmerman at the Rail Golf Club, Springfield, IL, during the 1984 Rail Charity Golf Classic; Pat Bradley at the Green Gables Country Club, Denver, CO, during the 1984 Columbia Savings Classic; Muffin Spencer-Devlin at the Knollwood Country Club, Elmsford, NY, during the 1985 MasterCard International Pro-Am; Peggy Kirsch at the Squaw-Creek Country Club, Vienna, OH during the 1991 Phar-Mar in Youngstown; Renee Heiken at the Highland Meadows Golf Club, Sylvania, OH during the 1996 Jamie Farr Kroger Classic.

18 holes 62, by four players: Mickey Wright at Hogan Park Golf Club, Midland, TX, in the first round of the 1964 Tall City Open; Vicki Fergon at Alamaden Golf & Country Club, San Jose, CA, in the second round of the 1984 San Jose Classic; Laura Davies (Great Britain) at the Rail Golf Club, Springfield, IL, during the first round of the 1991 Rail Charity Golf Classic; and Hollis Stacy at the Meridian Valley Country Club, Kent, WA, during the second round of the 1992 Safeco Classic.

36 holes 129, by Judy Dickinson at Pasadena Yacht & Country Club, St. Petersburg, FL, during the first and second rounds of the 1985 S&H Golf Classic.

54 holes 197, by Pat Bradley at the Rail Golf Club, Springfield, IL, during all three rounds of the 1991 Rail Charity Golf Classic.

72 holes 267, by Betsy King at the Bethesda Country Club, MD, in the 1992 Mazda LPGA Championship.

AMATEUR GOLF

United States Amateur Championship

Inaugurated in 1895, the men's championship's initial format was match-play competition. In 1965, the format was changed to stroke-play; however, since 1972, the event has been played under the original match-play format. The women's championship also began in 1895 at 36 holes of stroke-play, then changed to match-play format the following year.

Most wins (men) Five, by Bobby Jones, 1924–25, 1927–28, 1930.

Most wins (women) Six, by Glenna Collette Vare, 1922, 1925, 1928–30, 1935..

Lowest score (stroke-play) 279, Lanny Wadkins, 1970.

Biggest winning margin (match-play: final) 12 & 11, Charles Macdonald, 1895.

NCAA Championship

The men's championship was initiated in 1897 as a match-play championship. In 1967 the format was switched to stroke-play.

Most titles (team) Yale has won the most team championships with 21 victories (1897–98, 1902, 1905–13, 1915, 1924–26, 1931–33, 1936, 1943).

Most titles (individual) Two golfers have won three individual titles: Ben Crenshaw (Texas), 1971–73; Phil Mickelson (Arizona State), 1989–90, 1992.

Ⅲ➡ Fantastic Feats

Consecutive birdies The official PGA record for consecutive birdies is 8, recorded by three players: Bob Goalby, during the fourth round of the 1961 St. Petersburg Open; Fuzzy Zoeller, during the opening round of the 1976 Quad Cities Open; and Dewey Arnette, during the opening round of the 1987 Buick Open. Goalby was the only one to win his event.

Longest drive (standard course) Michael Hoke Austin holds the record for longest recorded drive on a standard course. On September 25, 1974, Austin hit a golf ball 515 yards in the U.S. National Seniors Open Championship in Las Vegas, NV.

Longest drive (general) Niles Lied (Australia) drove a golf ball 2,640 yards (1 1/2 miles) across an ice cap at Mawson Base, Antarctica in 1962.

The greatest recorded carry of a golf ball is 458 yards, by Jack Hamm at Highlands Ranch, CO, July 20, 1993.

The greatest carry below 1,000 meters altitude is 364.8 yards, by Karl Woodward (Great Britain) at the Boca Raton (FL) Country Club, June 28, 1996.

Longest putt (tournament) The longest recorded holed putt in a professional tournament is 110 feet, by Jack Nicklaus in the 1964 Tournament of Champions; and by Nick Price in the 1992 United States PGA Championship.

Longest putt (general) Bob Cook (U.S.) sank a putt measured 140 feet 2 3/4 inches at St. Andrews, Great Britain in the International Fourball Pro Am Tournament on October 1, 1976.

Most balls hit in one hour The most balls driven in one hour—at least 100 yards and into a target area—is 2,146, by Sean Murphy at Wifts Practice Range, Carlisle, England on June 30, 1995.

Fastest round (individual)
With wide variations in the lengths of courses, speed records, even for rounds under par, are of little comparative value. The fastest round played with the golf ball coming to rest before each new stroke is 27 minutes 9 seconds, by James Carvil at Warrenpoint Golf Course, County Down, Northern Ireland, 18 holes 6,154 yards on June 18, 1987.

Fastest round (team)
The Fore Worcester's Children team of golfers completed 18 holes in 9 minutes 28 seconds at the Tatnuck Country Club, Worcester, MA on September 9, 1996. They scored 70.

Most holes (on foot) Ian Colston, 35, played 22 rounds plus five holes (401 holes in all) at Bendigo Gold Club, Victoria, Australia (par-73, 6,061 yards) on November 27–28, 1971.

Most holes (using golf cart) David Cavalier played 846 holes at Arrowhead Country Club, North Canton, OH (9 holes, 3,013 yards) on August 6–7, 1990.

Oldest hole in one Otto Bucher (Switzerland) was 99 years 244 days old when he sank the 130-yard 12th hole at La Manga Golf Club, Spain on January 13, 1985.

Fairway Phenom!

A pro rookie at the tender age of 20, golf wunderkind Eldrick "Tiger" Woods quickly proved he is no cub. The golf sensation of 1996, Woods hasn't slowed down since. In 1997, he won the season-starting Mercedes Championship and then annihilated the field and the record book at The Masters. His decision to turn pro, amid much fanfare, didn't intimidate the Amateur champion: "I had no fear. My decision was made so thoroughly, I knew it was the right decision. If I had made the decision on a whim, I might have had some fear."

Woods' end-of-season fireworks on the PGA Tour justified his decision to turn pro, but golf experts had never doubted his ability. An amateur phenom, Woods blazed a trail through golf's record books, displacing such legends as Bobby Jones and Jack Nicklaus. At 15, he became the youngest winner of the U.S. Junior title, and at 18, the youngest U.S. Amateur champion. He is the only player to win both events, and the only player to win each event three times. His attitude towards the game is indicative of his success: "Throughout my life, I 've never gone into an event without thinking I could win. That's the mind set I have. It's always to try to win," Woods says.

J. D. Cuban/Allsport

Tiger's biggest influence is his father, Earl Woods, who literally began teaching the game to his son when he was in the crib. At age two, Woods appeared on television, putting against Bob Hope. A retired Army officer, Earl Woods groomed his son to be a professional golfer and a role model. Woods doesn't duck the responsibility. "I've always felt like I've been blessed with that opportunity."

"I'm not out just to be the best black player. I want to be the best golfer ever." Declares Woods: "I'm just a golfer who happens to be black and Asian." Although Woods plays down the questions of race—his father is an African-American, his mother a native of Thailand—Woods is committed to boosting minority involvement in golf. "I want to go into inner cities to teach youth golf. This is something I've always been involved in. I want to show them [inner city kids] another outlet." Woods continues, "Golf's a great sport. It wasn't open to everyone at first, but now it is. Hopefully, more minorities will start playing."

So far Woods' career has rocketed towards the horizon like one of his prodigious drives, but he knows that "unplayable lies" lurk just around the next dogleg in golf. "Every time you step onto the golf course, you have failure. I will lose more out here than I win. That's part of it," says Woods.

Prior to turning pro, Woods had little success against the top players. His perspective on these experiences demonstrates his maturity. "My record was not very good. Most of the events were during high school and college. It's hard to get a rhythm or flow going that way."

Three tour victories and a Masters green jacket is a career for most golfers. Woods, however, is looking to the future. "On a weekly basis, my game will improve and my finishes will be better," predicts Woods. For the rest of the PGA Tour that prophecy is as scary as a slick downhill five-foot putt at Augusta National.

GREYHOUND RACING

Origins

The first greyhound meeting was staged in Hendon, England in September 1876. Modern greyhound racing originated with the perfecting of the mechanical hare by Own P. Smith in Emeryville, CA in 1919.

Fastest speed   The highest speed at which any greyhound has been timed is 41.83 mph (400 yards in 19.57 seconds), by Star Title on the straightaway track in Wyong, New South Wales, Australia, on March 5, 1994.

The fastest automatically timed speed for a full four-bend race is 38.89 mph (563 yards in 29.62 seconds), by Glen Miner in Hove, England, on May 4, 1982.

Most wins   The most career wins is 143 by JR's Ripper (U.S.), 1982–86.

Highest earnings (career)   The career record earnings mark is $297,000 by Homespun Rowdy, 1984–87.

Highest earnings (race)   The highest prize for a race is $125,000, won by the appropriately named Ben G Speedboat in the Greyhound Race of Champions at Seabrook, NH in August 1986.

GYMNASTICS

Origins

The ancient Greeks and Romans were exponents of gymnastics, as shown by demonstration programs in the ancient Olympic Games (776 B.C. to A.D. 393). Modern training techniques were developed in Germany toward the end of the 18th century. Johann Friedrich Simon was the first teacher of the modern methods, at Basedow's School, Dessau, Germany in 1776. Friedrich Jahn, who founded the Turnverein in Berlin, Germany in 1811, is regarded as the most influential of the gymnastics pioneers. The International Gymnastics Federation (FIG) was formed in 1891.

United States   Gymnastics was introduced to the United States in the 19th century. With the advent of the modern Olympic Games, interest in the sport grew in this country, and in 1920 the United States entered its first gymnastics team in the Games. The sport was governed by the Amateur Athletic Union (AAU) and then by the National Collegiate Athletic Association (NCAA) until 1963, when the United States Gymnastics Federation (USGF) was formed. The USGF changed its name to USA Gymnastics in 1994. It is still the governing body for the sport, and has its headquarters in Indianapolis, IN.

Olympic Games

Gymnastics was included in the first modern Olympic Games in 1896; however, women's competition was not included until 1928.

Most gold medals   Larissa Latynina (USSR) has won nine gold medals: six individual—all-around title, 1956 and 1960; floor exercise, 1956, 1960 and 1964; vault, 1956; and three team titles—1956, 1960 and 1964. In men's competition, Sawao Kato (Japan) has won eight gold medals: five individual—all-around title, 1968 and 1972; floor exercise, 1968; and parallel bars, 1972 and 1976; and three team titles—1968, 1972 and 1976.

Vera Caslavska (Czechoslovakia) has won a record seven individual gold medals: all-around title, 1964 and 1968; uneven bars, 1968; beam, 1964; floor exercise, 1968; and vault, 1964 and 1968. In men's competition, Boris Shakhlin and Nikolai Andrianov (both USSR) have each won six individual titles. Shakhlin won the all-around title, 1960; parallel bars, 1960; pommel horse, 1956, 1960; horizontal bar, 1964; vault, 1960. Andrianov won the all-around title, 1976; floor exercise, 1972, 1976; rings, 1976; and vault, 1976 and 1980.

Most medals   Larissa Latynina (USSR) has won 18 medals, the most of any athlete in any sport. She has won nine gold (six in individual events [see above] and one team event, 1980); five silver—all-around title, 1964; uneven bars, 1956 and 1960; beam, 1960; vault, 1964; and four bronze—uneven bars, 1964; beam, 1964; vault, 1964; and the portable apparatus team event (now discontinued) in 1956. Nikolai Andrianov holds the men's record at 15, which is the most by any male athlete in any sport. He won seven gold (six in individual events [see above] and one team event, 1980);

Perfect Poise

In the world of gymnastics, getting older is likened to a cardinal sin. But after winning three bronze and two silver medals in 1992 at the age of 15, Shannon Miller decided never to let her age undermine her potential to become a gold medalist at the 1996 Olympics. In fact, Miller clinched two golds at the Atlanta Games, upping her Guinness record of most medals from five to seven.

Over the four years between 1992 and 1996, she worked hard to incorporate new skills into her routine and show the world that she wasn't too old for the sport, "because in gymnastics, the normal thing to do is go to only one Olympics. I really wanted to get over the age thing and not worry about it. Right now I'm second oldest on the team."

How does Miller feel about her accomplishments? "It's different than I expected. It's been so much fun, traveling with the team, being on tour," she says. "Looking back on the records I broke, it's really cool but it's also a bit weird. When I go to competitions, I try to do the very best I can and the medals come after the fact. It's still not believable for me."

Miller began her career in gymnastics at the age of five and hasn't slowed down since. She doesn't

Mike Powell/Allsport

remember a time when tumbling was a chore—or a job. "I don't think there was ever a point when I decided that this was what I wanted to do. I've always loved doing gymnastics and kept on doing more and more of it," Miller recalls.

Growing up, the gymnast stayed in public school and never moved away from her family in Oklahoma. "The only thing I missed out on was growing up with my brother and sister," she explains. "I was away a whole lot—at competitions and at training."

"You always have to have a goal in life," she says. "It's great to have the Olympics as a goal, but only seven kids in the U.S. make the team, so there's got to be other goals along the way. It makes it easier to feel like you accomplish something every day you go into the gym."

The physical aspect of gymnastics is obviously important, but Miller also concentrates on other aspects of her sport. "I do my routines over and over in my head to get them perfect. I always try to keep a positive attitude so that if I do make a mistake I can learn from it and move on."

As for a philosophy of life, Miller keeps things simple. "I want to get everything I can out of every day and have fun with what I'm doing."

---

five silver—team event, 1972 and 1976; all-around title, 1980; floor exercise, 1980; parallel bars, 1976; and three bronze—pommel horse, 1976; horizontal bar, 1980; and vault, 1972.

World Championships

First held in Belgium in 1903, the championships were discontinued in 1913. Reintroduced in 1922, the event was held quadrennially until 1979, when the format became biennial. Until 1979 the Olympic Games served as the world championships, and results from Olympic competition are included in world championship statistics.

Most titles Larissa Latynina (USSR) won 17 world titles: five team and 12 individual, 1956–64. In men's

competition, Boris Shakhlin (USSR) has won 13 titles: three team and 10 individual, 1954–64.

United States Shannon Miller won a record five gold medals: all-around, uneven bars and floor exercise, 1993; and all-around and balance beam, 1994.

United States National Championships

Most titles Alfred A. Jochim won a record seven men's all-around U.S. titles, 1925–30 and 1933, and a total of 34 at all exercises between 1923 and 1934. The women's record is six all-around, 1945–46 and 1949–52, and 39 at all exercises, including 11 in succession at balance beam, 1941–51, by Clara Marie Schroth Lomady.

The U.S. women's gymnastic team acknowledged the roars of the home team crowd after receiving their Olympic gold medals.
(Doug Pensinger/Allsport)

NCAA Championships (Men)

The men's competition was first held in 1938.

Most team titles The most team championships won is nine, by two colleges: Illinois, 1939–42, 1950, 1955–56, 1958, 1989; Penn State, 1948, 1953–54, 1957, 1959–61, 1965, 1976.

Individual Records

Most titles (one year) Four, by two gymnasts: Jean Cronstedt, Penn State, won the all-around title, parallel bar, horizontal bar and floor exercise in 1954; Robert Lynn, Southern Cal., won the all-around title, parallel bar, horizontal bar and floor exercise in 1962.

Most titles (career) Seven, by two gymnasts: Joe Giallombardo, Illinois, won the tumbling, 1938–40; all-around title, 1938–40; and flying rings, 1938; Jim Hartung, Nebraska, won the all-around title, 1980–81; rings, 1980–82; and parallel bar, 1981–82.

NCAA Championships (Women)

The women's competition was first held in 1982.

Most team titles The most team championships won is nine, by Utah, 1982–86, 1990, 1992, 1994–95.

Individual Records

Most titles (one year) Four, by two gymnasts: Missy Marlowe, Utah, won the all-around, balance beam, uneven bars and floor exercise in 1992; and Jenny Hansen, Kentucky, won the all-around, vault, balance beam and floor exercise in 1995.

Most titles (career)   Eight, by Jenny Hansen, Kentucky. She won the all-around, 1993–95, vault, 1994–95, balance beam, 1994–95 and floor exercise, 1995.

RHYTHMIC GYMNASTICS

Rhythmic gymnastics involves complex body movements combined with handling of apparatus such as ropes, hoops, balls, clubs and ribbons. The performance must include required elements, and the choreography must cover the entire floor area and include elements such as jumps, leaps, balances, flexibility and pivots.

Origins

In 1962 the International Gymnastics Federation (FIG) officially recognized rhythmic gymnastics as a distinct sport. The first world championships were held in 1963 and the sport was included in the Olympic Games in 1984.

Olympic Games

Marina Lobach (USSR) won the 1988 Olympic title with a perfect score of 60.00 points in each of her events.

World Championships

Most titles (individual)   The most overall individual world championships is three, by two gymnasts: Maria Gigova (Bulgaria), 1969, 1971 and 1973 (tied); and Maria Petrova (Bulgaria), 1993–95.

Most titles (country)   Bulgaria has won nine team championships: 1969, 1971, 1981, 1983, 1985, 1987, 1989 (tie), 1993 and 1995.

Gymnastics Exercises

Exercise	Record	Name	Date
Chins—consecutive	370	Lee Chin-Yong (South Korea)	May 14, 1988
Chins—consecutive (one arm, from ring)	22	Robert Chrisnall (Canada)	December 3, 1982
Parallel bar dips— one hour	3,726	Kim Yang-ki (South Korea)	November 28, 1991
Push-ups—24 hours	46,001	Charles Servizio (U.S.)	April 24–25, 1993
Push-ups—five hours (one arm)	8,794	Paddy Doyle (Great Britain)	February 12, 1996
Push-ups—five hours (fingertip)	7,011	Kim Yang-ki (South Korea)	August 30, 1990
Push-ups—consecutive (one finger)	124	Paul Lynch (Great Britain)	April 21, 1992
Push-ups—one year	1,500,230	Paddy Doyle (Great Britain)	October 1988–October 1989
Leg lifts—12 hours	41,788	Lou Scripa Jr. (U.S.)	December 2, 1988
Somersaults— consecutive	8,341	Ashrita Furman (U.S.) (over 12 miles 390 yards)	April 30, 1986
Somersaults— backwards	54.68 yds./10.22 sec.	Vitaliy Scherbo (Belarus)	August 1, 1995
Squats—one hour	4,289	Paul Wai Man Chung (Hong Kong)	April 5, 1993
Squat thrusts—one hour	3,552	Paul Wai Man Chung (Hong Kong)	April 21, 1992
Burpees—one hour	1,840	Paddy Doyle (Great Britain)	February 6, 1994
Pummel horse double circles—consecutive	97	Tyler Farstad (Great Britain)	November 27, 1993

HARNESS RACING

Harness racing involves two styles of racing: trotting and pacing. The distinction between trotters and pacers is in the gait of the horses. The trotting gait requires the simultaneous use of the diagonally opposite legs, while pacers thrust out their fore and hind legs simultaneously on one side.

Origins

Trotting races were held in Valkenburg, Netherlands in 1554. There is also evidence of trotting races in England in the late 16th century.

United States Harness racing became popular in the United States in the mid-19th century. The National Trotting Association was founded in 1870, and is still the governing body for the sport in the United States.

TROTTING

HORSES' RECORDS

Most victories (career) Goldsmith Maid won an all-time record 350 races (including dashes and heats) from 1864 through 1877.

Most victories (season) Make Believe won a record 53 races in 1949.

Highest earnings (career) The greatest career earnings for any harness horse is $4,907,307, by Peace Corps, 1988–93.

Highest earnings (season) The single-season record for a trotter is $1,610,608, by Prakas in 1985.

Highest earnings (race) The richest race in the trotting calendar is the Hambletonian. The richest Hambletonian was the 1992 event, with a total purse of $1,380,000. The record first-place prize was $673,000 for the 1990 race, won by Harmonious.

THE TRIPLE CROWN

The Triple Crown for trotters consists of three races: Hambletonian, Kentucky Futurity and Yonkers Trot. Six trotters have won the Triple Crown.

Hambletonian

The most famous race in North American harness racing, the Hambletonian, was first run in 1926. The Hambletonian has been run at The Meadowlands, NJ since 1981. The Hambletonian is open to three-year-olds and is run over one mile.

Fastest time Continentalvictory, driven by Mike Lachance, finished in 1 minute 52$\frac{1}{5}$ seconds in 1996.

Most wins (driver) Four drivers have won the Hambletonian four times: Ben White, 1933, 1936, 1942 and 1943; Stanley Dancer, 1968, 1972, 1975 and 1983; William Haughton, 1974, 1976–77 and 1980; John Campbell, 1987–90 and 1995.

Kentucky Futurity

First held in 1893, the Kentucky Futurity is a one-mile race for three-year-olds, raced at The Red Mile, Lexington, KY.

Fastest time The fastest time is 1 minute 52$\frac{3}{5}$ seconds, by Pine Chip, driven by John Campbell, in 1993.

Most wins (driver) Ben White has driven the winning trotter seven times: 1916, 1922, 1924–25, 1933, 1936–37.

Yonkers Trot

First run in 1955, when it was known as "The Yonkers,"

Continentalvictory races down the stretch to win the 1996 Hambletonian.
(U.S. Trotting Association)

this race has been known since 1975 as the Yonkers Trot. Run over one mile for three-year-olds, the race is currently staged at Yonkers Raceway, NY.

Fastest time The fastest time is 1 minute 56 seconds, by CR Kay Suzie, driven by Rod Allen, in 1995.

Most wins (driver) Stanley Dancer has driven the winning trotter six times: 1959, 1965, 1968, 1971–72 and 1975.

PACING
HORSES' RECORDS

Most victories (career) Single G won 262 races (including dashes and heats), 1918–26.

Most victories (career–modern record) Symbol Allen won 241 races from 1943 through 1958.

Most victories (season) Victory Hy won a record 65 races in 1950.

Most consecutive wins Carty Nagle won 41 consecutive races from 1937 through 1938.

Highest earnings (career) The all-time earnings record for a pacer is $3,225,653, by Nihilator, 1984–85.

Highest earnings (season) The season record for a pacer is $2,264,714, by Cam's Card Shark in 1994.

Highest earnings (race) The richest race in harness racing history was the 1984 Woodrow Wilson, which carried a total purse of $2,161,000. The winner, Nihilator, earned a record $1,080,500.

THE TRIPLE CROWN

The Triple Crown for pacers consists of three races: Cane Pace, Little Brown Jug and Messenger Stakes. Seven horses have won the Triple Crown.

Cane Pace

First run in 1955, this race was originally known as the Cane Futurity. Since 1975, it has been called the Cane Pace. Run over one mile, the race is open to three-year-olds, and is run at Yonkers Raceway, NY.

Fastest time The fastest time is 1 minute 51 2/5 seconds, by Riyadh, driven by Jim Morrill Jr., in 1993.

Most wins (driver) Stanley Dancer has driven the winning pacer four times: 1964, 1970–71 and 1976.

Little Brown Jug

First run in 1946, the Jug is raced annually at Delaware County Fair, Delaware, OH The race is for three-year-olds and is run over one mile.

Fastest time The fastest time is 1 minute 51 2/5 seconds, shared by two horses: Nick's Fantasy, driven by John Campbell, in 1995; and Ambro Operative, driven by Mike Lachance, 1996.

Most wins (driver) William Haughton has driven five winning pacers, in 1955, 1964, 1968–69 and 1974.

Messenger Stakes

First run in 1956, this race has been staged at various locations during its history. The race is run over one mile and is open to three-year-olds only.

Fastest time The fastest time is 1 minute 51 seconds, by Cam's Card Shark, driven by John Campbell in 1994.

Most wins (drivers) William Haughton has driven seven winners, in 1956, 1967–68, 1972 and 1974–76.

DRIVERS' RECORDS

Most wins (career) Herve Filion (Canada) had won 14,783 harness races as of February 25, 1997.

Most wins (season) Tony Morgan won a record 853 races in 1996.

Most wins (day) Mike Lachance won 12 races at Yonkers Raceway, NY on June 23, 1987.

Highest earnings (career) John Campbell has won a career record $147,101,299 in prize money, 1972–February 25, 1997.

Highest earnings (season) John Campbell won a season record $11,620,878 in 543 races in 1990.

⇒ Fantastic Feats

Oldest driver Eighty-three-year-old George McCandless of Vineland, NJ guided Kehm's Scooter to victory at Freehold Raceway in 1994.

HOCKEY

Origins

There is pictorial evidence that a hockey-like game (*kalv*) was played on ice in the early 16th century in the Netherlands. The game was probably first played in North America on December 25, 1855 in Kingston, Ontario, Canada, but Halifax also lays claim to priority. The International Ice Hockey Federation was founded in 1908.

NATIONAL HOCKEY LEAGUE (NHL)

Origins

The National Hockey League (NHL) was founded on November 22, 1917 in Montreal, Canada. The formation of the NHL was precipitated by the collapse of the National Hockey Association of Canada (NHA). Four teams formed the original league: the Montreal Canadiens, Montreal Wanderers, Ottawa Senators and Quebec Bulldogs. The Toronto Arenas were admitted as a fifth team, but the Bulldogs were unable to operate, and the league began as a four-team competition. The first NHL game was played on December 19, 1917. The NHL now comprises 26 teams, six from Canada and 20 from the United States, divided into two divisions within two conferences: Northeast and Atlantic Divisions in the Eastern Conference; Pacific and Central Division in the Western Conference. At the end of the regular season, 16 teams compete in the Stanley Cup playoffs to decide the NHL Championship. (For further details of the Stanley Cup, see pages 156–162.)

TEAM RECORDS

Most wins (season) The Detroit Red Wings won 62 games during the 1995–96 season. In 82 games, the Red Wings won 62, lost 13 and tied 7.

Highest winning percentage (season) The 1929–30 Boston Bruins set an NHL record .875 winning percentage. The Bruins' record was 38 wins, 5 losses and 1 tie.

Most points (season) The Montreal Canadiens accumulated 132 points during their record-setting campaign of 1976–77, when they won a record 60 games.

Most losses (season) The San Jose Sharks hold the unenviable record of having lost the most games in one season. During the 1992–93 season, the second for the franchise, the Sharks lost 71 of 84 games played.

Most goals (game) The NHL record for goals in one game is 21, which has occurred on two occasions. The mark was set on January 10, 1920, when the Montreal Canadiens defeated the Toronto St. Patricks, 14–7, at Montreal. This record was matched on December 11, 1985, when the Edmonton Oilers beat the Chicago Blackhawks, 12–9, at Chicago.

Most goals (game–one team) The Montreal Canadiens pounded the Quebec Bulldogs 16–3 on March 3, 1920 to set the single-game scoring record. To make matters worse for Quebec, the game was on home ice.

Most goals (season) The Edmonton Oilers scored 446 goals in 80 games during the 1983–84 season.

Most assists (season) The Edmonton Oilers recorded 737 assists during the 1985–86 season.

Most points (season) The Edmonton Oilers amassed 1,182 points (446 goals, 736 assists) during the 1983–84 season.

Most power-play goals scored (season) The Pittsburgh Penguins scored 119 power-play goals during the 1988–89 season.

Most shorthand goals scored (season) The Edmonton Oilers scored 36 shorthand goals during the 1983–84 season.

Most penalty minutes in one game At the Boston Garden on February 26, 1981, the Boston Bruins and the Minnesota North Stars received a combined 406 penalty minutes, a record for one game. The Bruins received 20 minors, 13 majors, three 10-minute misconducts and six game misconducts for a total of 195 penalty minutes; the North Stars received 18 minors, 13 majors, four 10-minute misconducts and seven game misconducts for a total of 211 penalty minutes. It is also reported that a hockey game broke out between the fights, which the Bruins won 5–1.

Longest winning streak The Pittsburgh Penguins won 17 consecutive games from March 9 through April 10, 1993.

Longest undefeated streak The longest undefeated streak in one season is 35 games by the Philadelphia Flyers. The Flyers won 25 games and tied 10 from October 14, 1979–January 6, 1980.

Longest losing streak Two teams share the unwanted honor of losing 17 consecutive games: Washington Capitals from February 18–March 26, 1975; San Jose Sharks, January 4–February 12, 1993.

Longest winless streak
The Winnipeg Jets set the mark for the longest winless streak at 30 games. From October 19 to December 20, 1980, the Jets lost 23 games and tied seven.

Longest game The longest game was played between the Detroit Red Wings and the Montreal Maroons at the Forum Montreal and lasted 2 hours 56 minutes 30 seconds. The Red Wings won when Mud Bruneteau scored the only goal of the game in the sixth period of overtime at 2:25 A.M. on March 25, 1936. Norm Smith, the Red Wings goaltender, turned aside 92 shots for the NHL's longest shutout.

Penguins superstar Mario Lemieux led Pittsburgh to two Stanley Cup titles and featured prominently in the team's NHL record-breaking winning streak in 1993.
(Rick Stewart/Allsport)

National Hockey League Records

Goals

		Player(s)	Team(s)	Date(s)
Period	4	Busher Jackson	Toronto Maple Leaf vs. St. Louis Eagles	November 20, 1934
		Max Bentley	Chicago Blackhawks vs. New York Rangers	January 28, 1943
		Clint Smith	Chicago Blackhawks vs. Montreal Canadiens	March 4, 1945
		Red Berenson	St. Louis Blues vs. Philadelphia Flyers	November 7, 1968
		Wayne Gretzky	Edmonton Oilers vs. St. Louis Blues	February 18, 1981
		Grant Mulvey	Chicago Blackhawks vs. St. Louis Blues	February 3, 1982
		Bryan Trottier	New York Islanders vs. Philadelphia Flyers	February 13, 1982
		Al Secord	Chicago Blackhawks vs. Toronto Maple Leafs	January 7, 1987
		Joe Nieuwendyk	Calgary Flames vs. Winnipeg Jets	January 11,1989
		Peter Bondra	Washington Capitals vs. Tampa Bay Lightning	February 5, 1994
Game	7	Joe Malone	Quebec Bulldogs vs.Toronto St. Patricks	January 31,1920
Season	92	Wayne Gretzky	Edmonton Oilers	1981–82
Career	854	Wayne Gretzky	Edmonton Oilers; Los Angeles Kings St. Louis Blues; New York Rangers	1979–97*

Assists

		Player(s)	Team(s)	Date(s)
Period	5	Dale Hawerchuk	Winnipeg Jets vs. Los Angeles Kings	March 6, 1984
Game	7	Billy Taylor	Detroit Red Wings vs. Chicago Blackhawks	March 16, 1947
		Wayne Gretzky	Edmonton Oilers vs. Washington Capitals	February 15, 1980
		Wayne Gretzky	Edmonton Oilers vs. Chicago Blackhawks	December 11, 1985
		Wayne Gretzky	Edmonton Oilers vs. Quebec Nordiques	February 14, 1986
Season	163	Wayne Gretzky	Edmonton Oilers	1985–86
Career	1,832	Wayne Gretzky	Edmonton Oilers,Los Angeles Kings St. Louis Blues; New York Rangers	1979–97*

Points

		Player(s)	Team(s)	Date(s)
Period	6	Bryan Trottier	New York Islanders vs. New York Rangers	December 23, 1978
Game	10	Darryl Sittler	Toronto Maple Leafs vs. Boston Bruins	February 7, 1976
Season	215	Wayne Gretzky	Edmonton Oilers	1985–86
Career	2,686	Wayne Gretzky	Edmonton Oilers; Los Angeles Kings St. Louis Blues; New York Rangers	1979–97*

GOALTENDERS

Shutouts

		Player(s)	Team(s)	Date(s)
Season	22	George Hainsworth	Montreal Canadiens	1928–29
Career	103	Terry Sawchuk	Detroit Red Wings, Boston Bruins Toronto Maple Leafs, Los Angeles Kings, New York Rangers	1949–70

Wins

		Player(s)	Team(s)	Date(s)
Season	47	Bernie Parent	Philadelphia Flyers	1973–74
Career	447	Terry Sawchuk	Detroit Red Wings, Boston Bruins, Toronto Maple Leafs, Los Angeles Kings, New York Rangers	1949–70

* As of February 23, 1997

Source: NHL

INDIVIDUAL RECORDS

Most games played Gordie Howe played 1,767 games over a record 26 seasons for the Detroit Red Wings (1946–71) and Hartford Whalers (1979–80). The most games played by a goaltender is 971, by Terry Sawchuk, who played 21 seasons for five teams: Detroit Red Wings, Boston Bruins, Toronto Maple Leafs, Los Angeles Kings and New York Rangers (1949–70).

Most consecutive games played Doug Jarvis played 964 consecutive games from October 8, 1975 to October 10, 1987. During the streak, Jarvis played for three teams: the Montreal Canadiens, Washington Capitals and Hartford Whalers.

Fastest goal The fastest goal from the start of a game is 5 seconds, a feat performed by three players: Doug Smail (Winnipeg Jets) vs. St. Louis Blues at Winnipeg on December 20, 1981; Bryan Trottier (New York Islanders) vs. Boston Bruins at Boston on March 22, 1984; and Alexander Mogilny (Buffalo Sabres) vs. Toronto Maple Leafs at Toronto on December 21, 1991. The fastest goal from the start of any period was after 4 seconds, achieved by two players: Claude Provost (Montreal Canadiens) vs. Boston Bruins in the second period at Montreal on November 9, 1957, and by Denis Savard (Chicago Blackhawks) vs. Hartford Whalers in the third period at Chicago on January 12, 1986.

Most hat tricks The most hat tricks (three or more goals in a game) in a career is 49, by Wayne Gretzky (Edmonton Oilers, Los Angeles Kings, St. Louis Blues, New York Rangers), from 1979 through February 24, 1997. Gretzky also holds the record for most hat tricks in a season, 10, in both the 1981–82 and 1983–84 seasons for the Edmonton Oilers.

Longest consecutive goal-scoring streak The most consecutive games scoring at least one goal in a game is 16, by Harry (Punch) Broadbent (Ottawa Senators) in the 1921–22 season. Broadbent scored 25 goals during the streak.

Longest consecutive assist-scoring streak The record for most consecutive games recording at least one assist is 23 games, by Wayne Gretzky (Los Angeles Kings) in 1990–91. Gretzky was credited with 48 assists during the streak.

Most consecutive 50-or-more-goal seasons Mike Bossy (New York Islanders) scored at least 50 goals in nine consecutive seasons from 1977–78 through 1985–86.

Longest consecutive point-scoring streak The most consecutive games scoring at least one point is 51, by Wayne Gretzky (Edmonton Oilers) between October 5, 1983 and January 27, 1984. During the streak, Gretzky scored 61 goals, 92 assists for 153 points.

Longest shutout sequence by a goaltender Alex Connell (Ottawa Senators) played 461 minutes, 29 seconds without conceding a goal in the 1927–28 season.

Longest undefeated streak by a goaltender Gerry Cheevers (Boston Bruins) went 32 games (24 wins, 8 ties) undefeated during the 1971–72 season.

Defensemen Paul Coffey (Edmonton Oilers, 1980–87; Pittsburgh Penguins, 1987–91; Los Angeles Kings, 1991–93; Detroit Red Wings, 1993–96; Hartford Whalers, 1996; Philadelphia Flyers, 1996–97) holds the all-time records for goals, assists and points by a defenseman. As of February 23, 1997, Coffey's career marks were 377 goals, 1,057 assists and 1,434 points. Coffey also holds the single-season record for goals scored by a defenseman, 48, which he scored in 1985–86 when he played for the Edmonton Oilers. Bobby Orr (Boston Bruins) holds the single-season marks for assists (102) and points (139), both of which were set in 1970–71.

COACHES

Most wins As of February 24, 1997, Scotty Bowman has coached his teams to 1,004 victories (110 wins, St. Louis Blues, 1967–71; 419 wins, Montreal Canadiens, 1971–79; 210 wins, Buffalo Sabres, 1979–87; 95 wins, Pittsburgh Penguins, 1991–93; 170 wins, Detroit Red Wings, 1993–97).

Most games coached As of February 24, 1997, Scotty Bowman has coached a record 1,714 games with five teams: St. Louis Blues, 1967–71; Montreal Canadiens, 1971–79; Buffalo Sabres, 1979–87; Pittsburgh Penguins, 1991–93; Detroit Red Wings, 1993–97. Bowman's career record is 1,004 wins, 453 losses, 257 ties.

Flexibility: The Coaching Edge

"There's no formula that says 'If I do this, I can coach,'" says Scotty Bowman. The National Hockey League's winningest coach, Bowman attributes his success to his willingness to adopt new methods. "My philosophy is that you have to be an innovator. You have to try new things. The biggest thing is that a coach has to be a chance-taker."

Bowman has racked up the most regular-season career wins of any NHL coach, and also the most playoff victories. His record of six Stanley Cup wins ranks second to Toe Blake, the Montreal Canadiens' legend. These accomplishments are no small feat for a man whose own playing career ended prematurely when he fractured his skull. "The injury helped me get into coaching before my time," Bowman recalled. "I was fortunate that I began at a young age. When I was 21, I was coaching 'Junior Hockey.' There wasn't much age difference between the players and me, but it didn't bother me."

The Red Wings' skipper emphasizes that a coach must get the most out of individual players and meld them into a team. "The coach can't say we didn't win because so and so didn't do this or that. You have to get players to know their roles. You have to strive for perfection, and you do that by running repetitious drills in practice." Bowman adds, "Everybody can play under any system as long as you are on the same page and going in the same direction."

Last season, 1995–96, Bowman led the Detroit Red Wings to a 62-win regular season mark, breaking his own single season record of 60 wins, set while he led the Montreal Canadiens in 1976–77. Hockey critics have downplayed the 62-win campaign since the Red Wings fell short in their bid for the Stanley Cup. Bowman bristles at such comments: "I don't care what reporters say. We still set the record for most team wins. It's a meaningful record. We played nearly .800 and it's not easy to get there."

During his long career in the NHL Bowman has encountered many changes in tactics, players, and rules. But for him hockey remains fundamentally the same. "It's a skating game," he says. "You can't make it if you don't skate with your head, heart and feet. You need a head on your shoulders to think, a heart to play under tough situations, and feet to skate with."

For aspiring coaches, Bowman offers these tips: "Don't live in fear of defeat. You can't do any job with negative vibes. You have to be positive and have confidence." He adds, "Above all you have to adapt to stay with the job." After a pause he quips, "I never worry. There is nothing so uncertain as a sure thing."

Glenn Cratty/Allsport

Hart Memorial Trophy Winners

The Hart Trophy has been awarded annually since the 1923–24 season by the Professional Hockey Writers Association to the Most Valuable Player of the NHL. Wayne Gretzky has won the award a record nine times, 1980–87 and 1989.

Year	Player	Team	Year	Player	Team
1924	Frank Nighbor	Ottawa Senators	1961	Bernie Geoffrion	Montreal Canadiens
1925	Billy Burch	Hamilton Tigers	1962	Jacques Plante	Montreal Canadiens
1926	Nels Stewart	Montreal Maroons	1963	Gordie Howe	Detroit Red Wings
1927	Herb Gardiner	Montreal Canadiens	1964	Jean Beliveau	Montreal Canadiens
1928	Howie Morenz	Montreal Canadiens	1965	Bobby Hull	Chicago Blackhawks
1929	Roy Worters	New York Americans	1966	Bobby Hull	Chicago Blackhawks
1930	Nels Stewart	Montreal Maroons	1967	Stan Mikita	Chicago Blackhawks
1931	Howie Morenz	Montreal Canadiens	1968	Stan Mikita	Chicago Blackhawks
1932	Howie Morenz	Montreal Canadiens	1969	Phil Esposito	Boston Bruins
1933	Eddie Shore	Boston Bruins	1970	Bobby Orr	Boston Bruins
1934	Aurel Joliat	Montreal Canadiens	1971	Bobby Orr	Boston Bruins
1935	Eddie Shore	Boston Bruins	1972	Bobby Orr	Boston Bruins
1936	Eddie Shore	Boston Bruins	1973	Bobby Clarke	Philadelphia Flyers
1937	Babe Siebert	Montreal Canadiens	1974	Phil Esposito	Boston Bruins
1938	Eddie Shore	Boston Bruins	1975	Bobby Clarke	Philadelphia Flyers
1939	Toe Blake	Montreal Canadiens	1976	Bobby Clarke	Philadelphia Flyers
1940	Ebbie Goodfellow	Detroit Red Wings	1977	Guy Lafleur	Montreal Canadiens
1941	Bill Cowley	Boston Bruins	1978	Guy Lafleur	Montreal Canadiens
1942	Tom Anderson	Brooklyn Americans	1979	Bryan Trottier	New York Islanders
1943	Bill Cowley	Boston Bruins	1980	Wayne Gretzky	Edmonton Oilers
1944	Babe Pratt	Toronto Maple Leafs	1981	Wayne Gretzky	Edmonton Oilers
1945	Elmer Lach	Montreal Canadiens	1982	Wayne Gretzky	Edmonton Oilers
1946	Max Bentley	Chicago Blackhawks	1983	Wayne Gretzky	Edmonton Oilers
1947	Maurice Richard	Montreal Canadiens	1984	Wayne Gretzky	Edmonton Oilers
1948	Buddy O'Connor	New York Rangers	1985	Wayne Gretzky	Edmonton Oilers
1949	Sid Abel	Detroit Red Wings	1986	Wayne Gretzky	Edmonton Oilers
1950	Charlie Rayner	New York Rangers	1987	Wayne Gretzky	Edmonton Oilers
1951	Milt Schmidt	Boston Bruins	1988	Mario Lemieux	Pittsburgh Penguins
1952	Gordie Howe	Detroit Red Wings	1989	Wayne Gretzky	Los Angeles Kings
1953	Gordie Howe	Detroit Red Wings	1990	Mark Messier	Edmonton Oilers
1954	Al Rollins	Chicago Blackhawks	1991	Brett Hull	St. Louis Blues
1955	Ted Kennedy	Toronto Maple Leafs	1992	Mark Messier	New York Rangers
1956	Jean Beliveau	Montreal Canadiens	1993	Mario Lemieux	Pittsburgh Penguins
1957	Gordie Howe	Detroit Red Wings	1994	Sergei Fedorov	Detroit Red Wings
1958	Gordie Howe	Detroit Red Wings	1995	Eric Lindros	Philadelphia Flyers
1959	Andy Bathgate	New York Rangers	1996	Mario Lemieux	Pittsburgh Penguins
1960	Gordie Howe	Detroit Red Wings			

STANLEY CUP

The Stanley Cup is currently the oldest competition in North American professional sports. The cup was donated to the Canadian Amateur Hockey Association (AHA) by Sir Frederick Arthur Stanley, Lord Stanley of Preston in 1893. The inaugural championship was presented to the AHA champion, but since 1894 there has always been a playoff. The playoff format underwent several changes until 1926, when the National Hockey League (NHL) playoffs became the permanent forum to decide the Stanley Cup champion.

Most championships The Montreal Canadiens have won the Stanley Cup a record 24 times: 1916, 1924, 1930–31, 1944, 1946, 1953, 1956–60, 1965–66, 1968–69, 1971, 1973, 1976–79, 1986, 1993.

Most consecutive wins The Montreal Canadiens won the Stanley Cup for five consecutive years, 1956–60.

Most games played Larry Robinson has played in 227 Stanley Cup playoff games for the Montreal Canadiens (1973–89, 203 games) and the Los Angeles Kings (1990–92, 24 games).

Goal Scoring Records

Fastest goal The fastest goal from the start of any playoff game was scored by Don Kozak (Los Angeles Kings) past Gerry Cheevers (Boston Bruins) with 6 seconds elapsed. The Kings went on to win 7-4; the game was played on April 17, 1977. Kozak's goal shares the mark for fastest goal from the start of any period with one scored by Pelle Eklund (Philadelphia Flyers). Eklund scored in the second period of a game against the Pittsburgh Penguins in Pittsburgh on April 25, 1989; his effort was in vain, however, as the Penguins won 10–7.

Shorthanded Goals Scored

Period The most shorthanded goals scored in a single period is two, shared by three players. Bryan Trottier was the first player to perform this feat, on April 8, 1990 for the New York Islanders vs. the Los Angeles Kings. His goals came in the second period of an 8–1 Islanders victory. Bobby Lalonde (Boston Bruins) matched Trottier on April 11, 1981. His double came in the third period of a Bruins 6–3 loss to the Minnesota North Stars. Jari Kurri (Edmonton Oilers) joined this club on April 24, 1983. His goals came in the third period of an Oilers 8–4 win over the Chicago Blackhawks.

Series The record for most shorthanded goals in a playoff series is three, shared by two players: Bill Barber (Philadelphia Flyers) in a Flyers 4–1 series victory over the Minnesota North Stars in 1980; and Wayne Presley (Chicago Blackhawks) in a series vs. the Detroit Red Wings in 1989.

Season The record for shorthanded goals in one season is three, shared by five players: Derek Sanderson (Boston Bruins) in 1969; Bill Barber (Philadelphia Flyers) in 1980; Lorne Henning (New York Islanders) in 1980; Wayne Gretzky (Edmonton Oilers) in 1983; and Wayne Presley (Chicago Blackhawks) in 1989.

Career Mark Messier (Edmonton Oilers, New York Rangers) holds the mark for career playoff goals at 14 in 221 games (1979–96).

In 1996, Wayne Gretzky joined the New York Rangers as a free agent. He continues to extend his NHL career marks for the Broadway Blues from the Great White Way.
(Nathaniel Butler/Allsport)

DEFENSEMEN RECORDS

Goal Scoring

Game The most goals scored by a defenseman in a playoff game is three, by nine players: Bobby Orr, Boston Bruins vs. Montreal Canadiens, April 11, 1971; Dick Redmond, Chicago Blackhawks vs. St. Louis Blues, April 4, 1973; Denis Potvin, New York Islanders vs. Edmonton Oilers, April 17, 1981; Paul Reinhart, Calgary Flames, who performed the feat twice, vs. Edmonton Oilers, April 14, 1983; vs. Vancouver Canucks, April 8, 1984; Doug Halward, Vancouver Canucks vs. Calgary Flames, April 7, 1984; Al Ioufrate, Washington Capitals vs. New York Islanders, April 26, 1993; Eric DesJardins, Montreal Canadiens vs. Los Angeles Kings, June 3, 1993; Gary Suter, Chicago Black Hawks vs. Toronto Maple Leafs, April 24, 1994; and Brian Leetch, New York Rangers vs. Philadelphia Flyers, May 22, 1995.

Season Paul Coffey (Edmonton Oilers) scored 12 goals in 18 games during the 1985 playoffs.

Career Paul Coffey (Edmonton Oilers, 1980–87; Pittsburgh Penguins, 1987–91; Los Angeles Kings, 1991–93; Detroit Red Wings, 1993–96) has scored a playoff record 58 goals.

Assists

Game The most assists in a game is five, by two players: Paul Coffey, Edmonton Oilers vs. Chicago Blackhawks on May 14, 1985; and Risto Siltanen, Quebec Nordiques vs. Hartford Whalers on April 14, 1987.

Season The most assists in one playoff year is 25 in 18 games, by Paul Coffey, Edmonton Oilers in 1985.

Career The most assists by a defenseman in a career is 128, by Paul Coffey (Edmonton Oilers, 1980–87; Pittsburgh Penguins, 1987–91; Los Angeles Kings, 1991–93; Detroit Red Wings, 1993–96). Coffey played in 172 games.

Point Scoring

Game Paul Coffey earned a record six points on one goal and five assists, for the Edmonton Oilers vs. the Chicago Blackhawks on May 14, 1985.

Season Paul Coffey also holds the record for most points by a defenseman in a season, with 37 in 1985 for the Edmonton Oilers. Coffey's total comprised 12 goals and 25 assists in 18 games.

Career Paul Coffey (Edmonton Oilers, 1980–87; Pittsburgh Penguins, 1987–91; Los Angeles Kings, 1991–93; Detroit Red Wings, 1993–96) has scored a playoff record 186 points. Coffey scored 58 goals and 128 assists in 172 games.

Consecutive Records

Point-scoring streak Bryan Trottier (New York Islanders) scored a point in 27 consecutive playoff games over three seasons (1980–82), scoring 16 goals and 26 assists for 42 points.

Goal-scoring streak Reggie Leach (Philadelphia Flyers) scored at least one goal in nine consecutive playoff games in 1976. The streak started on April 17 vs. the Toronto Maple Leafs, and ended on May 9 when he was shut out by the Montreal Canadiens. Overall, Leach scored 14 goals during his run.

Longest shutout sequence In the 1936 semi-final contest between the Detroit Red Wings and the Montreal Maroons, Norm Smith, the Red Wings goaltender, shut out the Maroons for 248 minutes, 32 seconds. The Maroons failed to score in the first two games (the second game lasted 116 minutes, 30 seconds, the longest overtime game in playoff history), and finally breached Smith's defenses at 12:02 of the first period in game three. The Red Wings swept the series 3–0.

Coaches

Most championships Toe Blake coached the Montreal Canadiens to eight Stanley Cups, 1956–60, 1965–66, 1968.

Most playoff wins Through the 1995–96 season the record for playoff wins is 162 games, by Scotty Bowman, St. Louis Blues, 1967–71 (26 wins), Montreal Canadiens, 1971–79 (70 wins), Buffalo Sabres, 1979–87 (18 wins), Pittsburgh Penguins, 1991–93 (23 wins), Detroit Red Wings, 1993–96 (25 wins).

Most games Scotty Bowman holds the mark for most games coached, at 263 with five teams: St. Louis Blues, 1967–71; Montreal Canadiens, 1971–79; Buffalo Sabres, 1979–87; Pittsburgh Penguins, 1991–93; Detroit Red Wings, 1993–96.

Stanley Cup Individual Records

Records in this section are listed only from the formation of the National Hockey League in 1917.

		Player(s)	Team(s)	Date(s)
Goals Scored				
Period	4	Tim Kerr	Philadelphia Flyers vs. New York Rangers	April 13, 1985
		Mario Lemieux	Pittsburgh Penguins vs. New York Rangers	April 25, 1989
Game	5	Newsy Lalonde	Montreal Canadiens vs. Ottawa Senators	March 1, 1919
		Maurice Richard	Montreal Canadiens vs. Toronto Maple Leafs	March 23, 1944
		Darryl Sittler	Toronto Maple Leafs vs. Philadelphia Flyers	April 22, 1976
		Reggie Leach	Philadelphia Flyers vs. Boston Bruins	May 6, 1976
		Mario Lemieux	Pittsburgh Penguins vs. Philadelphia Flyers	April 25, 1989
Series (any round)	12	Jari Kurri	Edmonton Oilers vs. Chicago Blackhawks	1985
Series (final)	9	Babe Dye	Toronto St. Patricks vs. Vancouver Millionaires	1922
Season	19	Reggie Leach	Philadelphia Flyers	1976
		Jari Kurri	Edmonton Oilers	1985
Career	112	Wayne Gretzky	Edmonton Oilers, Los Angeles Kings, St. Louis Blues	1979–96
Power-Play Goals Scored				
Period	3	Tim Kerr	Philadelphia Flyers vs. New York Rangers	April 13, 1985
Series	6	Chris Kontos	Los Angeles Kings vs. Edmonton Oilers	1989
Season	9	Mike Bossy	New York Islanders	1981
		Cam Neely	Boston Bruins	1991
Career	35	Mike Bossy	New York Islanders	1977–87
Points Scored				
Period	4	Maurice Richard	Montreal Canadiens vs. Toronto Maple Leafs	March 29, 1945
		Dickie Moore	Montreal Canadiens vs. Boston Bruins	March 25, 1954
		Barry Pederson	Boston Bruins vs. Buffalo Sabres	April 8, 1982
		Peter McNab	Boston Bruins vs. Buffalo Sabres	April 11, 1982
		Tim Kerr	Philadelphia Flyers vs. New York Rangers	April 13, 1985
		Ken Linseman	Boston Bruins vs. Montreal Canadiens	April 14, 1985
		Wayne Gretzky	Edmonton Oilers vs. Los Angeles Kings	April 12, 1987
		Glenn Anderson	Edmonton Oilers vs. Winnipeg Jets	April 6, 1988
		Mario Lemieux	Pittsburgh Penguins vs. Philadelphia Flyers	April 25, 1989
		Dave Gagner	Minnesota North Stars vs. Chicago Blackhawks	April 8, 1991
		Mario Lemieux	Pittsburgh Penguins vs. Washington Capitals	April 23, 1992
Game	8	Patrik Sundstrom	New Jersey Devils vs. Washington Capitals	April 22, 1988
		Mario Lemieux	Pittsburgh Penguins vs. Philadelphia Flyers	April 25, 1989
Series (any round)	19	Rick Middleton	Boston Bruins vs. Buffalo Sabres	1983
Series (final)	13	Wayne Gretzky	Edmonton Oilers vs. Boston Bruins	1988
Season	47	Wayne Gretzky	Edmonton Oilers	1985
Career	362	Wayne Gretzky	Edmonton Oilers, Los Angeles Kings, St. Louis Blues	1979–96
Assists				
Period	3	This feat has been achieved 64 times.		
Game	6	Mikko Leinonen	New York Rangers vs. Philadelphia Flyers	April 8, 1982
		Wayne Gretzky	Edmonton Oilers vs. Los Angeles Kings	April 9, 1987
Series (any round)	14	Rick Middleton	Boston Bruins vs. Buffalo Sabres	1983
		Wayne Gretzky	Edmonton Oilers vs. Chicago Blackhawks	1985
Series (final)	10	Wayne Gretzky	Edmonton Oilers vs. Boston Bruins	1988
Season	31	Wayne Gretzky	Edmonton Oilers	1988
Career	250	Wayne Gretzky	Edmonton Oilers, Los Angeles Kings, St. Louis Blues	1979–96

Source: NHL

King of the Crease

A two-time Smythe Trophy winner, Patrick Roy holds or shares several NHL goaltending records: including, most Stanley Cup games and minutes played, and most playoffs wins in a season. These achievements, however, mean little to the Quebec native: "The records are not very important to me. The important thing is winning," says Roy. "If you finish first overall and win the Cup, a lot of guys are going to get recognized. That is what is fun about winning. It's not just a one-guy thing. It's a group of guys who get credit for it."

Like most boys growing up in Canada, Roy became a devoted hockey fan at a young age. "I always wanted to be a goalie," declares Roy. "As a kid, I dreamed of wearing real goalie pads." His first hockey experience came in the family room not on the ice. "My brother and I played in the house with a tennis ball. I used a pillow with a belt tied around it for hockey pads." Laughs Roy, "The pillow was almost bigger than I was."

Once he had strapped on real pads, Roy's next goal was a Stanley Cup title. He has played on three winning teams and seeks more: "My objective when the season starts is to win the Stanley Cup and get myself ready for that." The keys to his success are confidence and concentration. Explains Roy:

Jed Jacobsohn/Allsport

"Confidence is a big part of the game. I get confidence from playing some good games." Concentration is vital too. "You have to be focused. I try to make myself hard to beat. If I give up a goal, I hope it will be a tough goal." Adds Roy, "The playoffs are more focused so concentration is a lot easier."

Roy rejects the notion that winning the Stanley Cup comes down to having a "hot goalie." "I have one problem with that," says Roy. "I didn't see any goalie score a goal in the final." The net-minder continues: "It's a little too much to single out a goaltender. John Vanbriesbrouck played outstanding in the finals last season, but we won because we made the big play and scored the big goal." He adds with emphasis: "Every player makes a contribution. It's teamwork that brings you to the Cup."

At 31, Roy has the opportunity to eclipse many NHL goalie records. But he doesn't think about that: "I don't need to put pressure on myself. I need to perform in the moment. It would be a distraction if you start to look at records," he says. The goalie maintains that his only wish is to "win the Stanley Cup every year." When pressed further, the modest goalie does admit to a secret peek at the record books. "I would like to pass Terry Sawchuk in career wins." Roy adds, "I know I can't reach his shutout record. The game is much more wide open today."

Stanley Cup Individual Records—Goaltenders

Shutouts

Season	4	Clint Benedict	Montreal Maroons	1926
		Clint Benedict	Montreal Maroons	1928
		Dave Kerr	New York Rangers	1937
		Frank McCool	Toronto Maple Leafs	1945
		Terry Sawchuk	Detroit Tigers	1952
		Bernie Parent	Philadelphia Flyers	1975
		Ken Dyrden	Montreal Canadiens	1977
		Mike Richter	New York Rangers	1994
		Kirk McLean	Vancouver Canucks	1994
Career	15	Clint Benedict	Ottawa Senators, Montreal Maroons	1917–30

Wins

Season	16	Grant Fuhr	Edmonton Oilers	1988
		Mike Vernon	Calgary Flames	1989
		Bill Ranford	Edmonton Oilers	1990
		Tom Barrasso	Pittsburgh Penguins	1992
		Patrick Roy	Montreal Canadiens	1993
		Mike Richter	New York Rangers	1994
		Martin Brodeur	New Jersey Devils	1995
		Patrick Roy	Colorado Avalanche	1996
Career	88	Billy Smith	Los Angeles Kings, New York Islanders	1971–89

Source: NHL

Stanley Cup Champions

Year	Champion	Loser	Series
1893	Montreal A.A.A.	(no challenger)	–
1894	Montreal A.A.A.	Ottawa Generals	3–1*
1895	Montreal Victorias	(no challenger)	–
1896	Winnipeg Victorias (February)	Montreal Victorias	2–0*
	Montreal Victorias (December)	Winnipeg Victorias	6–5*
1897	Montreal Victorias	Ottawa Capitals	15–2*
1898	Montreal Victorias	(no challenger)	–
1899	Montreal Victorias (February)	Winnipeg Victorias	2–0
	Montreal Shamrocks (March)	Queen's University	6–2*
1900	Montreal Shamrocks	Halifax Crescents	**
		Winnipeg Victorias	
1901	Winnipeg Victorias	Montreal Shamrocks	2–0
1902	Winnipeg Victorias (January)	Toronto Wellingtons	2–0
	Montreal A.A.A. (March)	Winnipeg Victorias	2–1
1903	Montreal A.A.A. (February)	Winnipeg Victorias	2–1
	Ottawa Silver Seven (March)	Rat Portage Thistles	**
		Montreal Victorias	
1904	Ottawa Silver Seven	Brandon Wheat Kings	**
		Montreal Wanderers	
		Toronto Marlboros	
		Winnipeg Rowing Club	
1905	Ottawa Silver Seven	Rat Portage Thistles	**
		Dawson City Nuggets	
1906	Ottawa Silver Seven (February)	Queen's University	**
		Smith's Falls	
	Montreal Wanderers (March)	New Glasgow Clubs	**
		Ottawa Silver Seven	
1907	Kenora Thistles (January)	Montreal Wanderers	2–0
	Montreal Wanderers (March)	Kenora Thistles	1–1†
1908	Montreal Wanderers	Edmonton Eskimos	**
		Toronto Maple Leafs	
		Winnipeg Maple Leafs	
		Ottawa Victorias	
1909	Ottawa Senators	(no challenger)	
1910	Ottawa Senators (January)	Galt	**
		Edmonton Eskimos	
	Montreal Wanderers (March)	Berlin (Kitchener)	7–3*
1911	Ottawa Senators	Galt	**
		Port Arthur	
1912	Quebec Bulldogs	Moncton Victorias	2–0
1913	Quebec Bulldogs	Sydney Miners	2–0

* Final score of single challenge game.
** Multiple challenger series.
† Series decided on total goals scored.

Stanley Cup Champions (continued)

Year	Champion	Loser	Series
1914	Toronto Blueshirts	Victoria Cougars	**
	Montreal Canadiens		
1915	Vancouver Millionaires	Ottawa Senators	3–0
1916	Montreal Canadiens	Portland Rosebuds	3–21
1917	Seattle Metropolitans	Montreal Canadiens	3–1
1918	Toronto Arenas	Vancouver Millionaires	3–2
1919	*no decision*		‡
1920	Ottawa Senators	Seattle Metropolitans	3–2
1921	Ottawa Senators	Vancouver Millionaires	3–2
1922	Toronto St. Patricks	Vancouver Millionaires	3–2
1923	Ottawa Senators	Vancouver Maroons	**
		Edmonton Eskimos	
1924	Montreal Canadiens	Vancouver Maroons	**
		Calgary Tigers	
1925	Victoria Cougars	Montreal Canadiens	3–1
1926	Montreal Maroons	Victoria Cougars	3–1
1927	Ottawa Senators	Boston Bruins	2–0
1928	New York Rangers	Montreal Maroons	3–2
1929	Boston Bruins	New York Rangers	2–0
1930	Montreal Canadiens	Boston Bruins	2–0
1931	Montreal Canadiens	Chicago Blackhawks	3–2
1932	Toronto Maple Leafs	New York Rangers	3–0
1933	New York Rangers	Toronto Maple Leafs	3–1
1934	Chicago Blackhawks	Detroit Red Wings	3–1
1935	Montreal Maroons	Toronto Maple Leafs	3–0
1936	Detroit Red Wings	Toronto Maple Leafs	3–1
1937	Detroit Red Wings	New York Rangers	3–2
1938	Chicago Blackhawks	Toronto Maple Leafs	3–1
1939	Boston Bruins	Toronto Maple Leafs	4–1
1940	New York Rangers	Toronto Maple Leafs	4–2
1941	Boston Bruins	Detroit Red Wings	4–0
1942	Toronto Maple Leafs	Detroit Red Wings	4–3
1943	Detroit Red Wings	Boston Bruins	4–0
1944	Montreal Canadiens	Chicago Blackhawks	4–0
1945	Toronto Maple Leafs	Detroit Red Wings	4–3
1946	Montreal Canadiens	Boston Bruins	4–1
1947	Toronto Maple Leafs	Montreal Canadiens	4–2
1948	Toronto Maple Leafs	Detroit Red Wings	4–0
1949	Toronto Maple Leafs	Detroit Red Wings	4–0
1950	Detroit Red Wings	New York Rangers	4–3
1951	Toronto Maple Leafs	Montreal Canadiens	4–1
1952	Detroit Red Wings	Montreal Canadiens	4–0

** Multiple challenger series.
‡ Due to an influenza epidemic in Seattle, the final series between the Montreal Canadiens and the Seattle Metropolitans was canceled. The series was tied 2–2–1 in games.

Stanley Cup Champions (continued)

Year	Champion	Loser	Series
1953	Montreal Canadiens	Boston Bruins	4–1
1954	Detroit Red Wings	Montreal Canadiens	4–3
1955	Detroit Red Wings	Montreal Canadiens	4–3
1956	Montreal Canadiens	Detroit Red Wings	4–1
1957	Montreal Canadiens	Boston Bruins	4–1
1958	Montreal Canadiens	Boston Bruins	4–2
1959	Montreal Canadiens	Toronto Maple Leafs	4–1
1960	Montreal Canadiens	Toronto Maple Leafs	4–0
1961	Chicago Blackhawks	Detroit Red Wings	4–2
1962	Toronto Maple Leafs	Chicago Blackhawks	4–2
1963	Toronto Maple Leafs	Detroit Red Wings	4–1
1964	Toronto Maple Leafs	Detroit Red Wings	4–3
1965	Montreal Canadiens	Chicago Blackhawks	4–3
1966	Montreal Canadiens	Detroit Red Wings	4–2
1967	Toronto Maple Leafs	Montreal Canadiens	4–2
1968	Montreal Canadiens	St. Louis Blues	4–0
1969	Montreal Canadiens	St. Louis Blues	4–0
1970	Boston Bruins	St. Louis Blues	4–0
1971	Montreal Canadiens	Chicago Blackhawks	4–3
1972	Boston Bruins	New York Rangers	4–2
1973	Montreal Canadiens	Chicago Blackhawks	4–2
1974	Philadelphia Flyers	Boston Bruins	4–2
1975	Philadelphia Flyers	Buffalo Sabres	4–2
1976	Montreal Canadiens	Philadelphia Flyers	4–0
1977	Montreal Canadiens	Boston Bruins	4–0
1978	Montreal Canadiens	Boston Bruins	4–2
1979	Montreal Canadiens	New York Rangers	4–1
1980	New York Islanders	Philadelphia Flyers	4–2
1981	New York Islanders	Minnesota North Stars	4–1
1982	New York Islanders	Vancouver Canucks	4–0
1983	New York Islanders	Edmonton Oilers	4–0
1984	Edmonton Oilers	New York Islanders	4–1
1985	Edmonton Oilers	Philadelphia Flyers	4–1
1986	Montreal Canadiens	Calgary Flames	4–1
1987	Edmonton Oilers	Philadelphia Flyers	4–3
1988	Edmonton Oilers	Boston Bruins	4–0
1989	Calgary Flames	Montreal Canadiens	4–2
1990	Edmonton Oilers	Boston Bruins	4–1
1991	Pittsburgh Penguins	Minnesota North Stars	4–2
1992	Pittsburgh Penguins	Chicago Blackhawks	4–0
1993	Montreal Canadiens	Los Angeles Kings	4–1
1994	New York Rangers	Vancouver Canucks	4–3
1995	New Jersey Devils	Detroit Red Wings	4–0
1996	Colorado Avalanche	Florida Panthers	4–0

OLYMPIC GAMES

Hockey was included in the 1920 Summer Olympics in Antwerp, Belgium, and has been an integral part of the Winter Olympics since its introduction in 1924.

Most gold medals (country) The USSR/Unified Team has won eight Olympic titles, in 1956, 1964, 1968, 1972, 1976, 1984, 1988 and 1992.

World Championships (Men)

The world championships were first held in 1920 in conjunction with the Olympic Games. Since 1930, the world championships have been held annually. Through the 1964 Olympics, the Games were considered the world championships, and records for those Games are included in this section. Since 1976, the championships have been open to professionals.

Most titles The USSR has won the world championship 22 times: 1954, 1956, 1963–71, 1973–75, 1978–79, 1981–83, 1986, 1989–90.

Most consecutive titles The USSR won nine consecutive championships from 1963–71.

World Championships (Women)

The inaugural tournament was held in 1990.

Most wins Canada has won three times: 1990, 1992 and 1994.

NCAA Championships

A men's Division I hockey championship was first staged in 1948, and has been held annually since then.

Most wins Michigan has won the title eight times: 1948, 1951–53, 1955–56, 1964 and 1996 .

The Swedish team celebrates its 1994 Olympic victory.
(Chris Cole/Allsport)

HORSE RACING

Origins

Horsemanship was an important part of the Hittite culture of Anatolia, Turkey, dating from 1400 B.C. The 33rd ancient Olympic Games of 648 B.C. in Greece featured horse racing. Horse races can be traced in England from the 3rd century. The first sweepstakes race was originated by the 12th Earl of Derby at his estate in Epsom in 1780. The Epsom Derby is still run today and is the classic race of the English flat racing season.

United States Horses were introduced to the North American continent from Spain by Cortés in 1519. In colonial America, horse racing was common. Colonel Richard Nicholls, commander of English forces in New York, is believed to have staged the first organized race at Salisbury Plain, Long Island, NY in 1665. The first jockey club to be founded was in Charleston, SC in 1734. Thoroughbred racing was first staged in Saratoga Springs, NY in 1863.

RACING RECORDS (UNITED STATES)

HORSES

Career Records

Most wins The most wins in a racing career is 89, by Kingston, from 138 starts, 1986–94.

Most wins (graded stakes races) John Henry won 25 graded stakes races, including 16 Grade I races, 1978–84.

Highest Earnings

Career The career record for earnings is $9,999,815, by Cigar, 1992–96. Cigar's career record was 19 wins, four seconds and five thirds from 33 races.

Season The single-season earnings record is $4,910,000, by Cigar, in 1996, from eight starts (five wins, two seconds and one third).

Single race The richest race in the United States is the Breeders' Cup Classic, which carries a purse of $4 million, with first-place prize money of $2,080,000 to the winner.

JOCKEYS (MEN)
Career Records

Most wins Bill Shoemaker rode a record 8,833 winners from 40,350 mounts. "The Shoe" made his debut aboard Waxahachie on March 19, 1949, and raced for the last time on Patchy Groundfog on February 3, 1990. His first victory came on April 20, 1949 aboard Shafter V, his last on January 20, 1990 aboard Beau Genius at Gulfstream Park, FL.

Season Records

Most wins Kent Desormeaux rode a season record 598 winners, from 2,312 mounts, in 1989.

Most wins (stakes races) Mike Smith rode a season record 67 stakes race winners in 1994.

Daily Records

Most wins (single day) The most winners ridden in one day is nine, by Chris Antley on October 31, 1987. Antley rode four winners in the afternoon at Aqueduct, NY and five in the evening at The Meadowlands, NJ.

Most wins (one card) The most winners ridden on one card is eight, achieved by four jockeys: Hubert Jones, from 13 rides, in Caliente, CA, on June 11, 1944; Dave Gall, from 10 rides, at Cahokia Downs, East St. Louis, IL, on October 18, 1978; Robert Williams, from 10 rides, in Lincoln, NE, on September 29, 1984; and Pat Day, from nine rides, in Arlington, IL, on September 13, 1989.

Consecutive wins The longest consecutive winning streak by a jockey is nine races, by two jockeys. Albert Adams won nine races at Marlboro Racetrack, MD, over three days, September 10–12, 1930. He won the last two races on September 10,

Day at the Races

"I always loved horses," says champion jockey Pat Day. Horse racing, however, was not his first love: "Through my adolescent years, I pursued a career in rodeo. That was my first dream." Confesses Day, "I wanted to be a bull rider." When Day's rodeo ambitions spluttered, friends suggested he had the skills to be a jockey. At 19, Pat Day secured his first mount in a horse race. That day a record-breaking career broke from the stalls.

The Colorado native has won triple crown races and ridden winners at tracks across North America. His particular forte, however, is the Breeders's Cup races. Day dominates the record book of horse racing's biggest card of races. He leads all jockeys in victories and earnings, and has ridden two Classic winners—North America's richest race. Day is self-effacing about his success. "I have never thought about records," he says.

In a career of many highlights, eight wins in one day is a particularly memorable feat even for a jockey of Day's stature. "It was rainy and the track was muddy," recalls the jockey. "It was a great accomplishment, but to be honest I've had no time to reflect on it. My intention is always to try and win." Adds Day, "It thrust my career upward. Success begets success in whatever

Andy Lyons/Allsport

walk of life you happen to be in."

Like race car drivers, jockeys must confront the danger inherent in their profession. "The danger element is ever present but not one that any of us consciously think about." Observes the champion jockey: "You can't ride a good heavy race if you're overly concerned about it. Otherwise, you become a wreck looking for a place to happen." A deeply religious man, Day credits this stoicism to his faith: "I've been made by God to be a jockey," he says.

Day cautions aspiring jockeys that their career track will be heavy going. "It's very competitive. Start with a job on a farm and begin to make connections." Day advises, "You need to do the menial tasks on the farm and remember that there is a natural progression from the farms to the race tracks." Day followed this path himself. He got his start mucking out stalls and brushing horses at a thoroughbred farm in Riverside, CA before moving to Las Vegas Downs where he exercised horses and gained his first rides. Day exhorts young jockeys to never give up. "Don't lose focus, you might be only one step away from your dream." He adds, "Life is 10 percent of happens and 90 percent how you react to it."

---

all six races on September 11, and the first race on September 12. Tony Black won nine races on July 30–31, 1993. He won three races at Atlantic City Racecourse on July 30, two at Philadelphia Park on July 31 and four at Atlantic City on July 31.

Highest Earnings

Career Laffit Pincay Jr. has won a career record $190,538,811 from 1964 through the end of 1996.

Season The greatest prize money earned in a single season is $19,465,376, by Jerry Bailey in 1996.

JOCKEYS (WOMEN)

Most wins Julie Krone has won a record 3,158 races from 1980 through 1996.

Highest earnings Julie Krone has won a record $70,560,436 from 1980 through the end of 1996.

Triple Crown Winners

The races that make up the Triple Crown are the Kentucky Derby, the Preakness Stakes and the Belmont Stakes. The Triple Crown is for three-year-olds only and has been won by 11 horses.

Year	Horse	Jockey	Trainer	Owner
1919	Sir Barton	Johnny Loftus	H. Guy Bedwell	J. K. L. Ross
1930	Gallant Fox	Earl Sande	J. E. Fitzsimmons	Belair Stud
1935	Omaha	Willie Saunders	J. E. Fitzsimmons	Belair Stud
1937	War Admiral	Chas. Kurtsinger	George Conway	Samuel Riddle
1941	Whirlaway	Eddie Arcaro	Ben A. Jones	Calumet Farm
1943	Count Fleet	Johnny Longden	Don Cameron	Mrs. J. D. Hertz
1946	Assault	Warren Mehrtens	Max Hirsch	King Ranch
1948	Citation	Eddie Arcaro	Ben A. Jones	Calumet Farm
1973	Secretariat	Ron Turcotte	Lucien Laurin	Meadow Stable
1977	Seattle Slew	Jean Cruguet	Billy Turner	Karen Taylor
1978	Affirmed	Steve Cauthen	Laz Barrera	Harbor View Farm

Jim Fitzsimmons and Ben Jones are the only trainers to have trained two Triple Crown winners. Eddie Arcaro is the only jockey to have ridden two Triple Crown winners.

Grindstone won the 1996 "Run for the Roses."
(Simon Bruty/Allsport)

Kentucky Derby Winners

This event is held on the first Saturday in May at Churchill Downs, Louisville, Ky. The first race was run in 1875 over 1 1/2 miles; the distance was shortened to 1 1/4 miles in 1896 and is still run at that length.

Most Wins

Jockey   Five, by two jockeys: Eddie Arcaro (1938, 1941, 1945, 1948, 1952); Bill Hartack (1957, 1960, 962, 1964, 1969).

Trainer   Six, by Ben Jones (1938, 1941, 1944, 1948–49, 1952).

Owner   Eight, by Calumet Farm (1941, 1944, 1948–49, 1952, 1957–58, 1968).

Fastest Time

1 minute 59 2/5 seconds, by Secretariat, 1973.

Largest Field

23 horses in 1974.

Year	Horse	Year	Horse	Year	Horse	Year	Horse
1875	Aristides	1905	Agile	1936	Bold Venture	1967	Proud Clarion
1876	Vagrant	1906	Sir Huon	1937	War Admiral	1968	Forward Pass
1877	Baden-Baden	1907	Pink Star	1938	Lawrin	1969	Majestic Prince
1878	Day Star	1908	Stone Street	1939	Johnstown	1970	Dust Commander
1879	Lord Murphy	1909	Wintergreen	1940	Giallahadian	1971	Canonero II
1880	Fonso	1910	Donau	1941	Whirlaway	1972	Riva Ridge
1881	Hindoo	1911	Meridian	1942	Shut Out	1973	Secretariat
1882	Apollo	1912	Worth	1943	Count Fleet	1974	Cannonade
1883	Leonatus	1913	Donerail	1944	Pensive	1975	Foolish Pleasure
1884	Buchanan	1914	Old Rosebud	1945	Hoop Jr.	1976	Bold Forbes
1885	Joe Cotton	1915	Regret	1946	Assault	1977	Seattle Slew
1886	Ben Ali	1916	George Smith	1947	Jet Pilot	1978	Affirmed
1887	Montrose	1917	Omar Khayyam	1948	Citation	1979	Spectacular Bid
1888	Macbeth II	1918	Exterminator	1949	Ponder	1980	Genuine Risk
1889	Spokane	1919	Sir Barton	1950	Middleground	1981	Pleasant Colony
1890	Riley	1920	Paul Jones	1951	Count Turf	1982	Gato Del Sol
1891	Kingman	1921	Behave Yourself	1952	Hill Gail	1983	Sunny's Halo
1892	Azra	1922	Morvich	1953	Dark Star	1984	Swale
1893	Lookout	1923	Zev	1954	Determine	1985	Spend a Buck
1894	Chant	1924	Black Gold	1955	Swaps	1986	Ferdinand
1895	Halma	1925	Flying Ebony	1956	Needles	1987	Alysheba
1896	Ben Brush	1926	Bubbling Over	1957	Iron Liege	1988	Winning Colors
1897	Typhoon II	1927	Whiskery	1958	Tim Tam	1989	Sunday Silence
1898	Plaudit	1928	Reigh Count	1959	Tomy Lee	1990	Unbridled
1899	Manuel	1929	Clyde Van Dusen	1960	Venetian Way	1991	Strike the Gold
1900	Lieut. Gibson	1930	Gallant Fox	1961	Carry Back	1992	Lil E. Tee
1901	His Eminence	1931	Twenty Grand	1962	Decidedly	1993	Sea Hero
1902	Alan-a-Dale	1932	Burgoo King	1963	Chateaugay	1994	Go for Gin
1903	Judge Himes	1933	Brokers Tip	1964	Northern Dancer	1995	Thunder Gulch
1904	Elwood	1934	Cavalcade	1965	Lucky Debonair	1996	Grindstone
		1935	Omaha	1966	Kauai King		

Preakness Stakes Winners

Inaugurated in 1873, this event is held annually at Pimlico Race Course, Baltimore., Md. Originally run at 1 1/2 miles, the distance was changed several times before being settled at the current length of 1 3/16 miles in 1925.

Most Wins

Jockey Six, by Eddie Arcaro (1941, 1948, 1950–51, 1955, 1957).

Trainer Seven, by Robert Wyndham Walden (1875, 1878–82, 1888).

Owner Five, by George Lorillard (1878–82).

Fastest Time

1 minute 53 2/5 seconds, by Tank's Prospect, 1985 and by Louis Quatorze, 1996.

Largest Field

18 horses in 1928.

Year	Horse	Year	Horse	Year	Horse	Year	Horse
1873	Survivor	1904	Bryn Mawr	1935	Omaha	1967	Damascus
1874	Culpepper	1905	Cairngorm	1936	Bold Venture	1968	Forward Pass
1875	Tom Ochiltree	1906	Whimsical	1937	War Admiral	1969	Majestic Prince
1876	Shirley	1907	Don Enrique	1938	Dauber	1970	Personality
1877	Cloverbrook	1908	Royal Tourist	1939	Challedon	1971	Canonero II
1878	Duke of Magenta	1909	Effendi	1940	Bimelech	1972	Bee Bee Bee
1879	Harold	1910	Layminister	1941	Whirlaway	1973	Secretariat
1880	Grenada	1911	Watervale	1942	Alsab	1974	Little Current
1881	Saunterer	1912	Colonel Holloway	1943	Count Fleet	1975	Master Derby
1882	Vanguard	1913	Buskin	1944	Pensive	1976	Elocutionist
1883	Jacobus	1914	Holiday	1945	Polynesian	1977	Seattle Slew
1884	Knight of Ellerslie	1915	Rhine Maiden	1946	Assault	1978	Affirmed
1885	Tecumseh	1916	Damrosch	1947	Faultless	1979	Spectacular Bid
1886	The Bard	1917	Kalitan	1948	Citation	1980	Codex
1887	Dunboyne	1918	War Cloud*	1949	Capot	1981	Pleasant Colony
1888	Refund	1918	Jack Hare Jr.*	1950	Hill Prince	1982	Aloma's Ruler
1889	Buddhist	1919	Sir Barton	1951	Bold	1983	Deputed Testamony
1890	Montague	1920	Man o'War	1952	Blue Man	1984	Gate Dancer
1891	*not held*	1921	Broomspun	1953	Native Dancer	1985	Tank's Prospect
1892	*not held*	1922	Pillory	1954	Hasty Road	1986	Snow Chief
1893	*not held*	1923	Vigil	1955	Nashua	1987	Alysheba
1894	Assignee	1924	Nellie Morse	1956	Fabius	1988	Risen Star
1895	Belmar	1925	Coventry	1957	Bold Ruler	1989	Sunday Silence
1896	Margrave	1926	Display	1958	Tim Tam	1990	Summer Squall
1897	Paul Kauvar	1927	Bostonian	1959	Royal Orbit	1991	Hansel
1898	Sly Fox	1928	Victorian	1960	Bally Ache	1992	Pine Bluff
1899	Half Time	1929	Dr. Freeland	1961	Carry Back	1993	Prairie Bayou
1900	Hindus	1930	Gallant Fox	1962	Greek Money	1994	Tabasco Cat
1901	The Parader	1931	Mate	1963	Candy Spots	1995	Timber Country
1902	Old England	1932	Burgoo King	1964	Northern Dancer	1996	Louis Quatorze
1903	Flocarline	1933	Head Play	1965	Tom Rolfe		
		1934	High Quest	1966	Kauai King		

* The 1918 race was run in two divisions.

Belmont Stakes Winners

This race is the third leg of the Triple Crown, first run in 1867 at Jerome Park, N.Y. Since 1905 the race has been staged at Belmont Park, NY. Originally run over 1 mile 5 furlongs, the current distance of 1 1/2 miles has been set since 1926.

Most Wins

Jockey Six, by two jockeys: Jim McLaughlin (1882–84, 1886–88); Eddie Arcaro (1941–42, 1945, 1948, 1952, 1955).

Trainer Eight, by James Rowe Sr. (1883–84, 1901, 1904, 1907–08, 1910. 1913).

Owner Six, by three owners: Belmont Family (1869, 1896, 1902, 1916–17, 1983); James R. Keene (1879, 1901, 1904, 1907–08, 1910); Belair Stud (1930, 1932, 1935–36, 1939, 1955).

Fastest Time

2 minutes 24 seconds, by Secretariat, 1973.

Largest Field

15 horses, in 1983.

Year	Horse				
1867	Ruthless	1899	Jean Bereaud	1932	Faireno	1965	Hail to All
1868	General Duke	1900	Ildrim	1933	Hurryoff	1966	Amberoid
1869	Fenian	1901	Commando	1934	Peace Chance	1967	Damascus
1870	Kingfisher	1902	Masterman	1935	Omaha	1968	Stage Door Johnny
1871	Harry Bassett	1903	Africander	1936	Granville	1969	Arts and Letters
1872	Joe Daniels	1904	Delhi	1937	War Admiral	1970	High Echelon
1873	Springbok	1905	Tanya	1938	Pasteurized	1971	Pass Catcher
1874	Saxon	1906	Burgomaster	1939	Johnstown	1972	Riva Ridge
1875	Calvin	1907	Peter Pan	1940	Bimelech	1973	Secretariat
1876	Algerine	1908	Colin	1941	Whirlaway	1974	Little Current
1877	Cloverbrook	1909	Joe Madden	1942	Shut Out	1975	Avatar
1878	Duke of Magenta	1910	Sweep	1943	Count Fleet	1976	Bold Forbes
1879	Spendthrift	1911	*not held*	1944	Bounding Home	1977	Seattle Slew
1880	Grenada	1912	*not held*	1945	Pavot	1978	Affirmed
1881	Saunterer	1913	Prince Eugene	1946	Assault	1979	Coastal
1882	Forester	1914	Luke McLuke	1947	Phalanx	1980	Temperence Hill
1883	George Kinney	1915	The Finn	1948	Citation	1981	Summing
1884	Panique	1916	Friar Rock	1949	Capot	1982	Conquistador Cielo
1885	Tyrant	1917	Hourless	1950	Middleground	1983	Caveat
1886	Inspector B.	1918	Johren	1951	Counterpoint	1984	Swale
1887	Hanover	1919	Sir Barton	1952	One Count	1985	Creme Fraiche
1888	Sir Dixon	1920	Man o'War	1953	Native Dancer	1986	Danzig Connection
1889	Eric	1921	Grey Lag	1954	High Gun	1987	Bet Twice
1890	Burlington	1922	Pillory	1955	Nashua	1988	Risen Star
1891	Foxford	1923	Zev	1956	Needles	1989	Easy Goer
1892	Patron	1924	Mad Play	1957	Gallant Man	1990	Go and Go
1893	Commanche	1925	American Flag	1958	Cavan	1991	Hansel
1894	Henry of Navarre	1926	Crusader	1959	Sword Dancer	1992	A.P. Indy
1895	Belmar	1927	Chance Shot	1960	Celtic Ash	1993	Colonial Affair
1896	Hastings	1928	Vito	1961	Sherluck	1994	Tabasco Cat
1897	Scottish Chieftain	1929	Blue Larkspur	1962	Jaipur	1995	Thunder Gulch
1898	Bowling Brook	1930	Gallant Fox	1963	Chateaugay	1996	Editor's Note
		1931	Twenty Grand	1964	Quadrangle		

BREEDERS' CUP CHAMPIONSHIP

The Breeders' Cup Championship has been staged annually since 1984. It was devised by John R. Gaines, a leading thoroughbred owner and breeder, to provide a season-ending championship for each division of thoroughbred racing.

The Breeders' Cup Championship consists of seven races: Juvenile, Juvenile Fillies, Sprint, Mile, Distaff, Turf and the Classic, with a record purse of $11 million.

CHAMPIONSHIP RECORDS

Horses

Most wins   Three horses have won two Breeders' Cup races: Bayakoa, which won the Distaff in 1989 and 1990; Miesque, which won the Mile in 1987 and 1988; and Lure, which won the Mile in 1992 and 1993.

Highest earnings   Alysheba has won a record $2,133,000 in Breeders' Cup races, from three starts, 1986–88.

Jockeys

Most wins   Two jockeys have ridden seven winners in the Breeders' Cup Championship: Laffit Pincay Jr., Juvenile (1985, 1986, 1988), Classic (1986), Distaff (1989, 1990), Juvenile Fillies (1993); and Eddie Delahoussaye, Distaff (1984, 1993), Turf (1989), Juvenile Fillies (1991), Sprint (1992, 1993).

Highest earnings   Pat Day has won a record $13,503,000 in Breeders' Cup racing, 1984–96.

Breeders' Cup Classic

This race, the principal event of the Breeders' Cup Championship, is run over 1 1/4 miles. The Classic offers a single-race record $4 million purse, with $2,080,000 to the winner.

Most wins (horse)   The Classic has been won by a different horse on each occasion.

Most wins (jockey)   Jerry Bailey has won the Classic three times: 1991, 1993 and 1995.

One of the world's oldest sports, horse racing can be traced to the ancient Greeks. Today the biggest race weekend is the annual Breeders' Cup races, which were staged in Toronto in 1996.
(Gray Mortimore/Allsport)

INTERNATIONAL RACES

VRC Melbourne Cup

This contest, Australia's most prestigious classic race, has been staged annually since 1861. The race is run almost two miles at the Flemington Racetrack, Victoria.

Fastest time The fastest time is 3 minutes 16.3 seconds, by Kingston Rule, ridden by Darren Beadman in 1990.

Most wins (jockeys) Two jockeys have won the race four times: Bobby Lewis, 1902, 1915, 1919 and 1927; Harry White, 1974–75 and 1978–79.

Italian jockey Frankie Dettori swept the complete seven-race card at Ascot Race Course, the home of British horse racing.
(Allsport)

Derby

England's most prestigious classic race has been staged annually since 1780. The race is contested over 1 mile 4 furlongs at Epsom Downs, Surrey.

Fastest time The fastest time is 2 minutes 32.31 seconds, by Lammtarra, ridden by Walter Swinburn, in 1995.

Most wins (jockey) Lester Piggott has won the Derby a record nine times: 1954, 1957, 1960, 1968, 1970, 1972, 1976–77 and 1983.

Grand National

England's most famous steeplechase race, and most beloved sporting event, has been staged annually since 1839. The race is contested over a 4-mile course of 30 fences at Aintree, Liverpool.

Fastest time Mr. Frisk, ridden by Marcus Armytage, finished in 8 minutes 47.8 seconds in 1990.

Most wins (jockey) George Stevens won the National five times: 1856, 1863–64 and 1869–70.

Prix de l'Arc de Triomphe

France's most prestigious classic race, and Europe's richest thoroughbred race, has been staged annually since 1920. The race is contested over 1 mile 864 yards at Longchamps, Paris.

Fastest time The fastest time is 2 minutes 26.3 seconds, by Trempolino, ridden by Pat Eddery, in 1987.

Most wins (jockeys) Four jockeys have won the Arc four times: Jacques Doyasbere, 1942, 1944, 1950–51; Freddy Head, 1966, 1972, 1976, 1979; Yves Saint-Martin, 1970, 1974, 1982, 1984; Pat Eddery, 1980, 1985–87.

Irish Derby

Ireland's most prestigious classic race has been staged annually since 1866. The race is contested over 1 1/2 miles at The Curragh, County Kildare.

Fastest time The fastest time is 2 minutes 25.6 seconds, by St. Jovite, ridden by Christie Roche in 1992.

Most wins (jockey) Morny Wing has won the Irish Derby a record six times: 1921, 1923, 1930, 1938, 1942 and 1946.

HURLING

Most titles The greatest number of All-Ireland Championships won by one team is 27, by Cork, between 1890 and 1990. The greatest number of successive wins is four, by Cork (1941–44).

Most appearances The most appearances in All-Ireland finals is 10, shared by Christy Ring (Cork and Munster); John Doyle (Tipperary); and Frank Cummins (Kilkenny). Ring and Doyle also share the record of All-Ireland medals won, with eight each. Ring's appearances on the winning side were in 1941–44, 1946 and 1952–54, while Doyle's were in 1949–51, 1958, 1961–62 and 1964–65. Ring also played in a record 22 interprovincial finals (1942–63), and was on the winning side 18 times.

The traditional Irish sport of hurling dates to the 19th century. The All-Ireland Final takes place each September.
(Simon Bruty/Allsport)

Highest and lowest scores

The highest score in an All-Ireland final (60 minutes) was in 1989, when Tipperary, 41 (4 goals, 29 points) beat Antrim, 18 (3 goals, 9 points).

The record aggregate score was when Cork, 39 (6 goals, 21 points) defeated Wexford, 25 (5 goals, 10 points), in the 80-minute final of 1970.

The highest recorded individual score was by Nick Rackard (Wexford), who scored 7 goals and 7 points against Antrim in the 1954 All-Ireland semifinal.

The lowest score in an All-Ireland final was when Tipperary (1 goal, 1 point) beat Galway (zero) in the first championship at Birr in 1887.

Largest crowd The largest crowd was 84,865 for the All-Ireland Final between Cork and Wexford at Croke Park, Dublin in 1954.

JAI ALAI
(PELOTA VASCA)

World Championships

The *Federación Internacional de Pelota Vasca* stages World Championships every four years (the first in 1952). The most successful pair has been Roberto Elias and Juan Labat (Argentina), who won the Trinquete Share four times, 1952, 1958, 1962 and 1966. Labat won a record seven world titles in all between 1952 and 1966. Riccardo Bizzozero (Argentina) also won seven world titles in various Trinquete and Frontón Corto events, 1970–1982. The most wins in the long court game Cesta Punta is three, by José Hanuy (Mexico; 1934–83), with two different partners, 1958, 1962 and 1966.

Fastest speed An electronically measured ball velocity of 188 mph was recorded by José Ramon Areitio (Spain) at the Newport (RI) Jai Alai on August 3, 1979.

Longest domination The longest domination as the world's No. 1 player was enjoyed by Chiquito de Cambo (France; born Joseph Apesteguy) from the beginning of the century until 1938.

Largest frontón The world's largest frontón (enclosed stadium) is the Palm Beach Jai Alai, West Palm Beach, which has a seating capacity of 6,000 and covers three acres.

Largest crowd The record attendance for a jai alai contest was 15,052 people at the World Jai Alai in Miami, FL on December 7, 1975. The frontón has seating capacity for only 3,884.

LACROSSE

LACROSSE (MEN)

Origins

The sport is of Native American origin, derived from the intertribal game of baggataway, which has been recorded as being played by Iroquois tribes as early as

The world's fastest racket sport is jai alai. The speed of the ball has been electronically measured at 188 mph.
(Jean Guyot/Vandystadt/Allsport)

1492. French settlers in North America coined the name "La Crosse" (the French word for a crozier or staff). The National Lacrosse Association was formed in Canada in 1867. The United States Amateur Lacrosse Association was founded in 1879. The International Federation of Amateur Lacrosse (IFAL) was founded | in 1928.

World Championships

The men's world championships were first staged in Toronto, Canada in 1967.

Most titles The United States has won six world titles, in 1967, 1974, 1982, 1986, 1990 and 1994.

NCAA Campionships (Division I)

The men's NCAA championship was first staged in 1971.

Most titles Johns Hopkins has won seven lacrosse titles, in 1974, 1978–80, 1984–85 and 1987.

NCAA Championships (Division II)

The men's division began play in 1974.

Most titles Adelphi has won four titles: 1979, 1981, 1993, and 1995.

NCAA Championships (Division III)

The men's division started in 1980.

Most titles Hobart College has won 13 titles, 1980–91 and 1993.

LACROSSE (WOMEN)

Origins

Women were first reported to have played lacrosse in 1886. The women's game evolved separately from the men's, developing different rules; thus two distinct games were created: the women's game features 12-a-side and six-a-side games, while men's games field 10-a-side teams.

World Championships

A women's world championship was first held in 1969. Since 1982 the world championships have been known as the World Cup.

Most titles The United States has won four world titles, in 1974, 1982, 1989, and 1993.

NCAA Championships (Division I)

The NCAA first staged a women's national championship in 1982.

Most titles Maryland has won four titles: 1986, 1992, and 1995–96.

NCAA Championships (Division III)

The women's division began play in 1985.

Most titles Trenton State has won eight titles, 1985, 1987–88, 1991, 1993–96.

MARTIAL ARTS

JUDO

Origins

Judo is a modern combat sport that developed from an amalgam of several old Japanese martial arts, the most popular of which was ju-jitsu (jiujitsu), which is thought to be of Chinese origin. Judo has developed greatly since 1882, when it was first devised by Dr. Jigoro Kano. The International Judo Federation was founded in 1951.

Highest grades　The efficiency grades in judo are divided into pupil (kyu) and master (dan) grades. The highest grade awarded is the extremely rare red belt judan (10th dan), given to only 13 men so far. The judo protocol provides for an 11th dan (juichidan) who also would wear a red belt, a 12th dan (junidan) who would wear a white belt twice as wide as an ordinary belt, and the highest of all, shihan (doctor), but these have never been bestowed, save for the 12th dan, to the founder of the sport, Dr. Jigoro Kano.

Olympic Games

Judo was first included in the Games in 1964 in Tokyo, Japan, and has been included in every Games since 1972. Women's events were first included as official events at the Barcelona Games in 1992.

Most gold medals　Four men have won two gold medals: Willem Ruska (Netherlands), open class and over 93 kilograms class, in 1972; Hiroshi Saito (Japan), over 95 kilograms class, in 1984 and 1988; Peter Seisenbacher (Austria), up to 86 kilograms class, in 1984 and 1988; and Waldemar Legien (Poland), up to 78 kilograms class, in 1988 and up to 86 kilograms class, in 1992.

Most medals (individual)　Angelo Parisi has won a record four Olympic medals, while representing two countries. In 1972 Parisi won a bronze medal in the open class, representing Great Britain. In 1980 Parisi represented France and won a gold, over 95 kilograms class, and a silver, open class; and won a second silver in the open class in 1984.

World Championships

The first men's world championships were held in Tokyo, Japan in 1956. The event has been staged biennially since 1965. A world championship for women was first staged in New York City in 1980.

Most titles (women)　Ingrid Berghmans (Belgium) has won a record six world titles: open class, 1980, 1982, 1984 and 1986; under 72 kilograms class, 1984 and 1989.

Most titles (men)　Three men have won four world titles: Yasuhiro Yamashita (Japan), open class, 1981; over 95 kilograms class, 1979, 1981, 1983; Shozo Fujii (Japan), under 80 kilograms class, 1971, 1973, 1975; under 78 kilograms class, 1979; and Naoya Ogawa (Japan), open class, 1987, 1989, 1991 and over 95 kilograms class, 1989.

➠ Fantastic Feats

Judo throws　Lee Finney and Gary Foster (both Great Britain) completed 27,803 throwing moves in 10 hours at the Forest Judo Club, Leicester, England on September 25, 1993.

KARATE

Origins

Karate is a martial art developed in Japan. Karate (empty hand) techniques evolved from the Chinese art of shoalin boxing, known as kempo, which was popularized in Okinawa in the 16th century as a means of self-defense, and became known as Tang Hand. Tang Hand was introduced to Japan by Funakoshi Gichin in the 1920s, and the name karate was coined in the 1930s. Gichin's style of karate, known as shotokan, is one of five major styles adapted for competition, the others being wado-ryu, gojuryu, shito-ryu and kyo-kushinkai. Each style places different emphasis on the elements of technique, speed and power. Karate's popularity grew in the West in the late 1950s.

World Championships

The first men's world championships were staged in Tokyo, Japan in 1970; a women's competition was first

David Douillet (France) won the 95+ kg division gold medal at the Atlanta Games.
(Ross Kinnaird/Allsport)

staged in 1980. Both tournaments are now staged biennially. The competition consists of two types: kumite, in which combatants fight each other, and kata events, in which contestants perform routines.

Kumite Championships (Men)

Most titles (team)   Great Britain has won six kumite world team titles, in 1975, 1982, 1984, 1986, 1988 and 1990.

Most titles (individual)   Four men have won two world titles: Pat McKay (Great Britain) in the under 80 kilograms class, 1982, 1984; Emmanuel Pinda (France), in the open class, 1984, and the over 80 kilograms class, 1988; Thierry Masci (France), in the under 70 kilograms class, 1986, 1988; Jose Manuel Egea (Spain), in the under 80 kilograms class, 1990, 1992.

Kata Championships (Men)

Most titles (team)   Japan has won four kata world team titles, in 1986, 1988, 1992 and 1994.

Most titles (individual)   Tsuguo Sakumoto (Japan) has won three world titles, in 1984, 1986 and 1988.

Kumite Championships (Women)

Most titles (individual)   Guus van Mourik (Netherlands) has won four world titles in the over 60 kilograms class, in 1982, 1984, 1986 and 1988.

Kata Championships (Women)

Most titles (individual)   Two women have won three world titles: Mie Nakayama (Japan), in 1982, 1984 and 1986; and Yuki Mimura (Japan), in 1988, 1990 and 1992.

TAEKWONDO

Origins

Taekwondo is a martial art, with all activities based on defensive spirit, developed over 20 centuries in Korea. It was officially recognized as part of Korean tradition and culture on April 11, 1955. The first World Taekwondo Championships were organized by the Korean Taekwondo Association and were held at Seoul, South Korea in 1973. The World Taekwondo Federation was then formed and has organized biennial championships.

United States   The United States Taekwondo Union was founded in 1974.

Olympic Games

Taekwondo was included as a demonstration sport at the 1988 and 1992 Games. It will be a full-medal sport at the 2000 Games.

World Championships

These biennial championships were first held in Seoul, South Korea in 1973, when they were staged by the Korean Taekwondo Association. Women's events were first staged unofficially in 1983 and have been officially recognized since 1987.

Most titles   Chung Kook-hyun (South Korea) has won a record four world titles: light middleweight, 1982–83; welterweight 1985, 1987. The women's record is three titles, achieved by Lynette Love (U.S.), 1985, 1987 and 1991.

MODERN PENTATHLON

Origins

The modern pentathlon is made up of five activities: fencing, horseback riding, pistol shooting, swimming and cross-country running. The sport derives from military training in the 19th century, which was based on a messenger's being able to travel across country on horseback, fight his way through with sword and pistol, and swim across rivers and complete his journey on foot if necessary.

Each event is scored on points, determined either against other contestants or against scoring tables. There is no standard course; therefore, point totals are not comparable. *L'Union Internationale de Pentathlon Moderne* (UIPM) was formed in 1948 and expanded to include the administration of the biathlon in 1957. (For further information on the biathlon, see page 66.)

United States The United States Modern Pentathlon and Biathlon Association was established in 1971, but this body was split to create the U.S. Modern Pentathlon Association in 1978.

Olympic Games

Modern pentathlon was first included in the 1912 Games held in Stockholm, Sweden, and has been part of every Olympic program since.

Most gold medals Andras Balczo (Hungary) has won three gold medals in Olympic competition: team event, 1960 and 1968; individual title, 1972.

Most gold medals (team event) Two countries have won the team event four times: Hungary, 1952, 1960, 1968 and 1988; USSR, 1956, 1964, 1972 and 1980.

Most medals (individual) Pavel Lednev (USSR) has won a record seven medals in Olympic competition: two gold—team event, 1972 and 1980; two silver—team event, 1968; individual event, 1976; and three bronze—individual event, 1968, 1972 and 1980.

World Championships

An official men's world championship was first staged in 1949, and has been held annually since. In Olympic years the Games are considered the world championships, and results from those events are included in world championship statistics. A women's world championship was inaugurated in 1981.

Men's Championship

Most titles (overall) Andras Balczo (Hungary) has won a record 13 world titles, including a record six individual titles: seven team, 1960, 1963, 1965–68 and 1970; six individual, 1963, 1965–67, 1969 and 1972.

Most titles (team event) The USSR has won 17 world championships: 1956–59, 1961–62, 1964, 1969, 1971–74, 1980, 1982–83, 1985 and 1991.

United States The United States won its only team world title in 1979, when Bob Nieman became the first American athlete, and so far the only American man, to win an individual world championship.

Women's Championship

Most titles (individual event) Eva Fjellerup (Denmark) is the only woman to win the individual title four times, in 1990, 1991, 1993 and 1994.

Most titles (team event) Poland has won five world titles: 1985, 1988–91.

United States The best result for the U.S. in the team event is

second place, which has been achieved twice, in 1981 and 1989. Lori Norwood won the individual championship in 1989.

United States National Championships

The men's championship was inaugurated in 1955, and the women's in 1977.

Most titles (men)   Mike Burley has won four men's titles, in 1977, 1979, 1981 and 1985.

Most titles (women)   Kim Arata (née Dunlop) has won nine titles, in 1979–80, 1984–89 and 1991.

Aleksandr Parygin celebrates his modern pentathlon Olympic title.
(Stu Forster/Allsport)

MOTORCYCLE RACING

Origins

The first recorded motorcycle race took place in France on September 20, 1896, when eight riders took part in a 139-mile race from Paris to Nantes and back. The winner was M. Chevalier on a Michelin-Dion tricycle; he covered the course in 4 hours 10 minutes 37 seconds. The first race for two-wheeled motorcycles was held on a one-mile oval track at Sheen House, Richmond, England on November 29, 1897. *The Fédération Internationale Motorcycliste* (FIM) was founded in 1904 and is the world governing body.

WORLD CHAMPIONSHIPS

The FIM instituted world championships in 1949 for 125, 250, 350 and 500cc classes. In 1962, a 50cc class was introduced; it was upgraded to 80cc in 1984. The 350cc class was discontinued in 1982 and the 80cc class was discontinued in 1989.

Most championships—125cc   7, by Angel Nieto (Spain), 1971–72, 1979, 1981–84.

Most championships—250cc   4, by Phil Read (Great Britain), 1964–65, 1968, 1971.

Most championships—500cc   8, by Giacomo Agostini (Italy), 1966–72, 1975.

Multiple titles   The only rider to win more than one world championship in one year is Freddie Spencer (U.S.), who won the 250cc and 500cc titles in 1985.

United States   The most world titles won by an American rider is four, by Eddie Lawson at 500cc in 1984, 1986, 1988–89.

Most Grand Prix wins—125cc   62, by Angel Nieto (Spain).

Most Grand Prix wins—250cc   33, by Anton Mang (West Germany).

Most Grand Prix wins—500cc   68, by Giacomo Agostini (Italy).

Most successful machines   Japanese Yamaha machines won 45 world championships between 1964 and 1993.

Fastest circuits   The highest average lap speed attained on any closed circuit is 160.288 mph, by Yvon du Hamel (Canada) on a modified 903cc four-cylinder Kawasaki Z1 at the 31-degree banked 2.5 mile Daytona International Speedway, FL in March 1973. His lap time was 56.149 seconds.

The fastest road circuit was the Francorchamps circuit near Spa, Belgium, then 8.74 miles long. It was lapped in 3 minutes 50.3 seconds (average speed 137.150 mph) by Barry Sheene (Great Britain) on a 495cc four-cylinder Suzuki during the Belgian Grand Prix on July 3, 1977. On that occasion he set a record time for this 10-lap (87.74-mile) race of 38 minutes 58.5 seconds (average speed 135.068 mph).

MOTOCROSS RACING

World Championships

Joel Robert (Belgium) won six 250cc Motocross World Championships (1964, 1968–72). Between April 25, 1964 and June 18, 1972 he won a record fifty 250cc Grand Prix. Eric Geboers (Belgium) has uniquely won all three categories of the Motocross World Championships, at 125cc in 1982 and 1983, 250cc in 1987 and 500cc in 1988 and 1991.

The most successful American rider is Eddie Lawson. He won four 500-cc titles between 1984 and 1989.
(Yann Guichaoua/Vandystadt)

Youngest champion The youngest motocross world champion was Sébastien Tortelli (France), who won the 125cc title at the age of 17 years 343 days on July 28, 1996.

United States The youngest-ever female motocross champion in the United States was Kristy Shealy, who, at age 14, won the women's division in the 1993 AMA Amateur/Youth National Motocross. In the same year, at the GNC Motocross 21st Annual Texas Series, she became the youngest racer to win the 125 Novice Class. In 1994, at age 15, Shealy became the youngest to win in the Ladies' class at the GNC International Motocross Final.

Eric Geboers is the most versatile motocross world champion. He has won world titles in three categories.
(Mike Powell/Allsport)

NETBALL

Origins

Invented in 1891, netball is a variation on basketball. In this passing and shooting game, netball players shoot the ball into a basketball-style net, but are not allowed to dribble the ball. The oldest club in continuous existence is the Polytechnic Netball Club of London, England, founded in 1907.

World Championships

Most titles Australia has won the world championships a record seven times, 1963, 1971, 1975, 1979, 1983, 1991 and 1995.

Most international appearances Kendra Slawinski (England) played in a record 128 international matches from 1981 to 1995.

Highest score The highest score in a World Championship game occurred when the Cook Islands defeated Vanuatu 120–38 on July 9, 1991 in Sydney, Australia.

Most goals The record number of goals by an individual at one World Championship tourney is 543 by Irene van Dyk (South Africa) in 1995.

POWERBOAT RACING

Origins

A gasoline engine was first installed in a boat by Jean Lenoir on the River Seine, Paris, France in 1865. Organized powerboat races were first run at the turn of the 20th century.

The first major international competition was the Harnsworth Trophy, launched in 1903. Modern powerboat racing is broken down into two main types: circuit racing in sheltered waterways, and offshore racing. Offshore events were initially for displacement (nonplaning) cruisers, but in 1958 the 170-mile Miami, FL-to-Nassau, Bahamas race was staged for planing cruisers.

United States The American Power Boat Association (APBA) was founded on April 22, 1903 in New York City. In 1913 the APBA issued the "Racing Commission" rules, which created its powers for governing the sport in North America. In 1924 the APBA set rules for boats propelled by outboard detachable motors and became the governing body for both inboard and outboard racing in North America. The APBA is currently based in Eastpointe, MI.

Powerboat Speed Records

Distance: One Kilometer

Type	Class	Speed (mph)	Driver	Location	Year
Inboard	GP	170.024	Kent MacPhail	Decatur, IL	1979
Inboard	KRR	146.649	Gordon Jennings	Lincoln City, OR	1989
Offshore	Super Boat	158.452	Dennis Kaiser	Sarasota, FL	1995
Offshore	Open	157.428	Tom Gentry	San Diego, CA	1994
PR Outboard	500ccH	121.940	Daniel Kirts	Moore Haven, FL	1987
PR Outboard	700ccH	118.769	Billy Rucker Jr.	Waterford, CA	1992
Performance	Champ Boat	143.716	Todd Bowden	Parker, AZ	1996
Performance	Mod U	142.968	Bob Wartinger	Moore Haven, FL	1989
Special Event	World Outboard Assault	176.551	Bob Wartinger	Parker, AZ	1989
Special Event	Jet	317.600	Ken Warby	Tumut, Australia	1976

Unlimited in Competition

Type	Distance	Speed (mph)	Driver	Location	Year
Qualifying Lap	2 miles	165.975	Chip Hanauer	Evansville, IN	1993
Lap	2 miles	156.713	Chip Hanauer	Evansville, IN	1993
Qualifying Lap	2.5 miles	172.166	Chip Hanauer	San Diego, CA	1995
Lap	2.5 miles	166.296	Steve David	Honolulu, HI	1992

Source: APBA

David Mischke set the electric powerboat speed record of 70.597 mph in October 1995.
(Courtesy of the American Power Boat Association)

APBA Gold Cup

The APBA held its first Gold Cup race at the Columbia Yacht Club on the Hudson River, NY in 1904, when the winner was *Standard*, piloted by C. C. Riotto at an average speed of 23.6 mph.

Most wins (driver) The most wins is 10, by Chip Hanauer, 1982–88, 1992–93 and 1995.

Most wins (boat) The most successful boat has been *Miss Budweiser* with 10 wins, driven by Bill Sterett Sr. in 1969; by Dean Chenoweth in 1970, 1973 and 1980–81; by Tom D'Eath in 1989–90; and by Chip Hanauer in 1992–93 and 1995.

Consecutive wins Chip Hanauer has won a record seven successive victories, 1982–88.

Fastest winner The highest average speed for the race is 147.943 mph by Mark Tate, piloting *Smokin' Joe's* in June 1994.

RACQUETBALL

Origins

Racquetball, using a 40-foot x 20-foot court, was invented in 1950 by Joe Sobek at the Greenwich YMCA, Greenwich, CT. Sobek designed a "strung paddle racquet" and combined the rules of squash and handball to form the game of "paddle rackets."

The International Racquetball Association (IRA) was founded in 1960 by Bob Kendler, and was renamed the American Amateur Racquetball Association (AARA) in 1979. The AARA changed its name in 1997 to the United States Racquetball Association (USRA).

The International Amateur Racquetball Federation (IARF) was founded in 1979 and staged its first world championship in 1981. The IARF was renamed the International Racqetball Federation (IRF) in 1988.

World Championships

First held in 1981, the IRF world championships have been held biennially since 1984.

Most titles (team) The United States has won all eight team titles, in 1981, 1984, 1986 (tie with Canada), 1988, 1990, 1992, 1994 and 1996.

Most titles (women) Michelle Gould (U.S.) has won three singles titles, in 1992, 1994 and 1996.

Most titles (men) Egan Inoue (U.S.) has won two singles titles, in 1986 and 1990.

REAL TENNIS

Origins

Real (meaning "royal") tennis was derived from the game *jeu de paume*, which was played in monastery cloisters in the 11th century. The architecture of the cloisters is reflected in the features of the courts, such as the sloping roofs and side gallery. During play, the ball can be hit against the roof-slopes. The scoring system is the same as that used in lawn tennis, which derived from real tennis in the late 19th century.

The Women's World Championships has been won three times by Penny Lumley (Great Britain), in 1989, 1991, and 1995.

RODEO

Origins

Rodeo originated in Mexico and moved north to the United States and Canada with the expansion of the North American cattle industry in the 18th and 19th centuries. There are several claims to the earliest organized rodeo. The Professional Rodeo Cowboys Association (PRCA) sanctions the West of the Pecos Rodeo, Pecos, TX as the oldest; it was first held in 1883. The development of rodeo as a regulated national sport can be traced to the formation of the Cowboys' Turtle Association in 1936. In 1945 the Turtles became the Rodeo Cowboy Association, which in 1975 was renamed the Professional Rodeo Cowboys Association (PRCA).

Roughstock The roughstock events are saddle bronc riding, bareback riding, and bull riding. In these events the cowboy is required to ride the mount for eight seconds to receive a score. The cowboy must use only one hand to grip the "rigging" (a handhold secured to the animal), and is disqualified if the free hand touches the animal or equipment during the round. The performance is judged on the cowboy's technique and the animal's bucking efforts.

Timed The timed events are calf roping, steer roping, team roping, and steer wrestling. In these events the cowboy chases the calf or steer, riding a registered quarter horse, catches up to the animal, and then captures the animal performing the required feat. The cowboy's performance is timed, with the fastest time winning the event.

World Championships

The Rodeo Association of America organized the first world championships in 1929. The championship has been organized under several different formats and sponsored by several different groups throughout its existence. The current championship is a season-long competition based on PRCA earnings. The PRCA has organized the championship since 1945 (as the Rodeo Cowboy Association through 1975).

Most titles (overall) Jim Shoulders has won 16 rodeo world championship events: all-around, 1949, 1956–59; bareback riding, 1950, 1956–58; bull riding, 1951, 1954–59.

Individual Events

All-around   Three cowboys have won six all-around titles: Larry Mahan, 1966–70, 1973; Tom Ferguson, 1974–79; and Ty Murray, 1989–94.

Saddle bronc riding   Casey Tibbs won six saddle bronc titles, in 1949, 1951–54 and 1959.

Bareback riding   Two cowboys have won five titles: Joe Alexander, 1971–75; Bruce Ford, 1979–80, 1982–83, 1987.

Bull riding   Don Gay has won eight bullriding titles: 1975–81 and 1984.

Calf roping   Dean Oliver has won eight titles: 1955, 1958, 1960–64 and 1969.

Steer roping   Guy Allen has won 11 titles: 1977, 1980, 1982, 1984, 1989, 1991–96.

Steer wrestling   Homer Pettigrew has won six titles: 1940, 1942–45 and 1948.

Team roping   The team of Jake Barnes and Clay O'Brien Cooper has won seven titles, 1985–89, 1992 and 1994.

Women's barrel racing   Charmayne Rodman has won 10 titles, 1984–93.

Oldest world champion   Ike Rude won the 1953 steer roping title at age 59 to became the oldest rodeo titleholder.

Youngest champions   The youngest winner of a world title is Anne Lewis, who won the WPRA barrel racing title in 1968 at 10 years of age. Ty Murray, 20, became the youngest cowboy to win the PRCA World Champion All-Around Cowboy title in 1989.

Riding Records

Bull riding   Wade Leslie scored 100 points riding Wolfman Skoal at Central Point, OR in 1991.

Saddle bronc riding   Two riders have scored 95 points: Doug Vold, riding Transport, in Meadow Lake, Saskatchewan, Canada in 1979; and Glen O'Neill, riding Skoal's Airwolf, in Innisfail, Alberta, Canada in June 1996.

Bareback riding   Joe Alexander scored 93 points riding Marlboro in Cheyenne, WY in 1974.

The youngest-ever rodeo world champion, Ty Murray also holds the PRCA single-season earnings mark.
(Scott Ridgway/Allsport)

Fastest Times

Calf roping   The fastest time in this event is 5.7 seconds, by Lee Phillips in Assinoia, Saskatchewan, Canada in 1978.

Steer wrestling   Without a barrier, the fastest time is 2.2 seconds by Oral Zumwalt in the 1930s. With a barrier, the record time is 2.4 seconds, achieved by three cowboys: Jim Bynum, Marietta, OK, 1955; Gene Melton, Pecatonia, IL, 1976; and Carl Deaton, Tulsa, OK, 1976.

Team roping   The team of Bob Harris and Tee Woolman performed this feat in a record 3.7 seconds in Spanish Fork, UT in 1986.

Steer roping   The fastest time in this event is 8.1 seconds, by Guy Allen in Coffeyville, KS in 1996.

Highest Earnings

Career   Roy Cooper holds the career PRCA earnings mark at $1,742,278, 1976–96.

Season   The single-season PRCA mark is $297,896 by Ty Murray in 1993.

⟫ Fantastic Feats

Texas skips   Vince Bruce (U.S.) performed 4,001 Texas skips (jumping back and forth through a large, vertical spun hoop) on July 22, 1991 in New York City.

Largest loop   Kalvin Cook spun a 95-foot loop in Las Vegas, NV on March 27, 1994.

ROWING

Origins

Forms of rowing can be traced back to ancient Egypt; however, the modern sport of rowing dates to 1715, when the Doggett's Coat and Badge scull race was established in London, England. Types of regattas are believed to have taken place in Venice, Italy in 1300, but the modern regatta can also be traced to England, where races were staged in 1775 on the River Thames at Ranleigh Gardens, Putney. The world governing body is the *Fédération Internationale des Sociétés d'Aviron* (FISA), founded in 1892. Rowing has been part of the Olympic Games since 1900.

United States   The first organized boat races in the United States were reportedly races staged between boatmen in New York harbor in the late 18th century. The first rowing club formed in the United States was the Castle Garden Amateur Boat Club Association, New York City, in 1834. The oldest active boat club is the Detroit Boat Club, founded in 1839. The first collegiate boat club was formed at Yale University in 1843. The National Association of Amateur Oarsmen (NAAO) was formed in 1872. The NAAO merged with the National Women's Rowing Association in 1982 to form the United States Rowing Association.

Fastest speed   The fastest recorded speed on nontidal water for 2,000 meters is by an eight from the Netherlands, in 5 minutes 23.90 seconds in Duisberg, Germany on May 19, 1996.

Olympic Games

Men's rowing events have been included in the Olympic Games since 1900. In 1976 women's events were introduced.

Most gold medals   Steven Redgrave (Great Britain) won four gold medals: coxed fours, 1984, coxless pairs, 1988, 1992 and 1996.

Most medals   Two oarsmen have won five medals in rowing competition: Jack Beresford (Great Britain), three gold (single sculls, 1924, coxless fours, 1932, and double sculls, 1936) and two silver (single sculls, 1920, and eights, 1928); and Steven Redgrave (Great Britain), four gold (see above) and one bronze (coxed pairs, 1988).

World Championships

World rowing championships staged separately from the Olympic Games were first held in 1962. Since 1974 the championships have been staged annually. In Olympic years the Games are considered the world championships, and results from the Olympics are included in this section.

Most titles   Steven Redgrave (Great Britain) has won 10 titles: coxed fours, 1984; coxed pairs, 1986; coxless pairs, 1987–88 and 1991–96. Yelena Tereshina (USSR) won seven titles: eights, 1978–79, 1981–83 and 1985–86.

Single sculls   Three oarsmen have won five single sculls titles: Peter-Michael Kolbe (West Germany), 1975, 1978, 1981, 1983 and 1986; Pertti Karppinen (Finland), 1976, 1979–80 and 1984–85; and Thomas Lange (Germany), 1988–92. Christine Hahn (née Scheiblich; East Germany) has won five women's titles, 1974–78.

Eights   Since 1962, East German crews have won seven men's eights titles—1970, 1975–80. In women's competition the USSR has won seven titles—1978–79, 1981–83, 1985–86.

Collegiate Championships

Harvard and Yale staged the first intercollegiate boat race in 1852. The Intercollegiate Rowing Association (IRA) was formed in 1895, and in 1898 inaugurated the Varsity Challenge Cup, which was recognized as the premier event in college racing. In 1979, a women's national championship was inaugurated, followed by an official men's event in 1982. The University of Washington has won the women's title a record seven times: 1981–85 and 1987–88. Since 1982 Harvard University has won the most men's titles, with five: 1983, 1985 and 1987–89.

Most wins (men)   Cornell has won 24 titles: 1896–97 (includes two wins in 1897), 1901–03, 1905–07, 1909–12, 1915, 1930, 1955–58, 1962–63, 1971, 1977, and 1981. Since 1982, Harvard has won six titles, 1983, 1985, 1987–89, and 1992.

Most wins (women)   Washington has won seven titles—1981–85, 1987–88.

RUGBY

Origins

As with baseball in the United States, the origins of rugby are obscure. The tradition is that the game began when William Webb Ellis picked up the ball during a soccer game at Rugby School in November 1823 and ran with it. Whether or not there is any truth to this legend, the "new" handling code of soccer developed, and the game was played at Cambridge University in 1839. The first rugby club was formed at Guy's Hospital, London, England in 1843, and the Rugby Football Union (RFU) was founded in January 1871. The International Rugby Football Board (IRFB) was founded in 1886.

OLYMPIC GAMES

Rugby was played at four Games from 1900 to 1924. The only double gold medalist was the U.S., which won in 1920 and 1924.

WORLD CUP

The Rugby World Cup is the world championship for rugby and is staged every four years. The first World Cup was staged in 1987. The first Women's World Cup was held in Wales in 1991.

Most wins   No team has won more than one World Cup in either men's or women's events.

Team Records

Most points (game)   The most points in a Rugby World Cup finals tournament game is 145, scored by New Zealand against Japan (17 points) in Bloemfontein, South Africa on June 4, 1995.

Most points (game, aggregate score)   The highest aggregate score in a Rugby World Cup finals tournament is 162 points, New Zealand defeating Japan 145–17 (see above).

Individual Records

Most points (game)   Simon Culhane (New Zealand) scored 45 points (one try and 20 conversions) vs. Japan in Bloemfontein, South Africa, June 4, 1995.

Most points (tournament)   Grant Fox (New Zealand) scored 126 points in 1987.

Most points (career)   Gavin Hastings (Scotland) scored 227 points in three finals, 1987, 1991 and 1995.

INTERNATIONAL RECORDS

Australian winger David Campese is rugby's all-time try-scoring leader.
(Mike Hewitt/Allsport)

Highest score   The highest score by a team in a full international game is 164, by Hong Kong against Singapore in Kuala Lumpur, Malaysia on October 27, 1994.

Most points (game)   Ashley Billington (Hong Kong) scored 50 points (10 tries) on October 27, 1994.

Most points (career)   Michael Lynagh (Australia) scored a record 911 points in international rugby competition, 1984–95.

Most tries (game)   Ashley Billington (Hong Kong) scored 10 tries on October 27, 1994.

Most tries (career)   David Campese (Australia) scored 64 tries in international competition, 1982–97.

Most penalty goals (game)   8, tied by five: Mark Wyatt (Canada) vs. Scotland in St. John, New Brunswick, May 25, 1991; Neil Jenkins (Wales) vs. Canada in Cardiff, Wales, November 10, 1993; Santiago Meson (Argentina) vs. Canada in Buenos Aires, Argentina, March 12, 1995; Gavin Hastings (Scotland) vs. Tonga in Pretoria, South Africa, May 30, 1995; Thierry Lacroix (France) vs. Ireland in Durban, South Africa, June 10, 1995.

Most internationals   Philippe Sella (France) played a record 111 international matches, 1982–95.

Consecutive internationals   Sean Fitzpatrick (New Zealand) played in 63 consecutive games, 1986–95.

SHOOTING

The National Rifle Association recognizes four categories of shooting competition: conventional, international, silhouette, and action pistol. This section reports records for international style shooting—the shooting discipline used at the Olympic Games.

Origins

The earliest recorded shooting club is the Lucerne (Switzerland) Shooting Guild, formed c. 1466. The first shooting competition was held in Zurich, Switzerland in 1472. The international governing body, the *Union International de Tir* (UIT), was formed in Zurich in 1907.

United States   The National Rifle Association (NRA) was founded in 1871 and designated as the national governing body for shooting sports in the United States by the U.S. Olympic Committee. Since 1995, USA Shooting has been the national governing body.

International Style Shooting

International or Olympic-style shooting is composed of four disciplines: rifle, pistol, running target, and shotgun. Running target events are limited to male competitors. Shotgun shooting (also known as trap and skeet) requires the competitor to hit clay targets released from a trap machine.

Olympic Games

Shooting has been part of the Olympic program since the first modern Games in 1896. Women were allowed to compete against men at the 1968 Games, and separate women's events were included in 1984.

Shooting—Individual World Records

The table below shows the world records for the 13 Olympic shooting disciplines, giving in parentheses the score for the number of shots specified plus the score in the additional round.

Men

Event	Points	Marksman (Country)	Date
Free rifle 50 m 3 x 40 shots	1,287.9 (1,186 + 101.9)	Rajmond Debevec (Slovenia)	August 29,1992
Free rifle 50 m 60 shots prone	704.8 (600 + 104.8)	Christian Klees (Germany)	July 25, 1996
Air rifle 10 m 60 shots	699.4 (596 + 103.4)	Rajmond Debevec (Yugoslavia)	June 7, 1990
Free pistol 50 m 60 shots	675.3 (580 + 95.3)	Taniu Kiriakov (Bulgaria)	April 21, 1995
Rapid-fire pistol 25 m 60 shots	699.7 (596 + 103.7)	Ralf Schumann (Germany)	June 8, 1994
Air pistol 10 m 60 shots	695.1 (593 + 102.1)	Sergei Pyzhianov (USSR)	October 13, 1989
Running target 10 m 30 + 30 shots	687.9 (586 + 101.9)	Ling Yang (China)	June 6, 1996
Trap 125 targets	150 (125 + 25)	Marcello Tittarelli (Italy)	June 11, 1996
Skeet 125 targets	150 (125 + 25)	Jan Henrik Heinrich (Germany.)	June 5, 1996

Women

Event	Points	Markswoman (Country)	Date
Standard rifle 50 m 3 x 20 shots	689.7 (592 + 97.7)	Vessela Letcheva (Bulgaria)	June 15, 1995
Air rifle 10 m 40 shots	501.5 (398 + 103.5)	Vessela Letcheva (Bulgaria)	April 12, 1996
Sport pistol 25 m 60 shots	696.2 (594 + 102.2)	Diana Jorgova (Bulgaria)	May 31, 1994
Air pistol 10 m 40 shots	492.7 (392 + 100.7)	Jasna Sekaric (Yugoslavia)	September 22, 1996

The first world record by a woman at any sport for a category in direct and measurable competition with men was by Margaret Murdock (née Thompson; U.S.), who set a world record for smallbore rifle (kneeling position) of 391 in 1967.

Right On Target

Most 17-year-olds are busy studying algebra, getting their driver's license and going to proms. But Kimberly Rhode can add something else to her list of things to do. In the past six years, Rhode has succeeded in becoming the youngest Olympic shooting champion in history.

"I've put a lot of time, a lot of effort and a lot of hard work into this. I practice anywhere from five to six hours every day, seven days a week. And on the weekends, I practice even more," she says happily.

Rhode started her shooting career as a recreational sport and from there, things just mushroomed for her.

"It started off at club shoots— little shoots just for the fun of it. From there, before I knew it, I was at the State, and then the World, and the World Cup, and then the Olympics."

Getting to the Olympics didn't take as long as Rhode thought it would. "I'd only been shooting the [double trap] for two years before I made it to the Olympics," she explains. "I love all the traveling and all the people I meet along the way. It was always such a great, challenging sport and to this day, there still isn't anyone who's run a straight in this event. It's a real challenge for me to keep it that way."

So what words of wisdom does Rhode have for the younger generation of shooters?

"I have one thing to say to kids who want to get into this sport. Dreams really do come true with a lot of hard work and effort. It does pay off. Working this hard didn't bother me a bit. I got to do it all. The football games, dances. I was very organized with my plans. If something was on Friday night, I'd rearrange my schedule so I could make it."

The future is more than bright for Rhode. She looks forward to college, a career and the prospect of many more Olympic titles. "I'm hoping to become a veterinarian or a doctor and to continue to shoot for the Olympics again and again and again. I know that by the time I'm 36 or 37, I could go to six Olympics—and that's a lot."

Rick Stewart/Allsport

Most gold medals Seven marksmen have won five gold medals: Konrad Staheli (Switzerland), 1900–1906; Louis Richardet (Switzerland), 1900–06; Alfred Lane (U.S.), 1912–20; Carl Osburn (U.S.), 1912–24; Ole Lilloe-Olsen (Norway), 1920–24; Morris Fisher (U.S.), 1920–24; and Willis Lee (U.S.), 1920. Marina Logvinenko (Unified Team) is the only woman to win two gold medals: sport pistol and air pistol, both in 1992.

Most medals Carl Osburn (U.S.) won 11 medals: five gold, four silver and two bronze. The greatest tally by a woman competitor is three medals, by Jasna Sekaric (Yugoslavia/Independent Olympic Participant). She won one gold and one bronze in 1988, and one silver in 1992.

NCAA Championships

A combined NCAA rifle championship was inaugurated in 1980, and the contest is now held annually.

Most titles (team) West Virginia has won 11 NCAA team titles, 1983–84, 1986, 1988–93, 1995–96.

Most titles (individual) Eight competitors have won two individual titles: Rod Fitz-Randolph, Tennessee Tech, smallbore and air rifle, 1980; Kurt Fitz-Randolph, Tennessee Tech, smallbore, 1981–82; John Rost, West Virginia, air rifle, 1981–82; Pat Spurgin, Murray State, air rifle, 1984, smallbore, 1985; Web Wright, West Virginia, smallbore, 1987–88; Michelle Scarborough, South Florida, air rifle, 1989, smallbore, 1990; Ann-Marie Pfiffner, West Virginia, air rifle, 1991–92; Trevor Gathman, West Virginia, air rifle, 1993, 1996.

SKIING

Origins

Skiing traces its history to Scandinavia; ski is the Norwegian word for snowshoe. A ski discovered in a peat bog in Hoting, Sweden dates to c. 2500 B.C., and records note the use of skis at the Battle of Isen, Norway in A.D. 1200. The first ski races were held in Norway and Australia in the 1850s and 1860s. Two men stand out as pioneers of the development of skiing in the 19th century: Sondre Nordheim, a Norwegian, who designed equipment and developed skiing techniques; and Mathias Zdarsky, an Austrian, who pioneered Alpine skiing. The first national governing body was that of Norway, formed in 1833. The International Ski Commission was founded in 1910 and was succeeded as the world governing body in 1924 by the International Ski Federation (FIS).

United States The first ski club in the United States was formed at Berlin, N.H. in January 1872. The United States Ski Association was originally founded as the National Ski Association in 1905; in 1962, it was renamed the United States Ski Association, and in 1990 it was renamed U.S. Skiing.

In the modern era, skiing has evolved into two main categories, Alpine and Nordic. Alpine skiing encompasses downhill and slalom racing. Nordic skiing covers ski jumping events and cross-country racing.

ALPINE SKIING

Olympic Games

Downhill and slalom events were first included at the 1936 Olympic Games.

Most gold medals In men's competition, the most gold medals won is three, by three skiers: Anton Sailer (Austria), who won all three events, downhill, slalom and giant slalom, in 1956; Jean-Claude Killy (France), who matched Sailer's feat in 1968; and Alberto Tomba (Italy), who won the slalom and giant slalom in 1988 and the giant slalom in 1992. For women the record is also three golds, by Vreni Schneider (Switzerland), who won the giant slalom and slalom in 1988 and the slalom in 1994.

Most medals Two men have won five Olympic medals: Alberto Tomba (Italy), three gold and two silver, 1988–94; Kjetil Andre Aamodt (Norway), one gold, two silver and two bronze, 1992–94. The most by a woman is also five, by Vreni Schneider (Switzerland): three gold, one silver and one bronze, 1994.

World Championships

This competition was inaugurated in 1931 in Murren, Switzerland. From 1931 to 1939 the championships were held annually; from 1950 they were held biennially. Up to 1980, the Olympic Games were considered the world championships, except in 1936. In 1985, the championship schedule was changed so as not to coincide with an Olympic year.

Most gold medals Christel Cranz (Germany) won 12 titles: four slalom, 1934, 1937–39; three downhill, 1935, 1937, 1939; five combined, 1934–35, 1937–39. Anton Sailer (Austria) holds the men's record with seven titles: one slalom, 1956; two giant slalom, 1956, 1958; two downhill, 1956, 1958; two combined, 1956, 1958.

World Cup

Contested annually since 1967, the World Cup is a circuit of races where points are earned during the season, with the champion being the skier with the most points at the end of the season.

Individual Racing Records

Most wins (men) Ingemar Stenmark (Sweden) won a record 86 races (46 giant slalom, 40 slalom) from 287 contested, 1974-89.

Most wins (women) Annemarie Moser-Pröll (Austria) won a record 62 races, 1970–79.

Katja Seizinger has won a record four Super-G World Cup titles.
(Simon Bruty/Allsport)

Picabo Street is the only American to win the women's downhill World Cup title.
Simon Bruty/Allsport

Most wins (season) Ingemar Stenmark (Sweden) won 13 races in 1978–79 to set the men's mark. Vreni Schneider (Switzerland) won 13 races in 1988–89 to set the women's mark.

Consecutive wins Ingemar Stenmark (Sweden) won 14 successive giant slalom races from March 18, 1978 to January 21, 1980. The women's record is 11 wins by Annemarie Moser-Pröll (Austria) in the downhill from December 1972 to January 1974.

United States National Championships

Most titles Tamara McKinney won seven slalom titles, 1982–84, 1986–89—the most by any skier in one discipline. Phil Mahre won five giant slalom titles, 1975, 1977–79, 1981—the most by a male skier in one event.

NCAA Championships

The NCAA skiing championship was introduced in 1954. Teams compete in both Alpine and cross-country events, with cumulative point totals determining the national champion. Teams are composed of both men and women.

Most titles (team) Denver has won 14 titles, 1954–57, 1961–67, and 1969–71.

Most titles (individual) Chiharu Igaya of Dartmouth won a record six NCAA titles: Alpine, 1955–56; downhill, 1955; slalom, 1955–57.

NORDIC SKIING

CROSS-COUNTRY SKIING

Olympic Games Cross-country racing has been included in every Winter Olympic Games.

Most gold medals The most gold medals won in Nordic events is six, by Lyubov Yegorova (Unified Team/Russia), 15 km, 4 x 5 km relay and 5 x 10 km relay, 1992; 5 km, 4 x 5 km relay and 5 x 10 km combined, 1994. Bjorn Daehlie (Norway) holds the men's record five gold medals: 50 km, 10 + 15 km pursuit, and 4 x 10 km relay, 1992; 10 km and 10 + 15 km pursuit, 1994.

Most medals The most medals won in Nordic events is 10, by Raisa Smetanina (four gold, five silver and one bronze, 1976–92). Sixten Jernberg (Sweden) holds the men's record with nine (four gold, three silver, two bronze, 1956–64).

World Cup

A season series of World Cup races was instituted in 1981.

Most titles Gunde Svan (Sweden) has won five overall cross-country skiing titles, 1984–86 and 1988–89. Yelena Valbe (USSR/Russia) has won four overall titles, 1989, 1991–92 and 1995.

United States National Championships

Most titles Martha Rockwell has won a record 14 national titles, 1969–75. The record in men's competition is 12, by Audun Endestad, 1984–90.

SKI JUMPING

Olympic Games

Ski jumping has been included in every Winter Games.

Most gold medals Matti Nykanen (Finland) has won four gold medals: 70-meter hill, 1988; 90-meter hill, 1984 and 1988; 90-meter team, 1988.

Most medals Matti Nykanen has won five medals in Olympic competition: four gold (see above) and one silver, 70-meter hill, 1984.

World Cup

A season series of ski jumping events was instituted in 1981.

Most titles Matti Nykanen (Finland) has won four World Cup titles, 1983, 1985–86 and 1988.

United States National Championships

Most titles Lars Haugen has won seven ski jumping titles, 1912–28.

FREESTYLE SKIING

Freestyle skiing is composed of three skiing disciplines: moguls, aerials and ballet. Moguls was included as an Olympic event for the first time at the 1992 Games.

MOGULS

Skiers race down a slope marked with small snow hills (moguls). The skiers are required to perform two jumps during the run. The score is calculated by combining the speed of the run and marks awarded for performance.

Olympic Games

Moguls was a full-medal sport for the first time at the 1992 Games. No skier has won more than once.

World Championship

First staged in 1986, the event has been staged biennially since 1989.

Most wins (men) Edgar Grospiron (France) has won the event three times, in 1989, 1991 and 1995.

Most wins (women) No skier has won the women's event more than once.

AERIALS

World Championship

Most wins (men) Two men have won the title twice: Lloyd Langlois (Canada), 1986 and 1989; and Philippe Laroche (Canada), 1991 and 1993.

Most wins (women) No skier has won this event more than once.

BALLET

World Championship

Most wins (men) No skier has won the event more than once.

Most wins (women) Two women have won the event twice: Jan Bucher (U.S.) , 1986 and 1989; and Ellen Breen (U.S.), 1991 and 1993.

SPEED AND DISTANCE RECORDS

Fastest speed (men) The official world record is 150.028 mph by Jeffrey Hamilton (U.S.), April 14, 1995.

Fastest speed (women) The fastest speed by a woman is 140.864 mph, by Karine Dubouchet (France) on April 20, 1996.

Fastest speed—one-legged On April 16, 1988 Patrick Knaff set a one-legged record at 115.306 mph.

Fastest speed—cross-country The world record time for a 50 km race is 1 hour 54 minutes 46 seconds by Aleksei Prokurorov (Russia) at Thunder Bay, Canada on March 19, 1994 at an average speed of 16.24 mph.

Distance—24 hours cross-country Seppo-Juhani Savolainen skied 258.2 miles at Saariselka, Finland on April 8–9, 1988.

The fastest-growing alpine sport in the United States is snowboarding.
(Nathan Bilow/Allsport)

SLED DOG RACING

Origins

Racing between harnessed dog teams (usually huskies) is believed to have been practiced by Inuits in North America, and also by the peoples of Scandinavia, long before the first recorded formal race, the All-America Sweepstakes, which took place in 1908. Sled dog racing was a demonstration sport at the 1932 Olympic Games. The best known race is the Iditarod Trail Sled Dog Race, first run in 1973.

Longest trail   The longest race is the 1,243-mile Benergia Trail from Esso to Markovo, Russia. The 1991 race was won by Pavel Lazarev in 10 days 18 hours 17 minutes 56 seconds.

Iditarod Trail Sled Dog Race

The annual race from Anchorage to Nome, AK commemorates the 1925 midwinter emergency mission to get medical supplies to Nome during a diphtheria epidemic. Raced over alternate courses, the northern and southern trails, the Iditarod was first run in 1973.

Most wins   Rick Swenson has won the event five times: 1977, 1979, 1981–82, 1991. The most wins by a woman is four, by Susan Butcher, in 1986–88, 1990.

Record time   The fastest time was set by Doug Swingley (U.S.) in 1995, with 9 days 2 hours 42 minutes 19 seconds.

Iditarod Winners

Year	Musher	Elapsed Time	Year	Musher	Elapsed Time
1973	Dick Wilmarth	20 days, 00:49:41	1985	Libby Riddles	18 days, 00:20:17
1974	Carl Huntington	20 days, 15:02:07	1986	Susan Butcher	11 days, 15:06:00
1975	Emmitt Peters	14 days, 14:43:45	1987	Susan Butcher	11 days, 02:05:13
1976	Gerald Riley	18 days, 22:58:17	1988	Susan Butcher	11 days, 11:41:40
1977	Rick Swenson	16 days, 16:27:13	1989	Joe Runyan	11 days,05:24:34
1978	Rick Mackey	14 days, 18:52:24	1990	Susan Butcher	11 days, 01:53:23
1979	Rick Swenson	15 days, 10:37:47	1991	Rick Swenson	12 days, 16:34:39
1980	Joe May	14 days, 07:11:51	1992	Martin Buser	10 days, 19:36:17
1981	Rick Swenson	12 days, 08:45:02	1993	Jeff King	10 days, 15:38:17
1982	Rick Swenson	16 days, 04:40:10	1994	Martin Buser	10 days, 13:02:39
1983	Rick Mackey	12 days,14:10:44	1995	Doug Swingley	9 days, 02:42:19
1984	Dean Osmar	12 days, 15:07:33	1996	Jeff King	9 days, 05:43:13
			1997	Martin Buser	9 days, 08:30:45

SOCCER

Origins

A game with some similarities to soccer, called *Zu-qui* ("to kick a ball of stuffed leather"), was played in China in the fourth and third centuries B.C. The ancestry of the modern game is traced to England. In 1314 King Edward II prohibited the game because of excessive noise. Three subsequent monarchs also banned the game. Nevertheless, soccer continued its development in England. In 1848, the first rules of the game were drawn up at Cambridge University. In 1863, the Football Association was founded in England to govern the sport. By the turn of the 20th century, soccer had become a worldwide phenomenon, and an international governing body, FIFA (*Fédération Internationale de Football*) was formed in Paris, France in 1904.

United States The first international games played outside the British Isles were played between the United States and Canada in 1885 and 1886. The United States Football Association was one of the earliest national soccer associations and became a FIFA affliate in 1913. Since 1974, the governing body has been known as U.S. Soccer.

FIFA WORLD CUP

The first World Cup was staged in Uruguay in 1930. The Finals tournament is staged every four years. The World Cup championship game is the most widely watched event in the world, with over one billion viewers watching the 1994 World Cup Final between Brazil and Italy.

Team Records

Most wins   Brazil has won four World Cups, 1958, 1962, 1970 and 1994.

Most appearances   Brazil is the only country to qualify for all 15 World Cup tournaments.

Most goals (qualifying game)   13, by New Zealand. The Kiwis defeated Fiji 13–0 in a qualifying match in Auckland on August 15, 1981.

Most goals (finals game)   10, by Hungary in a 10–1 defeat of El Salvador in Elche, Spain on June 15, 1982.

The first MLS championship game ended in dramatic fashion, with DC United claiming the title with a goal in sudden-death overtime.
(Simon Bruty/Allsport)

Soccer Centenarian

David Leah/Allsport

"I've been playing soccer since I could walk," says Marcelo Balboa. Born in Chicago, Balboa is the son of Luis Balboa, an Argentinian who played for the Chicago Mustangs of the North American Professional Soccer League. "Soccer is in the blood," he muses. A tough-tackling, intimidating defender, Balboa debuted on the national eleven versus Guatemala on January 10, 1988. He rapidly established himself as the anchor of the defense. As of January 1, 1997, Balboa had played 113 times for Team USA. He and Paul Caligiuri are tied for the most appearances ever on the team.

On June 11, 1995, Balboa became the first player to gain 100 appearances for the U.S. national team. Balboa is modest in his assessment of attaining one of soccer's greatest milestones. "I really didn't think I'd be the first one to break the century mark. There was someone else on the team who was up to 97 times," recalls the defender. "I was very excited to find out that I had done it. To me that was something extremely special." So special that he celebrated by scoring the second goal in the team's 3–2 victory over Nigeria.

While Balboa is proud of his appearance record, his main desire was to play in the finals of the World Cup. "My focus was always to make the World Cup. I think that's everyone's dream in this sport. I played in two of them and you just can't top that," declares Balboa. He played in each of the US team's three games in Italy '90, and played every minute of the team's run in USA '94. Reflects Balboa, "I think that's what I strove for my whole life."

Currently a member of the MLS's Colorado Rapids, Balboa has been one of the pioneers in soccer's resurgence in the United States. Ironically, his place in the national team is now under threat from an exciting generation of young players emerging from the college and MLS ranks. This just motivates the defender even more. "Every individual has their own way of making themselves better. I need to be playing at a high level... acquiring skills from other players and coaches. Once you stop learning, it's time to stop. As a professional athlete, there's always time to grow and get better." Adds Balboa, "Soccer's brought me a lot of success and joy. I plan to be in it another six or seven years."

Women's soccer player of the year Mia Hamm led the United States in its successful Olympic gold medal campaign.
(Stephen Dunn/Allsport)

Most goals (finals tournament) 27, by Hungary in 1954. The Mighty Magyars tallied their record total in five games, but lost in the Final to Germany, 3–2.

Most goals (all finals tournaments) 159, by Brazil in 73 games over 15 tournaments.

Individual Records

Most appearances (finals) 5, by Antonio Carbajal (Mexico). The goalkeeper played in 11 games in the 1950, 1954, 1958, 1962 and 1966 finals tournaments.

Most games (finals) 21, by four players: Uwe Seeler (West Germany), 1958–70; Wladyslaw Zmuda (Poland), 1974–86; Diego Maradona (Argentina), 1982–94; and Lothar Matthaus (West Germany/ Germany), 1982–94.

Most goals (game) 5, by Oleg Salenko (Russia) in a 6–1 defeat of Cameroon in 1994.

Most goals (tournament) 13, by Just Fontaine (France), in 1958, in six games.

Most goals (career) 14, by Gerd Muller (West germany), 10 in 1970 and four in 1974.

Most goals (World Cup Final) 3, by Geoff Hurst (England) in a 4–2 defeat of West Germany on July 30, 1966.

EUROPEAN CHAMPIONSHIP

First held in 1960, the tournament is staged every four years.

Most wins 3, West Germany/Germany, 1972, 1980 and 1996.

COPA AMERICA

The South American Championship was first staged in 1916. In 1975 the tournament was restructured and relaunched as the Copa America. Staged every two years, the 1995 tournament was expanded to include the United States.

Most wins 14, by Argentina, 1921, 1925, 1927, 1929, 1937, 1941, 1945–47, 1955, 1957, 1959, 1991 and 1993.

AFRICAN NATIONS CUP

First staged in 1957, the tournament is played biennially.

Most wins 4, by Ghana, 1963, 1965, 1978 and 1982.

MAJOR LEAGUE SOCCER (MLS)

As a condition of gaining the rights to host World Cup '94, U.S. Soccer agreed to form a professional league. Major League Soccer, after several postponements, was inaugurated in 1996. With a season average attendance of 17,416, the 10-team MLS was a huge success. D.C. United won the championship game in sudden death overtime 3–2 over the Los Angles Galaxy.

Individual Records

Most goals (season) 27, Roy Lassiter, Tampa Bay Mutiny, 1996.

Most assists (season) 19, Marco Etcheverry, D.C. United, 1996.

Most points (season) 58 (27 goals, 4 assists), Roy Lassiter, Tampa Bay Mutiny, 1996.

FIFA WORLD CUP (WOMEN)

The first women's World Cup was staged in China in 1991. The tournament is held every four years.

Most wins
One, by two countries: United States, 1991, and Norway, 1995.

OLYMPIC GAMES

A men's soccer tournament has been officially included in the Olympic program since 1908; however, "unofficial" tournaments were staged in 1896, 1900 and 1904. Women's soccer was first included in the 1996 Atlanta Games.

Most wins (men) 3, by Hungary, 1952, 1964 and 1968.

Most wins (women) The United States won the inuagural 1996 women's tournament, defeating China, 2–1 in sudden-death overtime.

NCAA DIVISION I

The NCAA Division I men's championship was first staged in 1959. A women's tournament was introduced in 1982.

Most titles (men) 10, including one tie game, University of St. Louis, 1959–60, 1962–63, 1965, 1967, 1969–70, 1972–73.

Most titles (women) 13, University of North Carolina, 1982–84, 1986–94, 1996.

Euro '96, staged in England, was the biggest event of the 1996 soccer year. Germany defeated the Czech Republic to gain a record third European championship.
(Shaun Botterill/Allsport)

⏩ Fantastic Feats

Ball juggling (duration) Ricardinho Neves (Brazil) juggled a regulation soccer ball nonstop with his feet, legs and head, without the ball touching the ground, for 19 hours 5 minutes 31 seconds at the Los Angeles Convention Center, July 15–16, 1994. The women's record is 7 hours 5 minutes 25 seconds by Claudia Martini (Brazil) at Caxias do Sul, Brazil on July 12, 1996.

Heading (duration) Godzerzi Maakharadze (Georgia) headed a ball for 8 hours 12 minutes 25 seconds on May 26, 1996 in Tibilisi, Georgia.

Marathon The fastest time for completing a marathon while juggling a soccer ball is 7 hours 18 minutes 55 seconds by Jan Skorkovsky (Czechoslovakia) on July 8, 1990 when he "ran" the Prague Marathon.

Most red cards It was reported on June 1, 1993 that in a league soccer game between Sportivo Ameliano and General Caballero in Paraguay, referee William Weiler ejected 20 players. Trouble flared after two Sportivo players were thrown out, a 10-minute fight ensued and Weiler then dismissed a further 18 players, including the rest of the Sportivo team. Not suprisingly, the game was abandoned.

SOFTBALL

Origins

Softball, a derivative of baseball, was invented by George Hancock at the Farragut Boat Club, Chicago, IL in 1887. Rules were first codified in Minneapolis, MN in 1895 under the name kitten ball. The name "softball" was introduced by Walter Hakanson at a meeting of the National Recreation Congress in 1926. The name was adopted throughout the United States in 1930.

Rules were formalized in 1933 by the International Joint Rules Committee for Softball and adopted by the Amateur Softball Association of America (ASA), the governing body for softball in this country. Located in Oklahoma City, the ASA is also home to the National Softball Hall of Fame.

A competing organization, the United States Slo-Pitch Softball Association (U.S.S.S.A.), was formed in 1968 and is concerned exclusively with slow pitch. The International Softball Federation (ISF) was formed in 1950 as governing body for both fast pitch and slow pitch.

FAST PITCH SOFTBALL

World Championships

A women's fast pitch world championship was first staged in 1965, and a men's tournament in 1966. Both tournaments are held quadrennially.

Most titles (men)   The United States has won five world titles: 1966, 1968, 1976 (tied), 1980 and 1988.

Most titles (women)   The United States has won five world titles: 1974, 1978, 1986, 1990 and 1994.

Amateur Softball Association National Championship

The first ASA national championship was staged in 1933 for both men's and women's teams.

Most titles (women)   The Raybestos Brakettes (Stratford, CT) won 23 women's fast pitch titles from 1958 through 1992.

Most titles (men)   The Clearwater (FL) Bombers won 10 championships between 1950 and 1973.

NCAA Championships

The first NCAA Division I women's championship was staged in 1982.

Most titles   UCLA has won eight titles: 1982, 1984–85, 1988–90, 1992 and 1995.

SLOW PITCH SOFTBALL

World Championships

A slow pitch world championship was staged for men's teams in 1987. The United States team won this event. So far a second tournament has not been scheduled. No world championship has been staged for women's teams.

Amateur Softball Association National Championship

The first men's ASA national championship was staged in 1953. The first women's event was staged in 1962.

Most titles (men—major slow pitch)
Two teams have won three major slow pitch championships: Skip Hogan A.C. (Pittsburgh, PA), 1962, 1964–65; Joe Gatliff Auto Sales (Newport, KY), 1956–57, 1963.

Most titles (men—super slow pitch)   Steele's Silver Bullets (Grafton, OH) won four super slow pitch titles, 1985–87 and 1990.

Most titles (women)   The Dots of Miami (FL) have won five major slow pitch titles, playing as the Converse Dots in 1969, as Marks Brothers North Miami Dots, 1974–75, and as Bob Hoffman Dots, 1978–79.

⇒ Fantastic Feats

Perfect game   Carol Christ Hampton, pitcher for Les's Legacy, Seattle, WA, pitched an entire game with all strikes except for three balls called at the ASA Class C Women's National Softball Championship, St. Augustine, FL on September 25, 1994.

Softball Championship Records (Men)

	Fast Pitch	Super Slow Pitch	Major Slow Pitch
Individual Batting Records			
Batting average	.632, Ted Hicks, CMI, Springfield, MO, 1978	.900 tied by two: Carl Rose, Lighthouse/Sunbelt, 1990; and Wes Lord, Budweiser,1994 San Francisco, CA, 1990	.947, David Bear, Reece Astros, Indianapolis, IN
Home runs	5, tied by two: Jody Hennigan, Farm Tavern, Madison, WI, 1990; and Bob McClish, Springfield, MO, 1973	20, tied by two: Doug Roberson, Superior/Apollo, Windsor Locks, CT, 1990; and Rick Scheer, Howard's-Western Steer, Denver, NC, 1984	23, Stan Harvey, Howard's-Western Steer, Denver, NC, 1978
RBI	13, Bob McClish Springfield, MO, 1973	35, Doug Roberson, Superior/Apollo, Windsor Locks, CT, 1990	54, Russ Earnest, Back Porch, Niceville, FL, 1994

Pitching Records (Fast Pitch)

Wins	8, tied by four: Peter Meredith, Tran-Aire, Elkhart, IN, 1988; Grame Robertson, Pay 'n Pak, Seattle, WA, 1987; Harvey Sterkel, Aurora, IL, 1959; and Bonnie Jones, Butch Grinders, Detroit, MI, 1959
Strikeouts (total)	140, Mike Piechnik, Farm Tavern, Madison, WI, 1988
Strikeouts (game)	55 in 21 innings, Herb Dudley, Bombers, Clearwater, FL, 1949

Team USA won the first women's Olympic softball tournament. The players celebrate their victory over China in the gold medal game.
(Rusty Jarrett/Allsport)

Softball Championship Records (Women)

	Fast Pitch	Major Slow Pitch
Individual Batting Records		
Batting average	Not available	.857, Princess Carpenter, Rutenschroer Floral, Cincinnati, OH, 1973
Home runs	5, Kim Maher, Redding, CA, 1994	5, tied by two: Patsy Danson, Carter's Rebel, Jacksonville, FL, 1970; and Sue Taylor, Huntington (NY) YMCA, 1970
RBI	12, Kim Maher, Redding, CA, 1994	Not available

Pitching (Fast Pitch)

Wins	8, Joan Joyce, Stratford, CT, 1973
Strikeouts (total)	134, Joan Joyce, Stratford, CT, 1973
Strikeouts (game)	40 in 19 innings, Joan Joyce, Stratford, CT, 1961
Strikeouts (consecutive)	18, Michele Granger, Orange County (CA) Majestics, 1988

Source: Amateur Softball Association

SPEED SKATING

Origins

The world's longest skating race, the 124-mile *Elfstedentocht* ("Tour of the Eleven Towns"), is said to commemorate a race staged in the Netherlands in the 17th century. The first recorded skating race was staged in 1763, from Wisbech to Whittlesey, England. The International Skating Union (ISU) was founded in the Netherlands in 1892 and is the governing body for both speed skating and figure skating.

Olympic Games

Men's speed skating events have been included in the Olympic Games since 1924. Women's events were first staged in 1960.

Most gold medals Lydia Skoblikova (USSR) has won six gold medals: 500-meter, 1964; 1,000-meter, 1964; 1,500-meter, 1960, 1964; 3,000-meter, 1960, 1964. The men's record is five, shared by two skaters: Clas Thunberg (Finland), 500-meter, 1928; 1,500-meter, 1924, 1928; 5,000-meter, 1924; all-around title, 1924; and Eric Heiden (U.S.), 500-meter, 1,000-meter, 1,500-meter, 5,000-meter, and 10,000-meter, all in 1980.

The United States' most successful Olympian, Bonnie Blair still holds the 500-m speedskating world record.
(Shaun Botterill/Allsport)

Speed Skating World Records

MEN

Meters	Time	Name and Country	Date
500	0:35.39	Hiroyasu Shimizu (Japan)	March 1, 1996
1,000	1:11.67	Manabu Horli (Japan)	March 1, 1996
1,500	1:50.61	Hiroyuki Noake (Japan)	March 2, 1996
3,000	3:53.06	Bob De Jong (Netherlands)	March 8, 1996
5,000	6:34.96	Johann Olav Koss (Norway)	February 13, 1994
10,000	13:30.55	Johann Olav Koss (Norway)	February 20, 1994

WOMEN

Meters	Time	Name and Country	Date
500	0:38.69	Bonnie Blair (U.S.)	February 12, 1995
1,000	1:17.65†	Christa Rothenburger (now Luding; East Germany)	February 26, 1988
1,500	1:59.30†	Karin Kania (East Germany)	March 22, 1986
3,000	4:09.32	Gunda Niemann (née Kleeman; Germany)	March 25, 1994
5,000	7:03.26	Gunda Niemann	March 26, 1994

† Set at high altitude

World Championships

Speed skating world championships were first staged in 1893.

Most titles Oscar Mathisen (Norway) and Clas Thunberg (Finland) have won a record five overall world titles. Mathisen won titles in 1908–09 and 1912–14; Thunberg won in 1923, 1925, 1928–29 and 1931. Karin Enke-Kania (East Germany) holds the women's mark, also at five. She won in 1982, 1984 and 1986–88.

United States Eric Heiden won three overall world titles, 1977–79, the most by any U.S. skater. His sister Beth became the only American woman to win an overall championship in 1979.

SHORT TRACK

Origins

Short track speed skating was developed in North America in the 1960s. Besides being held indoors and on a smaller track, short track racing also differs from the longer version in that there are usually a pack of four skaters in a race, and a certain amount of bumping between the competitors is allowed. World championships were first staged unofficially in 1978, and the sport gained official Olympic status at the 1992 Games.

World Championships

Unofficial world championships were first staged in 1978. Since 1981 the championships have been recognized by the ISU. The event is staged annually. Two championships were staged in 1987.

Most wins (men) Mark Gagnon (Canada) has won three titles, 1994–96.

Most wins (women) Sylvie Daigle (Canada) has won four world titles, 1983, 1988–90.

Olympic Games Short track speed skating was included as a demonstration sport at the 1988 Calgary Games, and gained official status at the 1992 Games in Albertville.

Most gold medals Kim Ki-hoon (South Korea) won three gold medals: 1,000 meters and 5,000 meter relay, 1992; 1,000 meters, 1994.

Speed Skating World Records—Short Track

MEN

Meters	Time	Name and Country	Date
500	0:42.68	Mirko Vuillermin (Italy)	March 29, 1996
1,000	1:28.47	Mike McMillen (New Zealand)	April 4, 1992
1,500	2:18.16	Mark Gagnon (Canada)	March 11, 1996
3,000	4:56.29	Chae Ji-hoon (South Korea)	March 19, 1995
5,000 relay	6:59.63	Italy	February 9, 1997

WOMEN

Meters	Time	Name and Country	Date
500	0:45.25	Isabel Charest (Canada)	March 2, 1996
1,000	1:32.24	Chun Lee-kyung (South Korea)	October 20, 1996
1,500	2:27.38	Chun Lee-kyung (South Korea)	February 23, 1995
3,000	5:02.18	Chun Lee-kyung South Korea)	March 19, 1995
3,000 relay	4:20.42	South Korea	October 26, 1996

SQUASH

Origins

Squash is an offshoot of rackets and is believed to have been first played at Harrow School, London, England in 1817. The International Squash Rackets Federation (ISRF) was founded in 1967. The Women's International Squash Rackets Federation was formed in 1976. These two groups merged in 1985. In 1992 the ISRF was renamed the World Squash Federation (WSF).

United States The U.S. Squash Racquets Association was formed in 1907, and staged the first U.S. amateur championships that year.

World Open Championships

Both the men's and women's events were first held in 1976. The men's competition is an annual event, but the women's tournament was biennial until 1989, when it switched to the same system as the men's event. There was no championship in 1978.

Most titles Jansher Khan (Pakistan) has won eight titles, 1987, 1989–90, and 1992–96. Susan Devoy (New Zealand) holds the mark in the women's event with five victories, 1985, 1987, 1990–92.

United States Amateur Championships

The U.S. Amateur Championships were first held for men in 1907, and for women in 1928.

Most titles G. Diehl Mateer won 11 men's doubles titles between 1949 and 1966 with five different partners. Joyce Davenport won eight women's doubles titles with two different partners, 1969–90.

Most titles (singles) Alicia McConnell has won seven women's singles titles, 1982–88. Stanley Pearson won a record six men's titles, 1915–17, 1921–23.

SURFING

Origins

The Polynesian sport of surfing in a canoe (*ehorooe*) was first recorded by British explorer Captain James Cook in Tahiti in 1771. The modern sport developed in Hawaii, California and Australia in the 1950s. Hawaii is allowed to compete separately from the U.S. in international surfing competition.

World Amateur Championships

First held in May 1964 in Sydney, Australia, the open championship is the most prestigious event in both men's and women's competition.

Most titles The women's title has been won twice by two surfers: Joyce Hoffman (U.S.), 1965–66; and Sharon Weber (Hawaii), 1970 and 1972. The men's title has been won by a different surfer each time.

Barton Lynch is pro surfing's career earnings leader.
(Jean-Pierre L'Enfant/
Agence Vandystadt)

World Professional Championships

First held in 1970, the World Championship has been organized by the Association of Surfing Professionals (ASP) since 1976. The World Championship is a circuit of events held throughout the year; the winning surfer is the one who gains the most points over the year.

Most titles Two surfers have won four titles: Mark Richards (Australia), in 1979–82; and Kelly Slater (U.S.), in 1992 and 1994–96. The women's record is also four, by two surfers: Frieda Zamba (U.S.), 1984–86, 1988; Wendy Botha (Australia), 1987, 1989, 1991–92.

Youngest champion The youngest surfing world champion was Frieda Zamba, who was 19 years old when she won in 1984. The youngest men's champion was Kelly Slater, who won the 1992 crown at age 20.

Career earnings Barton Lynch (Australia) has the highest career earnings with $582,787. The women's leader is Pam Burridge (Australia) with $227,375.

SWIMMING

Origins

The earliest references to swimming races were in Japan in 36 B.C. The first national swimming association, the Metropolitan Swimming Clubs Association, was founded in England in 1791. The international governing body for swimming, diving and water polo—the *Fédération Internationale de Natation Amateur* (FINA)—was founded in 1908.

Olympic Games

Swimming events have been included in every modern Games since the first one in 1896.

Most gold medals The most Olympic gold medals won is nine, by Mark Spitz (U.S.): 100-meter and 200-meter freestyle, 1972; 100-meter and 200-meter butterfly, 1972; 4 x 100-meter freestyle, 1968 and 1972; 4 x 200-meter freestyle, 1968 and 1972; 4 x 100-meter medley, 1972. The record number of gold medals won by a woman is six, by Kristin Otto (East Germany) at Seoul, South Korea in 1988: 100-meter freestyle, backstroke and butterfly, 50-meter freestyle, 4 x 100-meter freestyle and 4 x 100-meter medley.

Most medals The most medals won by a swimmer is 11, by two competitors: Mark Spitz (U.S.): nine gold (see above), one silver and one bronze, 1968–72; and Matt Biondi (U.S.), eight gold, two silver and one bronze, 1984–92. The most medals won by a woman is eight, by three swimmers: Dawn Fraser (Australia), four gold, four silver, 1956-64; Kornelia Ender (East Germany), four gold, four silver, 1972-76; Shirley Babashoff (U.S.), two gold, six silver, 1972-76.

Most medals (one Games) The most medals won at one Games is seven, by two swimmers: Mark Spitz (U.S.), seven golds in 1972; and Matt Biondi (U.S.), five gold, one silver and one bronze in 1988. Kristin Otto (East Germany) won six gold medals at the 1988 Games, the most for a woman swimmer.

World Championships

The first world swimming championships were held in Belgrade, Yugoslavia in 1973. The championships have been held quadrennially since 1978.

100 meter world record holder Aleksandr Popov celebrates his 1996 Olympic win.
(Pascal Rondeau/Allsport)

Most gold medals Kornelia Ender (East Germany) won eight gold medals, 1973–75. Jim Montgomery (U.S.) won six gold medals, 1973–75, the most by a male swimmer.

Most medals Michael Gross (West Germany) has won 13 medals: five gold, five silver and three bronze, 1982–90. The most medals won by a female swimmer is 10, by Kornelia Ender, who won eight gold and two silver, 1973–75.

Most medals (one championship) Matt Biondi (U.S.) won seven medals—three gold, one silver and three bronze—in 1986 in Madrid, Spain. Two swimmers share the women's record of six medals: Shirley Babashoff (U.S.), two gold, three silver, one bronze, 1975; and Tracy Caulkins (U.S.), five gold, one silver in 1978.

SWIMMING—Men's World Records
(set in 50-meter pools)

Event	Time	Swimmer (Country)	Date
Freestyle			
50 meters	21.81	Tom Jager (U.S.)	March 24, 1990
100 meters	48.21	Alexander Popov (Russia)	June 18, 1994
200 meters	46.69	Giorgio Lamberti (Italy)	August 15, 1989
400 meters	3:43.80	Kieren Perkins (Australia)	September 9, 1994
800 meters	7:46.00	Kieren Perkins (Australia)	August 24, 1994
1,500 meters	14:41.66	Kieren Perkins (Australia)	August 24, 1994
4 x 100-meter relay	3:15.11	U.S. (Dave Fox, Joe Hudipohi, John Olsen and Gary Hall Jr.)	August 12, 1995
4 x 200-meter relay	7:11.95	Unified Team (Dmitri Lepikov, Vladimir Pychenko, Veniamin Taianovitch, Yevgeni Sadovyi)	July 27, 1992
Breaststroke			
100 meters	1:00.60	Frederik Deburghgraeve (Belgium)	July 20, 1996
200 meters	2:10.16	Michael Barrowman (U.S.)	July 29, 1992
Butterfly			
100 meters	52.27	Denis Pankratov (Russia)	July 24, 1996
200 meters	1:55.22	Denis Pankratov (Russia)	June 14, 1995
Backstroke			
100 meters	53.86	Jeff Rouse (U.S.)	July 31, 1992
200 meters	1:56.57	Martin Lopez-Zubero (Spain)	November 23, 1991
Individual Medley			
200 meters	1:58.16	Jani Sievinen (Finland)	September 11, 1994
400 meters	4:12.30	Tom Dolan (U.S.)	September 6, 1994
4 x 100-meter relay	3:34.84	U.S. (Jeff Rouse, Jeremy Linn, Mark Henderson, Gary Hall Jr.)	July 26, 1996

Source: USA Swimming

United States National Championships

The first United States swimming championships were staged by the Amateur Athletic Union on August 25, 1888.

Most titles Tracy Caulkins has won a record 48 national swimming titles, 1977–84. The most titles for a male swimmer is 36, by Johnny Weissmuller, 1921–28.

Fastest swimmer In a 25-yard pool, Tom Jager (U.S.) achieved an average speed of 5.37 mph, swimming 50 yards in 19.05 seconds at Nashville, TN on March 23, 1990. The women's fastest average speed is by Le Jingyi (China) in her 50-meter world record (see World Records table).

SWIMMING—Women's World Records
(set in 50-meter pools)

Event	Time	Swimmer (Country)	Date
Freestyle			
50 meters	24.51	Le Jingyi (China)	September 11, 1994
100 meters	54.01	Le Jingyi (China)	September 5, 1994
200 meters	1:56.78	Franziska Van Almsick (Germany)	September 6, 1994
400 meters	4:03.85	Janet Evans (U.S.)	September 22, 1988
800 meters	8:16.22	Janet Evans (U.S.)	August 20, 1989
1,500 meters	15:52.10	Janet Evans (U.S.)	March 26, 1988
4 x 100-meter relay	3:37.91	China (Le Jingyi, Shan Ying, Le Ying, Lu Bin)	September 10, 1994
4 x 200-meter relay	7:55.47	East Germany (Manuella Stellmach, Astrid Strauss, Anke Möhring, Heike Freidrich)	August 18, 1987
Breaststroke			
100 meters	1:07.02	Penny Heyns (South Africa)	July 21, 1996
200 meters	2:24.76	Rebecca Brown (Australia)	March 16, 1994
Butterfly			
100 meters	57.93	Mary T. Meagher (U.S.)	August 16, 1981
200 meters	2:05.96	Mary T. Meagher (U.S.)	August 13, 1981
Backstroke			
100 meters	1:00.16	He Cihong (China)	September 10, 1994
200 meters	2:06.82	Krizstina Egerszegi (Hungary)	August 26, 1991
Individual Medley			
200 meters	2:11.65	Lin Li (China)*	July 30, 1992
400 meters	4:36.10	Petra Schneider (East Germany)	August 1, 1982
4 x 100-meter relay	4:01.67	China (He Cihong, Dai Guohong, Liu Limin, Le Jingyi)	September 10, 1994

* Lu Bin (China) swam 2:11:57 on October 7, 1994, but she was disqualified for using drugs.

Source: USA Swimming

⟩ Fantastic Feats

Manhattan swim The fastest swim around Manhattan Island, New York City is 5 hours 53 minutes 57 seconds, achieved by Kris Rutford (U.S.), on August 29, 1992. (Rutford also holds the record for swimming clockwise around Manhattan, 17 hours 48 minutes 30 seconds.) Shelley Taylor set the women's record, 6 hours 12 minutes 29 seconds, on October 15, 1985.

English Channel swim Chad Hundeby (Irvine, CA) swam the English Channel in a record time of 7 hours 17 minutes on September 27, 1994. The official women's record is 7 hours 40 minutes by Penny Dean (U.S.).

Alison Streeter (Great Britain) swam the Channel 32 times between 1982 and 1995, including a record seven crossings in one year in 1992. The men's record is 31, by Michael Reed (Great Britain), 1969–84.

Swimming Against the Tide

Talk about The Little Engine That Could. When Amy Van Dyken was six, her doctor advised her that swimming would help her asthma. Struggling to stay afloat, Van Dyken worked for six years to finish one single lap in the pool.

Who would have guessed this young beginner trying to improve her health would one day become an Olympic gold medalist and Guinness record-holder? Well, Van Dyken did it. After her struggle to finish her first lap at age 12, she won her first gold medal at 13. "I just wanted to make my high school team," she says. "That was my first step. I always took things step by step in my life. Of course I watched the Olympics and wanted to be like those swimmers, but I never thought it would happen."

So Van Dyken tried out for her high school team. They took 28 swimmers and she was the 28th. "My freshman and sophomore years were tough because I was just terrible. My teammates would say things like 'I don't want Van Dyken on my team' because I was so bad. But by my junior

Tony Duffy/NBC/Allsport

year, I turned it around. I started breaking state records. By my senior year I had offers for college scholarships," she recalls.

Although swimming is an intense sport for a teenager, Van Dyken remembers all the fun she had with her buddies on the team. "I just loved what I was doing. We goofed around a lot after practice—you know, seeing how long we could hold our breath and stuff like that," she reminisces. "It was very hard to juggle swimming and high school in terms of work. But in the end, I think it actually gives you a shot of discipline. You have to wake up early and go to practices. When you come home, you're tired, but you realize you need to get good grades for college. So you do your work and go to sleep and wake up early again for practice. Even now, it's hard not to have a structure in my life—I had one for so long."

So what's Van Dyken's secret to success? Nothing too complicated, she admits. She just hates to lose. "I do anything I can to make sure I'm the best at what I do. I'm so competitive in everything. That's what keeps me going."

SYNCHRONIZED SWIMMING

In international competition, synchronized swimmers compete in three events: solo, duet and team. A technical routine in each event of the competitive program is now included at the World Cup, World Championships and Olympic Games. In all three events the swimmers perform to music a series of moves that are judged for technical merit and artistic impression. In solo events the swimmer must be synchronized with the music; in duet and team events the swimmers must be synchronized with each other as well as with the music.

Origins

Annette Kellerman and Kay Curtis are considered the pioneers of synchronized swimming in the United States. Kellerman's water ballet performances drew widespread attention throughout the U.S. at the beginning of the 20th century. Curtis was responsible for establishing synchronized swimming as part of the physical education program at the University of Wisconsin.

In 1945 the Amateur Athletic Union recognized the sport. In 1973 the first world championship was staged, and in 1984 synchronized swimming was recognized as an official Olympic sport. The governing body for the sport in this country is United States Synchronized Swimming, formed in 1978.

Olympic Games

Synchronized swimming was first staged as an official sport at the 1984 Games.

Most gold medals Two swimmers have won two gold medals: Tracie Ruiz-Conforto (U.S.), solo and duet, 1984; Carolyn Waldo (Canada), solo and duet, 1988.

Most medals Two swimmers have won three medals: Tracie Ruiz-Conforto (U.S.), two gold and one silver, 1984–88; Carolyn Waldo (Canada), two gold and one silver, 1984–88.

World Championships

The world championships were first held in 1973, and have been held quadrennially since 1978.

Most titles The solo title has been won by a different swimmer on each occasion.

Most titles (team) The United States has won five team titles, 1973, 1975, 1978, 1991 and 1994.

United States National Championships

The first national championships were staged in 1946, and the competition is now an annual event.

Most titles Gail Johnson has won 11 national titles: six solo (two indoors, four outdoors), 1972–75; and five duet (two indoors, three outdoors), 1972–74.

Most titles (duet) The team of Karen and Sarah Josephson has won seven national duet titles, 1985–88, and 1990–92.

Grand Slams

Most grand slams Becky Dyroen Lancer (U.S.) has won a record nine Grand Slams (solo, duet team and figures) consecutively in five international and four national competitions, 1992–95.

The United States team won the 1996 Olympic synchronized swimming gold medal.
(Pascal Rondeau/Allsport)

TABLE TENNIS

Origins

The earliest evidence relating to a game resembling table tennis (also commonly known as Ping-Pong) has been found in the catalogs of London sporting goods manufacturers from the 1880s. The International Table Tennis Federation (ITTF) was founded in 1926.

United States The United States Table Tennis Association was established in 1933. In 1971, a U.S. table tennis team was invited to play in the People's Republic of China, thereby initiating the first officially sanctioned Chinese–American cultural exchange in almost 20 years.

Olympic Games

Table tennis was included in the Olympic Games in 1988 for the first time.

Most gold medals Deng Yapin (China) has won four gold medals, 1992–96.

Most medals Two players have won four medals in Olympic competition: Yoo Nam-kyu (South Korea), one gold, three bronze, 1988–96; and Deng Yapin (see above).

World Championships

The ITTF instituted European championships in 1926 and later designated this event the world championship. The tournament was staged annually until 1957, when the event became biennial.

Swaythling Cup

The men's team championship is named after Lady Swaythling, who donated the trophy in 1926.

Most titles The most wins is 12, by Hungary (1926, 1928–31, 1933 [two events were held that year, with Hungary winning both times], 1935, 1938, 1949, 1952, 1979).

Corbillon Cup

The women's team championship is named after Marcel Corbillon, president of the French Table Tennis Association, who donated the trophy in 1934.

Most titles China has won the most titles, with 11 wins (1965, 1975, 1977, 1979, 1981, 1983, 1985, 1987, 1989, 1993 and 1995).

Men's singles The most victories in singles is five, by Viktor Barna (Hungary), 1931, 1932-35.

Women's singles The most victories is six, by Angelica Rozeanu (Romania), 1950–55.

Men's doubles The most victories is eight, by Viktor Barna (Hungary), 1929–35, 1939. The partnership that won the most titles is Viktor Barna and Miklos Szabados (Hungary), 1929–33, 1935.

Women's doubles The most victories is seven, by Maria Mednyanszky (Hungary), 1928, 1930–35. The team that won the most titles is Maria Mednyanszky and Anna Sipos (Hungary), 1930–35.

Mixed doubles Maria Mednyanszky (Hungary) won a record six mixed doubles titles: 1927–28, 1930-31, 1933 (twice). The pairing of Miklos Szabados and Maria Mednyanszky (Hungary) won the title a record three times: 1930–31, 1933.

United States National Championships

U.S. national championships were first held in 1931.

Most titles Leah Neuberger (née Thall) won a record 21 titles between 1941 and 1961: nine women's singles, 12 women's doubles. Richard Mills won a record 10 men's singles titles between 1945 and 1962.

➠ Fantastic Feats

Most hits The record number of hits in 60 seconds is 173, by Jackie Bellinger and Lisa Lomas (née Bellinger) in Great Britain on February 7, 1993.

With a paddle in each hand, S. Ramesh Babu (India) completed 5,000 consecutive volleys over the net in 41 minutes 27 seconds on April 14, 1995.

Youngest championship player Joy Foster (Jamaica) was eight years old when she played at the West Indies Championships in Port of Spain, Trinidad in August 1988.

TEAM HANDBALL

Origins

Team handball developed around the turn of the 20th century. It evolved from a game devised by soccer players in northern Germany and Denmark designed to keep them fit during the winter months. An outdoors version of the game was included in the 1936 Olympic Games as a demonstration sport. In 1946 the International Handball Federation (IHF) was formed. The growth of team handball has been rapid since its reintroduction into the Olympic Games in 1972 as an indoor game with seven players on each side. The IHF claims 4.2 million members from 88 countries, second only to soccer in terms of worldwide membership.

United States Team handball was first introduced to the United States in the 1920s, and a national team entered the 1936 Olympic demonstration competition. In 1959 the United States Team Handball Federation USTHF) was formed, and it still governs the sport in this country.

Olympic Games

Most wins In men's competition the USSR/Unified Team has won the Olympic gold medal three times—1976, 1988 and 1992.

In women's competition, introduced in 1976, two countries have won the gold medal twice: the USSR in 1976 and 1980; and South Korea in 1988 and 1992.

World Championship

This competition was instituted in 1938.

Most titles (country) Romania has won four men's and three women's titles (two outdoor, one indoor) from 1956 to 1974. East Germany has also won three women's titles, in 1971, 1975 and 1978.

Ziatco Savacevic led Croatia to its Olympic team handball gold medal.
(Mike Hewitt/Allsport)

TENNIS

Origins

The modern game evolved from the indoor sport of real tennis. There is an account of a game called "field tennis" in an English sports periodical dated September 29, 1793; however, the "father" of lawn tennis is considered to be Major Walter Wingfield, who patented a type of tennis called "sphairistike" in 1874. The Marylebone Cricket Club, England revised Wingfield's initial rules in 1877, and the famed All-England Croquet Club (home of the Wimbledon Championships) added the name Lawn Tennis to its title in 1877. The "open" era of tennis, when amateurs were permitted to play with and against professionals, was introduced in 1968.

GRAND SLAM

The grand slam is achieved by winning all four grand slam events—the Australian Open, French Open, Wimbledon and U.S. Open—in one calendar year.

Most Grand Slam Titles

Singles   The most singles championships won in grand slam tournaments is 24, by Margaret Court (née Smith; Australia): 11 Australian, five French, three Wimbledon, five U.S. Open between 1960 and 1973. The men's record is 12, by Roy Emerson (Australia): six Australian, two French, two Wimbledon, two U.S. Open between 1961 and 1967.

Doubles   The most wins by a doubles partnership is 20, by two teams: Louise Brough (U.S.) and Margaret Du Pont (U.S.), who won three French, five Wimbledon and 12 U.S. Opens, 1942–57; and by Martina Navratilova (U.S.) and Pam Shriver (U.S.). They won seven Australian, four French, five Wimbledon, four U.S. Opens,1981–89.

AUSTRALIAN OPEN CHAMPIONSHIPS

The first Australasian championships were held in 1905, with New Zealand hosting the event in 1906 and 1912. A women's championship was not introduced

Martina Hingis holds up the Australian Open trophy following her victory in the 1997 event. At 16 years old, she is the youngest champion.
(Clive Brunskill/Allsport)

until 1922. The tournament was changed to the Australian Open in 1925 and is counted as a grand slam event from that year. There were two championships in 1977 because the event was moved from early season (January) to December. It reverted to a January date in 1987, which meant there was no championship in 1986. Currently the tournament is held at the Australian Tennis Center in Melbourne and is the first leg of the grand slam.

Most wins (men)   The most wins is six, by Roy Emerson (Australia), 1961, 1963–67.

Most wins (women)   The most wins is 11, by Margaret Court (née Smith) of Australia, 1960–66, 1969–71, 1973.

Men's doubles   The most wins by one pair is eight, by John Bromwich and Adrian Quist (Australia), 1938–40, 1946–50. In addition, Quist holds the record for most wins by one player with 10, winning in 1936–37 with Don Turnbull, to add to his triumphs with Bromwich.

Australian Open Champions
Men's Singles

Year	Player		Year	Player		Year	Player
1905	Rodney Heath		1936	Adrian Quist		1968	Bill Bowrey
1906	Tony Wilding		1937	V. B. McGrath		1969	Rod Laver
1907	Horace Rice		1938	Don Budge		1970	Arthur Ashe
1908	Fred Alexander		1939	John Bromwich		1971	Ken Rosewall
1909	Tony Wilding		1940	Adrian Quist		1972	Ken Rosewall
1910	Rodney Heath		1941	*not held*		1973	John Newcombe
1911	Norman Brookes		1942	*not held*		1974	Jimmy Connors
1912	J. Cecil Parke		1943	*not held*		1975	John Newcombe
1913	E. F. Parker		1944	*not held*		1976	Mark Edmondson
1914	Pat O'Hara Wood		1945	*not held*		1977	Roscoe Tanner*
1915	Francis Lowe		1946	John Bromwich		1977	Vitas Gerulaitis*
1916	*not held*		1947	Dinny Pails		1978	Guillermo Vilas
1917	*not held*		1948	Adrian Quist		1979	Guillermo Vilas
1918	*not held*		1949	Frank Sedgman		1980	Brian Teacher
1919	A. Kingscote		1950	Frank Sedgman		1981	Johan Kriek
1920	Pat O'Hara Wood		1951	Dick Savitt		1982	Johan Kriek
1921	Rhys Gemmell		1952	Ken McGregor		1983	Mats Wilander
1922	Pat O'Hara Wood		1953	Ken Rosewall		1984	Mats Wilander
1923	Pat O'Hara Wood		1954	Mervyn Rose		1985	Stefan Edberg
1924	James Anderson		1955	Ken Rosewall		1986	*not held*
1925	James Anderson		1956	Lew Hoad		1987	Stefan Edberg
1926	John Hawkes		1957	Ashley Cooper		1988	Mats Wilander
1927	Gerald Patterson		1958	Ashley Cooper		1989	Ivan Lendl
1928	Jean Borotra		1959	Alex Olmedo		1990	Ivan Lendl
1929	John Gregory		1960	Rod Laver		1991	Boris Becker
1930	Gar Moon		1961	Roy Emerson		1992	Jim Courier
1931	Jack Crawford		1962	Rod Laver		1993	Jim Courier
1932	Jack Crawford		1963	Roy Emerson		1994	Pete Sampras
1933	Jack Crawford		1964	Roy Emerson		1995	Andre Agassi
1934	Fred Perry		1965	Roy Emerson		1996	Boris Becker
1935	Jack Crawford		1966	Roy Emerson		1997	Pete Sampras
			1967	Roy Emerson			

* There were two championships in 1977 because the event was moved from early season (January) to December.

Women's doubles The most wins by one pair is 10, by Nancye Bolton (née Wynne) and Thelma Long (née Coyne), both Australian. Their victories came in 1936–40, 1947–49, 1951–52. Long also holds the record for most wins, with 12, winning in 1956 and 1958 with Mary Hawton.

Mixed doubles The most wins by one pair is four, by two teams: Harry Hopman and Nell Hopman (née Hall; Australia), 1930, 1936–37, 1939; Colin Long and Nancye Bolton (née Wynne; Australia), 1940, 1946–48. Thelma Long (Australia) shares the women's record of four wins, 1951–52, 1954–55.

Australian Open Champions
Women's Singles

Year	Player		Year	Player		Year	Player
1905	*no event*		1938	Dorothy M. Bundy		1972	Virginia Wade
1906	*no eventt*		1939	Emily Westacott		1973	Margaret Court
1907	*no event*		1940	Nancye Wynne		1974	Evonne Goolagong
1908	*no event*		1941	*not held*		1975	Evonne Goolagong
1909	*no event*		1942	*not held*		1976	Evonne Cawley [4]
1910	*no event*		1943	*not held*		1977	Kerry Reid*
1911	*no event*		1944	*not held*		1977	Evonne Cawley*
1912	*no event*		1945	*not held*		1978	Christine O'Neill
1913	*no event*		1946	Nancye Bolton [1]		1979	Barbara Jordan
1914	*no event*		1947	Nancye Bolton		1980	Hana Mandlikova
1915	*no event*		1948	Nancye Bolton		1981	Martina Navratilova
1916	*not held*		1949	Doris Hart		1982	Chris Evert
1917	*not held*		1950	Louise Brough		1983	Martina Navratilova
1918	*not held*		1951	Nancye Bolton		1984	Chris Evert
1919	*no event*		1952	Thelma Long		1985	Martina Navratilova
1920	*no event*		1953	Maureen Connolly		1986	*not held*
1921	*no event*		1954	Thelma Long		1987	Hana Mandlikova
1922	Margaret Molesworth		1955	Beryl Penrose		1988	Steffi Graf
1923	Margaret Molesworth		1956	Mary Carter		1989	Steffi Graf
1924	Sylvia Lance		1957	Shirley Fry		1990	Steffi Graf
1925	Daphne Akhurst		1958	Angela Mortimer		1991	Monica Seles
1926	Daphne Akhurst		1959	Mary Reitano [2]		1992	Monica Seles
1927	Esna Boyd		1960	Margaret Smith		1993	Monica Seles
1928	Daphne Akhurst		1961	Margaret Smith		1994	Steffi Graf
1929	Daphne Akhurst		1962	Margaret Smith		1995	Mary Pierce
1930	Daphne Akhurst		1963	Margaret Smith		1996	Monica Seles
1931	Coral Buttsworth		1964	Margaret Smith		1997	Martina Hingis
1932	Coral Buttsworth		1965	Margaret Smith			
1933	Joan Hartigan		1966	Margaret Smith			
1934	Joan Hartigan		1967	Nancy Richey			
1935	Dorothy Round		1968	Billie Jean King			
1936	Joan Hartigan		1969	Margaret Court [3]			
1937	Nancye Wynne		1970	Margaret Court			
			1971	Margaret Court			

1—Nancye Bolton (née Wynne)
2—Mary Reitano (née Carter)
3—Margaret Court (née Smith)
4—Evonne Cawley (née Goolagong)

* There were two championships in 1977 because the event was moved from early season (January) to December.

Most titles (overall) Margaret Court (née Smith) won 21 Australian Open titles, 1960–73: 11 singles, eight doubles and two mixed doubles.

Youngest champion The youngest singles champion is Martina Hingis (Switzerland), who won the 1997 event at age 16 years 117 days.

FRENCH OPEN CHAMPIONSHIPS

The first French championships were held in 1891; however, entry was restricted to members of French clubs until 1925. Grand slam records include the French Open only from 1925. This event has been staged at the Stade Roland Garros since 1928 and currently is the second leg of the grand slam.

Most wins (women) Chris Evert has won a record seven French titles: 1974–75, 1979–80, 1983, 1985–86.

Most wins (men) Bjorn Borg (Sweden) has won the French title a record six times: 1974–75, 1978–81.

Men's doubles The most wins by one pair is three, by Henri Cochet and Jacques Brugnon (both France). They won in 1927, 1930 and 1932. The most wins by one player is six, by Roy Emerson (Australia), 1960–65, with five different partners.

Women's doubles

Three teams have won the doubles title three times: Doris Hart and Shirley Fry (both U.S.), 1950–53; Martina Navratilova and Pam Shriver (both U.S.), 1984–85, 1987–88; and Gigi Fernandez (U.S.) and Natasha Zvereva (Belarus), 1992–95. The most wins by an individual player is seven, by Martina Navratilova—four times with Pam Shriver, 1984–85, 1987–88; and with three other players, in 1975, 1982 and 1986.

Mixed doubles Two teams have won the mixed title three times: Ken Fletcher and Margaret Smith (Australia), 1963–65; Jean-Claude Barclay and Francoise Durr (France), 1968, 1971, 1973. Margaret Court (née Smith) has won the title the most times, with four wins, winning with Marty Riessen (U.S.)

in 1969, in addition to her wins with Fletcher. Fletcher and Barclay share the men's record of three wins.

Most titles (overall) Margaret Court (née Smith) has won a record 13 French Open titles, 1962–73: five singles, four doubles and four mixed doubles.

Youngest champions The youngest singles champion at the French Open was Monica Seles (Yugoslavia) in 1990, at 16 years 169 days. The youngest men's winner was Michael Chang (U.S.), who was 17 years 109 days when he won the 1989 title.

WIMBLEDON CHAMPIONSHIPS

The "Lawn Tennis Championships" at the All-England Club, Wimbledon are generally regarded as the most prestigious in tennis and currently form the third leg of the grand slam events. They were first held in 1877 and, until 1922, were organized on a challenge round system (the defending champion automatically qualified for the following year's final and played the winner of the challenger event). Wimbledon became an open championship (professionals could compete) in 1968.

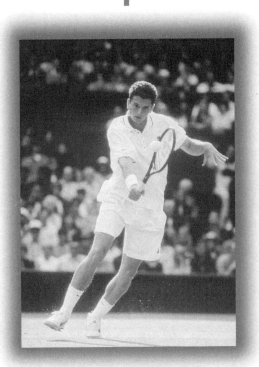

1996 Wimbledon men's champion Richard Krajicek won the first final contested between unseeded players in the tournament's long history.
(Gary M. Prior/Allsport)

Most titles (men) Overall, the most titles is seven, by William Renshaw (Great Britain), 1881–86, 1889. Since the abolition of the Challenge Round in 1922, the most wins is five, by Bjorn Borg (Sweden), 1976–80.

Most titles (women) Martina Navratilova has won a record nine titles: 1978–79, 1982–87, 1990.

Men's doubles Lawrence and Reginald Doherty (Great Britain) won the doubles title eight times: 1897–1901, 1903–05. *(continued on page 216)*

French Open Champions
Men's Singles

Year	Player		Year	Player
1925	Rene Lacoste		1962	Rod Laver
1926	Henri Cochet		1963	Roy Emerson
1927	Rene Lacoste		1964	Manuel Santana
1928	Henri Cochet		1965	Fred Stolle
1929	Rene Lacoste		1966	Tony Roche
1930	Henri Cochet		1967	Roy Emerson
1931	Jean Borotra		1968	Ken Rosewall
1932	Henri Cochet		1969	Rod Laver
1933	Jack Crawford		1970	Jan Kodes
1934	Gottfried Von Cramm		1971	Jan Kodes
1935	Fred Perry		1972	Andres Gimeno
1936	Gottfried Von Cramm		1973	Ilie Nastase
1937	Henner Henkel		1974	Bjorn Borg
1938	Don Budge		1975	Bjorn Borg
1939	Donald McNeil		1976	Adriano Panatta
1940	not held		1977	Guillermo Vilas
1941	Bernard Destremau*		1978	Bjorn Borg
1942	Bernard Destremau*		1979	Bjorn Borg
1943	Yvon Petra*		1980	Bjorn Borg
1944	Yvon Petra*		1981	Bjorn Borg
1945	Yvon Petra*		1982	Mats Wilander
1946	Marcel Bernard		1983	Yannick Noah
1947	Jozsef Asboth		1984	Ivan Lendl
1948	Frank Parker		1985	Mats Wilander
1949	Frank Parker		1986	Ivan Lendl
1950	Budge Patty		1987	Ivan Lendl
1951	Jaroslav Drobny		1988	Mats Wilander
1952	Jaroslav Drobny		1989	Michael Chang
1953	Ken Rosewall		1990	Andres Gomez
1954	Tony Trabert		1991	Jim Courier
1955	Tony Trabert		1992	Jim Courier
1956	Lew Hoad		1993	Sergei Bruguera
1957	Sven Davidson		1994	Sergei Bruguera
1958	Mervyn Rose		1995	Thomas Muster
1959	Nicola Pietrangeli		1996	Yevgeny Kafelnikov
1960	Nicola Pietrangeli			
1961	Manuel Santana			

* From 1941 through 1945 the event was called Tournoi de France and was open only to French citizens.

French Open Champions
Women's Singles

Year	Player
1925	Suzanne Lenglen
1926	Suzanne Lenglen
1927	Kea Bouman
1928	Helen Moody [1]
1929	Helen Moody
1930	Helen Moody
1931	Cilly Aussem
1932	Helen Moody
1933	Margaret Scriven
1934	Margaret Scriven
1935	Hilde Sperling
1936	Hilde Sperling
1937	Hilde Sperling
1938	Simone Mathieu
1939	Simone Mathieu
1940	*not held*
1941	*not held*
1942	*not held*
1943	*not held*
1944	*not held*
1945	*not held*
1946	Margaret Osborne
1947	Pat Todd
1948	Nelly Landry
1949	Margaret Du Pont [2]
1950	Doris Hart
1951	Shirley Fry
1952	Doris Hart
1953	Maureen Connolly
1954	Maureen Connolly
1955	Angela Mortimer
1956	Althea Gibson
1957	Shirley Bloomer
1958	Zsuzsi Kormoczy
1959	Christine Truman
1960	Darlene Hard
1961	Ann Haydon
1962	Margaret Smith
1963	Lesley Turner
1964	Margaret Smith
1965	Lesley Turner
1966	Ann Jones [3]
1967	Francoise Durr
1968	Nancy Richey
1969	Margaret Court [4]
1970	Margaret Court
1971	Evonne Goolagong
1972	Billie Jean King
1973	Margaret Court
1974	Chris Evert
1975	Chris Evert
1976	Sue Barker
1977	Mima Jausovec
1978	Virginia Ruzici
1979	Chris Evert
1980	Chris Evert
1981	Hana Mandlikova
1982	Martina Navratilova
1983	Chris Evert
1984	Martina Navratilova
1985	Chris Evert
1986	Chris Evert
1987	Steffi Graf
1988	Steffi Graf
1989	Arantxa Sánchez Vicario
1990	Monica Seles
1991	Monica Seles
1992	Monica Seles
1993	Steffi Graf
1994	Arantxa Sánchez Vicario
1995	Steffi Graf
1996	Steffi Graf

1 — Helen Moody (née Wills)
2 — Margaret Du Pont (née Osborne)
3 — Ann Jones (née Haydon)
4 — Margaret Court (née Smith)

Wimbledon Champions
Men's Singles

Year	Player	Year	Player	Year	Player
1877	Spencer Gore	1917	*not held*	1957	Lew Hoad
1878	Frank Hadlow	1918	*not held*	1958	Ashley Cooper
1879	Rev. John Hartley	1919	Gerald Patterson	1959	Alex Olmedo
1880	Rev. John Hartley	1920	Bill Tilden	1960	Neale Fraser
1881	William Renshaw	1921	Bill Tilden	1961	Rod Laver
1882	William Renshaw	1922	Gerald Patterson	1962	Rod Laver
1883	William Renshaw	1923	William Johnston	1963	Chuck McKinley
1884	William Renshaw	1924	Jean Borotra	1964	Roy Emerson
1885	William Renshaw	1925	Rene Lacoste	1965	Roy Emerson
1886	William Renshaw	1926	Jean Borotra	1966	Manuel Santana
1887	Herbert Lawford	1927	Henri Cochet	1967	John Newcombe
1888	Ernest Renshaw	1928	Rene Lacoste	1968	Rod Laver
1889	William Renshaw	1929	Henri Cochet	1969	Rod Laver
1890	Willoughby Hamilton	1930	Bill Tilden	1970	John Newcombe
1891	Wilfred Baddeley	1931	Sidney Wood	1971	John Newcombe
1892	Wilfred Baddeley	1932	Ellsworth Vines	1972	Stan Smith
1893	Joshua Pim	1933	Jack Crawford	1973	Jan Kodes
1894	Joshua Pim	1934	Fred Perry	1974	Jimmy Connors
1895	Wilfred Baddeley	1935	Fred Perry	1975	Arthur Ashe
1896	Harold Mahoney	1936	Fred Perry	1976	Bjorn Borg
1897	Reginald Doherty	1937	Don Budge	1977	Bjorn Borg
1898	Reginald Doherty	1938	Don Budge	1978	Bjorn Borg
1899	Reginald Doherty	1939	Bobby Riggs	1979	Bjorn Borg
1900	Reginald Doherty	1940	*not held*	1980	Bjorn Borg
1901	Arthur Gore	1941	*not held*	1981	John McEnroe
1902	Lawrence Doherty	1942	*not held*	1982	Jimmy Connors
1903	Lawrence Doherty	1943	*not held*	1983	John McEnroe
1904	Lawrence Doherty	1944	*not held*	1984	John McEnroe
1905	Lawrence Doherty	1945	*not held*	1985	Boris Becker
1906	Lawrence Doherty	1946	Yvon Petra	1986	Boris Becker
1907	Norman Brookes	1947	Jack Kramer	1987	Pat Cash
1908	Arthur Gore	1948	Bob Falkenburg	1988	Stefan Edberg
1909	Arthur Gore	1949	Ted Schroeder	1989	Boris Becker
1910	Tony Wilding	1950	Budge Patty	1990	Stefan Edberg
1911	Tony Wilding	1951	Dick Savitt	1991	Michael Stich
1912	Tony Wilding	1952	Frank Sedgman	1992	Andre Agassi
1913	Tony Wilding	1953	Vic Seixas	1993	Pete Sampras
1914	Norman Brookes	1954	Jaroslav Drobny	1994	Pete Sampras
1915	*not held*	1955	Tony Trabert	1995	Pete Sampras
1916	*not held*	1956	Lew Hoad	1996	Richard Krajicek

Wimbledon Champions
Women's Singles

Year	Player
1877	*no event*
1878	*no event*
1879	*no event*
1880	*no event*
1881	*no event*
1882	*no event*
1883	*no event*
1884	Maud Watson
1885	Maud Watson
1886	Blanche Bingley
1887	Lottie Dod
1888	Lottie Dod
1889	Blanche Hillyard [1]
1890	Helene Rice
1891	Lottie Dod
1892	Lottie Dod
1893	Lottie Dod
1894	Blanche Hillyard
1895	Charlotte Cooper
1896	Charlotte Cooper
1897	Blanche Hillyard
1898	Charlotte Cooper
1899	Blanche Hillyard
1900	Blanche Hillyard
1901	Charlotte Sterry [2]
1902	Muriel Robb
1903	Dorothea Douglass
1904	Dorothea Douglass
1905	May Sutton
1906	Dorothea Douglass
1907	May Sutton
1908	Charlotte Sterry
1909	Dora Boothby
1910	Dorothea Lambert-Chambers [3]
1911	Dorothea Lambert-Chambers
1912	Ethel Larcombe
1913	Dorothea Lambert-Chambers
1914	Dorothea Lambert-Chambers
1915	*not held*
1916	*not held*
1917	*not held*
1918	*not held*
1919	Suzanne Lenglen
1920	Suzanne Lenglen
1921	Suzanne Lenglen
1922	Suzanne Lenglen
1923	Suzanne Lenglen
1924	Kathleen McKane
1925	Suzanne Lenglen
1926	Kathleen Godfree [4]
1927	Helen Wills
1928	Helen Wills
1929	Helen Wills
1930	Helen Moody [5]
1931	Cilly Aussem
1932	Helen Moody
1933	Helen Moody
1934	Dorothy Round
1935	Helen Moody [5]
1936	Helen Jacobs
1937	Dorothy Round
1938	Helen Moody
1939	Alice Marble
1940	*not held*
1941	*not held*
1942	*not held*
1943	*not held*
1944	*not held*
1945	*not held*
1946	Pauline Betz
1947	Margaret Osborne
1948	Louise Brough
1949	Louise Brough
1950	Louise Brough
1951	Doris Hart
1952	Maureen Connolly
1953	Maureen Connolly
1954	Maureen Connolly
1955	Louise Brough
1956	Shirley Fry
1957	Althea Gibson
1958	Althea Gibson
1959	Maria Bueno
1960	Maria Bueno
1961	Angela Mortimer
1962	Karen Susman
1963	Margaret Smith
1964	Maria Bueno
1965	Margaret Smith
1966	Billie Jean King
1967	Billie Jean King
1968	Billie Jean King
1969	Ann Jones
1970	Margaret Court [6]
1971	Evonne Goolagong
1972	Billie Jean King
1973	Billie Jean King
1974	Chris Evert
1975	Billie Jean King
1976	Chris Evert
1977	Virginia Wade
1978	Martina Navratilova
1979	Martina Navratilova
1980	Evonne Cawley [7]
1981	Chris Evert
1982	Martina Navratilova
1983	Martina Navratilova
1984	Martina Navratilova
1985	Martina Navratilova
1986	Martina Navratilova
1987	Martina Navratilova
1988	Steffi Graf
1989	Steffi Graf
1990	Martina Navratilova
1991	Steffi Graf
1992	Steffi Graf
1993	Steffi Graf
1994	Conchita Martinez
1995	Steffi Graf
1996	Steffi Graf

1 - Blanche Hillyard (née Bingley)
2 - Charlotte Sterry (née Cooper)
3 - Dorothea Lambert-Chambers (née Douglass)
4 - Kathleen Godfree (née McKane)
5 - Helen Moody (née Wills)
6 - Margaret Court (née Smith)
7 - Evonne Cawley (née Goolagong)

Women's doubles   Suzanne Lenglen (France) and Elizabeth Ryan (U.S.) won the doubles a record six times: 1919–23, 1925. Elizabeth Ryan was a winning partner on a record 12 occasions: 1914, 1919–23, 1925–27, 1930, 1933–34.

Mixed doubles   The team of Ken Fletcher and Margaret Court (née Smith), both of Australia, won the mixed doubles a record four times: 1963, 1965–66, 1968. Fletcher's four victories tie him for the men's record for wins, which is shared by two other players: Vic Seixas (U.S.), 1953–56; Owen Davidson (Australia), 1967, 1971, 1973–74. Elizabeth Ryan (U.S.) holds the women's record with seven wins: 1919, 1921, 1923, 1927–28, 1930, 1932.

Most titles (overall)   Billie Jean King (U.S.) won a record 20 Wimbledon titles from 1961–79: six singles, 10 doubles and four mixed doubles.

Youngest champions   The youngest champion was Lottie Dod (Great Britain), who was 15 years 285 days when she won in 1887. The youngest men's champion was Boris Becker (Germany), who was 17 years 227 days when he won in 1985.

UNITED STATES OPEN CHAMPIONSHIPS

The first official U.S. championships were staged in 1881. From 1884 to 1911, the contest was based on a challenger format. In 1968 and 1969, separate amateur and professional events were held. Since 1970, there has been only an Open competition. On the current schedule the U.S. Open is the fourth and final leg of the grand slam and is played at the U.S. National Tennis Center, Flushing Meadows, NY.

Most titles (men)   The most wins is seven, by three players: Richard Sears (U.S.), 1881–87; William Larned (U.S.), 1901–02, 1907–11; Bill Tilden (U.S.), 1920–25, 1929.

Most titles (women)   Molla Mallory (née Bjurstedt; U.S.) won a record eight titles: 1915–18, 1920–22, 1926.

Men's doubles   The most wins by one pair is five, by Richard Sears and James Dwight (U.S.), 1882–84, 1886–87. The most wins by an individual player is six, by two players: Richard Sears, 1882–84, 1886–87 (with Dwight) and 1885 (with Joseph Clark); Holcombe Ward, 1899–1901 (with Dwight Davis), 1904–06 (with Beals Wright).

Women's doubles   The most wins by a pair is 12, by Louise Brough and Margaret Du Pont (née Osborne), both of the U.S.. They won in 1942–50 and in 1955–57. Margaret Du Pont holds the record for an individual player with 13 wins; adding to her victories with Brough was the 1941 title with Sarah Fabyan (née Palfrey).

Mixed doubles   The most wins by one pair is four, by William Talbert and Margaret Osborne (U.S.), who won in 1943–46. The most titles won by any individual is nine, by Margaret Du Pont (née Osborne). She won in 1943-46, 1950, 1956, 1958-60. The most titles won by a man is four, accomplished by six players: Edwin Fischer (U.S.), 1894–96, 1898; Wallace Johnson (U.S.), 1907, 1909, 1911, 1920; Bill Tilden (U.S.), 1913–14, 1922–23; William Talbert (U.S.), 1943–46; Owen Davidson (Australia), 1966–67, 1971, 1973; and Marty Riessen (U.S.), 1969–70, 1972, 1980.

Most titles (overall)   Margaret Du Pont (née Osborne) won a record 25 U.S. Open titles, 1941–60— three singles, 13 doubles, and nine mixed doubles.

Youngest champions   The youngest singles champion was Tracy Austin (U.S.), who was 16 years 271 days when she won the women's singles in 1979. The youngest men's champion was Pete Sampras (U.S.), who was 19 years 28 days old when he won the 1990 title.

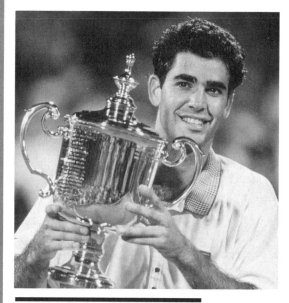

World number one Pete Sampras won only one Grand Slam event in 1996: the U.S. Open.
(Shaun Botterill/Allsport)

U.S. Open Champions
Men's Singles

Year	Player	Year	Player	Year	Player
1881	Richard Sears	1920	Bill Tilden	1961	Roy Emerson
1882	Richard Sears	1921	Bill Tilden	1962	Rod Laver
1883	Richard Sears	1922	Bill Tilden	1963	Raphael Osuna
1884	Richard Sears	1923	Bill Tilden	1964	Roy Emerson
1885	Richard Sears	1924	Bill Tilden	1965	Manuel Santana
1886	Richard Sears	1925	Bill Tilden	1966	Fred Stolle
1887	Richard Sears	1926	Rene Lacoste	1967	John Newcombe
1888	Henry Slocum Jr.	1927	Rene Lacoste	1968	Arthur Ashe*
1889	Henry Slocum Jr.	1928	Henri Cochet	1968	Arthur Ashe†
1890	Oliver Campbell	1929	Bill Tilden	1969	Stan Smith*
1891	Oliver Campbell	1930	John Doeg	1969	Rod Laver†
1892	Oliver Campbell	1931	Ellsworth Vines	1970	Ken Rosewall
1893	Robert Wrenn	1932	Ellsworth Vines	1971	Stan Smith
1894	Robert Wrenn	1933	Fred Perry	1972	Ilie Nastase
1895	Fred Hovey	1934	Fred Perry	1973	John Newcombe
1896	Robert Wrenn	1935	Wilmer Allison	1974	Jimmy Connors
1897	Robert Wrenn	1936	Fred Perry	1975	Manuel Orantes
1898	Malcolm Whitman	1937	Don Budge	1976	Jimmy Connors
1899	Malcolm Whitman	1938	Don Budge	1977	Guillermo Vilas
1900	Malcolm Whitman	1939	Bobby Riggs	1978	Jimmy Connors
1901	William Larned	1940	Donald McNeil	1979	John McEnroe
1902	William Larned	1941	Bobby Riggs	1980	John McEnroe
1903	Lawrence Doherty	1942	Ted Schroeder	1981	John McEnroe
1904	Holcombe Ward	1943	Joseph Hunt	1982	Jimmy Connors
1905	Beals Wright	1944	Frank Parker	1983	Jimmy Connors
1906	William Clothier	1945	Frank Parker	1984	John McEnroe
1907	William Larned	1946	Jack Kramer	1985	Ivan Lendl
1908	William Larned	1947	Jack Kramer	1986	Ivan Lendl
1909	William Larned	1948	Pancho Gonzalez	1987	Ivan Lendl
1910	William Larned	1949	Pancho Gonzalez	1988	Mats Wilander
1911	William Larned	1950	Arthur Larsen	1989	Boris Becker
1912	Maurice McLoughlin	1951	Frank Sedgman	1990	Pete Sampras
1913	Maurice McLoughlin	1952	Frank Sedgman	1991	Stefan Edberg
1914	Richard Williams	1953	Tony Trabert	1992	Stefan Edberg
1915	William Johnston	1954	Vic Seixas	1993	Pete Sampras
1916	Richard Williams	1955	Tony Trabert	1994	Andre Agassi
1917	Lindley Murray	1956	Ken Rosewall	1995	Pete Sampras
1918	Lindley Murray	1957	Malcolm Anderson	1996	Pete Sampras
1919	William Johnston	1958	Ashley Cooper		
		1959	Neale Fraser		
		1960	Neale Fraser		

* Amateur championship
† Open championship

U.S. Open Champions
Women's Singles

Year	Player
1881	*no event*
1882	*no event*
1883	*no event*
1884	*no event*
1885	*no event*
1886	*no event*
1887	Ellen Hansell
1888	Bertha Townsend
1889	Bertha Townsend
1890	Ellen Roosevelt
1891	Mabel Cahill
1892	Mabel Cahill
1893	Aline Terry
1894	Helen Helwig
1895	Juliette Atkinson
1896	Elisabeth Moore
1897	Juliette Atkinson
1898	Juliette Atkinson
1899	Marion Jones
1900	Myrtle McAteer
1901	Elisabeth Moore
1902	Marion Jones
1903	Elisabeth Moore
1904	May Sutton
1905	Elisabeth Moore
1906	Helen Homans
1907	Evelyn Sears
1908	Maud Bargar-Wallach
1909	Hazel Hotchkiss
1910	Hazel Hotchkiss
1911	Hazel Hotchkiss
1912	Mary Browne
1913	Mary Browne
1914	Mary Browne
1915	Molla Bjurstedt
1916	Molla Bjurstedt
1917	Molla Bjurstedt
1918	Molla Bjurstedt
1919	Hazel Wightman [1]
1920	Molla Mallory [2]
1921	Molla Mallory
1922	Molla Mallory
1923	Helen Wills
1924	Helen Wills
1925	Helen Wills
1926	Molla Mallory
1927	Helen Wills
1928	Helen Wills
1929	Helen Wills
1930	Betty Nuthall
1931	Helen Moody [3]
1932	Helen Jacobs
1933	Helen Jacobs
1934	Helen Jacobs
1935	Helen Jacobs
1936	Alice Marble
1937	Anita Lizana
1938	Alice Marble
1939	Alice Marble
1940	Alice Marble
1941	Sarah Cooke
1942	Pauline Betz
1943	Pauline Betz
1944	Pauline Betz
1945	Sarah Cooke
1946	Pauline Betz
1947	Louise Brough
1948	Margaret Du Pont
1949	Margaret Du Pont
1950	Margaret Du Pont
1951	Maureen Connolly
1952	Maureen Connolly
1953	Maureen Connolly
1954	Doris Hart
1955	Doris Hart
1956	Shirley Fry
1957	Althea Gibson
1958	Althea Gibson
1959	Maria Bueno
1960	Darlene Hard
1961	Darlene Hard
1962	Margaret Smith
1963	Maria Bueno
1964	Maria Bueno
1965	Margaret Smith
1966	Maria Bueno
1967	Billie Jean King
1968	Margaret Court* [4]
1968	Virginia Wade†
1969	Margaret Court*
1969	Margaret Court†
1970	Margaret Court
1971	Billie Jean King
1972	Billie Jean King
1973	Margaret Court
1974	Billie Jean King
1975	Chris Evert
1976	Chris Evert
1977	Chris Evert
1978	Chris Evert
1979	Tracy Austin
1980	Chris Evert
1981	Tracy Austin
1982	Chris Evert
1983	Martina Navratilova
1984	Martina Navratilova
1985	Hanna Mandlikova
1986	Martina Navratilova
1987	Martina Navratilova
1988	Steffi Graf
1989	Steffi Graf
1990	Gabriela Sabatini
1991	Monica Seles
1992	Monica Seles
1993	Steffi Graf
1994	Arantxa Sánchez Vicario
1995	Steffi Graf
1996	Steffi Graf

1 - Hazel Wightman (née Hotchkiss)
2 - Molla Mallory (née Bjurstedt)
3 - Helen Moody (née Wills)
4 - Margaret Court (née Smith)
* Amateur championship
† Open championship

Olympic Games

Tennis was reintroduced to the Olympic Games in 1988, having originally been included at the Games from 1896 to 1924. It was also a demonstration sport in 1968 and 1984.

Most gold medals Max Decugis (France) won four gold medals: men's singles, 1906; men's doubles, 1906; mixed doubles, 1906 and 1920.

Most medals Max Decugis (France) won a record six medals in Olympic competition: four gold (see above), one silver and one bronze, 1900–20. Kitty McKane (Great Britain) won a women's record five medals: one gold, two silver and two bronze, 1920–24.

Davis Cup

The Davis Cup, the annual men's international team championship, was first held in 1900.

Most wins The U.S. team has won the Davis Cup a record 31 times, 1900–96.

Most matches (career) Nicola Pietrangeli (Italy) played a record 163 matches (66 ties), 1954 to 1972, winning 120. He played 109 singles (winning 78) and 54 doubles (winning 42).

Most matches (season) The most wins is 18, by two players: Manuel Santana (Spain), 11 of 12 singles matches and seven of eight doubles matches in 1965; and Ilie Nastase (Romania), 13 of 14 singles matches and five of six doubles matches in 1971.

United States Team Records

Most selections John McEnroe has played for the U.S. team on 31 occasions, 1978–92.

Most wins John McEnroe has won 60 matches in Davis Cup competition—41 singles and 19 doubles.

Federation Cup

The Federation Cup, the women's international team championship, was first held in 1963 and is an annual event.

Most wins The United States has won the Federation Cup a record 15 times.

Men's Professional Tour Records

Most singles titles (career) Jimmy Connors (U.S.) has won 109 singles titles, 1972–89.

Most singles titles (season) Guillermo Vilas (Argentina) won 16 titles in 1977.

Most consecutive match wins Bjorn Borg (Sweden) won 49 consecutive matches in 1978.

Most consecutive weeks ranked number one Jimmy Connors (U.S.) held the number one ranking on the ATP computer from July 29, 1974 to August 23, 1977, a total of 160 weeks.

Highest earnings (career) Pete Sampras (U.S.) has won a career record $25,562,347, 1988–96.

Highest earnings (season) Pete Sampras (U.S.) earned a season record $5,415,066 in 1995.

Women's Professional Tour Records

Most singles titles (career) Martina Navratilova (U.S.) won 167 titles, 1975–94.

Most singles titles (season) Martina Navratilova won 16 titles in 1983.

Most consecutive matches won Martina Navratilova won 74 consecutive matches in 1984.

Most consecutive weeks ranked number one Steffi Graf (Germany) held the number one computer ranking from August 17, 1987 to March 11, 1991, a total of 186 weeks.

Highest earnings (career) Martina Navratilova (U.S.) won a career record $20,344,061, 1972–94.

Highest earnings (season) Arantxa Sánchez Vicario (Spain) won $2,943,665 in 1994.

➠ Fantastic Feats

Fastest serve Mark Philippoussis (Australia) completed a serve of 142 mph at the Franklin Templeton Tennis Classic in Scottsdale, AZ on March 7, 1997. The women's record is 121.8 mph, by Brenda Schultz-McCarthy (Netherlands) at the Australian Open in Melbourne on January 22, 1996.

TRACK AND FIELD

Origins

Competition in running, jumping and throwing must have occurred from the earliest days of humankind. The earliest evidence of organized running is from 3800 B.C. in Egypt. The ancient Olympic Games were cultural festivals that highlighted the ancient Greek ideal of perfection of mind and body.

The first modern Olympic Games, staged in 1896, focused on athletic achievement and the spirit of competition, and the Games have provided the focus for track and field as a sport ever since. In 1983, a separate world championship was introduced.

Olympic Games

The first modern Olympic Games were staged in Athens, Greece, April 6–15, 1896. Fifty-nine athletes from 10 nations competed; women's events were not added until 1928.

Most gold medals   Ray Ewry (U.S.) holds the all-time record for most appearances atop the winners' podium, with 10 gold medals: standing high jump (1900, 1904, 1906, 1908); standing long jump (1900, 1904, 1906, 1908); standing triple jump (1900, 1904). The women's record is four, shared by four athletes: Fanny Blankers-Koen (Netherlands): 100 m, 200 m, 80 m hurdles and 4 x 100 m relay in 1948; Betty Cuthbert (Australia): 100 m, 200 m, 4 x 100 m relay in 1956, and 400 m in 1964; Barbel Wockel (née Eckert; East Germany): 200 m and 4 x 100 m relay in both 1976 and 1980; Evelyn Ashford (U.S.): 100 m and 4 x 100 m relay in 1984, 4 x 100 m relay in 1988, 4 x 100 m relay in 1992.

Most gold medals (one Games)   Paavo Nurmi (Finland) won five gold medals at the 1924 Games. His victories came in the 1,500 m, 5,000 m, 10,000 m cross-country, 3,000 m team, and cross-country team. The most wins at individual events (not including relay or other team races) is four, by Alvin Kraenzlein (U.S.) in 1900 at 60 m, 110 m hurdles, 200 m hurdles and the long jump.

Most medals won   Paavo Nurmi (Finland) won a record 12 medals (nine gold, three silver) in the Games of 1920, 1924 and 1928. The women's record is seven, shared by three athletes: Shirley de la Hunty (Australia), three gold, one silver, three bronze in the 1948, 1952 and 1956 Games; Irena Szewinska (Poland), three gold, two silver, two bronze in the 1964, 1968, 1972 and 1976 Games; Merlene Ottey (Jamaica), two silver, five bronze in the 1980, 1984, 1992 and 1996 Games.

Canada's Donovan Bailey crosses the finish line in the new world record time of 9.84 seconds to win the 1996 Olympic 100-m title.
(Mike Powell/Allsport)

Svetlana Masterkova won the Olympic 800-m title and later in the season set a world record for the mile.
(Al Bello/Allsport)

Individual Records (U.S. Athletes)

Most medals   Ray Ewry's 10 gold medals are the most won by any U.S. athlete (see above). Florence Griffith-Joyner has won a women's record five medals in track and field—three golds, two silver in the 1984 and 1988 Games.

Most gold medals   Ray Ewry holds the Olympic mark for most golds (see above). The women's record for gold medals is four, by Evelyn Ashford—100m and 4 x 100 m relay in 1984, 4 x 100 m relay in 1988, 4 x 100 m relay in 1992.

Most gold medals (one Games)   The most gold medals won at one Olympics is four, by three men: Alvin Kraenzlein (see above); Jesse Owens, 100 m, 200 m, long jump and 4 x 100 m relay in 1936; Carl Lewis, 100 m, 200 m, long jump and 4 x 100 m relay in 1984. The women's record is three golds, by three women: Wilma Rudolph, 100 m, 200 m and 4 x 100 m relay in 1960; Valerie Brisco, 200 m, 400 m and 4 x 100 m relay in 1984; Florence Griffith-Joyner, 100 m, 200 m and 4 x 100 m relay in 1988.

World Championships

Quadrennial world championships distinct from the Olympic Games were first held in 1983 in Helsinki, Finland.

Most medals   The most medals won is 13, by Merlene Ottey (Jamaica), three gold, four silver and six bronze, 1983–95. The most medals won by a man is 10, by Carl Lewis (U.S.), a record eight gold, one silver and one bronze, 1983–93.

Most consecutive titles   Sergei Bubka (USSR/ Ukraine) is the only athlete to win four consecutive world titles, winning the pole vault, 1983, 1987, 1991 and 1993.

United States National Championships

Most titles   The most American national titles won at all events, indoors and out, is 65, by Ronald Owen Laird at various walking events between 1958 and 1976. Excluding the walks, the record is 41, by Stella Walsh (née Walasiewicz), who won 41 women's events between 1930 and 1954: 33 outdoors and eight indoors.

Longest winning sequence   Iolanda Balas (Romania) won a record 140 consecutive competitions at high jump from 1956 to 1967. The record at a track event was 122, at 400 meter hurdles, by Edwin Moses (U.S.) between his loss to Harald Schmid (West Germany) in Berlin, Germany on August 26, 1977 and his loss to to Danny Lee Harris (U.S.) in Madrid, Spain on June 4, 1987.

track and field

World Records—Men

World records are for the men's events scheduled by the International Amateur Athletic Federation. Full *automatic electronic timing is mandatory for events up to 400 meters.*

RUNNING

Event	Time	Athlete	Place	Date
100 meters	00:09.84	Donovan Bailey (Canada)	Atlanta, GA	July 27, 1996
200 meters	00:19.32	Michael Johnson (U.S.)	Atlanta, GA	August 1, 1996
400 meters	00:43.29	Butch Reynolds (U.S.)	Zurich, Switzerland	August 17, 1988
800 meters	01:41.73	Sebastian Coe (Great Britain)	Florence, Italy	June 10, 1981
1,500 meters	03:27.37	Noureddine Morcelli (Algeria)	Nice, France	July 12, 1995
1 mile	03:44.39	Noureddine Morcelli (Algeria)	Rietti, Italy	September 5, 1993
2,000 meters	04:47.88	Noureddine Morcelli	Paris, France	July 13, 1995
5,000 meters	12:44.39	Haile Gebrselassie (Ethiopia)	Zürich, Switzerland	August 16, 1995
10,000 meters	26:38.08	Salah Hissou (Morocco)	Brussels, Belgium	August 23, 1996
110 meter hurdles	00:12.91	Colin Jackson (Great Britain)	Stuttgart, Germany	August 20, 1993
400 meter hurdles	00:46.78	Kevin Young (U.S.)	Barcelona, Spain	August 6, 1992
3,000-m steeplechase	07:59.18	Moses Kiptanui (Kenya)	Zürich, Switzerland	August 16, 1995
4 x 100 meters	00:37.40	United States (Mike Marsh, Leroy Burrell, Dennis Mitchell, Carl Lewis)	Barcelona, Spain	August 8, 1992
	00:37.40	United States (John Drummond, Andre Cason, Dennis Mitchell, Leroy Burrell)	Stuttgart, Germany	August 21, 1993
4 x 400 meters	02:54.29	United States (Andrew Valmon, Quincy Watts, Butch Reynolds, Michael Johnson)	Stuttgart, Germany	August 22, 1993

FIELD EVENTS

Event	Distance	Athlete	Place	Date
High jump	8' 1/2"	Javier Sotomayor (Cuba)	Salamanca, Spain	July 27, 1993
Pole vault	20' 1 3/4"	Sergei Bubka (Ukraine)	Sestriere, Italy	July 31, 1994
Long jump	29' 4 1/2"	Mike Powell (U.S.)	Tokyo, Japan	August 30, 1991
Triple jump	60' 1/4"	Jonathan Edwards (Great Britain)	Göteborg, Sweden	August 7, 1995
Shot	75' 10 1/4"	Randy Barnes (U.S.)	Los Angeles, CA	May 20, 1990
Discus	243' 0"	Jurgen Schult (East Germany)	Neubrandenburg, Germany	June 6, 1986
Hammer	284' 7"	Yuriy Sedykh (USSR)	Stuttgart, Germany	August 30, 1986
Javelin	323' 1"	Jan Zelezny (Czech Republic)	Jena, Germany	May 25, 1996
Decathlon	8,891 points	Dan O'Brien (U.S.) (1st day: 100m 10.43 sec, Long jump 26' 6 1 1/4", Shot put 54' 9 1/4", High jump 6' 9 1/2", 400 m 48.51 sec), (2nd day: 110 m hurdles 13.98 sec, Discus 159' 4", Pole vault 16' 4 3/4", Javelin 205' 4", 1,500 m 4:42.10 sec)	Talence, France	September 4–5, 1992

WALKING

Event	Time	Athlete	Place	Date
20 km	01:17:25.5	Bernardo Segura (Mexico)	Bergen, Norway	May 7, 1994
50 km	03:40:57.9	Thierry Toutain (France)	Hencourt, France	September 29, 1996

The World's Greatest Athlete

"You talk about what is the essence of sports, which is running, jumping and throwing, and to be the best at those, you have to be the world's greatest athlete," says Olympic decathlon champion Dan O'Brien. The world record holder in the 10-sport event, O'Brien believes that the rigors of the decathlon require a peculiarly natural talent. "I think the decathlon finds people. You don't find it, it finds you," he says.

O'Brien's triumph at the 1996 Atlanta Games didn't set a world record, but it did erase a terrible memory. Four years earlier, O'Brien failed to make the U.S. Olympic team for the '92 Barcelona Games when he failed to clear a height in the pole vault segment of the decathlon. He was the world champion at the time, and his failure stunned the track and field world. In typical fashion, O'Brien rebounded from the shock. In a specially arranged meet in Talence, France, he set a new decathlon world record a month after the Barcelona Olympics. "I needed to get my number one status back," he recalls. "I was there to regain my world ranking."

Such focus and candor are typical of O'Brien. "I always think of the possibility of breaking the world record. I want to do more than win. I want to be the first man to score 9,000 points." O'Brien dedicated himself to his event as a teenager. "I was 15 the first time I tried the decathlon. Track and field has always been a natural sport for me. I saw an opening in the decathlon." The champion adds, "I told myself that I wanted to be the next Bruce Jenner."

Success was not instant for the future world record-holder. "Be prepared to fail many, many times, because you are dealing in events that you are not very good at." O'Brien advises: "Failure and hard work go together. You are constantly working on things, constantly trying to learn new things, and you have to accept coming up short almost every day." The Olympic champion points to the javelin as his most difficult event. "I grew up throwing baseballs and footballs and you have to change the way you throw for the javelin."

His favorite event is the 400 meters. "I think it's one of the hardest events since you really have to be in shape to run the 400. When you are in good 400-meter shape, it's the best shape you can be in." O'Brien adds, "You can really tell you're fit. You sleep and eat better and can walk up a flight of stairs without feeling tired." His least favorite event? "The mile run," he says.

O'Brien doesn't limit his sporting prowess to the track. "I take a lot of pride that there hasn't been a sport that I couldn't learn. I play golf, tennis and racquetball. I was a good baseball and football player in high school. I'm also an avid skier," he claims. The athlete urges kids to try many sports. "So many kids grow up with the idea that they'll be Michael Jordan or Emmitt Smith. They should try everything and that way won't miss their calling." Above all, O'Brien counsels aspiring athletes to follow their dreams. "If you have a dream, and it's a strong dream and a goal, just never give up. Never give up no matter what."

World Records—Women

World records are for the women's events scheduled by the International Amateur Athletic Federation. Full *automatic electronic timing* is mandatory for events up to 400 meters.

RUNNING

Event	Time	Athlete	Place	Date
100 meters	00:10.49	Florence Griffith-Joyner (U.S.)	Indianapolis, IN	July 16, 1988
200 meters	00:21.34	Florence Griffith-Joyner (U.S.)	Seoul, South Korea	September 29, 1988
400 meters	00:47.60	Marita Koch (East Germany)	Canberra, Australia	October 6, 1985
800 meters	01:53.28	Jarmila Kratochvilov (Czechoslovakia)	Munich, Germany	July 26, 1983
1,500 meters	03:50.46	Qu Yunxia (China)	Beijing, China	September 11, 1993
1 mile	04:12.56	Svetlana Masterkova (Russia)	Zürich, Switzerland	August 14, 1996
2,000 meters	05:25:36	Sonia O'Sullivan (Ireland)	Edinburgh, Scotland	July 8, 1994
3,000 meters	08:06.11	Wang Junxia (China)	Beijing, China	September 13, 1993
5,000 meters	14:36.45	Fernanda Ribeiro (Portugal)	Hechtel, Belgium	July 22, 1995
10,000 meters	29:31.78	Wang Junxia (China)	Beijing, China	September 8, 1993
100 m hurdles	00:12.21	Yordanka Donkova (Bulgaria)	Stara Zagora, Bulgaria	August 20, 1988
400 m hurdles	00:52.61	Kim Batten (U.S.)	Göteborg, Sweden	August 11, 1995
4 x 100 m	00:41.37	East Germany (Silke Gladisch, Sabine Rieger, Ingrid Auerswald, Marlies Göhr)	Canberra, Australia	October 6, 1985
4 x 400 m	03:15.17	USSR (Tatyana Ledovskaya, Olga Nazarova, Maria Pinigina, Olga Bryzgina)	Seoul, South Korea	October 1, 1988

FIELD EVENTS

Event	Distance	Athlete	Place	Date
High jump	6' 10 1/4"	Stefka Kostadinova (Bulgaria)	Rome, Italy	August 30, 1987
Long jump	24' 8 1/4"	Galina Chistyakova (USSR)	Leningrad, USSR	June 11, 1988
Triple jump	50' 10 1/4"	Inessa Kravets (Ukraine)	Göteborg, Sweden	August 10, 1995
Shot	74' 3"	Natalya Lisovskaya (USSR)	Moscow, USSR	June 7, 1987
Discus	252' 0"	Gabriele Reinsch (East Germany)	Neubrandenburg, Germany	July 9, 1988
Javelin	262' 5"	Petra Felke (East Germany)	Potsdam, Germany	September 9, 1988
Heptathlon	7,291 points	Jacqueline Joyner-Kersee (U.S.) (100 m hurdles 12.69 sec; High jump 6' 1 1/4"; Shot put 51' 10"; 200 m 22.56 sec; Long jump 23' 10 1/4"; Javelin 149' 10"; 800 m 2:08.51 sec)	Seoul, South Korea	September 23–24, 1988

WALKING

Event	Time	Athlete	Place	Date
5 km	20:13.26	Kerry Saxby-Junna (Australia)	Hobart, Australia	February 25, 1996
10 km	41:56.23	Nadezhda Ryashkina (USSR)	Seattle, WA	July 24, 1990

ROAD RUNNING

MARATHON

The marathon is run over a distance of 26 miles 385 yards. This distance was the one used for the race at the 1908 Olympic Games, run from Windsor to the White City stadium, London, England, and it became standard from 1924 on. The marathon was introduced at the 1896 Olympic Games. The 1896 Olympic marathon was preceded by trial races that year. The first Boston Marathon, the world's oldest annual marathon race, was held on April 19, 1897 at 24 miles 1,232 yards. The first national marathon championship was that of Norway in 1897. The first championship marathon for women was organized by the Road Runners Club of America on September 27, 1970.

Most marathons run Horst Preisler (Germany) had run 631 marathons of 26 miles or more as of May 29, 1996.

World Records

There are as yet no official records for the marathon, and it should be noted that courses may vary in severity. The following are the best times recorded, all on courses with verified distances: for men, 2 hours 6 minutes 50 seconds, by Belayneh Dinsamo (Ethiopia) in Rotterdam, Netherlands on April 17, 1988; for women, 2 hours 21 minutes 6 seconds, by Ingrid Kristiansen (née Christensen; Norway) in London, England on April 21, 1985.

United States USA Track and Field recognizes the following U.S. records: for men, Pat Peterson, 2 hours 10 minutes 4 seconds, in London, England on April 23, 1989 and Jerry Lawson in Chicago, IL on October 20, 1996; for women, Joan Benoit Samuelson, 2 hours 21 minutes 21 seconds, in Chicago, IL on October 20, 1985.

Olympic Games

The marathon has been run at every Olympic Games of the modern era; however, a women's race was not included in the Games until 1984.

Most gold medals The record for most wins in the men's race is two, by two marathoners: Abebe Bikila (Ethiopia), 1960 and 1964; Waldemar Cierpinski (East Germany), 1976 and 1980. The women's event has been run four times, with different winners each time.

World Championship

The marathon has been included as part of both the men's and women's programs at every World Track and Field championship.

Most wins No athlete in either the men's or women's division has won the world title more than once.

Boston Marathon

The world's oldest annual running race, the Boston Marathon was first staged on April 19, 1897.

Most wins (men) Clarence De Mar (U.S.) won the race seven times—1911, 1922–24, 1927–28, 1930.

Most wins (women) The women's division has been won three times by two women: Rosa Mota (Portugal), 1987–88, 1990, and Uta Pippig (Germany), 1994–96. Prior to 1972, when the marathon was opened to women, two women "unofficially" won the women's division three times each: Roberta Gibb (U.S.) 1966–68; and Sarah Mae Berman (U.S.) in 1969–71.

Fastest time The course record for men is 2 hours 7 minutes 15 seconds, by Cosmas Ndeti (Kenya) in 1994. The women's record is 2 hours 21 minutes 45 seconds, by Uta Pippig (Germany) in 1994.

New York City Marathon

The race was run in Central Park each year from 1970 to 1976, when, to celebrate the U.S. Bicentennial, the course was changed to a route through all five boroughs of the city. From that year, when there were 2,090 runners, the race has become one of the world's great sporting occasions; in 1994 there were a record 29,735 finishers.

Most wins Grete Waitz (Norway) has won nine times—1978–80, 1982-86 and 1988. Bill Rodgers has a men's record four wins—1976–79.

Fastest time The course record for men is 2 hours 8 minutes 1 second, by Juma Ikangaa (Tanzania) in 1989, and for women, 2 hours 24 minutes 40 seconds, by Lisa Ondieki (Australia) in 1992.

TRAMPOLINING

Origins

Trampolining has been part of circus acts for many years. The sport of trampolining dates from 1936, when the prototype "T" model trampoline was designed by George Nissen of the United States. The first official tournament took place in 1947.

World Championships

Instituted in 1964, championships have been staged biennially since 1968. The world championships recognize champions, both men and women, in four events: individual, synchronized pairs, tumbling, and double mini trampoline.

Most titles Judy Wills (U.S.) has won a record five individual world titles, 1964–68. The men's record is two, shared by six trampolinists: Wayne Miller (U.S.), 1966 and 1970; Dave Jacobs (U.S.), 1967–68; Richard Tisson (France), 1974 and 1976; Yevgeniy Yanes (USSR), 1976 and 1978; Lionel Pioline (France), 1984 and 1986; and Alexander Maskalenko (USSR/Russia), 1990 and 1992.

United States National Championships

The American Trampoline & Tumbling Association staged the first national championship in 1947. The inaugural event was open only to men; a women's event was not introduced until 1961. The association changed its name to USA Trampoline & Tumbling in 1995.

Most titles Two people have won a record 12 national titles: Stuart Ransom—six individual, 1975–76, 1978–80, 1982; three synchronized, 1975, 1979–80; and three double mini-tramp, 1979–80 and 1982; and Karl Heger—four individual, 1991–94; two synchronized, 1982 and 1986; and six double mini-tramp, 1986–87, 1991–94. Leigh Hennessy has won a record 10 women's titles: one individual, 1978; eight synchronized, 1972–73, 1976–78, 1980–82; one double mini-tramp, 1978.

TRIATHLON

Origins

The triathlon combines long distance swimming, cycling, and running. The sport was developed by a group of athletes who founded the Hawaii Ironman in 1974. After a series of unsuccessful attempts to create a world governing body, *L'Union Internationale de Triathlon* (UIT) was founded in Avignon, France in 1989. The UIT staged the first official world championships in Avignon on August 6, 1989. The UIT was renamed the International Triathlon Union (ITU) and moved to North Vancouver, Canada in 1989.

World Championships

The ITU has established various competition standards for the sport. In 1989 the official Olympic distance (now known as triathlon distance) of 1.5 km swim, 40 km bike and 10 km run was staged at the first Triathlon World Championship in France (see above).

Most titles Simon Lessing (Great Britain) has won a record three times, 1992–95. Michellie Jones (Australia) has won a record two women's titles, 1992–93.

Hawaii Ironman

This is the first, and best known, of the triathlons. Instituted on February 18, 1978, the first race was contested by 15 athletes. The Ironman grew rapidly in popularity, and 1,000 athletes entered the 1984 race. Contestants must swim 2.4 miles, then cycle 112 miles, and finally run a full marathon of 26 miles 385 yards.

Most titles Two men have won the Ironman a record six times: Dave Scott (U.S.), 1980, 1982–84, 1986–87; and Mark Allen (U.S.), 1989–93 and 1995. The women's event has been won a record eight times by Paula Newby-Fraser (Zimbabwe/U.S.) in 1986, 1988–89, 1991–94 and 1996.

Fastest times Luc Van Lierde (Belgium) holds the course record at 8 hours 4 minutes 8 seconds in 1996. Paula Newby-Fraser holds the women's record at 8 hours 55 seconds in 1992.

Largest field The most competitors to finish a triathlon race were the 5,030 who completed the 1995 Mrs. T's Chicago Triathlon in Chicago, IL.

VOLLEYBALL

Origins

The game was invented as mintonette in 1895 by William G. Morgan at the YMCA gymnasium in Holyoke, MA. The International Volleyball Association (IVA) was formed in Paris, France in April 1947. The United States Volleyball Association was founded in 1922 and is the governing body for the sport in this country. The United States National Championships were inaugurated for men in 1928, and for women in 1949.

Olympic Games

Volleyball became an official Olympic sport in 1964, when both men's and women's tournaments were staged in Tokyo, Japan.

Most gold medals (country) The USSR has won three men's titles, 1964, 1968 and 1980; and four women's titles, 1968, 1972, 1980 and 1988.

Most medals (individual) Inna Ryskal (USSR) has won four medals in Olympic competition: two gold, 1968, 1972; and two silver, 1964, 1976. The men's record is three, won by three players: Yuriy Poyarkov (USSR), two golds, 1964 and 1968, one bronze, 1972; Katsutoshi Nekoda (Japan), one gold, 1972, one silver, 1968, and one bronze, 1964; and Steve Timmons (U.S.), two gold, 1984 and 1988, and one bronze, 1992.

World Championships

World championships were instituted in 1949 for men and in 1952 for women.

Most titles The USSR has won six men's titles, 1949, 1952, 1960, 1962, 1978 and 1982, and five women's titles, 1952, 1956, 1960, 1970 and 1990.

BEACH VOLLEYBALL

In professional beach volleyball the court dimensions are the same as in the indoor game: 30 feet by 60 feet, or 30 feet by 30 feet on each side, with the net set at a height of eight feet; however, teams play two-a-side, as opposed to six-a-side for the indoor game.

Origins

Beach volleyball originated in California in the 1940s. The sport grew rapidly in the 1960s, and the first world championships were staged in 1976. In 1981 the Association of Volleyball Professionals was founded, and the AVP/Miller Lite Tour was formed that year.

UNITED STATES CHAMPIONSHIPS

Most titles Four players are tied with five: Sinjin Smith (U.S.), 1979 and 1981 (with Karch Kiraly), 1982, 1988 and 1990 (with Randy Stoklos); Mike Dodd (U.S.) and Tim Hovland (U.S.), 1983, 1985–87 and 1989; and Karch Kiraly (U.S.), 1979 and 1981 (with Sinjin Smith), and 1992–94 (with Kent Steffes).

AVP/Miller Lite Tour Records

Most tour wins Sinjin Smith has won 139 tour events, 1977–94.

Highest earnings Karch Kiraly had earned a career record $2,578,840 as of March 16, 1997.

The 1996 Olympic indoor volleyball champions were the Netherlands (above) in the men's event and Cuba (right) in the women's.
(Gary M. Prior/Allsport; Jed Jacobsohn/Allsport)

WATER POLO

Origins

This game was originally played in England as "water soccer" in 1869. The first rules were drafted in 1876. Water polo has been an Olympic event since 1900. In 1908, FINA (see Swimming) became the governing body for water polo. The first world championships were held in 1973.

Olympic Games

Water polo was first included at the 1900 Games, and has been included in every Games since.

Most gold medals (country) Hungary has won six Olympic titles, 1932, 1936, 1952, 1956, 1964 and 1976.

Most gold medals (players) Five players have won three gold medals: George Wilkinson (Great Britain), 1900, 1908, 1912; Paul Radmilovic (Great Britain), 1908,

1912, 1920; Charles Smith (Great Britain), 1908, 1912, 1920; Deszo Gyarmati (Hungary), 1952, 1956, 1964; Gyorgy Karpati (Hungary), 1952, 1956, 1964.

World Championships

A competition was first held at the World Swimming Championships in 1973. A women's event was included from 1986.

Most titles Two countries have won two men's titles: USSR, 1975 and 1982; Yugoslavia, 1986 and 1991. The women's competition was won by Australia in 1986, and by the Netherlands in 1991.

United States National Championships

The first men's national championship was held in 1891. A women's tournament was first held in 1926.

Most titles The New York Athletic Club has won 25 men's titles: 1892-96, 1903-04, 1906-08, 1922, 1929–31, 1933–35, 1937–39, 1954, 1956, 1960–61, and 1971. The Industry Hills Athletic Club (CA) has won nine women's titles: 1980–81 and 1984–88 (outdoors), 1987–88 (indoors).

Spain won the 1996 Olympic water polo tournament. (Michael Cooper/ Allsport)

WATERSKIING

Origins

Modern waterskiing was pioneered in the 1920s. Ralph Samuelson, who skied on Lake Pepin, MN in 1922 using two curved pine boards, is credited as being the father of the sport. Forms of skiing on water can be traced back centuries to people attempting to walk on water with planks. The development of the motorboat to tow skiers was the largest factor in the sport's growth. The world governing body is the International Water Ski Federation (IWSF), which replaced the World Water Ski Union (WWSU) in 1988. WWSU had succeeded the *Union Internationale de Ski Nautique*, which had been formed in Geneva, Switzerland in 1946. The American Water Ski Association was founded in 1939 and held the first national championships that year.

World Championships

The first world championships were held in 1949.

Most titles Sammy Duvall (U.S.) has won four overall titles, in 1981, 1983, 1985 and 1987. Two women have won three overall titles: Willa McGuire (née Worthington; U.S.), 1949–50 and 1955; Liz Allan-Shetter (U.S.), 1965, 1969 and 1975.

Most individual titles Liz Allan-Shetter has won a record eight individual championship events and is the only person to win all four titles—slalom, jumping, tricks, and overall—in one year, in Copenhagen, Denmark in 1969. Patrice Martin (France) has won a men's record seven titles: three overall, 1989, 1991, 1993, and four tricks, 1979, 1985, 1987 and 1991.

United States National Championships

National championships were first held at Jones Beach State Park, Long Island, NY on July 22, 1939.

Most titles The most overall titles is nine, tied by two individuals: Carl Roberge, 1980–83, 1985–88 and 1990; and Willa McGuire, 1946–51 and 1953–55.

Waterskiing World Records

SLALOM

Buoys	Line	Skier	Location	Date
Men				
4	10.25m	Andrew Mapple (Great Britain)	Charleston, SC	September 4, 1994
Women				
2.25	10.75m	Susi Graham (Canada)	Santa Rosa, FL	September 25, 1994

TRICKS

Points	Skier	Location	Date
Men			
11,590	Aymeric Benet (France)	West Palm Beach, FL	October 30, 1994
Women			
8,580	Tawn Larsen (U.S.)	Groveland, FL	July 4, 1992

JUMPING

Distance	Skier	Location	Date
Men			
220 feet	Sammy Duvall (U.S.)	Santa Rosa Beach, FL	October 10, 1993
Women			
156 feet	Deena Mapple (U.S.)	Charlotte, MI	July 9, 1988

WEIGHTLIFTING

There are two standard lifts in weightlifting: the "snatch" and the "clean and jerk." Totals of the best two lifts determine competition results. The "press," which had been a standard lift, was abolished in 1972.

Origins

Competitions for lifting weights of stone were held at the ancient Olympic Games. In the 19th century, weightlifting consisted of professional exhibitions in which some of the advertised poundages were open to doubt. The *Fédération Internationale Haltérophile et Culturiste*, now the International Weightlifting Federation (IWF), was established in 1905, and its first official championships were held in Tallinn, Estonia on April 29–30, 1922.

Youngest world record holder
Naim Suleimanov set 56-kg world records for clean and jerk (160 kg) and total (285 kg), at 16 years 62 days, in Allentown, NJ on March 26, 1983.

Oldest world record holder
The oldest is Norbert Schemansky (U.S.), who snatched 164.2 kg in the then unlimited Heavyweight class, aged 37 years 333 days, in Detroit, MI on April 28, 1962.

Heaviest lift to body weight   Stefan Topurov (Bulgaria) managed to clean and jerk more than three times his body weight when he lifted 396 3/4 pounds in Moscow, USSR on October 24, 1983.

Olympic Games

Weightlifting events were included in the first modern Games in 1896.

Most gold medals   Naim Suleymanoglu (Turkey), featherweight, won three gold medals, in 1988, 1992 and 1996

Most medals   Norbert Schemansky (U.S.) won four medals: one gold, one silver and two bronze, 1960–64.

Andrei Chemerkin set new world records in winning the super-heavyweight Olympic title.
(Jed Jacobsohn/Allsport)

World Championships

The IWF held its first world championships in Tallinn, Estonia in 1922, but has subsequently recognized 20 championships held in Vienna, Austria and London, England between 1898 and 1920. The championships have been held annually since 1946, with the Olympic Games recognized as world championships in the year of the Games until 1988, when a championship separate from the Olympics was staged. A women's championship was introduced in 1987.

Most titles (men)   The record for most titles is eight, held by three lifters: John Davis (U.S.), 1938, 1946–52; Tommy Kono (U.S.), 1952–59; and Vasiliy Alekseyev (USSR), 1970–77.

Most titles (women)   The most gold medals is 12, by Peng Li Ping (China) with snatch, jerk and total in the 52-kg class each year, 1988–89 and 1991–92; and Milena Tendafilova (Bulgaria), 67.5-kg/70-kg classes, 1989–93.

United States   Two American women have won world titles. In the 82-kg category, Karyn Marshall won a title in 1987 by lifting a total of 220 kg (a 95-kg snatch and a 125-kg clean and jerk). In 1994, Robin Byrd-Goad won a 50-kg title with a total weight of 175 kg.

United States National Championships

Most titles   The most titles won is 13, by Anthony Terlazzo at 137 pounds, 1932 and 1936, and at 148 pounds, 1933, 1935, 1937–45.

⟫ Fantastic Feats

24-hour team deadlift   A team of 10 deadlifted 6,705,241 pounds in 24 hours at the Forum Health Club, Birmingham, England on March 30–31, 1996.

24-hour individual deadlift   The 24-hour individual deadlift record is 818,121 pounds, by Anthony Wright at Her Majesty's Prison, Featherstone, England, August 31–September 1, 1990.

12-hour individual bench press   An individual bench press record of 1,181,312 pounds was set by

Turkey's "Pocket Hercules," Naim Suleymanoglu, made Olympic Games history when he won his third consecutive weightlifting gold medal in Atlanta.
(Tony Duffy/NBC/Allsport)

Chris Lawton at the Waterside Wine Bar, Solihull, England on June 3, 1994.

Team bench press   A bench press record of 8,873,860 pounds was set by a 9-man team from the Forum Health Club, Chelmsleywood, England, March 19–20, 1994.

Team squat   A squat record of 4,780,994 pounds was set by a 10-man team at St. Albans Weightlifting Club and Ware Boys Club, Hertfordshire, England, July 20–21, 1986.

Team arm curling   A record 133,380 arm-curling repetitions using three 48 1/4-pound weightlifting bars and dumbbells was achieved by a team of nine from Intrim Health and Fitness Club in Gosport, England, August 4–5, 1989.

World Weightlifting Records

From January 1, 1993, the International Weightlifting Federation (IWF) introduced modified weight categories, thereby making the then-world records redundant.

MEN

Bodyweight	Lift	kg	Name and Country	Place	Date
54 kg (119 lb)	Snatch	132.5	Halil Mutlu (Turkey)	Atlanta, GA	July 20, 1996
	Clean and Jerk	160	Halil Mutlu (Turkey)	Istanbul, Turkey	November 18, 1994
	Total	290	Halil Mutlu (Turkey)	Istanbul, Turkey	November 18, 1994
59 kg (130 lb)	Snatch	140	Hafiz Suleymanoglu (Turkey)	Warsaw, Poland	May 3, 1995
	Clean and Jerk	170	Nikolai Pershalov (Bulgaria)	Warsaw, Poland	May 3, 1995
	Total	307.5	Tang Ningsheng (China)	Atlanta, GA	July 21, 1996
64 kg (141 lb)	Snatch	148.5	Wang Guohua (China)	Yachiyo, Japan	April 5, 1996
	Clean and Jerk	187.5	Valerios Leonidis (Greece)	Atlanta, GA	July 22, 1996
	Total	335	Naim Suleymanoglu (Turkey)	Atlanta, GA	July 22, 1996
70 kg (154 lb)	Snatch	162.5	Zhan Xugang (China)	Atlanta, GA	July 23, 1996
	Clean and Jerk	195	Zhan Xugang (China)	Atlanta, GA	July 23, 1996
	Total	357.5	Zhan Xugang (China)	Atlanta, GA	July 23, 1996
76 kg (167 lb)	Snatch	170	Ruslan Savchenko (Ukraine)	Melbourne, Australia	November 16, 1993
	Clean and Jerk	208	Pablo Lara (Cuba)	Szekszard, Hungary	April 20, 1996
	Total	372.5	Pablo Lara (Cuba)	Szekszard, Hungary	April 20, 1996
83 kg (183 lb)	Snatch	180	Pyrros Dimas (Greece)	Atlanta, GA	July 26, 1996
	Clean and Jerk	213.5	Marc Huster (Germany)	Atlanta, GA	July 26, 1996
	Total	392.5	Pyrros Dimas (Greece)	Atlanta, GA	July 26, 1996
91 kg (200 lb)	Snatch	187.5	Alexei Petrov (Russia)	Atlanta, GA	July 27, 1996
	Clean and Jerk	228.5	Kakhi Kakhisahvili (Greece)	Warsaw, Poland	May 6, 1995
	Total	412.5	Alexei Petrov (Russia)	Sokolov, Czech Republic	May 7, 1994
99 kg (218 lb)	Snatch	192.5	Sergei Syrtsov (Russia)	Istanbul, Turkey	November 25, 1994
	Clean and Jerk	235	Akakide Kakhiashvilis (Greece)	Atlanta, GA	July 28, 1996
	Total	420	Akakide Kakhiashvilis (Greece)	Atlanta, GA	July 28, 1996
108 kg (238 lb)	Snatch	200	Timur Taimazov (Ukraine)	Istanbul, Turkey	November 26, 1994
	Clean and Jerk	236	Timur Taimazov (Ukraine)	Atlanta, GA	July 29, 1996
	Total	435	Timur Taimazov (Ukraine)	Istanbul, Turkey	November 26, 1994
Over 108 kg	Snatch	205	Alexander Kurlovich (Belarus)	Istanbul, Turkey	November 27, 1994
	Clean and Jerk	260	Andrei Chemerkin (Russia)	Atlanta, GA	July 30, 1996
	Total	457.5	Alexander Kurlovich (Belarus)	Istanbul, Turkey	November 27, 1994

World Weightlifting Records

WOMEN

Bodyweight	Lift	kg	Name and Country	Place	Date
46 kg (101 lb)	Snatch	81	Guang Hong (China)	Guangzhou, China	November 17, 1995
	Clean and Jerk	105	Guang Hong (China)	Yachiyo, Japan	April 4,1996
	Total	185	Guang Hong (China)	Yachiyo, Japan	April 4,1996
50 kg (110 lb)	Snatch	88	Baoyu Jiang (China)	Pusan, South Korea	July 3, 1995
	Clean and Jerk	110.5	Liu Xiuhua (China)	Hiroshima, Japan	October 3, 1994
	Total	197.5	Liu Xiuhua (China)	Hiroshima, Japan	October 3, 1994
54 kg (119 lb)	Snatch	92.5	Zhang Juhua (China)	Hiroshima, Japan	October 3, 1994
	Clean and Jerk	113.5	Zhang Xixiang (China)	Yachiyo, Japan	April 5, 1996
	Total	202.5	Zhang Juhua (China)	Hiroshima, Japan	October 3, 1994
59 kg (130 lb)	Snatch	99	Chen Xiaomin (China)	Warsaw, Poland	May 6, 1996
	Clean and Jerk	124	Xiu Xiongying (China)	Warsaw, Poland	May 6, 1996
	Total	220	Chen Xiaomin (China)	Hiroshima, Japan	October 4, 1994
64 kg (141 lb)	Snatch	106	Li Hongyun (China)	Warsaw, Poland	May 7, 1996
	Clean and Jerk	130	Li Hongyun (China)	Istanbul, Turkey	November 22, 1994
	Total	235	Li Hongyun (China)	Istanbul, Turkey	November 22, 1994
70 kg (154 lb)	Snatch	103	Lin Weining (China)	Seoul, South Korea	November 23,1996
	Clean and Jerk	129	Tang Weifang (China)	Guangzhou, China	November 22, 1995
	Total	230	Tang Weifang (China)	Hiroshima, Japan	October 4,1994
76 kg (167 lb)	Snatch	106.5	Gao Xiaoyan (China)	Seoul, South Korea	November 24, 1996
	Clean and Jerk	140	Zhang Guimei (China)	Shilong, China	December 18, 1993
	Total	235	Zhang Guimei (China)	Shilong, China	December 18, 1993
83 kg (183 lb)	Snatch	110	Wei Xiangying (China)	Warsaw, Poland	May 11, 1996
	Clean and Jerk	135	Chen Shu-Chih (Taiwan)	Guangzhou, China	November 24, 1995
	Total	242.5	Wei Xiangying (China)	Warsaw, Poland	May 11, 1996
Over 83 kg	Snatch	108.5	Wang Yanmei (China)	Warsaw, Poland	May 12, 1996
	Clean and Jerk	155	Li Yajuan (China)	Melbourne, Australia	November 20, 1993
	Total	260	Li Yajuan (China)	Melbourne, Australia	November 20, 1993

WINDSURFING

Boardsailing (windsurfing) World Championships were first held in 1973 and the sport was added to the Olympic Games in 1984, when the winner was Stephan van den Berg (Netherlands), who also won five world titles 1979–83.

⟫⟫➡ Fantastic Feats

Longest sailboard A sailboard of 165 feet was constructed in Fredrikstad, Norway. It was first sailed on June 28, 1986.

The longest snake of sailboards was made by 70 windsurfers in a row at the Sailboard Show '89 event in Narrabeen Lakes, Manly, Australia on October 21, 1989.

Lai Shan Lee won the women's mistral event in Atlanta. She is the first Hong Kong athlete to win a gold medal at the Olympic Games.
(Thierry Martinez/Allsport)

WRESTLING

Origins

Wrestling was the most popular sport in the ancient Olympic Games; wall drawings dating to c. 2600 B.C. show that the sport was popular long before the Greeks. Wrestling was included in the first modern Games. The International Amateur Wrestling Association (FILA) was founded in 1912. There are two forms of wrestling at the international level: freestyle and Greco-Roman. The use of the legs and holds below the waist are prohibited in Greco-Roman.

Olympic Games

Wrestling events have been included in all the Games since 1896.

Most gold medals Four wrestlers won three Olympic titles: Carl Westergren (Sweden) in 1920, 1924 and 1932; Ivar Johansson (Sweden) in 1932 (two) and 1936; Aleksandr Medved (USSR) in 1964, 1968 and 1972; and Aleksandr Karelin (USSR/Unified Team/Russia) 1988–96.

Most medals (individual) Wilfried Dietrich (Germany) won five medals in Olympic competition: one gold, two silver and two bronze, 1956–68. The most Olympic medals won by a U.S. wrestler is four, by freestyler Bruce Baumgartner: two gold, one silver and one bronze, 1984–96.

World Championships

The United States has competed in the freestyle World Women's Championships since 1989.

Most titles (men's individual) The freestyler Aleksandr Medved (USSR) won a record seven world championships, 1962–63, 1966–67 and 1969–71, in three weight categories. The most world titles won by any U.S. wrestler is four, by the freestyler John Smith, 1987 and 1989–91.

Most titles (women's individual) Yayoi Urano (Japan) has won five titles, 1990–91, 1993–94 and 1996.

Most titles (women's team) Japan has won all six women's world titles (1989–94) since 1989, when women first competed.

Bruce Baumgartner's bronze medal showing at the Atlanta Games made him the most successful American wrestler in Olympic competetion.
(Simon Bruty/Allsport)

U.S. National Titles

Most titles (men's) 17, by Bruce Baumgartner (Cambridge Springs, PA), who won all of his titles in freestyle events: 1980 and 1982 in AAU Championships and 1981, 1983–96 in USA Wrestling Championships.

Most titles (women's) Seven, by Tricia Sanders (Phoenix, AZ), 1990–96.

SUMO

Heaviest sumo wrestler The heaviest-ever rikishi, or wrestler, is Samoan-American Salevaa Fuali Atisnoe of Hawaii, alias Konishiki, who weighed in at 589 pounds as of January 3, 1994. He is the only foreign rikishi to attain the second highest rank of ozeki, or champion.

Highest winning percentage *Ozeki* Tameemon Torokichi, known as Raiden, compiled a .962 winning percentage—254 wins in 264 bouts—from 1789 to 1810.

Most wins *Yokozuna* Mitsugu Akimoto, known as Chiyonofuji, set a record for domination of one of the six annual tournaments by winning the Kyushu Basho for eight years, 1981–88. He also holds the record for most career wins, 1,045, and Makunoiuchi (top division) wins, 807.

Most bouts *Yokozuna* Kenji Hatano, known as Oshio, contested a record 1,891 bouts in his 26-year career, 1962–88, the longest in modern sumo history.

YACHTING

Origins

Sailing as a sport dates from the 17th century. Originating in the Netherlands, it was introduced to England by Charles II, who participated in a 23-mile race along the River Thames in 1661. The oldest yacht club in the world is the Royal Cork Yacht Club, which claims descent from the Cork Harbor Water Club, founded in Ireland in 1720. The oldest continuously existing yacht club in the United States is the New York Yacht Club, founded in 1844.

Oldest race The oldest race that is still regularly run is the Chicago–Mackinac race on Lake Michigan and Lake Huron. First held in 1898, the race has been staged annually since 1920.

America's Cup

The America's Cup was originally won as an outright prize by the schooner *America* on August 22, 1851 at Cowes, England and was later offered by the New York Yacht Club as a challenge trophy. On August 8, 1870, J. Ashbury's *Cambria* (Great Britain) failed to capture the trophy from *Magic*, owned by F. Osgood (U.S.). The Cup has been challenged 27 times. The U.S. was undefeated until 1983, when *Australia II*, skippered by John Bertrand and owned by a Perth syndicate headed by Alan Bond, beat *Liberty* 4–3, the narrowest series victory, at Newport, RI.

Most wins (skipper) Three skippers have won the cup three times: Charlie Barr (U.S.), who defended in 1899, 1901 and 1903; Harold S. Vanderbilt (U.S.), who defended in 1930, 1934 and 1937; and Dennis Conner (U.S.), who defended in 1980, challenged in 1987, and defended in 1988.

Largest yacht The largest yacht to have competed in the America's Cup was the 1903 defender, the gaff-rigged cutter *Reliance*, with an overall length of 144 feet, a record sail area of 16,160 square feet and a rig 175 feet high.

Olympic Games

Bad weather caused the abandonment of yachting events at the first modern Games in 1896. However, the weather has stayed "fair" ever since, and yachting has been part of every Games.

Most gold medals Paul Elvstrom (Denmark) won a record four gold medals in yachting, and in the process became the first competitor in Olympic history to win individual gold medals in four successive Games. Elvstrom's titles came in the Firefly class in 1948, and in the Finn class in 1952, 1956 and 1960.

Most medals Paul Elvstrom's four gold medals are also the most medals won by any Olympic yachtsman.

The Spanish team of Jose Luis Ballester and Fernando Leon won the Tornado class at the 1996 Olympics.
(Allsport)

ROUND-THE-WORLD RACING

Longest race (nonstop)   The world's longest nonstop sailing race is the Vendée Globe Challenge, the first of which started from Les Sables d'Olonne, France on November 26, 1989. The distance circumnavigated without stopping was 22,500 nautical miles. The race is for boats of between 50 and 60 feet, sailed single-handed. The record time on the course is 105 days 20 hours 31 minutes, by Christophe Auguin (France) in the sloop *Geodis*, which finished at Les Sables on February 17, 1997.

Longest race (total distance)   The longest and oldest regular sailing race around the world is the quadrennial Whitbread Round the World race (instituted August 1973), organized by the Royal Naval

Sailing Association (Great Britain). It starts in England, and the course around the world and the number of legs with stops at specified ports vary from race to race. The distance for 1993–94 was 32,000 nautical miles. The record time for the race is 120 days 5 hours 9 minutes, by New Zealand Endeavour, skippered by Grant Dalton (New Zealand) on June 3, 1994.

Fastest circumnavigation   *Enza New Zealand*, a catamaran skippered by Peter Blake (New Zealand) and Robin Knox-Johnston (Great Britain), completed the fastest nonstop circumnavigation at Ushart, France on April 1, 1994. The voyage took 74 days 22 hours 17 minutes.

French sailor Christophe Auguin returns to home port on February 17, 1997, having set a new solo round-the-world speed record.
(AP Photo/Francois Mori)

OLYMPIC GAMES

Records in this section include results from the
Intercalated Games staged in 1906.

Origins

The exact date of the first Olympic Games is
uncertain. The earliest date for which there is
documented evidence is July 776 B.C. By order of
Theodosius I, emperor of Rome, the Games were
prohibited in A.D. 394. The revival of the Games is
credited to Pierre de Fredi, Baron de Coubertin, a
French aristocrat, who was commissioned by his
government to form a universal sports association
in 1889. Coubertin presented his proposals for a
modern Games on November 25, 1892 in Paris; this
led to the formation of the International Olympic
Committee (IOC) in 1894 and thence to the staging
of the first modern Olympic Games, which were
opened in Athens, Greece on April 6, 1896. In 1906,
the IOC organized the Intercalated Games in Athens,
to celebrate the 10th anniversary of the revival of the
Games. In 1924, the first Winter Olympics were held
in Chamonix, France.

**The centennial Olympic Games staged in
Atlanta, GA were the largest ever held.
A record 10,768 athletes, representing
a record 197 countries, competed in
27 sports and 271 events. The opening
ceremony embraced the Games' ancient
tradition and honored its modern-day
champions.**
(Michael Cooper/Allsport; David Taylor/Allsport)

OLYMPIC GAMES
MEDAL RECORDS

Most gold medals

Ray Ewry (U.S.) has won 10 gold medals in Olympic competition: standing high jump, 1900, 1904, 1906 and 1908; standing long jump, 1900, 1904, 1906 and 1908; standing triple jump, 1900 and 1904. The most gold medals won by a woman is nine, by gymnast Larissa Latynina (USSR): all-around, 1956 and 1960; vault, 1956; floor exercise, 1956, 1960 and 1964; team title, 1956, 1960 and 1964.

Most medals

Gymnast Larissa Latynina (USSR) has won 18 medals (nine gold, five silver and four bronze), 1956–64. The most medals won by a man is 15 (seven gold, five silver and three bronze), by gymnast Nikolai Andrianov (USSR), 1972–80.

Most gold medals at one Olympics

Swimmer Mark Spitz (U.S.) won a record seven gold medals at Munich in 1972. His victories came in the 100-meter freestyle, 200-meter freestyle, 100-meter butterfly, 200-meter butterfly, and three relay events. The most gold medals won at one Games by a woman athlete is six, by swimmer Kristin Otto (East Germany), who won six gold medals at the 1988 Games. Her victories came in the 50-meter freestyle, 100-meter freestyle, 100-meter backstroke, 100-meter butterfly, and two relay events. The most individual events won at one Games is five, by speed skater Eric Heiden (U.S.) in 1980. Heiden won the 500 meters, 1,000 meters, 1,500 meters, 5,000 meters, and 10,000 meters.

Most medals at one Olympics

Gymnast Aleksandr Dityatin (USSR) won eight medals (three gold, four silver and one bronze) at Moscow, USSR in

Ekaterina Serebryanskaya (Ukraine) won the individual gold medal for rhythmic gymnastics at the Atlanta Games.
(Richard Martin/Vandystadt/Allsport)

1980. The most medals won by a woman athlete is seven (two gold and five silver), by gymnast Maria Gorokhovskaya (USSR) in 1952.

Most consecutive gold medals (same event)

Two athletes have won four consecutive individual titles in the same event: Al Oerter (U.S.), who won the discus 1956–68; and Carl Lewis (U.S.), who won the long jump 1984–96. Yachtsman Paul Elvstrom (Denmark) won four successive golds at monotype events, 1948–60, but there was a class change: Firefly in 1948; Finn class, 1952–60.

Oldest gold medalist

Oscar Swahn (Sweden) was aged 64 years 258 days when he won an Olympic gold medal in 1912 as a member of the team that won the running deer shooting single-shot title. The oldest woman to win a gold medal was Queenie Newall (Great Britain), who won the 1908 national round archery event at age 53 years 275 days.

Youngest gold medalist

The youngest-ever winner was an unnamed French boy who coxed the Netherlands pair to victory in the 1900 rowing event. He was believed to be 7–10 years old. The youngest-ever woman champion was Kim Yoon-mi (South Korea), who at age 13 years 83 days won the 1994 women's short-track speed skating relay event.

Most Games

The record for the most Olympic Games competed in by any one participant is nine, by yachtsman Hubert Raudaschl (Austria), 1964–96. The most appearances by a woman is seven, by fencer Kerstin Palm (Sweden), 1964–88.

Summer/Winter Games gold medalist

The only person to have won gold medals in both Summer and Winter Olympiads is Edward Eagan (U.S.), who won the 1920 light-heavyweight boxing title and was a member of the 1932 winning four-man bobsled team.

Track great Carl Lewis leaps into the record books, winning his fourth consecutive long-jump title.
(Mike Powell/Allsport)

Summer/Winter Games medalist (same year) The only athlete to have won medals at both the Winter and Summer Games held in the same year is Christa Rothenburger-Luding (East Germany). At the 1988 Winter Games in Calgary, Canada, Rothenburger-Luding won two speed skating medals: gold medal, 1,000 meters, and silver medal, 500 meters; and at the Seoul Games that summer she won a silver medal in the women's sprint cycling event.

UNITED STATES RECORDS

Most gold medals The records for most gold medals overall and at one Games are both held by American athletes (see page 239). The most gold medals won by an American woman is five, shared by two athletes: Bonnie Blair, speed skating 1988–94; and Jenny Thompson, swimming 1992–96.

Most medals The most medals won by an American Olympian is 11, by three athletes: Carl Osburn, shooting—five gold, four silver and two bronze (1912—24); Mark Spitz, swimming—nine gold, one silver and one bronze (1968–72); Matt Biondi, swimming—eight golds, two silver and one bronze (1984–92). The most medals won by an American woman is eight, by Shirley Babashoff, swimming-two gold and six silver (1972–76).

Oldest gold medalist The oldest U.S. Olympic champion was Galen Spencer, who won a gold medal in the Team Round archery event in 1904, at age 64 years 2 days.

Youngest gold medalist The youngest gold medalist was Jackie Fields, who won the 1924 featherweight boxing title at age 16 years 161 days.

Oldest medalist The oldest U.S. medalist was Samuel Duvall, who was a member of the 1904 silver-medal-winning team in the team round archery event, at age 68 years 194 days.

Youngest medalist The youngest American medal winner, and the youngest-ever participant, was Dorothy Poynton, who won a silver medal in springboard diving at the 1928 Games at age 13 years 23 days. The youngest men's medalist was Donald Douglas Jr., who won a silver medal at six-meter yachting in 1932, at age 15 years 40 days.

Most games Equestrian Michael Plumb has participated in seven Olympics, 1960–76, 1984 and 1992. He was selected for the 1980 team, but the Moscow Games were boycotted by the U.S. Fencer Janice Romary has appeared in six Games, 1948–68, the most for an American woman.

WINTER GAMES MEDAL RECORDS

Most gold medals The most gold medals won in Winter Games competition is six, by two women: speed skater Lydia Skoblikova (USSR) won 500 meters, 1964; 1,000 meters, 1964; 1,500 meters, 1960–64; 3,000 meters, 1960–64; cross-country skier Lyubov Egorova (Unified Team/Russia) won 5 km classical, 1994, 10 km freestyle pursuit, 1992–94, 15 km freestyle, 1992, 4 x 5 km mixed relay, 1992–94. The most gold medals won by a man is five, by three athletes: speed skater Clas Thunberg (Finland), 500 meters, 1928; 1,500 meters, 1924–28; 5,000 meters, 1924; all-around title, 1924; speed skater Eric Heiden (U.S.), 500, 1,000, 1,500, 5,000 and 10,000 meters, all in 1980; and cross-country skier Bjorn Dahlie (Norway), 10 km classical, 1994, 15 km freestyle pursuit, 1992–94, 50 km classical, 1992, 4 x 10 km mixed relay, 1992.

Most medals Cross-country skier Raisa Smetanina (USSR/Unified Team) has won 10 medals (four gold, five silver and one bronze), 1976–92. The most medals won by a man is nine (four gold, three silver and two bronze), by cross-country skier Sixten Jernberg (Sweden), 1956–64.

Oldest gold medalist Jay O'Brien (U.S.) was aged 48 years 359 days when he won an Olympic gold medal in 1932 in the four-man bobsled event. The oldest woman to win a gold medal was Raisa Smetanina (Unified Team), who was a member of the 1992 4 x 5 km relay team at age 39 years 352 days.

Youngest gold medalist Maxi Herber (Germany) was aged 15 years 128 days when she won the 1936 figure skating title. The youngest-ever men's champion was Toni Neiminen (Finland), who at age 16 years 259 days was a member of the winning ski jumping team in 1992.

1996 SUMMER OLYMPICS RESULTS

(W) = *world record*
(O) = *Olympic record*

ARCHERY

Individual (men)
Gold: Justin Huish (U.S.)
Silver: Magnus Petersson (Sweden)
Bronze: Oh Kyo-moon (South Korea)

Individual (women)
Gold: Kim Kyung-wook (South Korea)
Silver: He Ying (China)
Bronze: Olena Sadovnycha (Ukraine)

Team (men)
Gold: U.S.
Silver: South Korea
Bronze: Italy

Team (women)
Gold: South Korea
Silver: Germany
Bronze: Poland

BADMINTON

Men's singles
Gold: Poul-Erik Hoyer-Larsen (Denmark)
Silver: Dong Jiong (China)
Bronze: Rashid Sidek (Malaysia)

Men's doubles
Gold: Rexy Mainaky and Ricky Subagja (Indonesia)
Silver: Cheah Soon Kit and and Yap Kim Hock (Malaysia)
Bronze: Denny Kantono and S. Antonius (Indonesia)

Women's singles
Gold: Bang Soo-hyun (South Korea)
Silver: Mia Audina (Indonesia)
Bronze: Susi Susanti (Indonesia)

Women's doubles
Gold: Ge Fei and Gu Jun (China)
Silver: Gil Young-ah and Jang Hye-ock (South Korea)
Bronze: Qin Yiyuan and Tang Yongshu (China)

Mixed doubles
Gold: Kim Dong-moon and Gil Young-ah (South Korea)
Silver: Park Joo-bong and Ra Kyung-min (South Korea)
Bronze: Liu Jianjun and Sun Man (China)

BASEBALL

Gold: Cuba
Silver: Japan
Bronze: U.S.

BASKETBALL

Men

Gold: U.S.
Silver: Yugoslavia
Bronze: Lithuania

Women

Gold: U.S.
Silver: Brazil
Bronze: Australia

BOXING

48kg
Gold: Daniel Petrov Bojilov (Bulgaria)
Silver: Mansueto Velasco (Phillippines)
Bronze: Rafael Lozano (Spain)
Bronze: Oleg Kiryukhin (Ukraine)

51kg
Gold: Maikro Romero (Cuba)
Silver: Bulat Dzumadilov (Kazakhstan)
Bronze: Albert Pakeev (Russia)
Bronze: Zoltan Lunka (Germany)

54 kg
Gold: Istvan Kovacs (Hungary)
Silver: Arnaldo Mesa (Cuba)
Bronze: Raimkul Malakhbekov (Russia)
Bronze: Vichairachanon Khadpo (Thailand)

57kg
Gold: Somluk Kamsing (Thailand)
Silver: Serafim Todorov (Bulgaria)
Bronze: Pablo Chacon (Argentina)
Bronze: Floyd Mayweather (U.S.)

60kg
Gold: Hocine Soltani (Algeria)
Silver: Tontcho Tontchev (Bulgaria)
Bronze: Terrance Cauthen (U.S.)
Bronze: Leonard Doroftei (Romania)

63.5kg

Gold: Hector Vinent (Cuba)
Silver: Oktay Urkal (Germany)
Bronze: Bolat Niyazymbetov (Kazakhstan)
Bronze: Fathi Missaousi (Tunisia)

67kg

Gold: Oleg Saitov (Russia)
Silver: Juan Hernandez (Cuba)
Bronze: Marian Simion (Romania)
Bronze: Daniel Santos (Puerto Rico)

71kg

Gold: David Reid (U.S.)
Silver: Alfredo Duvergel (Cuba)
Bronze: Ezmouhan Ibzaimov (Kazakhstan)
Bronze: Karim Tulaganov (Uzbekistan)

75kg

Gold: Ariel Hernandez (Cuba)
Silver: Malik Beyleroglu (Turkey)
Bronze: Mohamed Bahari (Algeria)
Bronze: Rhoshii Wells (U.S.)

81kg

Gold: Vasilii Jirov (Kazakhstan)
Silver: Lee Seung-bae (South Korea)
Bronze: Antonio Tarver (U.S.)
Bronze: Thomas Ulrich (Germany)

91kg

Gold: Felix Savon (Cuba)
Silver: David Defiagbon (Canada)
Bronze: Nate Jones (U.S.)
Bronze: Luan Krasniqi (Germany)

91+ kg

Gold: Vladimir Klichko (Ukraine)
Silver: Paea Wolfgram (Tonga)
Bronze: Aleksei Lezin (Russia)
Bronze: Duncan Dokiwari (Nigeria)

CANOEING

Men

Slalom K1

Gold: Oliver Fix (Germany) 141.22 points
Silver: Andraz Vehovar (Slovenia) 141.65 points
Bronze: Thomas Becker (Germany) 142.79 points

Slalom C1

Gold: Michal Martikan (Slovakia) 151.03 points
Silver: Lukas Pollert (Czech Republic) 151.17 points
Bronze: Patrice Estanguet (France) 152.84 points

Slalom C2

Gold: Frank Addison/Wilfrid Forgues (France) 158.82 points
Silver: Jiri Rohan/Miroslav Simek (Czech Republic) 160.16 points
Bronze: Andre Ehrenberg/Michael Senft (Germany) 163.72 points

500 m (K1) (0)

Gold: Antonio Rossi (Italy) 1:37.42
Silver: Knut Holmann (Norway) 1:38.33
Bronze: Piotr Markiewicz (Poland) 1:38.61

500 m (K2)

Gold: Kay Bluhm/Torsten Gutsche (Germany) 1:28.69
Silver: Beniamino Bonomi/Daniele Scarpa (Italy) 1:28.72
Bronze: Danny Collins/Andrew Trim (Australia) 1:29.40

500 m (C1) (0)

Gold: Martin Doktor (Czech Republic) 1:49.93
Silver: Slavomir Knazovicky (Slovakia) 1:50.51
Bronze: Imre Pulai (Hungary) 1:50.75

500 m (C2) (0)

Gold: Csaba Horvath/Gyorgy Kolonics (Hungary) 1:40.42
Silver: Nikolai Juravschi/Victor Reneischi (Moldova) 1:40.45
Bronze: Gheorghe Andriev/Grigore Obreja (Romania) 1:41.33

1000 m (K1) (0)

Gold: Knut Holmann (Norway) 3:25.78
Silver: Beniamino Bonomi (Italy) 3:27.07
Bronze: Clint Robinson (Australia) 3:29.71

1,000 m (K2) (0)

Gold: Antonio Rossi/Daniele Scarpa (Italy) 3:09.19
Silver: Kay Bluhm/Torsten Gutsche (Germany) 3:10.51
Bronze: Milko Kazanov/Andrian Dushev (Bulgaria) 3:11.20

1,000 m (K4) (0)

Gold: Germany 2:51.52
Silver: Hungary 2:53.18
Bronze: Russia 2:53.99

1,000 m (C1) (O)

Gold: Martin Doktor (Czech Republic) 3:54.41
Silver: Ivan Klementyev (Latvia) 3:54.95
Bronze: Gyorgy Zala (Hungary) 3:56.36

1,000 m (C2) (O)

Gold: Andreas Dittmer/Gunar Kirchbach (Germany)
3:31.87
Silver: Antonel Borsan/Marcel Glavan (Romania) 3:32.39
Bronze: Csaba Horvath/Gyorgy Kolonics (Hungary)
3:32.51

Women

Slalom K1

Gold: Stepana Hilgertova (Czech Republic) 169.49
points
Silver: Dana Chladek (U.S.) 169.49 points
Bronze: Myriam Fox-Jerusalmi (France) 171.0 points

500 m (K1) (O)

Gold: Rita Koban (Hungary) 1:47.65
Silver: Caroline Brunet (Canada) 1:47.89
Bronze: Josefa Idem (Italy) 1:48.73

500 m (K2) (O)

Gold: Agneta Andersson/Susanne Gunnarsson
(Sweden) 1:39.32
Silver: Ramona Portwich/Birgit Fischer (Germany)
1:39.68
Bronze: Katrina Borchert/Anna Wood (Australia)
1:40.64

500 m (K4) (O)

Gold: Germany 1:31.07
Silver: Switzerland 1:32.70
Bronze: Sweden 1:32.91

CYCLING

Men

1,000-m time trial (O)

Gold: Florian Rousseau (France) 1:02.712
Silver: Erin Hartwell (U.S.) 1:02.940
Bronze: Takanobu Jumonji (Japan) 1:03.261

Sprint (200 m)

Gold: Jens Fiedler (Germany)
Silver: Marty Nothstein (U.S.)
Bronze: Curtis Harnett (Canada)

Individual pursuit (4,000 m)

Gold: Andrea Collinelli (Italy) 4:20.893
Silver: Philippe Ermenault (France) 4:22.714
Bronze: Bradley McGee (Australia) 4:26.121

Team pursuit (4,000 m) (O)

Gold: France 4:05.93
Silver: Russia 4:07.73
Bronze: Australia 4:07.535

Points race (40 km)

Gold: Silvio Martinello (Italy) 37 points
Silver: Brian Walton (Canada) 29 points
Bronze: Stuart O'Grady (Australia) 27 points

Road race (225 km)

Gold: Pascal Richard (Switzerland) 4:53:56
Silver: Rolf Sorensen (Denmark) 4:53:56
Bronze: Max Sciandri (Great Britain) 4:53:58

Road time trial individual (52 km)

Gold: Miguel Indurain (Spain) 1:04:05
Silver: Abraham Olano (Spain) 1:04:17
Bronze: Chris Boardman (Great Britain) 1:04:36

Mountain bike (47.7 km)

Gold: Bart Jan Brentjens (Netherlands) 2:17:38
Silver: Thomas Frischknecht (Switzerland) 2:20:14
Bronze: Miguel Martinez (France) 2:20:36

Women

Sprint (200 m)

Gold: Felicia Ballanger (France)
Silver: Michelle Ferris (Australia)
Bronze: Ingrid Haringa (Netherlands)

Individual pursuit (3 km)

Gold: Antonella Bellutti (Italy) 3:33.595
Silver: Marion Clignet (Canada) 3:38.571
Bronze: Judith Arndt (Germany) 3:38.744

Points race (25 km)

Gold: Nathalie Lancien (France) 24 points
Silver: Ingrid Haringa (Netherlands) 23 points
Bronze: Lucy Tyler Sharman (Australia) 17 points

Road race (106 km)

Gold: Jeannie Longo-Ciprelli (France) 2:36:13
Silver: Imelda Chiappa (Italy) 2:36:38
Bronze: Clara Hughes (Canada) 2:36:44

Road time trial individual (26 km)
Gold: Zulfiya Zabirova (Russia) 36:40
Silver: Jeannie Longo-Ciprelli (France) 37:00
Bronze: Clara Hughes (Canada) 37:13

Mountain bike (32 km)
Gold: Paola Pezzo (Italy) 1:50:51
Silver: Alison Sydor (Canada) 1:51:58
Bronze: Susan De Mattei (U.S.) 1:52:36

EQUESTRIAN SPORTS

SHOW JUMPING

Individual
Gold: Ullrich Korchhoff (Germany) 1.0 point
Silver: Willi Melliger (Switzerland) 4.0 points
Bronze: Alexandra Ledermann (France) 4.0 points

Team
Gold: Germany 1.75 points
Silver: U.S. 12.0
Bronze: Brazil 17.25

DRESSAGE

Individual
Gold: Isabell Werth (Germany) 235.09 points
Silver: Anky Van Grunsven (Netherlands) 233.02 points
Bronze: Sven Rothenberger (Netherlands) 224.94 points

Team
Gold: Germany 5,553 points
Silver: Netherlands 5,437 points
Bronze: U.S. 5,309 points

THREE-DAY EVENT

Individual
Gold: Blyth Tait (New Zealand) 56.8 points
Silver: Sally Clark (New Zealand) 60.4 points
Bronze: Kerri Millikin (U.S.) 73.7

Team
Gold: Australia 203.85 points
Silver: U.S. 261.1 points
Bronze: New Zealand 268.55 points

FENCING

Men

Foil, individual
Gold: Alessandro Puccini (Italy)
Silver: Lionel Plumenail (France)
Bronze: Franck Boidin (France)

Foil, team
Gold: Russia
Silver: Poland
Bronze: Cuba

Epee, individual
Gold: Aleksandr Beketov (Russia)
Silver: Ivan Perez Trevejo (Cuba)
Bronze: Geza Imre (Hungary)

Epee, team
Gold: Italy
Silver: Russia
Bronze: France

Saber, individual
Gold: Stanislav Pozdnyakov (Russia)
Silver: Sergey Sharikov (Russia)
Bronze: Damien Touya (France)

Saber, team
Gold: Russia
Silver: Hungary
Bronze: Italy

Women

Foil, individual
Gold: Laura Badea (Romania)
Silver: Valentina Vezzali (Italy)
Bronze: Giovanna Trillini (Italy)

Foil, team
Gold: Italy
Silver: Romania
Bronze: Germany

Epee, individual
Gold: Laura Flessel (France)
Silver: Valeriy Barlois (France)
Bronze: Gyoengyi Szalay Horvathne (Hungary)

Epee, team
Gold: France
Silver: Italy
Bronze: Russia

FIELD HOCKEY

Men

Gold: Netherlands
Silver: Spain
Bronze: Australia

Women

Gold: Australia
Silver: South Korea
Bronze: Netherlands

GYMNASTICS

Men

Team
Gold: Russia 576.778 points
Silver: China 575.539 points
Bronze: Ukraine 571.541 points

Individual all-around
Gold: Li Xiaoshuang (China) 58.423 points
Silver: Aleksei Nemov (Russia) 58.374 points
Bronze: Vitaliy Scherbo (Belarus) 58.197 points

Floor exercise
Gold: Ioannis Melissanidis (Greece) 9.85 points
Silver: Li Xiaoshuang (China) 9.837 points
Bronze: Aleksei Nemov (Russia) 9.8

Parallel bars
Gold: Rustam Sharipov (Ukraine) 9.837 points
Silver: Jair Lynch (U.S.) 9.825 points
Bronze: Vitaliy Scherbo (Belarus) 9.8 points

Pommel horse
Gold: Li Donghua (Switzerland) 9.875 points
Silver: Marius Urzica (Romania) 9.825 points
Bronze: Aleksei Nemov (Russia) 9.787 points

Rings
Gold: Yuri Chechi (Italy) 9.887 points
Silver: Szilvesztzter Csollany (Hungary) and Dan Burinca (Romania) 9.812 points

Vault
Gold: Aleksei Nemov (Russia) 9.787 points
Silver: Yeo Hong-chul (South Korea) 9.756 points
Bronze: Vitaliy Scherbo (Belarus) 9.724 points

Horizontal bar
Gold: Andreas Wecker (Germany) 9.85 points
Silver: Krasimir Dounev (Bulgaria) 9.825 points
Bronze: Vitaliy Scherbo (Belarus), Aleksei Nemov (Russia) and Fan Bin (China) 9.8 points

Women

Team
Gold: U.S. 389.225 points
Silver: Russia 388.404 points
Bronze: Romania 388.246 points

Individual all-around
Gold: Lilia Podkopayeva (Ukraine) 39.255 points
Silver: Gina Gogean (Romania) 39.075 points
Bronze: Simona Amanar (Romania) and Lavinia Milosovici (Romania) 39.067 points

Uneven bars
Gold: Svetlana Chorkina (Russia) 9.85 points
Silver: Bi Wenjiing (China) and Amy Chow (U.S.) 9.837 points

Floor exercise
Gold: Lilia Podkopayeva (Ukraine) 9.887 points
Silver: Simona Amanar (Romania) 9.85 points
Bronze: Dominique Dawes (U.S.) 9.837 points

Balance beam
Gold: Shannon Miller (U.S.) 9.862 points
Silver: Lilia Podkopayeva (Ukraine) 9.825 points
Bronze: Gina Gogean (Romania) 9.787 points

Vault
Gold: Simona Amanar (Romania) 9.825 points
Silver: Mo Huilan (China) 9.768 points
Bronze: Gina Gogean (Romania) 9.750 points

Rhythmic all-around individual
Gold: Ekaterina Serebryanskaya (Ukraine) 39.863 points
Silver: Ianina Batyrchina (Russia) 39.382 points
Bronze: Elena Vitrichenko (Ukraine) 39.331 points

Rhythmic all-around team
Gold: Spain 38.933 points
Silver: Bulgaria 38.866 points
Bronze: Russia 38.365 points

JUDO

Men

60kg
Gold: Tadahiro Nomura (Japan)
Silver: Girolamo Giovinazzo (Italy)
Bronze: Dorjpalam Narmandakh (Mongolia)
Bronze: Richard Trautmann (Germany)

65kg
Gold: Udo Quellmalz (Germany)
Silver: Yukimasa Nakamura (Japan)
Bronze: Israel Hernandez Plana (Cuba)
Bronze: Henrique Guimaraes (Brazil)

71kg
Gold: Kenzo Nakamura (Japan)
Silver: Kwak Dae-sung (South Korea)
Bronze: James Pedro (U.S.)
Bronze: Christophe Gagliano (France)

78kg
Gold: Djamel Bouras (France)
Silver: Toshihiko Koga (Japan)
Bronze: Soso Liparteliani (Georgia)
Bronze: Cho In-chul (South Korea)

86kg
Gold: Jeon Ki-young (South Korea)
Silver: Armen Bagdasarov (Uzbekistan)
Bronze: Marko Spittka (Germany)
Bronze: Mark Huizinga (Netherlands)

95kg
Gold: Pawel Nastula (Poland)
Silver: Kim Min-soo (South Korea)
Bronze: Miguel Fernandes (Brazil)
Bronze: Stephane Traineau (France)

95+ kg
Gold: David Douillet (France)
Silver: Ernesto Perez (Spain)
Bronze: Harry van Barneveld (Belgium)
Bronze: Frank Moeller (Germany)

Women

48kg
Gold: Kye Sun (North Korea)
Silver: Ryoko Tamura (Japan)
Bronze: Amarilis Savon Carmenaty (Cuba)
Bronze: Yolanda Soler (Spain)

52kg
Gold: Marie-Claire Restoux (France)
Silver: Hyung Sook-hee (South Korea)
Bronze: Noriko Sugawara (Japan)
Bronze: Legna Verdecia (Cuba)

56kg
Gold: Driulis Gonzalez (Cuba)
Silver: Jung Sun-yong (South Korea)
Bronze: Isabel Fernandez (Spain)
Bronze: Marisabel Lomba (Belgium)

61kg
Gold: Yuko Emoto (Japan)
Silver: Gella Vandecaveye (Belgium)
Bronze: Jenny Gal (Netherlands)
Bronze: Jung Sung-sook (South Korea)

66kg
Gold: Cho Min-sun (South Korea)
Silver: Aneta Szczepanska (Poland)
Bronze: Wang Xianbo (China)
Bronze: Claudia Zwiers (Netherlands)

72kg
Gold: Ulla Werbrouck (Belgium)
Silver: Yoko Tanabe (Japan)
Bronze: Ylenia Scapin (Italy)
Bronze: Diadenis Luna (Cuba)

72+ kg
Gold: Sum Fuming (China)
Silver: Estela Rodriguez (Cuba)
Bronze: Johanna Hagn (Germany)
Bronze: Christine Cicot (France)

MODERN PENTATHLON

Gold: Aleksandr Parygin (Kazakhstan) 5,551 points
Silver: Eduard Zenkova (Russia) 5,530 points
Bronze: Janos Martinek (Hungary) 5,501 points

ROWING

Men

Single sculls (0)
Gold: Xeno Mueller (Switzerland) 6:44.85
Silver: Derek Porter (Canada) 6:47.45
Bronze: Thomas Lange (Germany) 6:47.72

Double sculls

Gold: Davide Tizzano/Agostino Abbagnale (Italy)
6:16.98
Silver: Kjetil Undset/Steffen Stoerseth (Norway) 6:18.42
Bronze: Frederic Kowal/Samuel Barathay (France)
6:19.85

Double sculls (lightweight)

Gold: Markus Gier/Michael Gier (Switzerland) 6:23.47
Silver: Maarten van der Linden/Pepijn Aardewijn
(Netherlands) 6:26.48
Bronze: Anthony Edwards/Bruce Hick (Australia)
6:26.69

Quad sculls

Gold: Germany 5:56.93
Silver: U.S. 5:59.10
Bronze: Australia 6:01.65

Coxless pairs (0)

Gold: Steven Redgrave/Matthew Pinsent (Great Britain)
6:20.09
Silver: David Weightman/Robert Scott (Australia)
6:21.02
Bronze: Michel Andrieux/Jean-Christophe Rolland
(France) 6:22.15

Coxless fours

Gold: Australia 6:06.37
Silver: France 6.07.03
Bronze: Great Britain 6:07.28

Coxless fours (lightweight)

Gold: Denmark 6:09.58
Silver: Canada 6:10.13
Bronze: U.S. 6:12.29

Eights

Gold: Netherlands 5:42.74
Silver: Germany 5:44.58
Bronze: Russia 5:45.77

Women

Single sculls

Gold: Yekaterina Khodotovich (Belarus) 7:32.21
Silver: Silken Laumann (Canada) 7:35.15
Bronze: Trine Hansen (Denmark) 7:37.20

Double sculls

Gold: Marnie McBean/Kathleen Heddle (Canada)
6:56.84
Silver: Cao Mianying/Zhang Xiuyuan (China) 6:58.35
Bronze: Irene Eijs/Eeke van Nes (Netherlands) 6:58.72

Double sculls (lightweight)

Gold: Constanta Burcica/Camelia Macoviciuc (Romania)
7:12.78
Silver: Teresa Bell/Lindsay Burns (U.S.) 7:14.65
Bronze: Rebecca Joyce/Virginia Lee (Australia) 7:16.56

Quad sculls

Gold: Germany 6:27.44
Silver: Ukraine 6:30.36
Bronze: Canada 6:30.38

Coxless pairs (0)

Gold: Megan Still/Kate Slatter (Australia) 7:01.39
Silver: Missy Schwen/Karen Kraft (U.S.) 7:01.78
Bronze: Christine Gosse/Helene Cortin (France) 7:03.82

Eights

Gold: Romania 6:19.73
Silver: Canada 6:24.05
Bronze: Belarus 6:24.44

SHOOTING

Men

50 m free pistol (0)

Gold: Boris Kokorev (Russia) 666.4 points
Silver: Igor Basinski (Belarus) 662.0 points
Bronze: Roberto Di Donna (Italy) 661.8 points

25 m rapid-fire pistol (0)

Gold: Ralf Schumann (Germany) 698.0 points
Silver: Emil Milev (Bulgaria) 692.1 points
Bronze: Vladimir Vokmyanin (Kazakhstan) 691.5 points

10 m air pistol

Gold: Robert Di Donna (Italy) 684.2 points
Silver: Wang Yifu (China) 684.1 points
Bronze: Tanu Kiriakov (Bulgaria) 683.8 points

10 m air rifle (0)

Gold: Artem Khadzhibekov (Russia) 695.7 points
Silver: Wolfram Waibel Jr. (Austria) 695.2 points
Bronze: Jean-Pierre Amat (France) 693.1 points

10 m running game target (O)

Gold: Yang Ling (China) 685.8 points
Silver: Xiao Jun (Japan) 679.8 points
Bronze: Miroslav Janus (Czech Republic) 678.4 points

50 m free rifle, prone (O)

Gold: Christian Klees (Germany) 704.8 points
Silver: Sergey Beliaev (Kazakhstan) 703.3 points
Bronze: Josef Gonci (Slovakia) 701.9 points

50 m free rifle, three positions (O)

Gold: Jean-Pierre Amat (France) 1,273.9 points
Silver: Sergey Beliaev (Kazakhstan) 1,272.3 points
Bronze: Wolfram Waibel Jr. (Austria) 1,269.6 points

Trap

Gold: Michael Diamond (Australia) 149 points
Silver: Josh Lakatos (U.S.) 147 points
Bronze: Lance Bade (U.S.) 147 points

Double trap

Gold: Russell Mark (Australia) 189 points
Silver: Albano Pera (Italy) 183 points
Bronze: Zhang Bing (China) 183 points

Skeet (O)

Gold: Ennio Falco (Italy) 149 points
Silver: Miroslaw Rzepkowski (Poland) 148 points
Bronze: Andrea Benelli (Italy) 147 points

Women

25 m sport pistol (O)

Gold: Li Duihong (China) 687.9 points
Silver: Diana Yorgova (Bulgaria) 684.8 points
Bronze: Marina Logvinenko (Russia) 684.2 points

50 m small-bore rifle, three positions (O)

Gold: Aleksandra Ivosev (Yugoslavia) 686.1 points
Silver: Irina Gerasimenok (Russia) 680.1 points
Bronze: Renata Mauer (Poland) 679.8 points

10 m air pistol (O)

Gold: Olga Klochneva (Russia) 490.1 points
Silver: Marina Logvinenko (Russia) 488.5 points
Bronze: Mariya Grozdeva (Bulgaria) 488.5 points

10 m air rifle

Gold: Renata Mauer (Poland) 497.6 points
Silver: Petra Horneber (Germany) 497.4 points
Bronze: Aleksandra Ivosev (Yugoslavia) 497.2 points

Double trap

Gold: Kim Rhode (U.S.) 141 points
Silver: Susanne Kiermayer (Germany) 139 points
Bronze: Deserie Huddleston (Australia) 139 points

SOCCER

Men

Gold: Nigeria
Silver: Argentina
Bronze: Brazil

Women

Gold: U.S.
Silver: China
Bronze: Norway

SOFTBALL

Gold: U.S.
Silver: China
Bronze: Australia

SWIMMING

Men

50-m freestyle

Gold: Aleksandr Popov (Russia) 22.13
Silver: Gary Hall Jr. (U.S.) 22.26
Bronze: Fernando Scherer (Brazil) 22.29

100-m freestyle

Gold: Aleksandr Popov (Russia) 48.74
Silver: Gary Hall Jr. (U.S.) 48.81
Bronze: Gustavo Borges (Brazil) 49.02

200-m freestyle

Gold: Danyon Loader (New Zealand) 1:47.63
Silver: Gustavo Borges (Brazil) 1:48.08
Bronze: Daniel Kowalski (Australia) 1:48.25

400-m freestyle

Gold: Danyon Loader (New Zealand) 3:47.97
Silver: Paul Palmer (Great Britain) 3:49.00
Bronze: Daniel Kowalski (Australia) 3:49.39

1,500-m freestyle

Gold: Kieren Perkins (Australia) 14:56.40
Silver: Daniel Kowalski (Australia) 15:02.43
Bronze: Graeme Smith (Great Britain) 15:02.48

4 x 100-m freestyle (0)
Gold: U.S. 3:15.41
Silver: Russia 3:17.06
Bronze: Germany 3:17.20

4 x 200-m freestyle
Gold: U.S. 7:14.84
Silver: Sweden 7:17.56
Bronze: Germany 7:17.71

100-m breaststroke
Gold: Frederic Deburghgraeve (Belgium) 1:00.65
([W] 1:00.60 in qualifying)
Silver: Jeremy Linn (U.S.) 1:00.77
Bronze: Mark Warnecke (Germany) 1:01.33

200-m breaststroke
Gold: Norbert Rozsa (Hungary) 2:12.57
Silver: Karoly Guttler (Hungary) 2:13.03
Bronze: Andrey Korneyev (Russia) 2:13.17

100-m backstroke
Gold: Jeff Rouse (U.S.) 54.10
Silver: Rodolfo Falcon Cabrera (Cuba) 54.98
Bronze: Neisser Bent (Cuba) 55.02

200-m backstroke
Gold: Brad Bridgwater (U.S.) 1:58.54
Silver: Tripp Schwenk (U.S.) 1:58.99
Bronze: Emanuele Merisi (Italy) 1:59.18

100-m butterfly (W)
Gold: Denis Pankratov (Russia) 52.27
Silver: Scott Miller (Australia) 52.53
Bronze: Vladislav Kulikov (Russia) 53.13

200-m butterfly
Gold: Denis Pankratov (Russia) 1:56.51
Silver: Tom Malchow (U.S.) 1:57.44
Bronze: Scott Goodman (Australia) 1:57.48

200-m medley (0)
Gold: Attila Czene (Hungary) 1:59.91
Silver: Jani Sievinen (Finland) 2:00.13
Bronze: Curtis Myden (Canada) 2:01.13

400-m medley
Gold: Tom Dolan (U.S.) 4:14.90
Silver: Eric Namesnik (U.S.) 4:15.25
Bronze: Curtis Myden (Canada) 4:16.28

4 x 100-m medley (W)
Gold: U.S. 3:34.84
Silver: Russia 3:37.55
Bronze: Australia 3:39.56

Women

50-m freestyle
Gold: Amy van Dyken (U.S.) 24.87
Silver: Le Jingyi (China) 24.90
Bronze: Sandra Volker (Germany) 25.14

100-m freestyle (0)
Gold: Le Jingyi (China) 54.50
Silver: Sandra Volker (Germany) 54.88
Bronze: Angel Martino (U.S.) 54.93

200-m freestyle
Gold: Claudia Poll (Costa Rica) 1:58.16
Silver: Franziska van Almsick (Germany) 1:58.57
Bronze: Dagmar Hase (Germany) 1:59.56

400-m freestyle
Gold: Michelle Smith (Ireland) 4:07.25
Silver: Dagmar Hase (Germany) 4:08.30
Bronze: Kirsten Vlieghuis (Netherlands) 4:08.70

800-m freestyle
Gold: Brooke Bennett (U.S.) 8:27.89
Silver: Dagmar Hase (Germany) 8:29.91
Bronze: Kirsten Vlieghuis (Netherlands) 8:30.84

4 x 100-m freestyle (0)
Gold: U.S. 3:39.29
Silver: China 3:40.48
Bronze: Germany 3:41.48

4 x 200 m freestyle
Gold: U.S. 7:59.87
Silver: Germany 8:01.55
Bronze: Australia 8:05.47

100-m breaststroke
Gold: Penny Heyns (South Africa) 1:7.73 ([W] 1:07.02
in qualifying)
Silver: Amanda Beard (U.S.) 1:08.09
Bronze: Samantha Riley (Australia) 1:09.18

200-m breaststroke (0)
Gold: Penny Heyns (South Africa) 2:25.41
Silver: Amanda Beard (U.S.) 2:25.75
Bronze: Agnes Kovacs (Hungary) 2:26.57

100-m backstroke

Gold: Beth Botsford (U.S.) 1:01.19
Silver: Whitney Hedgepeth (U.S.) 1:01.47
Bronze: Marianne Kriel (South Africa) 1:02.12

200-m backstroke

Gold: Krisztina Egerszegi (Hungary) 2:07.83
Silver: Whitney Hedgepeth (U.S.) 2:11.98
Bronze: Cathleen Rund (Germany) 2:12.06

100-m butterfly

Gold: Amy Van Dyken (U.S.) 59.13
Silver: Liu Limin (China) 59.14
Bronze: Angel Martino (U.S.) 59.23

200-m butterfly

Gold: Susan O'Neil (Australia) 2:07.76
Silver: Petria Thomas (Australia) 2:09.82
Bronze: Michelle Smith (Ireland) 2:09.91

200-m medley

Gold: Michelle Smith (Ireland) 2:13.93
Silver: Marianne Limpert (Canada) 2:14.35
Bronze: Lin Li (China) 2:14.74

400-m medley

Gold: Michelle Smith (Ireland) 4:39.18
Silver: Allison Wagner (U.S.) 4:42.03
Bronze: Krisztina Egerszegi (Hungary) 4:42.53

4x100-m medley

Gold: U.S. 4:02.88
Silver: Australia 4:05.08
Bronze: China 4:07.34

DIVING

Men

Springboard

Gold: Xiong Ni (China) 701.46 points
Silver: Yu Zhoucheng (China) 690.93 points
Bronze: Mark Lenzi (U.S.) 689.49

Platform

Gold: Dmitriy Saoutine (Russia) 692.34 points
Silver: Jan Hempel (Germany) 663.27 points
Bronze: Xiao Hailiang (China) 658.20 points

Women

Springboard

Gold: Fu Mingxia (China) 547.68 points
Silver: Irina Lashko (Russia) 512.19 points
Bronze: Annie Pelletier (Canada) 509.64 points

Platform

Gold: Fu Mingxia (China) 521.58 points
Silver: Annika Walter (Germany) 479.22 points
Bronze: Mary Ellen Clark (U.S.) 472.95 points

SYNCHRONIZED SWIMMING

Gold: U.S. 99.720 points
Silver: Canada 98.367 points
Bronze: Japan 97.753 points

TABLE TENNIS

Men's singles

Gold: Lui Guoliang (China)
Silver: Wang Tao (China)
Bronze: Joerg Rosskopf (Germany)

Men's doubles

Gold: Kong Linghui and Lui Guoliang (China)
Silver: Lu Lin and Wang Tao (China)
Bronze: Lee Chun-seung and Yoo Nam-kyu (South Korea)

Women's singles

Gold: Deng Yaping (China)
Silver: Jing Chen (Taiwan)
Bronze: Qiao Hong (China)

Women's doubles

Gold: Deng Yaping and Qiao Hong (China)
Silver: Liu Wei and Qiao Yunping (China)
Bronze: Park Hae-jung and Ryu Ji-hae (South Korea)

TEAM HANDBALL

Men

Gold: Croatia
Silver: Sweden
Bronze: Spain

Women

Gold: Denmark
Silver: South Korea
Bronze: Hungary

TENNIS

Men's singles

Gold: Andre Agassi (U.S.)
Silver: Sergi Bruguera (Spain)
Bronze: Leander Paes (India)

Men's doubles

Gold: Todd Woodbridge and Mark Woodforde (Australia)
Silver: Neil Broad and Tim Henman (Great Britain)
Bronze: Marc-Kevin Goellner and David Prinosil (Germany)

Women's singles

Gold: Lindsay Davenport (U.S.)
Silver: Arantxa Sanchez Vicario (Spain)
Bronze: Jana Novotna (Czech Republic)

Women's doubles

Gold: Gigi Fernandez and Mary Joe Fernandez (U.S.)
Silver: Jana Novotna and Helena Sukova (Czech Republic)
Bronze: Conchita Martinez and Arantxa Sanchez Vicario (Spain)

TRACK AND FIELD

Men

100 m (W)

Gold: Donovan Bailey (Canada) 9.84
Silver: Frank Fredericks (Namibia) 9.89
Bronze: Ato Boldon (Trinidad and Tobago) 9.90

200 m (W)

Gold: Michael Johnson (U.S.) 19.32
Silver: Frank Fredericks (Namibia) 19.68
Bronze: Ato Boldon (Trinidad and Tobago) 19.80

400 m (0)

Gold: Michael Johnson (U.S.) 43.49
Silver: Roger Black (Great Britain) 44.41
Bronze: Davis Kamoga (Uganda) 44.53

800 m (0)

Gold: Vebjoern Rodal (Norway) 1:42.58
Silver: Hezekiel Sepeng (South Africa) 1:42.74
Bronze: Fred Onyancha (Kenya) 1:42.79

1,500 m

Gold: Noureddine Morceli (Algeria) 3:35.78
Silver: Fermin Cacho (Spain) 3:36.40
Bronze: Stephen Kipkorir (Kenya) 3:36.72

5,000 m

Gold: Venuste Niyongabo (Burundi) 13:07.96
Silver: Paul Bitok (Kenya) 13:08.16
Bronze: Khalid Boulami (Morocco) 13:08.37

10,000 m (0)

Gold: Haile Gebrselassie (Ethiopia) 27:07.34
Silver: Paul Tergat (Kenya) 27:08.17
Bronze: Salah Hissou (Morocco) 27:24.67

Marathon

Gold: Josia Thugwane (South Africa) 2:12:36
Silver: Lee Bong-ju (South Korea) 2:12:39
Bronze: Eric Wainaina (Kenya) 2:12:44

110-m hurdles (0)

Gold: Allen Johnson (U.S.) 12.95
Silver: Mark Crear (U.S.) 13.09
Bronze: Florian Schwarthoff (Germany) 13.17

400-m hurdles

Gold: Derrick Adkins (U.S.) 47.54
Silver: Samuel Matete (Zambia) 47.78
Bronze: Calvin Davis (U.S.) 47.96

4x100-m

Gold: Canada 37.69
Silver: U.S. 38.05
Bronze: Brazil 38.41

4x400-m

Gold: U.S. 2:55.99
Silver: Great Britain 2:56.60
Bronze: Jamaica 2:59.42

Steeplechase

Gold: Joseph Keter (Kenya) 8:07.12
Silver: Moses Kiptanui (Kenya) 8:08.33
Bronze: Alessandro Lambruschini (Italy) 8:11.28

20-km walk

Gold: Jefferson Perez (Ecuador) 1:20:07
Silver: Ilya Markov (Russia) 1:20:16
Bronze: Bernardo Segura (Mexico) 1:20:23

50-km walk

Gold: Robert Korzeniowski (Poland) 3:43:30
Silver: Mikhail Shchennikov (Russia) 3:43:46
Bronze: Valentin Massana (Spain) 3:44:19

High jump (O)

Gold: Charles Austin (U.S.) 2.39 m
Silver: Artur Partyka (Poland) 2.37 m
Bronze: Steve Smith (Great Britain) 2.35 m

Pole vault (O)

Gold: Jean Galfione (France) 5.92 m
Silver: Igor Trandenkov (Russia) 5.92 m
Bronze: Andri Tivontchik (Germany) 5.92 m

Long jump

Gold: Carl Lewis (U.S.) 8.50 m
Silver: James Beckford (Jamaica) 8.29 m
Bronze: Joe Greene (U.S.) 8.24 m

Triple jump (O)

Gold: Kenny Harrison (U.S.) 18.09 m
Silver: Jonathan Edwards (Great Britain) 17.88 m
Bronze: Yoelbi Quesada (Cuba) 17.44 m

Shot

Gold: Randy Barnes (U.S.) 21.62 m
Silver: John Godina (U.S.) 20.79 m
Bronze: Oleksandr Bagach (Ukraine) 20.75 m

Discus (O)

Gold: Lars Riedel (Germany) 69.40 m
Silver: Vladimir Dubrovshchik (Belarus) 66.60 m
Bronze: Vasiliy Kaptyukh (Belarus) 65.80 m

Hammer

Gold: Balazs Kiss (Hungary) 81.24 m
Silver: Lance Deal (U.S.) 81.12 m
Bronze: Oleksiy Krykun (Ukraine) 80.02 m

Javelin

Gold: Jan Zelezny (Czech Republic) 88.16 m
Silver: Steve Backley (Great Britain) 87.44 m
Bronze: Seppo Raty (Finland) 86.98 m

Decathlon

Gold: Dan O'Brien (U.S.) 8,824 points
Silver: Franke Busemann (Germany) 8,706 points
Bronze: Tomas Dvorak (Czech Republic) 8,664 points

Women

100 m

Gold: Gail Devers (U.S.) 0:10.94
Silver: Merlene Ottey (Jamaica) 0:10.94
Bronze: Gwen Torrence (U.S.) 0:10.96

200 m

Gold: Marie-Jose Perec (France) 0:22.12
Silver: Merlene Ottey (Jamaica) 0:22.24
Bronze: Mary Onyali (Nigeria) 0:22.38

400 m (O)

Gold: Marie-Jose Perec (France) 0:48.25
Silver: Cathy Freeman (Australia) 0:48.63
Bronze: Falilat Ogunkoya (Nigeria) 0:49.10

800 m

Gold: Svetlana Masterkova (Russia) 1:57.73
Silver: Ana Fidelia Quirot (Cuba) 1:58.11
Bronze: Maria Lurdes Mutola (Mozambique) 1:58.71

1,500 m

Gold: Svetlana Masterkova 4:00.83
Silver: Gabriela Szabo (Romania) 4:01.54
Bronze: Theresia Kiesl (Austria) 4:03.02

5,000 m

Gold: Wang Junxia (China) 14:59.88
Silver: Pauline Konga (Kenya) 15:03.49
Bronze: Roberta Brunet (Italy) 15:07.52

10,000 m (O)

Gold: Fernanda Ribeiro (Portugal) 31:01.63
Silver: Wang Junxia (China) 31:02.58
Bronze: Gete Wami (Ethiopia) 31:06.65

Marathon

Gold: Fatuma Roba (Ethiopia) 2:26:05
Silver: Valentina Yegerova (Russia) 2:28:05
Bronze: Yuko Arimori (Japan) 2: 28:39

100-m hurdles

Gold: Ludmila Engquist (Sweden) 0:12.58
Silver: Brigita Bukovec (Slovenia) 0:12.59
Bronze: Patricia Girard-Leno (France) 0:12.65

400-m hurdles (O)

Gold: Deon Hemmings (Jamaica) 0:52.82
Silver: Kim Batten (U.S.) 0:53.08
Bronze: Tonja Buford-Bailey (U.S.) 0:53.22

4 x 100 m
Gold: U.S. 0:41.95 seconds
Silver: Bahamas 0:42.14
Bronze: Jamaica 0:42.24

4 x 400
Gold: U.S. 3:20.91
Silver: Nigeria 3:21.04
Bronze: Germany 3:21.14

10-km walk
Gold: Yelena Nikolayeva (Russia) 41:49
Silver: Elisabetta Perrone (Italy) 42:12
Bronze: Wang Yan (China) 42:19

High Jump (0)
Gold: Stefka Kostadinova (Bulgaria) 2.05 m
Silver: Niki Bakogianni (Greece) 2.03 m
Bronze: Inga Babakova (Ukraine) 2.01 m

Long Jump
Gold: Chioma Ajunwa (Nigeria) 7.12 m
Silver: Fiona May (Italy) 7.02 m
Bronze: Jackie Joyner-Kersee (U.S.) 7.00 m

Triple Jump
Gold: Inessa Kravets (Ukraine) 15.33 m
Silver: Inna Lasovskaya (Russia) 14.98 m
Bronze: Sarka Kasparkova (Czech Republic) 14.98 m

Shot
Gold: Astrid Kumbernuss (Germany) 20.56 m
Silver: Sui Xinmei (China) 19.88 m
Bronze: Irina Khurdoroshkina (Russia) 19.35 m

Discus
Gold: Ilke Wyludda (Germany) 69.66 m
Silver: Natalya Sadova (Russia) 66.48 m
Bronze: Ellina Zvereva (Belarus) 65.64 m

Javelin
Gold: Heli Rantanen (Finland) 67.94 m
Silver: Louise McPaul (Australia) 65.54 m
Bronze: Trine Hattestad (Norway) 64.98 m

Heptathlon
Gold: Ghada Shouaa (Syria) 6,780 points
Silver: Natasha Sazanovich (Belarus) 6,563 points
Bronze: Denise Lewis (Great Britain) 6,489 points

VOLLEYBALL

Men
Gold: Netherlands
Silver: Italy
Bronze: Yugoslavia

Women
Gold: Cuba
Silver: China
Bronze: Brazil

BEACH VOLLEYBALL

Men
Gold: Kent Steffes and Karch Kiraly (U.S.)
Silver: Mike Whitmarsh and Michael Dodd (U.S.)
Bronze: John Child and Mark Heese (Canada)

Women
Gold: Jackie Silva Cruz and Sandra Pires Tavares (Brazil)
Silver: Monica Rodrigues and Adriana Samuel Ramos (Brazil)
Bronze: Natalie Cook and Kerri Ann Pottharst (Australia)

WATER POLO
Gold: Spain
Silver: Croatia
Bronze: Italy

WEIGHTLIFTING

54kg
Gold: Halil Mutlu (Turkey) 287.5 kg (Snatch: 132.5 kg [W])
Silver: Zhang Xiangsen (China) 280 kg
Bronze: Sevdalin Minchev (Bulgaria) 277.5 kg

59kg (W)
Gold: Tang Ningsheng (China) 307.5 kg
Silver: Leonidas Sabanis (Greece) 305 kg
Bronze: Nikolai Peshalov (Bulgaria) 302.5 kg

64kg (W)
Gold: Naim Suleymanoglu (Turkey) 335 kg
Silver: Valerios Leonidis (Greece) 332.5 kg (Clean and jerk: 187.5 kg [W])
Bronze: Xiao Jiangang (China) 322.5 kg

70kg (W)
Gold: Zhan Xugang (China) 357.5 kg (Snatch: 162.5 kg [W]; Clean and jerk: 195 kg [W])
Silver: Myong Kim (North Korea) 345 kg
Bronze: Attila Feri (Hungary) 340 kg

76kg
Gold: Pablo Lara (Cuba) 367.5 kg
Silver: Yoto Yotov (Bulgaria) 360 kg
Bronze: Jon Chol (North Korea) 357.5 kg

83kg (W)
Gold: Pyrros Dimas (Greece) 392.5 kg (Snatch:180 kg [W])
Silver: March Huster (Germany) 382.5 kg (Clean and jerk: 212.5 kg [W])
Bronze: Andrzej Cofalik (Poland) 372.5 kg

91kg
Gold: Alexey Petrov (Russia) 402.5 kg (Snatch: 187.5 kg [W])
Silver: Leonidis Kokas (Greece) 390 kg
Bronze: Oliver Caruso (Germany) 390 kg

99kg (W)
Gold: Akakide Kakhiasvilis (Greece) 420 kg (Clean and jerk: 235 kg [W])
Silver: Anatoliy Khrapaty (Kazakhstan) 410 kg
Bronze: Denis Gotfrid (Ukraine) 402.5 kg

108kg
Gold: Timur Taimazov (Ukraine) 430 kg (Clean and jerk: 235 kg [W])
Silver: Sergei Syrtsov (Russia) 420 kg
Bronze: Nicu Vlad (Romania) 420 kg

+ 108kg (W)
Gold: Andrei Chemerkin (Russia) 457.5 kg (Clean and jerk: 260 kg [W])
Silver: Ronny Weller (Germany) 455 kg
Bronze: Stefari Botev (Australia) 450 kg

WRESTLING

FREESTYLE

48kg
Gold: Il Kim (North Korea)
Silver: Armen Mkrchyan (Armenia)
Bronze: Alexis Vila Perdomo (Cuba)

52kg
Gold: Valentin Dimitrov Jordanov (Bulgaria)
Silver: Namik Abdullayev (Azerbaijan)
Bronze: Maulen Mamyrov (Kazakhstan)

57kg
Gold: Kendall Cross (U.S.)
Silver: Giuvi Sissaouri (Canada)
Bronze: Yong Sam Ri (North Korea)

62kg
Gold: Tom Brands (U.S.)
Silver: Jang Jae-sung (South Korea)
Bronze: Elbrus Tedeyev (Ukraine)

68kg
Gold: Vadim Bogiyev (Russia)
Silver: Townsend Saunders (U.S.)
Bronze: Zaza Zazirov (Ukraine)

74kg
Gold: Buvaysa Saytyev (Russia)
Silver: Park Jang-soon (South Korea)
Bronze: Takuya Ota (Japan)

82kg
Gold: Khadzhimurad Magomedov (Russia)
Silver: Yang Hyun-mo (South Korea)
Bronze: Amir Reza Khadem-Azghadi (Iran)

90kg
Gold: Rasull Khadem-Azghadi (Iran)
Silver: Makharbek Khadartsev (Russia)
Bronze: Eldari Kurtanidze (Georgia)

100kg
Gold: Kurt Angel (U.S.)
Silver: Abbas Jadidi (Iran)
Bronze: Arawat Sabejew (Germany)

130kg
Gold: Mahmut Demir (Turkey)
Silver: Aleksey Medvedev (Belarus)
Bronze: Bruce Baumgartner (U.S.)

GRECO-ROMAN

48kg
Gold: Sim Kwon-ho (South Korea)
Silver: Aleksandr Pavlov (Belarus)
Bronze: Zafar Gulyov (Russia)

52kg
Gold: Armen Nazaryan (Armenia)
Silver: Brandon Paulson (U.S.)
Bronze: Andriy Kalashnikov (Ukraine)

57kg
Gold: Yuri Melnichenko (Kazakhstan)
Silver: Dennis Hall (U.S.)
Bronze: Sheng Zetian (China)

62kg
Gold: Wlodzimierz Zawadzki (Poland)
Silver: Juan Luis Maren Delis (Cuba)
Bronze: Mehmet Pirim (Turkey)

68kg
Gold: Ryszard Wolny (Poland)
Silver: Ghani Yolouz (France)
Bronze: Aleksandr Tretyakov (Russia)

74kg
Gold: Feliberto Ascuy Aguilera (Cuba)
Silver: Marko Asell (Finland)
Bronze: Josef Tracz (Poland)

82kg
Gold: Hamza Yerlikaya (Turkey)
Silver: Thomas Zander (Germany)
Bronze: Valeriy Tsilent (Belarus)

90kg
Gold: Vyacheslav Oleynyk (Ukraine)
Silver: Jacek Fafinski (Poland)
Bronze: Maik Bullman (Germany)

100kg
Gold: Andrzej Wronski (Poland)
Silver: Sergey Lishtvan (Belarus)
Bronze: Mikael Lyungberg (Sweden)

130kg
Gold: Aleksandr Karelin (Russia)
Silver: Slamak Ghaffari (U.S.)
Bronze: Serguei Moureiko (Moldova)

YACHTING

Laser
Gold: Robert Scheidt (Brazil) 26 points
Silver: Ben Ainslie (Great Britain) 37 points
Bronze: Peer Moberg (Norway) 46 points

Tornado
Gold: Jose Luis Ballester/Fernando Leon (Spain)
30 points
Silver: Mitch Booth/Andrew Landenberger (Australia)
42 points
Bronze: Lars Grael/Kiko Pellicano (Brazil) 43 points

Soling
Gold: Germany
Silver: Russia
Bronze: U.S.

Star
Gold: Torben Grael/Marcelo Ferreira (Brazil) 25 points
Silver: Hans Wallen/Bobbie Lohse (Sweden) 29 ponts
Bronze: Colin Beashel/David Giles (Australia) 32 points

Finn
Gold: Mateusz Kusznierewicz (Poland) 32 points
Silver: Sebastien Godefroid (Belgium) 45 points
Bronze: Roy Heiner (Netherlands) 50 points

Europe
Gold: Kristine Roug (Denmark) 24 points
Silver: Margriet Matthijsse (Netherlands) 30 points
Bronze: Courtenay Becker-Dey (U.S.) 39 points

470 (Men)
Gold: Yevhen Braslavets/Igor Matviyenko (Ukraine)
40 points
Silver: Ian Walker/John Merricks (Great Britain)
61 points
Bronze: Vitor Rocha/Nuno Barreto (Portugal) 62 points

470 (Women)
Gold: Begona Via Dufresne/Theresa Zabell (Spain)
25 points
Silver: Yumiko Shige/Alicia Kinoshita (Japan) 36 points
Bronze: Olena Pakholchik/Ruslana Taran (Ukraine)
38 points

Mistral (Men)
Gold: Nikolaos Kaklamanakis (Greece) 17 points
Silver: Carlos Espinola (Argentina) 19 points
Bronze: Gal Fridman (Israel) 21 points

Mistral (Women)
Gold: Lee Lai Shan (Hong Kong) 16 points
Silver: Barbara Kendall (New Zealand) 24 points
Bronze: Alessandra Sensini (Italy) 28 points